HUMAN MEMORY

A Series of Books in Psychology

HUMAN MEMORY: Structures and Processes

Second Edition

Roberta L. Klatzky

University of California, Santa Barbara

W. H. FREEMAN AND COMPANY
San Francisco

Sponsoring Editor: W. Hayward Rogers
Project Editor: Nancy Flight
Copyeditor: Susan Weisberg
Designer: Sharon H. Smith
Production Coordinator: Fran Mitchell
Illustration Coordinator: Cheryl Nufer
Artists: John and Jean Foster
Compositor: Typesetting Services of California

Library of Congress Cataloging in Publication Data

Klatzky, Roberta L
    Human memory.

    (A Series of books in psychology)
    Bibliography: p.
    Includes indexes.
    1. Memory. I. Title.
BF371.K53 1980   153.1'2   79-20895
ISBN 0-7167-1113-3
ISBN 0-7167-1114-1 pbk.

Printed in the United States of America

  2 3 4 5 6 7 8 9

To the memory of Arnold Klatzky

Contents

Preface

Each of us has a memory. We use it with such ease that we rarely pause to marvel at our capacity for knowledge and the many ways we use what we know. The human memory is a remarkably complex entity, and psychologists are only beginning to understand its complexities. Still, in the last two decades or so, research has provided an ever-clearer representation of the memory system. It is that emerging representation which this book attempts to describe, an attempt that began in 1975 with the first edition and continues in the present revision.

The word *memory* has an abundance of meanings. As used in everyday parlance, it may refer to reminiscence, to an image or impression of things recalled, even to an individual's general ability to retain what has been learned. From the information-processing perspective adopted by this book, the term has even broader use. Human memory is depicted as a continuously active system that receives, modifies, stores, retrieves, and acts upon information. This perspective therefore includes in the study of memory, perception, learning, language, and problem solving, as well as the encoding, storage, and retrieval of information. A book on memory written from the information-processing approach can also be considered a book on cognitive psychology and shares an expanding range of topics with texts on psycholinguistics.

This book does not attempt to cover every topic of interest to researchers in the fields of memory, cognitive processes, or psycholinguistics, however. The goal is to provide a fairly broad view of the current state of memory research and theory while at the same time avoiding a purely superficial treatment and maintaining a manageable size. The word *current* is important here; this revision was necessitated by developments of the last several years that significantly expanded and modified the view of memory presented in the first edition. Among those developments are the application of new models from artificial intelligence to memory and cognitive processes, new theories and findings in text comprehension and memory, and information-processing analyses of alcohol-induced memory deficits. An exhaustive list would touch virtually every aspect of memory.

The book begins with topics in perception, including sensory memory, pattern recognition, and attention. It continues through a discussion of short-term memory, treating it not only as a temporary storehouse for information but as working memory, the site of active processing. The book concludes with a discussion of topics related to long-term memory, including theories of memory structure, memory for text and for visual stimuli, encoding and retrieval, and inaccuracies in memory resulting from forgetting and distortions.

This book has benefited substantially from the comments of reviewers of both editions. The first edition was reviewed by Robert Crowder, Douglas Hintzman, Earl Hunt, James Juola, Thomas Landauer, and Edward E. Smith, and I gratefully acknowledge their assistance. Nancy S. Johnson, Gale Martin, Gary Olson, Bill Putnam, Allen M. Raffetto, and Robert L. Solso commented at various stages in the preparation of the second edition, and I greatly appreciate their help. I thank Jim Geiwitz, who has now twice provided encouragement and friendship throughout a demanding but rewarding project.

October 1979   Roberta L. Klatzky

HUMAN MEMORY

1

Introduction

What does it mean to remember? The famous psychologist William James once said that to remember is to think about something that we previously experienced and that we were not thinking about immediately before (James, 1890). James's definition has intuitive appeal; still, the concept of memory is not readily captured in a single phrase.

This book will address such specific questions as how we mentally represent our knowledge about the world, how we get access to that knowledge when we need it, why we may fail to get access to it, and how we integrate new information with our existing body of knowledge. Each of these problems is a part of the study of memory, and this book will discuss some of the ways that psychologists have conducted that study. In doing so, it will present a variety of topics and ideas, each related to the central question—what does it mean to remember?

The approach to human memory taken by this book is often given the labels *cognitive psychology* and the *information-processing approach*. These labels become more meaningful if we compare the cognitive approach we will take to an older, and still viable, approach to the study of memory, that of *stimulus–response (S–R) theory*, or *associationism*. According to the S–R approach, the ability to remember depends on the formation of associations, or bonds, between stimuli and responses—the strength of those bonds (called habit strength) determining the ability to remember. If a particular bond is sufficiently strong (as the bond between "2+2=" and "4" usually is), we can be said to have a memory; the nature of the memory depends on the stimuli and the responses involved.

For example, most of us remember to stop our cars at red lights most of the time. This habit can be attributed to our having an association between a stimulus (a red light) and a response (stopping the car). Of course, our example is rather simple—almost any organism can learn to stop at a red light and, in that sense, has a memory. But associationists argue that the S–R theory can also account for more subtle and complex human behaviors. One way this is accomplished is by assuming that there are *internal* stimuli and responses. In essence, this means that there are stimuli and responses that are not directly observable (and are thus unlike red lights and the pressing down of brake pedals). In fact, many human responses to the environment are probably internal or, if external, too small to be noticed. These hidden responses may serve as stimuli for other responses, and, in this manner, unobserved S–R chains could come to exist. By this means, more complex mental events can be brought into the framework of S–R theory.

Stimuli and responses are not unimportant to cognitive psychologists; they are the observable entities that are manipulated and measured when experiments are performed. But the cognitive approach toward these entities is considerably different from the associationist approach. Associationists have focused on the contingencies between stimuli and responses and on the principles of conditioning (which describe how associations are formed and how habit strength can be manipulated). Cognitive psychologists have emphasized the internal activities that intervene between stimuli and responses. The word *cognitive* itself is derived from cognition, meaning knowledge—the internal representation of the world. According to Neisser, whose book *Cognitive Psychology* (1967) gave real impetus to the approach, the focus of a cognitive theory is knowledge—how it is acquired, modified, manipulated, used, stored; in short, how it is processed by the human organism. Thus, *information processing* (a term cognitive psychologists have borrowed from computer scientists) broadly refers to the human being's active interaction with information about the world. Of central importance in this processing are the mental activities that occur between a stimulus and a response. Those activities are not viewed simply as links in an S–R chain (although, as we shall see later, the concept of association does have a place in cognitive psychology).

A more precise description of the information-processing approach depends on the theorist who uses it. Thus, it is more useful to identify certain elements that information-processing theories often have in common than to try to specify a set of assumptions basic to all such theories. One characteristic assumption of an information-processing theory is that processing can be broken down into a series of subprocesses, or stages. In other words, the time between an S—information in the external world—and an R—some observable response—can be subdivided into smaller intervals, each of which corresponds to some subset of the events that intervene between S and R. The postulated sequence of events, or stages, is termed a *model* of the internal processing that occurs. (More generally, the term *model* will be used synonymously with *theory*.)

To construct a model for our red-light example, we might divide the total process into the following stages: First, the light registers in our visual system. Second, we recognize the visual sensation for what it is—a red traffic light. (To do this, we must use information stored in memory, that is, knowledge about what a red traffic light looks like.) Third, we apply a rule that we have in our memory— stop the car when you see a red light. Of course, we could break the process down further if we wished. But note that, in the course of the stages we have described, the original information—a visual event—has already undergone successive transformations. From a visual event, it was changed to a recognized category (red lights) and then changed again to a condition for applying a rule (stop the car when . . .). This illustrates a general point: Isolating a stage of information processing is not done arbitrarily; rather, a stage of processing (sometimes called a *level* of processing) generally corresponds to some representation of the stimulus information. As the information goes from one stage to another, its representation changes accordingly.

Information-processing models are often presented simply in words, as in the red-light example. Sometimes a model is specified in mathematical terms in order to make more precise quantitative predictions about behavior. Still another means of modeling is to program a computer to act as a theory dictates. This is called *computer simulation;* to the extent that the computer mimics the performance of a human, it may be said to simulate human processes. The study of how computers can be programmed to behave as humans do, or at least to approximate human behavior, is the area of artificial intelligence. This area is closely tied to cognitive psychology, and the use of computer simulations to model human psychological behavior has become quite common.

Even if an information-processing theory does not explicitly compare a human to a computer, the computer often serves as a general metaphor for human processing. To cite an important example, the activities that computers perform when they serve as memory systems may be divided into three areas—encoding, storage, and retrieval. These same terms have been applied to human memory. *Encoding* means putting information into a system. The process of encoding may include modifying the information so that it is in an appropriate form for the human or mechanical system it is being put into (for example, information may be encoded for a computer by punching holes into IBM cards). Information in an encoded form is often referred to as a memory *code*. *Storage* is just that—storing information in a system. Of course, things may happen to stored information. It may be affected by subsequent information, or it may be lost. *Retrieval* means getting at the stored information.

Information-processing models often separate these three aspects of memory. Consider, for example, the reason that we cannot remember some fact that we were once presented with. This could reflect a breakdown in any of the three processes. The fact might not have been encoded properly in the first place; it could have been lost from storage; or we may be unable to retrieve it, even though it was encoded and stored. All three processes must be intact in order for us to remember.

Still another characteristic of the information-processing approach is its breadth. Traditional theories of learning tended to focus on relatively narrow areas. To study learning was to study "the modification of behavior through experience," as many textbooks defined it; this was considered quite distinct from other aspects of human behavior. The cognitive approach, in contrast, views as its domain human memory in its broadest sense, and that is a very large domain indeed. It is applied to such seemingly diverse areas as perceiving, remembering, imaging, and solving problems, because all are seen as facets of the complex memory system. Perception, the original registration of a stimulus, is inseparable from memory in this view; it can be considered the first stage in the continuous processing of information. The act of imaging, constructing a mental picture of some object, requires the retrieval of stored information about its physical appearance. Problem solving uses stored information about the world, information not only about objects and events but also about rules for manipulating symbolic representations like numbers and words. All of these topics have been studied by cognitive psychologists.

Why is the label *cognitive psychology* applied to the approach we have been describing? The cognitive character of the approach lies, as has been mentioned, in the view of the human organism as an active seeker of knowledge and processor of information. That is, humans are seen as acting on information in various ways. For example, the processor can decide whether or not to recode information from one form to another, to select certain information for further processing, or to eliminate some information from the system. We shall see that this view of the human as an active information processor permeates the newer theories about memory. Cognitive theorists conceive of perceiving and remembering as acts of construction, by means of which people actively build mental representations of the world.

In the remaining chapters of this book, we will consider human memory from the cognitive viewpoint, in the context of a general model of the memory system to be described in Chapter 2. Subsequent chapters will examine this system in detail, spanning cognitive activities from the perception of an external event to memory for long-ago events and complex thought processes.

2

The Human
Information-Processing
System

In the first chapter, humans were characterized as processors of information, and human memory was called an information-processing system. We noted that an important characteristic of such a system is that it can be divided into a series of stages. In the present chapter, we shall look at the human memory system in more detail. A theoretical model of this system will be described and compared to alternative models; in subsequent chapters, this initial model will be developed further. At this point, it is important for us to get an overview of the system that will serve as the basis for our discussion of human memory.

THE SYSTEM AND ITS COMPONENTS

A model of the human information-processing system is illustrated in Figure 2.1. The figure shows how the system operates when information about a stimulus from the "real world" passes through it. (This is not the only way in which the system can operate, but it serves to illustrate the model.)

The memory system is divided into three principal storage structures, each corresponding to a stage of processing the given stimulus. In the first stage following stimulus presentation, a certain amount of information about the stimulus (which, in the figure, has just occurred outside the system) is registered, or entered, in the

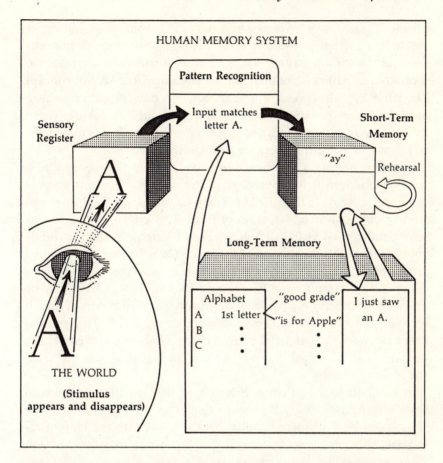

Figure 2.1 A model of the human information-processing system.

system. *Sensory register* is the name given to the site of that registration, because the information enters the system by one or more of the five senses and is held briefly in sensory form (for example, a sound is held in auditory form). Thus, there is a sensory register for each sense. The information can stay in a register only for a brief time. The longer it sits there, the weaker it gets, until it vanishes completely. This gradual weakening is called *decay*.

While information about the stimulus is in a sensory register (in Figure 2.1, the visual register) and before it is passed on to the next storage structure—short-term memory—an important component of the system comes into play. It is *pattern recognition*, a complex process that results in contact between the information in the sensory register and previously acquired knowledge. A pattern is said to be recognized when its sensory aspects are in some way equated with meaningful concepts. A more specific sense of pattern recognition is *naming*. Clearly, when we assign a name to a stimulus—"the letter ay" in this example—we have taken visual information (a representation of the stimulus as consisting of lines in particular orientations, connected at particular points) and equated it with a known concept (the letter ay). However, pattern recognition does not always mean naming (we can recognize some patterns without being able to name them), so it is better to think of pattern recognition in the more general sense of assigning meaning to a stimulus.

Pattern recognition is a means of encoding the stimulus so that it can be passed on to another stage of the system. That new stage is *short-term memory (STM)*. Unlike a sensory register, STM does not store information in a raw, sensory form. The letter A is held not as some unidentified visual stimulus, but as a letter, A. Another difference between the sensory registers and STM is the length of time a piece of information can be retained. An item in the visual register decays rather rapidly, say, in a second, but an item in STM may be maintained indefinitely by a holding process called *rehearsal*, which recycles material over and over again through STM. This process keeps renewing the material so that decay is never complete. However, without rehearsal information in STM is lost, as it is lost from the sensory register.

In addition to a limit on the length of time an item can remain without rehearsal, there is another limitation on STM—only a few stimuli can be held there simultaneously, even with the help of rehearsal. This has been demonstrated in laboratory experiments with a procedure called the *memory-span* or *immediate-memory* task. (*Immediate memory* is another name for STM.) In this task, a subject (participant in the experiment) receives a brief list of items—letters, for example—and is to repeat them immediately. In theory, this task draws on information in STM because the letters have been so recently presented. A common finding with this task is that performance is perfect as long as the items number about seven or less. As the list reaches seven items, however, the subject begins to make errors. It seems that STM has room for only about seven items; this limit is called the *memory span*. It can hold seven items perfectly for as long as it takes to report them. But if too many stimuli—more than the span—are presented, some will be lost from STM. This loss is one type of *forgetting*—a term that can refer to loss of information from any point of storage in the system.

The third storage structure in the memory system is long-term memory (LTM), an essentially permanent storehouse for knowledge about the world. Long-term memory is depicted in Figure 2.1 as entering into processing in two ways. First, after the stimulus has been recognized and has entered STM, it may be retained more permanently through storage in LTM. Second, knowledge stored in LTM was crucial to the process of recognizing the stimulus in the first place; it was this knowledge that was matched with the stimulus in order to recognize it as a known pattern.

A point to note about the system as a whole is that there are limitations on our ability to process information. Limits mentioned in our discussion so far include constraints on the time information can be retained in the sensory registers and STM and on the amount of information that can be held simultaneously in STM. In general, the system can be said to have a limited capacity to process information. This limitation can enter into many aspects of processing, so that it is difficult to associate the capacity with a particular stage. The name for this limited capacity is *attention*, as we use the term in an expression like "I can't pay attention to two things at once." Attentional capacity may be likened to a bank account, out of which only limited funds can be distributed; perhaps this is why we speak of "paying" attention.

With this brief look at the system, it becomes apparent that we have been talking about two types of features. The memory stores that hold information for some period—the sensory registers, STM, and LTM—are built-in, structural components of the system. On the other hand, we have also referred to processes, such as pattern recognition and rehearsal, that are used by the system to act on information in those structures. This distinction between memory structures and processes is a basic one that will recur in subsequent discussions. (Sometimes the word *structures* is used to refer to the memory stores themselves, but it can also refer to the information in a store.)

Let's go back a bit. We have traced the progress of some information from the real world into the deepest recesses of the human memory system, but, in doing so, we have touched upon only a few high points of an extremely complex entity. Before we continue our exploration of that complex entity, let's take a somewhat closer look at each of the structures and processes we have mentioned thus far.

The Sensory Registers

First, let's consider the sensory registers. A visual register for a stimulus entering via the sense of sight has been mentioned. We also assume there are registers for the other four senses: hearing, touch, smell, and taste. The two registers that psychologists have looked at most are the register for vision, called the *icon* by Neisser (1967), and the register for hearing, which we shall refer to as the *echo* (again, Neisser's term).

In general, a sensory register serves the function of briefly holding information about a stimulus in the system in what is called *veridical form*—that is, in much the same form it was initially presented— until it can be put into a new form and sent further on into the system. As mentioned above, the length of time that information is held there is quite brief under any circumstances, because information held in a register is subject to a process of very rapid decay. However, information can also be removed from a register (*masked* or *erased*) because new information came in. We can see why such a feature is necessary: If the icon (visual register), for example, had no such erasing feature, we would constantly be seeing sets of overlapping visual images rather than discrete scenes.

Pattern Recognition

Depicted as intervening between the sensory register and storage in short-term memory is pattern recognition, the process of matching incoming sensory information with previously learned information stored in LTM. The purpose of pattern recognition is to convert raw information (like visual forms or patterns of sound), relatively useless to the system, to something meaningful. This may mean assigning a name to a stimulus, but it need not. The importance of pattern recognition is easy to see. Just think of what might happen if you failed to categorize incoming visual information as "a bear" and instead categorized it as "a horse." Such a failure of the recognition system could be fatal.

Pattern recognition is not a simple process. Consider a fairly straightforward example: We see an immense variety of written, printed, and scrawled alphabet letters in our everyday lives. How are we able to recognize them in all of their multitudinous shapes and sizes? This particular problem is sufficiently complex that no one has been able to construct a machine to do the job—to read the handwritten addresses on letters, for example. As matters now stand, human beings must serve as pattern recognizers—as bank tellers, mail sorters, and so forth. What makes pattern recognition so difficult is that one category can include a great many patterns. For example, the letter A can also be written as A, a, or a. Also, the very same pattern can appear to the system in many sizes and orientations: A, A, ◁. Even more tricky to account for is the fact that novel patterns, never seen before, can be recognized: A̦! Indeed, most hand-printed letters are novel, even unique, in that each probably differs from every other. When you consider it this way, it is clear that there is an almost unlimited number of different patterns, all of which must be recognized as belonging to the same category, and it is this variety that makes machine recognition so difficult.

Short-Term Memory

Recognition of a pattern means that the resulting information can be sent on to STM. This store actually has a variety of names. In addition to short-term memory, it has been called *primary* (the first) memory, *immediate* memory, or *working* memory. The latter two labels reflect the view of STM as the site of what we are immediately thinking about or working on. In this same vein, STM has been equated with consciousness. Studies of STM have been largely confined to the use of verbal material—letters, words, and so on. Thus, most of our information about this store comes from the verbal domain. It has been suggested, for example, that a verbally coded item (that is, an item in the form of a word or label) will last less than a half-minute in STM if it is not rehearsed, and that about a half-dozen such items can be held in STM at one time.

Rehearsal itself is an immensely interesting and controversial STM phenomenon. Some theorists have proposed that the process of rehearsing is like subvocally, or silently, repeating the rehearsed item, and that each such repetition serves the same function as putting the item into STM in the first place; that is, the item returns fresh and unforgotten. Whether rehearsal is really implicit speech is an open question; however, rehearsal does seem to be used to maintain items in STM. A second function of rehearsal relates to the transfer of information to LTM. It has been suggested (for example, by Atkinson and Shiffrin, 1968) that the more an item is rehearsed in STM, and the longer it stays in STM, the more likely it is to be remembered later. This means, essentially, that the rehearsal process can provide an opportunity for adding to or enhancing a representation of the item in LTM, so that later it is more amenable to recall.

Theorists do not agree, however, on just how this strengthening process works. Some assume that each subvocal repetition of the item acts in a rather mechanical fashion to increase the strength of its LTM representation. Others assume that the effect of rehearsal is less direct. They propose that while repetitive or rote rehearsal maintains the item in STM, more active processing occurs, such as elaboration of the item's meaning or retrieval of associated items, and it is this more elaborative processing that enhances the LTM representation, rather than the maintenance of the item itself. This controversy is related to different views on the best way to study: Does rote repetition of a set of facts really enable us to recall it better for a test, or must we think about those facts in a more meaningful fashion?

Another oft-cited finding concerning STM is that a verbal label held in STM is usually coded acoustically. This means that the word is represented in terms of its sound, not as it appears to the visual sense. This occurs even if the word first entered the system visually, via the icon. We know this because, when retrieval from STM is inadequate and a wrong answer is reported (this is called a *confusion error*, because something *not* in STM is confused with something that was put in there), the confusion is between things that sound alike, rather than between things that look alike (Conrad, 1964). For example, when a V is visually presented and put into STM, B is more likely to be reported than X is, because B and V sound similar. This is true even though X may look more like V.

Long-Term Memory

Long-term memory, that immensely complex storehouse, has also been most extensively studied with the use of verbal materials, usually presented in the form of long lists. As we shall see, this approach has resulted in some extremely important findings, but it also has limitations. After all, remembering lists of words is somewhat different from remembering a conversation, principles of calculus, or the plot of a movie. Recently, LTM has been studied in the context of memory for language—not just isolated words, but meaningful linguistic discourse. Studying memory with stimulus material that is close to natural language leads to a much more extensive knowledge of how LTM works in everyday life.

We begin to get some idea of the complexities of LTM when we realize that stored in LTM is *everything* we know about the world. Washington could not tell a lie; dogs must eat to live; shoes are worn on the feet. Not only is this vast amount of information stored in LTM, each piece of it can be reached by a multitude of pathways. Just as an example, consider the single word *smile*. We can reach that word through its definition: "Tell me a word meaning configuration of the mouth that indicates happiness." We can reach it by filling in the blank in "Let a _____ be your umbrella." And we can reach it by other routes as well.

In general, information in LTM seems to be arranged in such a way that retrieval is accomplished with relative ease. For example, given a printed word like *smile*, we can easily find the spot in LTM where information about its meaning is stored. Moreover, we can quickly find related information in LTM (grin; frown; snicker). The very rapidity with which we can retrieve suggests both that retrieval is not a haphazard, undirected process and that LTM must be highly organized.

Some important ideas about LTM are worth mentioning here. One is that, unlike STM and the sensory registers, LTM is a *permanent* store. If this hypothesis is true, why is it that we can't remember everything we have ever known? Supporters of the hypothesis contend that forgetting is a retrieval problem—the information is there, but we can't get at it.

Another interesting hypothesis regarding LTM derives from the observation that many different types of information about items must reside there. Consider, for example, the word *train*. In our LTM for this item is information about how the word appears and how it is pronounced (graphemic and phonological information); information about the meaning of the word; information about the appearance of trains and the way they sound. Some theorists have proposed that LTM should be subdivided into different stores representing these different types of information: a lexicon, or store for words; a semantic memory for the meanings of concepts; and an imaginal memory for sounds and sights. Whether we accept the idea of separate LTMs or not, any theory must deal with the variety of information that can represent an item.

Attention

The concept of attention, the general limit on the capacity of the system to process information, has changed over the course of research on it. At one point, attention was viewed as a bottleneck or filter in the system, necessary because of the incredible amount of information impinging on the senses at any one time. For example, as you read this book, you are not only receiving the visual stimulation from the printed page, you are also receiving signals from your sense of touch, hearing sounds, and smelling odors. Some of the available information is important; some is not. Because the memory system cannot simultaneously recognize all of it and pass it on to STM, it was assumed that "attention" acted to filter out the less important inputs and select the more important ones for further processing. For this reason, it was called *selective* attention.

The concept of attention as a filter has given way to a relatively new concept of attention as a limited capacity that can occur at any of a variety of points in the system. This change has occurred in part because no one was able to find any one point in the system at which the bottleneck always occurred. Depending on the demands of the experiment that studied it, selection was found to operate in many different ways. It could occur before pattern recognition, for example, to select which patterns were recognized, or at the point of entry into STM.

The principal assumption of the limited-capacity view is that attention-demanding processing can be distinguished from another type of processing, called automatic. An *automatic* process is one that can handle as much information as is presented—for example, your ears automatically register sound waves whether one, two, three, or more sounds are presented. Although the sensory response to stimulation is automatic, at some point the system becomes unable to process all of its inputs because of limitations in its capacity. This is the point at which attention occurs. But note that this point may vary over different situations. Actually, the term *attention-demanding process* may be preferable to *attention*, to avoid suggesting a fixed location. For example, rehearsing items in STM is a process that demands attention.

Our overview of the human information-processing system has been rather simplistic so far; in the following chapters we shall see that many qualifications of the model are necessary. One qualification should be considered now, however, because it concerns one of the basic assumptions of the model: that postsensory memory can be divided into two stores, STM and LTM. This assumption is by no means accepted by all memory theorists.

THE DUPLEX THEORY—TWO MEMORIES OR ONE?

The theory that divides memory (after initial stimulus registration) into two stores is called the *duplex* theory. Evidence for it comes from a variety of sources, some logical, some from experimental research. Sigmund Freud is one theorist who made the distinction on logical grounds, separating conscious experience—what we are aware of thinking about—from unconscious thought, including our memories of past events. This distinction is analogous to the difference between STM and LTM.

Less intuitive lines of evidence are more commonly used to support the duplex theory. One is physiological. Brenda Milner (1959) described a group of behaviors accompanying damage to certain areas of the brain called the hippocampal regions. These behaviors, taken together, have come to be called *Milner's syndrome*. People with Milner's syndrome appear unable to remember events in the recent past—before the brain was damaged. Such brain-damaged patients have no loss of intelligence or of skills acquired before the damage. The patients can also remember information immediately after being given it; that is, they can repeat back what they are told and can even remember information for several minutes if permitted to say it over and over without interruption (rehearse). However, the patients seem unable to retain new information for any longer than they can rehearse it. All this suggests that the brain-damaged patients have a long-term store (where events of the remote past are held and *also* a short-term memory (used for immediate repetition and rehearsal). It is as if the patients have lost the connection between STM and LTM and, with it, the ability to transfer new information to LTM. Thus, Milner's syndrome fits in well with a duplex theory; in fact, such a theory helps to explain how such behavioral deficits could occur.

Other evidence for duplexity has come from experimental work on memory. One interesting series of findings has to do with confusion errors in recalling information. In a memory-span task, for example, a person is given a brief list of items such as letters and immediately asked to repeat them. A confusion error is said to occur if the subject reports a letter that was not in the list instead of a letter that was. As noted previously, such confusions are made more often between pairs like B and V, which sound similar, than between acoustically dissimilar pairs, even if the letters were presented visually.

Now consider the LTM analog of the immediate-memory experiment. We show a subject a list of words, say, and ask the subject to recall them an hour later. The typical confusions will be not acoustic, but semantic—based on meaning. For example, if the word *labor* was in the list, a subject is much more likely to report *work* than *later*. Thus, the subject confuses a word similar in meaning with the list word but does not confuse words on the basis of sound. In short, errors in recall from LTM are generally semantic (Baddeley and Dale, 1966), but most recall errors from STM are acoustic, suggesting that items are stored in STM by sound and in LTM by meaning.

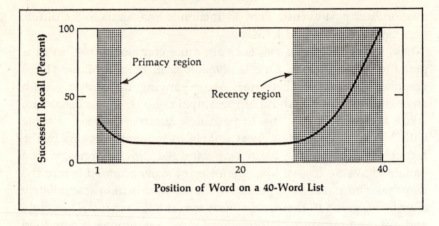

Figure 2.2   The serial-position function for free recall. The percentage of times that words were recalled, for words in each position in a 40-word list. The function is divided into a primacy region, a recency region, and a flat central region. [Data after Murdock, 1962.]

Other data used to support the duplex theory come from a common experimental procedure used to study memory called the *free-recall* paradigm. This is one of several procedures that require a subject to learn a list of items. The items are usually single words, although they may range from letters to sentences.The list is presented to the subject, who then attempts to "freely" recall the items, that is, recall them in any order. This presentation-test sequence is called a *trial*. The measured variable in this task is usually the percentage of items correctly recalled, averaged over many subjects and/or many lists.

The free-recall data particularly relevant to the duplex theory concern the serial-position function, which shows the percentage of correct recalls plotted against the serial positions of the to-be-recalled items. The serial position of an item is simply its numerical order in the list, the first item having serial-position one, the second having serial-position two, and so on. Serial position functions from free-recall experiments tend to have a common form, depicted in Figure 2.2. The items from the beginning and end positions of the list are recalled better than items in the middle, resulting in a U-shaped curve. As indicated in the figure, the various portions of this curve are given different names. The first portion of the curve, showing recall of items from early in the list, is called the *primacy region*. The last portion of the curve, showing recall of the last few items, is the *recency region.* The upturns of the function in those regions are called the *primacy effect* and the *recency effect.*

The duplex theory explains the free-recall serial-position curve as follows: The primacy effect is said to be a result of recall from LTM. It occurs because the first words in the list came into an "empty" STM; that is, the subject had nothing else to concentrate on and could therefore rehearse the first few words many times. But eventually—say after the first six words or so—the subject had more words to keep track of than could be held in STM at one time (owing to its limited capacity). Each subsequent word could be rehearsed only if a word in STM was dropped out, and the new word itself would be rehearsed only a few times before it too was lost from STM. Thus, the first words in the list were rehearsed more than later words and were therefore stored more effectively in LTM. In contrast, items in the middle of the list all came into a filled STM. All had about the same number of rehearsals before being dropped and were stored in LTM equally, so all are remembered at about the same relatively low rate.

The recency effect is explained this way: Items at the end of the list are still present in STM when the recall of the list begins; for this reason, the subject can report them immediately out of STM, and recall is very good for such items. This explanation is supported by the finding that subjects usually do report words from the end of the list right away when the test begins.

The duplex explanation of the form of the free-recall serial-position curve is supported by experiments showing that the primacy and recency portions of the curve can be separately manipulated. These manipulations supposedly affect LTM and STM respectively (see Figure 2.3). For example, suppose we present the list of words and then delay recall for a 30-second period. During that period, we ask the subject to do some arithmetic—presumably preventing rehearsal of the words in STM. We would expect the recency portion to be affected by this manipulation, because the subject would be unable to bring the last words in the list out of STM when recall begins. This, in fact, occurs: The recency effect disappears in such an experiment (for example, Postman and Phillips, 1965; Figure 2.3b).

On the other hand, suppose we attempt to affect LTM, by varying the rate at which words are presented. At a fast rate—one word per second—the subject has little time to rehearse, and LTM storage should be much less than for words presented at a slower rate of one word every two seconds. (However, STM storage should be un-

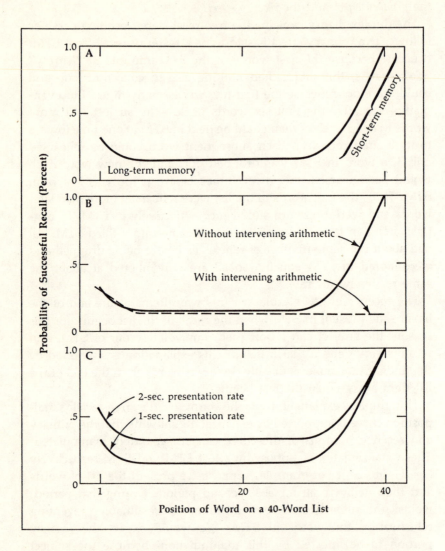

Figure 2.3 (A) The serial-position function for free recall, showing contributions of long-term memory (primacy region and central region) and short-term memory (recency region). (B) The effects of an arithmetic task interpolated between presentation of the list and free recall: With arithmetic, the serial-position function is flattened in the recency area. (C) The effects of presentation rate on the serial-position function for free recall: At faster rates, the primacy region and central region are lowered, but the recency portion is minimally affected by presentation rate. [Curves are idealized data, after experiments of Murdock, 1962; Postman and Phillips, 1965.]

affected, because the subject can hold the last few words in STM at either presentation rate.) Again, the hypothesis is confirmed. The primacy and middle portions of the free-recall serial-position curve are higher at the slow rate of presentation because more rehearsals could occur at that rate, leading to better LTM storage. At the same time, the recency portion of the curve is essentially unaffected by the rate of presentation (Murdock, 1962; Figure 2.3c).

The duplex theory has been accepted by many memory theorists, but it is not as problem-free as it might appear from the foregoing discussion. For one thing, much of the evidence for duplexity can be interpreted without postulating an STM that is separate from LTM. Wickelgren (1973) examined nine major lines of evidence favoring the duplex theory and rejected six of them on that basis. For example, consider the different effects that using an interpolated task (that is, a task that occurs between presentation of the list and free recall) has on the primacy and recency portions of the serial-position curve. We know that such a task wipes out the recency portion of the curve but has relatively small effects on the primacy portion; these different effects of interpolated material are used as evidence for duplexity. However, the evidence weakens when we recognize that items in the primacy portion of the list are always subjected to the negative effects of interpolated material. That is because the earliest items in the list are followed by all the subsequent items before those early items are recalled. Thus, the latter part of the list, that which intervenes between the presentation of the first items and their recall, actually serves as interpolated material. Moreover, as we shall see in Chapter 11, an interpolated task may greatly affect the recall of information that immediately preceded it; but, as more interpolated material is added, the effect of each additional piece of material is less than the effect of the piece before. It is not surprising, then, that a postlist task has little effect on recall of items from the first portion of the list, because that portion has already been subjected to the effects of the latter part of the list by the time the postlist task is performed. In other words, the effects of the postlist task on the recency portion of the list are comparable to the effects of the middle and recency parts of the list on the primacy portion. It can thus be seen that interpolated tasks do not necessarily have different effects on different areas of the serial-position curve and that, consequently, evidence for duplexity based on the effects of a postlist task cannot be considered conclusive.

Not only can data originally taken as evidence for the model be reinterpreted, additional experimental findings cast doubt on the initial interpretations. One finding (Bjork and Whitten, 1974) is that an arithmetic task interpolated between the end of a list and the free-recall test does not always eradicate the recency effect. This is inconsistent with the idea that the recency effect derives from items in short-term memory, which should be eliminated when such a task is performed. Another, related finding comes from an experiment in which subjects performed a series of memory-span tasks (each consisting of recalling a short list of items immediately after their presentation) at the same time as they heard a different list of items for later free recall. The memory-span items would be expected to fill STM and therefore keep the subject from storing the most recent items in the free-recall list there, thus eliminating the recency effect in free recall. However, the presence of the memory-span task was found to depress performance only in the primacy and central regions of the free-recall serial-position curve and not in the recency region (Baddeley and Hitch, 1974). This is certainly not what would be expected if the memory-span list and the last few items in the free-recall list competed for space in STM. Given data like these, it has been suggested that the recency effect in free recall does not arise from STM at all, but from some other source. One possibility is that the last items in the list, like the others, are retrieved from LTM in this task, but they stand out just because they were presented so recently, which gives them the advantage in recall. Whatever the interpretation, however, these results cast doubt on the duplex model's explanation of the serial-position curve.

The free-recall serial-position curve is not the only evidence for duplexity that has been criticized. The interpretation of Milner's syndrome according to the duplex model has been attacked as based on too simplistic a picture of the syndrome. Patients may deviate remarkably from the stereotype of intact-STM, intact-LTM, no-transfer. Such patients may show STM deficits, for example, or they may be able to introduce at least a small amount of new information to LTM (Marslen-Wilson and Teuber, 1975).

Another line of evidence cited for duplex theory is the difference between the representational format of information, or the memory *code*, of STM and that of LTM. STM, we have noted, represents information acoustically, whereas LTM codes information semantically. However, we will soon discuss experimental evidence for nonacoustic—visual and semantic—codes in STM, and we have already noted that LTM must contain acoustic and visual information (as well as information about smell, taste, and touch). Otherwise, how would we recognize faces or sounds that we had not seen or heard for some time? Thus, the acoustic-semantic distinction between the two memories is not as clear as some experiments have made it appear to be.

We have also said that items are stored in STM without rehearsal for only a few seconds but that items can be stored in LTM indefinitely. This might be a means of distinguishing between the stores, but estimates of the duration of STM vary widely. Furthermore, estimates vary about STM capacity, that is, the number of items that can be maintained there at any one time.

One source of this confusion is that STM and LTM—if they are actually separate entities—are highly interdependent. Not only is there a connection between the two, so that rehearsals in STM lead to building memories in LTM, but LTM contributes greatly to STM encoding. Consider the case where we put a visually presented letter in STM. How would we know it was indeed a letter without going to LTM for its visual appearance and its name? Because recognizing patterns involves LTM, STM encoding also involves LTM. In addition, the representation of items in STM can be affected by LTM after they are recognized. For example, the nonsense syllable WIS could be stored in STM as a word, Wisconsin. The process of mediation, which is what occurs when WIS is stored as Wisconsin, uses LTM information to convert the syllable to a more meaningful unit.

In trying to make these complex operations and memory codes fit a duplex framework, some psychologists have sometimes pulled, stretched, and distorted STM and LTM beyond recognition. This has led others to ask why we should bother with duplex theory at all.

THE LEVELS-OF-PROCESSING THEORY

Despite its flaws, the duplex model has the advantage of being a very general theory that can serve to integrate a large body of research on memory. As we will see in later chapters, this is a valuable function, for a great deal of research exists, and though theories of particular findings abound, theories that can incorporate many different findings do not. One alternative theoretical model that attempts to integrate findings across several areas of memory is called the *levels-of-processing theory* (Craik and Lockhart, 1972; Craik and Tulving, 1975; Lockhart, Craik, and Jacoby, 1976). This is a variant of the information-processing approach in that it isolates different stages (here called levels) of memory coding. However, in this approach there are no structural-component stages like STM and LTM. Instead, what we have described as structures are seen as processes, much like pattern recognition and rehearsal.

The fundamental assumption of the levels approach is that an incoming stimulus can be processed in many different ways (or levels), and that these various manners of processing can be viewed as forming a dimension called depth (or level) of processing. The processing of a stimulus is roughly divided into three broad domains: physical, acoustic, and semantic. These domains are best illustrated by considering the ways in which a single item, a word, can be processed. First, it can be processed at a physical, or perceptual, level—in terms of its appearance. The word *train*, for example, can be encoded as a string of lower-case (small) letters of a certain typeface. Second, the word can be processed in terms of its acoustic properties—how it sounds. *Train* rhymes with *pain* and begins with a sound like that beginning the word *trill*. Third, the meaningful attributes of the word can be processed. *Train* can be represented as a vehicle of transportation, related to car and bus.

Not only can these three types of processing be isolated, but they can also be ordered in terms of the depth, or elaborateness, of analysis they involve. It seems intuitively reasonable to say that processing the physical form of a word takes place at a more superficial, or shallow, level than processing its sound, and that processing sound, in turn, occurs at a more shallow level than processing meaning. Thus, the three domains can be ordered, with physical processing at the shallowest level, acoustic processing intermediate, and semantic processing deepest. When ordered in this way, the three levels obviously resemble the three memory stores of the duplex model: the sensory stores, acoustically coded STM, and meaningfully coded LTM. Just as the duplex model assumes that storage proceeds from the sensory store to LTM by progressive transformations of a stimulus, the levels theory assumes that processing increases in depth from the physical, to the acoustic, to the semantic level. However, it is important to note that the levels approach does not view the three levels as stores. For one thing, as noted above, they are depicted not as structures, but as processing variants. Second, it is assumed that each of these domains itself includes processes that vary in level. For example, we could subdivide semantic processing into a fairly "shallow" meaning analysis, such as a "a train is something you ride in," to a deeper, more elaborate analysis that includes different types of trains, the role of the train in public transportation, and the Amtrak system.

The levels-of-processing theory relates these distinctions among types of processing to memory by a very straightforward assumption: Deeper processing leads to better memory. It is as if the act of processing an item leaves behind it traces that are stored and can be retrieved later. The deeper these traces, the better the memory. However, the details of this assumption have been modified since the theory was first described in a paper by Craik and Lockhart (1972). For example, Craik and Lockhart initially assumed that the three domains of processing—physical, acoustic, and semantic— formed a continuum, so that acoustic processing could be reached only after physical processing had reached its deepest level, and semantic processing could be reached only after the deepest acoustic processing. However, later descriptions of the model (e.g., Lockhart, Craik, and Jacoby, 1976) changed the continuity assumption, stipulating only that the three domains could be ordered in depth and not that each ran continuously into the next. This change was necessitated by the realization that physical processing does not necessarily shade into acoustic; the two domains are quite distinct. Nor does it seem that in order to process the meaning of a word, you must first process its physical form in the utmost detail, as the continuum idea suggests.

In its initial version, the levels theory stated that *only* deeper processing leads to better memory. This assumption has two general implications for experiments. First, if we manipulate the depth to which items are processed, we should affect performance on tests of memory. Second, if an item is processed for a long time at a constant level, memory should be no better than if processing at that level occurred for a shorter time, because, as long as the level is constant, any extra time expended will not result in a deeper memory trace and thus will not increase the amount of information stored. This particular prediction is especially relevant to the duplex model's view of rehearsal. Recall that at least some duplex theorists view rehearsal as subvocal repetition of an item that increments its strength in LTM. The levels-of-processing theory would imply that this view is incorrect, because subvocal repetition of an item amounts simply to continuous processing at the acoustic level and cannot add to what is stored in memory.

A number of experiments have tested these implications of the levels theory and, in some tests, the model has fared quite well. One such study had subjects encode a list of words by processing the items to various levels (Craik and Tulving, 1975). As each word was presented, the subject answered one of three types of questions about it, such as (1) Is it printed in capital letters? This type of question (called the *case* question) was assumed to require processing of only the physical appearance of the word. (2) Does it rhyme with pain? This rhyme question was assumed to induce processing to an acoustic level, for it required knowing the sound of the word. (3) Does it fit in the sentence, "The girl placed the _____ on the table"? This sentence question clearly requires processing the meaning of the word. The levels theory predicts that the ability to remember the words in a subsequent test depends on the question with which they were encoded. Memory performance should improve from case, to rhyme, to sentence questions, because the depth of processing necessary for answering the question increases in that order, and deeper processing is supposed to lead to better memory. And this prediction was borne out in the study described: Subjects remembered words encoded with the sentence question best, the rhyme question next best, and the case question worst.

You may criticize the study as described because it does not take into account how long subjects took to answer the questions. Perhaps the sentence question took the longest time to answer and the case question the shortest. If so, the results could indicate merely that studying an item longer leads to better memory, a fact that is not unique to the levels theory; the duplex model makes the same point by saying that longer rehearsing leads to better memory. To eliminate this possible explanation of the results, Craik and Tulving (1975) distinguished between the time spent processing and the depth to which processing occurred. They did so by using shallow processing tasks that took a long time; for example, "Decide whether the word following this question has the pattern: consonant-vowel-consonant-vowel-consonant—RAVEL." Such tasks were found to lead to a relatively long processing time before the answer was given, but they did not produce better memory than more rapidly performed tasks that required processing at a deeper level, such as the sentence task. Thus, it was shown that *depth*, rather than *time* predicted memory performance.

Though the levels-of-processing approach was supported by such findings, other experiments pointed to the need for modification and expansion of the initial model. Consider first the model's prediction that deeper processing will lead to better retention in memory. It has been found that whether or not this is true depends on the type of test used to measure memory retention. In the experiments of Craik and Tulving (1975), for example, encoding items with the sentence task led to superior memory, as measured by tests such as free recall. However, we will see in later chapters that free recall is assumed to tap information about the meaning of items. This raises the possibility that the effectiveness of meaningful encoding, as induced by the sentence task, was due to the fact that the subsequent test tapped retention of meaning. What if we used a different test, for example, asking subjects if there was a word in the list that rhymed with a given test word ("Was there something that rhymed with pain?")? With this type of test, the rhyme task rather than the sentence task is found to lead to superior performance (Morris, Bransford, and Franks, 1977). Thus, the claim that deeper processing leads to better retention must be qualified; it depends on the type of test used to measure that retention.

Results like these have led levels-of-processing theorists to expand the theory to consider the role of retrieval—getting information out of memory. The initial theory, by emphasizing the processing of stimulus items at the time they occurred, focused on conditions of encoding into memory. In later discussions of the model (Moscovitch and Craik, 1976), it is assumed that the depth of processing at the time of encoding establishes a potential for subsequent memory performance, with deeper processing leading to better potential. Whether that potential is actually realized, however, is now seen to depend on the conditions at the time of retrieval, such as the type of test.

What of the model's second assumption, that only deeper processing, not continued processing at the same level, will facilitate memory? We will discuss this further in the context of rehearsal, in Chapter 4. For the present, it is sufficient to note that this assumption has been shown to be inaccurate. One contradictory finding is that of Nelson (1977), who gave subjects more than one presentation of an item but repeated the same encoding task. For example, subjects might be presented with *train* along with an acoustic question ("Does the item have an *n* sound?"), then later have a second presentation of *train* accompanied by the same question. According to the assumption stated above, this second presentation should have no effect, for it will induce more of the same old acoustic processing that the first presentation did. But, contrary to the levels prediction, two presentations, even with the same question, do in fact lead to better recall than one. If the number of presentations of an item as well as its level of processing can affect retention, it appears necessary to modify the levels theory to incorporate factors other than depth of processing in predicting memory performance (Craik and Tulving, 1975; Jacoby, Bartz, and Evans, 1978).

Not only has the initial version of the levels model been forced into modification by experimental outcomes that are incompatible with its predictions, antagonists to the levels theory have argued against it on logical grounds. In particular, it has been claimed (Baddeley, 1978; Nelson, 1977) that the definition of processing depth is inadequate because no objective measure of depth has been offered. The amount of time required for a process is not adequate to measure depth, for, as we have seen, physical processing can actually be slower than semantic processing. The idea that physical processing is shallow and semantic is deep may be intuitively appealing, the argument goes, but, without some independent definition of *depth*, all we know from observing that semantic processing leads to better retention than physical is that semantic is more effective than physical, not that deep is more effective than shallow.

From this discussion, it should be clear that the levels-of-processing theory, like the duplex model, is susceptible to criticism and controversy, to the point that some feel it should be abandoned. A more valuable approach, however, may be to combine the levels theory with the duplex model in order to develop theories of memory that incorporate the best points of both. The duplex theory has much to offer in its division of memory into short-term and long-term processing, into what we are currently thinking about and what we know but are not using at present. As we shall see, this division is very useful in organizing and integrating the large body of research on human memory. The levels theory points out, however, that the division of memory need not lead to the assumption of two completely separate memory structures like STM and LTM. We could alternatively distinguish between active processing and passive storage in memory, or between two types of memory codes, or between still other duplex processes or mechanisms. The levels approach also offers an expanded view of the active processing of stimulus items and its relationship to long-term storage and retrieval. As we shall see, the emphasis the levels model places on the importance of meaningful processing is consistent with what is known about effective encoding into LTM.

In all of this controversy, it is good to keep in mind that no matter what theory you may accept—and this statement goes beyond arguments about models of memory—it is a theory. As such, it is to be taken not as a rigid proclamation or literal description but as a useful tool for describing and explaining events, subject to modification when its predictions are inadequate. We will use the duplex framework as just such a tool in the chapters to come.

3

The Sensory
Registers

The model of human memory presented in Chapter 2 included as one type of component *sensory registers,* in which incoming information could be held for a brief period in veridical form—that is, as a faithful reproduction of the original stimulus—before it was recognized and passed on through the system. It was suggested that such a register existed for each sense. Sensory registers have been given a variety of names by psychologists: sensory-information stores, iconic stores, and precategorical stores. (The last label, *precategorical,* is used to indicate that the incoming information has not yet been recognized or matched with an appropriate category.)

THE VISUAL REGISTER

The most extensively studied sensory registers are the two that correspond to our visual and auditory senses. They have been called the *icon* and the *echo,* respectively (Neisser, 1967). Much of what we know about iconic storage comes from the work of George Sperling (1960; Averbach and Sperling, 1961). Sperling's research began with his observations of the results of experiments with immediate-memory tasks. In such experiments, subjects were asked to report back a series of letters that they had just viewed briefly. Sperling's results were quite consistent: How well the subjects performed depended on how many letters they viewed. If a list contained about four or fewer letters, the subjects could report them perfectly. But when the number of letters was increased to about five or more, performance broke down. The subjects could no longer report all of the letters in the list; in fact, they could report only an average of about four or five. The upper limit of about four or five, that is, the point at which performance on the immediate-memory task fell below 100 per cent accuracy, is what we earlier called the *memory span*. We could say that, as measured with the experimental conditions just described, the memory span, (or span of immediate memory) is about five. (The restriction to the particular experiment described is important, because the memory span varies somewhat with the nature of the material that is to be remembered and the conditions of its presentation.)

In such experiments, it matters little how the letters that the subject sees are arranged. For example, six letters might be arranged in a single row or in two rows of three each, and performance would not vary. Let us consider a specific experiment drawn from Sperling's work. Suppose the subject is presented with nine letters in the form of a three by three matrix (that is, three rows of three letters each). The letters are exposed for a very brief time, 50 milliseconds (msec.). (A millisecond is one 1/1000 second, so that would be .05 second, less time than the subject requires for an eye movement.) After the exposure, the subject reports as much as he or she can, with some (by now) predictable results: On the average, only four or five letters can be reported.

You might suspect that the subject could not report all nine letters because he or she didn't see them all; after all, .05 second is not much time. But briefness of exposure is not the reason for the subject's failure; if the exposure time is increased up to a half-second (plenty of time to see the letters), the results do not change.

These results indicate that the limit on the number of letters reported does not derive from a limit on the ability to perceive the letters, for if that were the case, changing the conditions of presentation (and thus the nature of what is to be perceived) by changing spacing or exposure duration should affect performance. Instead, the lack of such effects suggests that the limit is in memory rather than in perception. Presumably, the limit is on the number of items that can be held in STM simultaneously, long enough for them to be reported.

The procedure just described, in which a subject sees a list of letters and then attempts to recall as many as possible, is called the *whole-report procedure.* It is known by this name because the subject is requested to recall the whole list, or as much of it as he or she can. Sperling not only studied performance with whole reports, but he also developed a new procedure for studying immediate memory, called the *partial-report procedure.* In the partial-report experiment, the subject briefly views a display of letters arranged in three rows. Immediately after the letters vanish, the subject hears a tone of either high, medium, or low frequency. The tone is an instruction that tells the subject to report a single row of the matrix. A high tone indicates that the top row is to be reported; a middle tone, the middle row; a low tone, the bottom row. Then, immediately after the tone, the subject attempts to report the requested row of letters. The sequence of events (presentation of letters, then tone, then report) is called a *trial,* and the experiment itself comprises a series of such trials.

Another way to conduct a partial-report task is to ask subjects to report a specific letter from the matrix. In this case (Averbach and Coriell, 1961), the signal of what to report is not a tone, but a visual display that follows the matrix of letters: a white field containing a black bar. The bar, which occupies a position just above the previous position of one of the letters, indicates that the subject should report that letter. In general, the crucial feature of partial-report situations is that some kind of signal follows presentation of the letters and points out what part of the entire set of letters is to be recalled.

The results of the whole-report experiment reveal that no matter how many letters are in the list, subjects can report no more than about five of them. The results of the partial-report procedure are quite different, as can be seen in the data of Sperling's experiment (shown in Figure 3.1). Consider what happens when nine letters are shown. In the partial-report situation, subjects are nearly 100 percent accurate, no matter which row they were asked to report. But this means that the subjects must have had all nine of the letters available in memory at the time the tone sounded; otherwise, they would surely have made an error on some row at some time. That is, immediately after the letters were presented, at the time the tone sounded, the subjects must have had information in memory about all nine letters.

In general, we can use the rate of accuracy to estimate how many letters the subject had available in memory at the time of the tone. We simply multiply the accuracy rate (percentage correct) by the number of letters presented. For example, subjects performed with about 76 percent accuracy for displays of twelve letters (three rows of four each), indicating about nine of the letters were available

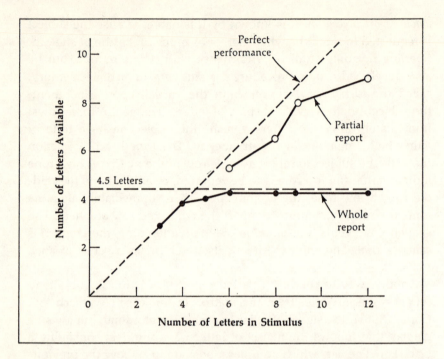

Figure 3.1 Performance in Sperling's experiments with whole-report and partial-report procedures. The partial-report results show letters available, calculated as the percentage of letters called for that are reported by observers, multiplied by the number of letters in the display. The whole-report results show letters available, calculated as the number of letters observers could correctly report. The diagonal line shows where performance would fall if subjects could report perfectly. [After Sperling, 1960. Copyright 1960 by the American Psychological Association. Reprinted by permission.]

in memory at the time of report, which agrees almost perfectly with the results of the experiment with nine letters.

The results of Sperling's experiment, shown in Figure 3.1, indicate that what is available in memory immediately after the stimulus is presented is much more than what can be reported in a whole-report situation. This conclusion leads to a question: Why is there such a discrepancy between partial report and whole report? Why do subjects have a memory span of only five letters, when they can actually remember nine?

Before answering that question, we should consider a variation on the partial-report procedure. As we described the procedure, the report signal followed immediately after the set of letters. It is possible, however, to delay the signal. The results of varying the delay of the signal are shown in Figure 3.2 (for a matrix of twelve letters). At

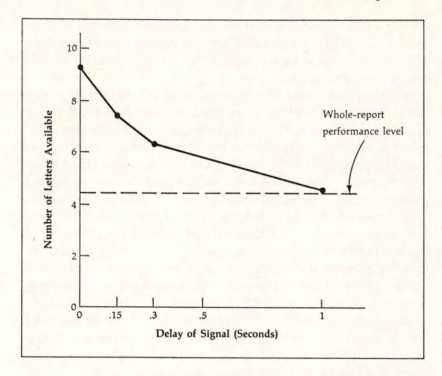

Figure 3.2 Letters available in the partial-report situation (calculated as for Figure 3.1) for various delays of the signal to report. Also shown is performance with a whole-report task for comparable material. [After Sperling, 1960. Copyright 1960 by the American Psychological Association. Reprinted by permission.]

no delay, performance indicates that about nine of the letters are available, as we have seen. But as the delay increases to 1.0 second, subjects make more and more errors, until finally their performance is about the same as it would be with the whole-report procedure; that is, about five letters.

Now, to return to our question. What Sperling's experiments show is that what is available in memory immediately after the visual presentation of a stimulus is more than what remains a second later. The results of the partial-report studies, with no delay of the signal to report, measure what is available immediately after the stimulus has been presented. The whole-report experiments, on the other hand, measure what is available in memory some time after the stimulus has terminated—much less than was there at first. And the results obtained when the partial-report signal is delayed show what happens in between those two points. What seems to happen is that the original, veridical representation of the stimulus gradually decays, so that less and less of the stimulus information is retained as time passes. In short, Sperling's results demonstrate the existence of a form of immediate visual storage that is highly accurate but that decays very rapidly.

This immediate visual storage corresponds to what we have been calling the sensory register, in this case the register for vision, the icon. The data described so far indicate that brief memory for visual information exists; however, our model postulates more about the icon. It assumes that the purpose of the icon is to hold visual information briefly in its original form, so that it can be recognized and passed on in the system. This makes iconic storage a rather primitive kind of memory, in which things are represented in much the same form as they occurred. This form is called *precategorical* (Crowder and Morton, 1969), indicating that it represents storage before the stimulus is assigned to a category during pattern recognition.

That the visual memory under study is in fact a primitive, pre-categorical store is supported by other data from partial-report experiments. In one study, instead of a cue to report information in a certain spatial area (a row), Sperling used a cue to report information from a certain category. In this case, the stimulus matrix consisted of a mixture of letters and digits, and the partial-report cue indicated which category of stimulus should be reported. If the icon is truly precategorical, such a partial-report cue should be of little use, for it relies on information that the icon does not convey. The cue says, "Pick out the letters," but in the icon letters are not differentiated from digits; all are just visual patterns. Sure enough, in this case, no more letters were available than in the whole-report case. This supports the idea that the icon is located prior to pattern recognition and does not portray the meaning (category) of items.

Other data indicate that, unlike STM, which remains fairly constant in span despite variations in stimulus presentation, the icon is affected by the conditions of stimulus occurrence. This is what we would expect if it portrayed the stimulus information in veridical form, as it actually occurred. Among the important variables affecting iconic storage are the illumination preceding and following the visual stimulus (in Sperling's experiments, the letters), the visual stimulation that follows the stimulus, and the exposure time.

We can investigate the effects of illumination by comparing two conditions: one in which a dark field precedes and follows the letters, the other in which a light field precedes and follows the letters. It appears that when the field is dark, the icon lasts longer. We infer this from the finding that the period of iconic decay (experimentally defined as the longest period between the stimulus and the partial-report signal where subjects still do better than with whole reports) is greater with dark fields. This suggests that the light fields may make it harder for the system to "see" the information in the icon—that the visual stimulation produced by the light fields somehow interferes with it. After all, a light field is a visual event in its own right.

This suggestion becomes even more plausible if we examine what happens when we follow the letters with something other than a tone or bar (Averbach and Coriell, 1961). Suppose we follow the letter matrix with a single circle that would encircle one of the letters if the letter were still there. The "circled" letter is then to be reported (as in the bar procedure described earlier). The effects of this manipulation are somewhat surprising, as shown in Figure 3.3. The figure shows that, when the signal marker is delayed either for a relatively long period (a half-second or so) or not at all, performance with the circle as a marker does not differ much from performance with a bar marker. However, in between the no-delay condition and the long-delay condition, the circle leads to much poorer performance than the bar does.

The data in Figure 3.3 have been interpreted as follows: When the circle follows immediately after the letters, it is effectively superimposed on a letter; what subjects "see" is that one letter has a circle *around* it, and they report that letter. (This is similar to what happens with the bar marker—at short delays, subjects see the letter with a bar *over* it.) At very long delays, both the circle and the bar appear after the icon has decayed, so neither marker improves performance over the whole-report level. In between, however, what happens is different. The circle actually erases and replaces the letter it was supposed to mark. Instead of seeing a letter and a circle, subjects see only a circle. This phenomenon is known as *backward masking*, because the circle acts backward in time to mask, or erase, the letter that preceded it. The bar, which is more offset from the letter's position, does not produce erasure.

The erasure phenomenon is related to the different effects of light and dark fields noted above. We suggested that a light field interfered with the icon because it was itself a visual stimulus. Now we find that a stimulus that immediately follows the letter array and is in the same position as a letter can act in much the same way. When we relate the phenomenon of erasure to our concept of the sensory register, we see that erasure could serve an important function, to prevent iconic representations from staying too long in the register.

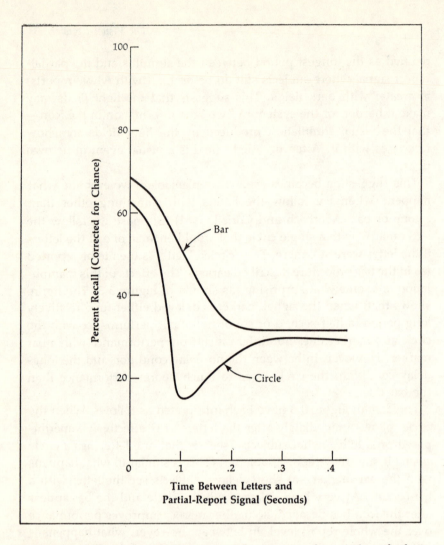

Figure 3.3 Effects of two different partial-report signals: a circle and a bar. They yield similar results when the delay of the signal is either small or large, but performance with the circle is markedly inferior for intermediate delays. [After Averbach and Coriell, 1961. Reprinted with permission from *The Bell System Technical Journal*. Copyright 1961, The American Telephone and Telegraph Company.]

If there were no erasure, then each iconic representation could fall on top of those which preceded it, leading to a piling up and scrambling of visual information. Erasure clears away the debris of preceding iconic storage as new information is registered.

So far, we have been restricting our discussion of the visual register to data from the partial-report versus whole-report techniques. But the icon's existence has been demonstrated by other procedures. A rather straightforward technique is based on the icon's function of extending brief stimuli. It essentially asks subjects to report how

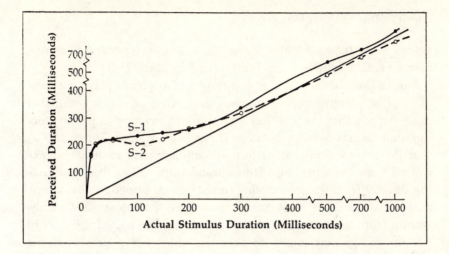

Figure 3.4 Perceived duration of a visual stimulus (measured by the interval between clicks set at its apparent onset and offset), as a function of its actual duration. Data are reported separately for two subjects; the diagonal line indicates performance if perceived duration were identical to actual duration. [After Haber and Standing, 1970. Copyright © 1970 Canadian Psychological Association. Reprinted by permission.]

long a briefly presented stimulus seems to persist. In one such experiment (Haber and Standing, 1970), subjects adjusted clicks of two types, one so that it seemed to occur just when a matrix of letters flashed on, another so that it seemed to occur when the matrix vanished. The subjects were not very accurate at perceiving the duration of brief stimuli, as Figure 3.4 shows. They perceived briefly presented stimuli as remaining long after they had actually vanished in the physical world. In the experimental condition shown in the figure, stimuli from 10 msec. to about 200 msec. were all perceived as lasting about 200 msec. Stimuli of durations beyond 200 msec., however, were seen more accurately, as lasting only about 40 msec. or so after they had terminated. These results suggest that the icon may serve a very specialized function, that of extending brief stimuli but not adding on to stimuli that already have a 200-msec. duration. (The time of extension observed varied somewhat with the illumination of the fields preceding and following the stimulus, although the general pattern was similar in all cases.) These data fit nicely with the purpose of the icon in our model (Chapter 2), namely, to hold visual information in its original form long enough so that it can be recognized and passed further into the system. If the stimuli are too brief, they need extending in order for recognition to occur; if they are already long enough, they do not need further persistence. And the icon accomplishes just these needs, according to the data of Haber and Standing. Moreover, the critical 200-msec. duration agrees with some estimates of the minimum time needed to recognize a visual stimulus (e.g., Eriksen and Eriksen, 1971).

Not all theorists accept this depiction of the icon as playing a critical role in pattern recognition, however. One argument against it concerns whether the icon has an important function in pattern recognition, as has been postulated. It has been argued (Turvey, 1977) that the assumption that pattern recognition uses information extracted from the world and stored in an icon, rather than proceeding directly from the information in the world, unnecessarily complicates matters. This is especially true where the information comes from a stimulus undergoing steady motion. The use of the icon in pattern recognition might obscure the motion if it presented the moving stimulus as a series of stationary "snapshots" for the pattern recognizer to operate on. Wouldn't it be better, it is argued, for the recognizer to look directly at the stimulus and use its movement as part of the information to be recognized? In this view, the demonstration that an icon exists is irrelevant. It is merely a coincidence, and rather an unfortunate one at that, insofar as it affects our theorizing about how patterns are perceived. It is as if we were theorizing about a physical process like the oxidation of iron. Observing that whenever iron decays, we always see rust, we might theorize that the rust was actually composed of tiny organisms that eat the metal. We would not realize that the rust was simply a by-product associated with oxidation, not a functional mechanism. The icon, similarly, might play no functional role in perception but rather be a relatively uninteresting part of the visual system.

Sakitt (1976; Sakitt and Long, 1978; 1979) has offered a view of the icon that is consistent with the above idea. She postulates that the icon is a visual persistence principally located in certain cells within the retina of the eye called *rods*. One observation on which she bases this assumption is that a person having only the function of rods, and not other retinal cells known to exist, can nevertheless show partial-report versus whole-report effects like those usually used to demonstrate the icon. This shows that rod cells are sufficient, at least, for the icon to exist. Another of Sakitt's findings is that the conditions of stimulus presentation that affect the rods—such as the wavelength of light used and its intensity—similarly affect the duration of the icon, as measured by the subjects' estimates. Thus, the icon seems to be closely related to the rods.

The importance of these results for our present discussion lies in what they indicate about the location of the icon. By placing it within the mechanical structure of the eye itself, much like the after-image from a popping flashbulb, these data seem to contrast with the view of the icon as a memory structure playing an intimate role in the assignment of the stimulus to known categories. This does not prove that the icon has no function in pattern recognition, as Turvey suggests, but it does indicate that the icon is a physical structure and not a memory store located beyond the sense organs in the processing system.

However, other findings conflict with Sakitt's work (Adelson, 1978; Banks and Barber, 1977; McCloskey and Watkins, 1978). Banks and Barber conducted partial-report and whole-report tasks using not only the usual black-and-white stimuli but also colored stimuli. One set of stimuli consisted of letters in one color on a background of another, where the shades had been chosen to seem identical shades of grey under dim light (when only the rod cells of the eye, which are insensitive to colors, are operative). If the rods were responsible for the icon, and thus the advantage for partial reports over whole reports, these stimuli should not give rise to a partial-report advantage, for they are "invisible" to the rods. However, the colored letters did give a partial-report effect, and one that declined over the same period as the partial-report effect with black letters on a white ground. This indicates that the iconic information did not reside solely in the rods.

As for the argument that the icon may not be functional in pattern recognition, that it would obscure perception rather than enhance it, counterarguments to this point have also been made (e.g., Hayes-Roth, 1977). One is that studies of the icon have primarily aimed at understanding perception under simplified conditions, where the stimulus does not move. Under these conditions at least, the icon can play a functional role. And understanding these conditions may help us to construct theories of more complex perception, such as the case of moving stimuli. We may or may not find that the icon plays a similar role there, but the attempt to argue against it with such complex stimuli is premature at this point.

Perhaps the best resolution of these arguments without further information is to retain an open mind but accept that it is plausible that the icon plays an important role in perception of patterns under at least simplified circumstances.

THE AUDITORY REGISTER

Without an icon, we would be able to "see" visual stimuli only while they were before our eyes. That could make it impossible to recognize briefly occurring stimuli, for recognition takes time, perhaps more time than the stimuli are exposed to view. Consider next what would happen if the sensory register for audition, the echo, did not exist. By the same reasoning, we would be able to "hear" sounds only when they were physically present. That limitation would have a striking effect: We would have great difficulties with the comprehension of speech. To illustrate the point, Neisser (1967, p. 201) gives an example of a foreigner who is told, "No, not zeal, *seal!*" He notes that the foreigner could not benefit from this advice unless he could retain the *z* in *zeal* long enough to compare it to the *s* in *seal*. Other examples of the usefulness of the echo can readily be seen. We could not recognize the rising intonation at the end of a question such as "You came?" if the first part of the rising-intonation pattern were not available for comparison when the second occurred. In general, because sounds occur over some period of time, there must be a place to store their components. That place is the sensory register for hearing.

The echo has been demonstrated in an experiment analogous to Sperling's demonstrations of the icon. Subjects in the echoic experiment (Moray, Bates, and Barnett, 1965) were "four-eared", which means they listened to as many as four messages simultaneously. The messages came via separate channels. To digress a bit, a *channel* means a source of information—in this case, sound. The concept may be familiar if you have a stereo system. There usually are two speakers, each reproducing its own distinct version of the music that is played. In the same vein, it is possible to construct a four-channel system for such an experiment. One way is to set up four loudspeakers and to put a listener in the middle of the four. Another method is to use headphones, splitting each phone so that it carries two sources of sound. Moray and his colleagues found that both systems—four loudspeakers or split headphones—worked about equally well. For our purposes, the main point about channels is that subjects are able to discriminate among them, that is, when directed to listen to one specific channel, they can do so. They do not hear a jumble of sound; rather, they can recognize the fact that there are different messages coming from different sources.

Now, to the four-eared subjects. In the Moray-et-al. experiment, the subjects took part in a series of trials. On each trial, they listened to messages played simultaneously on two, three, or four channels (loudspeakers). Each message consisted of one to four letters of the alphabet. The subjects' task was to recall the letters after they had heard them. In one condition of the experiment, they tried to recall all the letters; that was the whole-report case. In another condition, a partial-report procedure analogous to Sperling's was used. The signal to report was not a tone, but a light. On a board held by the subjects as they listened were two, three, or four lights, in positions corresponding to the positions of the loudspeakers being used. One second after the messages were over, one of the lights would flash, signaling the subjects to recall the letters spoken on that particular channel—in other words, to give a partial report. Moray and his colleagues found that subjects could recall a greater percentage of letters when a partial report was requested than when the whole report was requested, regardless of the number of channels or letters per channel. We can infer, as we did from Sperling's experiments, that shortly (1 second) after the letters had been presented, there was more information in memory about them than there was later. Presumably, that information was available in the auditory analogue of the icon, the echo.

We need more than the superiority of the partial report over the whole report, however, to conclude that the effect is in the echo. Just as in the case of the icon, it is important to show that the information that gives rise to the partial-report superiority is precategorical, that it has not yet undergone pattern recognition. The way to do this is to show that, when the partial-report cue indicates some aspect of the stimulus that becomes apparent only after it is categorized (as opposed to some perceptual attribute, such as spatial location, that is evident in an uncategorized stimulus), performance is no better than when subjects have no partial cue. Darwin, Turvey, and Crowder (1972) attempted to show this. They had subjects listen to simultaneously presented lists of three items each, one such list on each of three channels. The items were either letters or digits. The subjects either reported as many items as could be remembered (the whole-report condition) or were signaled with a visual indicator to report just some of the items (the partial-report condition). One outcome of this study was similar to that of Moray et al.: When the partial-report cue signaled the subjects to report items on just one channel, performance was superior to that of the whole-report condition. This situation uses the cue to select certain stimuli on the basis of perceptually evident attributes, which we expect to be conveyed in the sensory register. But, in another condition, the partial-report cue probed for a category of items, letters or digits. If the information being tapped is sensory, such a cue should be ineffective. Instead, Darwin et al. found a small advantage for such a partial-report indicator, which suggests that the experiment tapped at least some postcategorical information. Moreover, Massaro (1975) reanalyzed the data of the Darwin et al. study and pointed out that when the two partial-report conditions were directly compared, the category cue was not less effective than the channel cue, casting doubt on the interpretation of the experiment in terms of the echo. Instead, the information cued by partial report as well as whole report may have been in STM. In this case, the partial-report advantage could reflect the fact that it is easier to report just a couple of items from STM than several. When several are to be reported, in fact, the very act of recall can disrupt the retention in STM, a phenomenon called *output interference*.

Given these problems with interpretation of the partial-report procedure in the auditory domain, it is fortunate that other means of investigating the echo also exist. Some of these are again directly related to techniques used in the visual domain. For one, subjects can be asked to indicate when a sound seems to terminate, just as they can be asked to indicate when a visual event ends (Efron, 1970). And just as in the visual case, subjects perceive sounds as lasting longer than they are physically present, indicating that there is a source of persistence after termination. Presumably this is the echo.

Another technique mimics the backward-masking situation previously described for vision, in which a second stimulus acts to interfere with (mask) one that preceded it by some interval. Massaro (1970; Massaro, Cohen, and Idson, 1976) has conducted such experiments. He uses a task in which subjects are presented with two tones separated by an interval and asked to identify the first tone; for example, to indicate which of two previously learned tones (high or low) it was. The interest is in whether the second tone masks the first. The assumption behind these experiments is that in order for the second tone to have an effect on identification of the first, some sound must remain from the first when the second occurs. If the second, masking, tone is presented too late, after information about the first has vanished from the echo, it will be ineffective. As we would expect (see Figure 3.5), the masking tone is usually found to be less and less effective as more time elapses between the initial tone and the mask, until it is ineffective after a 250-msec. interval. Apparently, this is because the echoic information from the first sound decays over the interval, so that there is less and less to interfere with. The information being masked in this case is designated precategorical because the initial tone is assumed to be so brief (20 msec.) that pattern recognition is not completed during its presentation. The mask then must be interfering with the process of recognition by disrupting the echoic information that the recognition process requires.

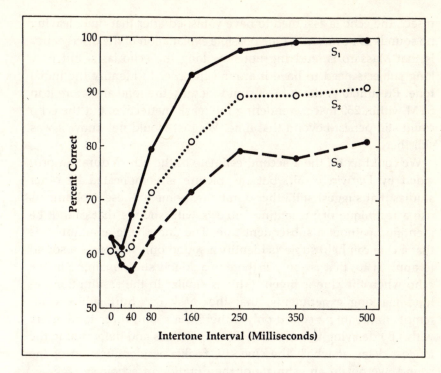

Figure 3.5 Percentage of correct identifications of a tone followed by a masking tone, for each of several intertone intervals, by each of three subjects. The masking tone is maximally effective at brief intervals, and its effect no longer changes after 250 milliseconds. [After Massaro, 1970. Copyright 1970 by the American Psychological Association. Reprinted by permission.]

Knowing, or at least presuming, that the echo exists, we can ask how long the representation of sound remains in it. The answer is not clear; estimates of the duration of echoic storage vary considerably. In the Darwin et al. paper discussed above, the duration was measured by presenting the partial-report signal from zero to 4 seconds after the messages ended. Performance in the partial-report condition was found to be superior to that of the whole-report as long as the signal followed within 2 seconds, but when it was delayed up to 4 seconds, the partial-report superiority vanished. This result, like the visual situation depicted in Figure 3.2, indicates that the echoic memory that produces the partial-report advantage lasts for about 2 seconds.

However, Massaro's experiments, in which a masking technique was used instead of the partial-report procedure, give a much shorter estimate. Because the mask is no longer effective after 250 msec., the echo is assumed to have vanished after that time, leaving no sounds to be masked. One possible explanation of the discrepancy is that Massaro is studying not how long the echo lasts, but how long subjects need to have it around in order to identify the initial tone. Presumably, the subject could identify the tone and store it in STM within 250 msec., rendering the mask ineffective, but the echo could still persist beyond that time. We just would not know it was still there.

We could fix on the 2-second estimate of the echo's duration provided by Darwin et al., but the picture is complicated by other studies that suggest still other durations. Some of these experiments use a technique of presenting subjects with sounds that cannot be identified without a subsequent clue. The underlying assumption is that a clue can help subjects identify a sound only if there is a sound to apply it to; that is, only if there is a sound still remaining in the echo when the clue is given. (This is similar to the assumption behind masking experiments, that the mask can hurt subjects' attempts to identify a sound only if there is a sound there to interfere with.) By delaying the clue for various intervals and determining the longest delay at which the clue still facilitates identification of the sound, we obtain an estimate of the duration of echoic storage.

Consider, for example, the experience of subjects listening to a word in a noisy background that obscures it, much as static obscures the sound of a radio broadcast (Pollack, 1959). The subjects cannot immediately identify the word because of the noise. Some time after the word is presented, the subjects are given a two-alternative, forced-choice recognition test. That is, they are shown two words, the one that was heard and a "distractor," and asked to identify the one heard. One of the words on the recognition test serves as the clue discussed above. It should assist in identification of the initial word to the extent that subjects can remember something about the sound they heard.

In this experiment and others similar in form (e.g., Crossman, 1958; Guttman and Julesz, 1963), the maximum delay at which the clue helps—and therefore the estimate of echoic storage—ranges from 1 second to 15 minutes—quite a range. Because of such variability in the estimates, it is difficult to determine just how long sounds remain in the auditory register. When an estimate as great as 15 minutes is obtained, however, we must question whether this technique actually taps precategorical information or whether the sounds being identified with the aid of the clue are in STM or LTM. The latter possibility is quite likely. It is possible, for example, that the subjects have actually made a partial identification of the sound, such as "It started with an s-sound and seemed to have two syllables." This sort of information is no longer sensory; it is a post-categorical, verbal description of the sound, which can easily be remembered for 15 minutes. Hearing "It is either 'second' or 'perform'," the subject can retrieve the postcategorical information and be aided by the clue. Thus, the technique may not always tap sounds in the echo.

What can we conclude about the duration of the echo? It seems safe to say that it lasts less than 15 minutes, but it is difficult to pin down its duration within the range of about 150 msec. to 2 seconds. One possibility is that some of the variation in estimates may be real; that is, the duration of echoic storage may actually vary with the kind of stimulus stored and the demands of the experimental situation. Thus, there may be no single duration for the echo.

We could reach a similar conclusion about the icon, given some data from Sakitt (1976). She used the technique of simply asking subjects to indicate when a visual stimulus—light letters against a dark background—seemed to terminate by having them adjust a click to coincide with its termination. She then determined how the duration of the icon, as measured by the interval between the true offset of the stimulus and the subject's adjusted click, varied with the intensity of the letters. When the intensity was great (relative to the lowest intensity where the stimulus can be seen with the rods), she found the duration of the icon to be estimated as long as 8 seconds. This is far greater than the approximately 250 msec. obtained by Haber and Standing (1970) with a similar technique. Though the locus of the inconsistency is uncertain, Sakitt's results make it clear that the icon's duration as well as the echo's is a matter of debate.

The echo and icon are both sensory registers. Thus, it is not surprising to discover they have a great deal in common, including short durations (whatever the actual value estimated) and the precategorical form of stored information. Furthermore, both can be interfered with by subsequent stimulation in the same modality, as we have seen from the experiments on backward masking of sounds and visually presented letters.

On the other hand, the icon and the echo do differ in that one deals with visual information and the other with sounds. We should therefore not expect them to operate identically. For one thing, the eye simultaneously takes in visual information over a region of space, and the information from successive looks at the world (fixations) may be quite unrelated, because the eye may move over a substantial area from one look to the next. In contrast, the auditory sense is specialized for integrating sequences of information that occur over time, such as patterns of speech. If information processed by the two senses differs with respect to its distribution over time and space, we might expect the sensory registers to differ accordingly. If the echo's duration is estimated as longer than the icon's, for example, it may be because the occurrence of speech over relatively long intervals requires that it be stored for longer periods than visual events.

In an ideal discussion of sensory registers, we would go on to consider how the other registers presumed to exist—those for taste, smell, and touch—are the same and yet different from one another. Unfortunately much less is known about the remaining sensory memories. Psychologists have concentrated on those most active in linguistic activity—the icon for reading and the echo for speech. Because we do not taste or smell words, and because most of us do not take in words by touch (though the Braille system exists), study of the remaining sensory systems lags behind. This remains one of the many exciting frontiers within cognitive psychology.

4

Pattern Recognition and Attention

PATTERN RECOGNITION

When you recognize a pattern, you derive meaning from a sensory experience. The process of pattern recognition is of fundamental importance to human behavior, for it is part of the interplay between the real world and the mind. For a pattern to be recognized, in terms of our model, information in one memory store, the sensory register, must be matched with information in another memory store, LTM. The first set of information comes from a stimulus; the second set is previously acquired knowledge about that stimulus. For example, given a stimulus consisting of three lines (/ \ and −) in certain positions, we may recognize a letter A. In that case, we can assign a label—a word or set of words—to the stimulus event. ("The letter ay" might be such a label.) Pattern recognition need not always mean labeling, for we can often recognize patterns and not name them. (For example, we may recognize that a face is familiar, or a certain smell may remind us of a place where we have experienced it.) In any case, information conveyed by the senses is matched with and related to what we know about the world.

It is easy to see that the study of pattern recognition is an important part of the study of memory. For one thing, it enhances our understanding of memory stores like the sensory registers and LTM.

For another, in discussing the process of recognizing patterns, it is necessary to consider the nature of memorial representations—the codes of information in memory. (In general, the memory *code* of some information refers to its representation in memory.) In fact, there are many different codes that can represent an item, codes for the sound, appearance, or meaning of a word, for instance. We will study the component processes of pattern recognition that work with these memory codes as well as the codes themselves.

Let us begin our discussion by considering what is essential to any model or theory of pattern recognition. We will start with a simplified situation, the case in which an isolated stimulus appears briefly and then vanishes. This situation is indeed simplified, as we shall see, for most naturally occurring stimuli appear in a meaningful context, and the context is very useful in recognition. Keeping this limitation in mind, however, we can consider a model of the simple situation (Figure 4.1).

The figure shows that the recognition of an incoming pattern utilizes two memory stores, the sensory register—which briefly stores the incoming information—and LTM—which holds the memory code to be paired with that information. It also uses three basic processes, called analysis, comparison, and decision. The first process, *analysis*, extracts information from the register. This may be a simple process, in which the information extracted is virtually unchanged from the original stimulus, or the analysis may break down the stimulus (in Figure 4.1, the letter A) into component parts (/–\). In the next stage, the *comparison* process, information extracted during analysis is compared to information about known patterns in LTM. This implies that the information in LTM must be in such a form that the stimulus can be compared with it. That is, the memory code of a stimulus must in some sense resemble or describe the information extracted from the actual stimulus. After the stimulus information is compared to various codes in LTM, a decision is made as to which of the memory codes provides the best match. This *decision* determines the output from the recognition system; the recognized pattern corresponds to the best matching code. Once the pattern is recognized, of course, more information in LTM concerning that pattern can be evoked. Once we have recognized the stimulus A, we can reconstruct what we know about it—for example, that it is the first letter of the alphabet or a grade we might like to obtain.

Pattern recognition, even in this simplified model, requires several stages. When a stimulus has undergone all of these stages—it is analyzed, compared to information in LTM, and a decision is made—it

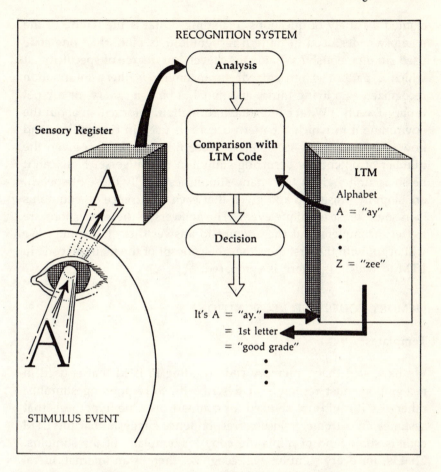

Figure 4.1 Basic components of pattern recognition: the sensory register; an analysis component, which extracts information from the register; a comparison component, which compares extracted information with known patterns; long-term memory, in which known patterns are stored; a decision component, which chooses the best match.

can be said to be *recognized*. As we shall see, however, in some situations the pattern recognition process may be incomplete. A stimulus may be analyzed, for example, and then processed no further. We shall therefore find it useful to distinguish between partial recognition, where a stimulus does not undergo all stages of pattern recognition, and full recognition, the outcome of the decision process.

The model of pattern recognition described in Figure 4.1 is at best a theoretical overview; it barely begins to describe what is an incredibly complex event. Cognitive psychologists have attempted to describe this event in much more detail, and have consequently confronted a variety of questions, including: What is the nature of the memory codes used in pattern recognition? Is more than one code used simultaneously? What is the "level," or degree of specificity, at which a pattern is recognized? (Is incoming feathery information recognized as a living thing, an animal, a bird, a canary, or my pet canary Tweety?) What contextual information, information about the environment in which a pattern occurs, is used in recognition, and how is it used? How can pattern recognition be so fast, given the number of potentially occurring stimuli in the universe? How can it be so accurate, given that many stimuli, especially those of speech, are sloppily presented and given that each occurrence of a stimulus is in some sense a unique event? The answers to these questions are as yet incomplete, but the attempt to answer them is exciting. We will begin with the first question, the concept of the memory code in LTM to which a pattern is compared.

MEMORY CODES AND RECOGNITION

Templates

We have said that a memory code residing in LTM that is used in recognition must resemble or describe its corresponding stimulus; otherwise it could not be used for comparison. One hypothesis that assumes an extremely close correspondence suggests that the LTM code is some kind of miniature copy (or template) of the stimulus. That is, for every stimulus we recognize, there is an internal, literal copy used for recognition. According to this hypothesis, known as the *template hypothesis*, little analysis of the stimulus is performed in the first stage of recognition. The pattern is passed on essentially unchanged to the comparison stage, during which it is compared with a vast array of templates in LTM. One matches the stimulus better than any other, and recognition occurs when this best-matching template is selected by the decision process.

But such a template hypothesis is too simple—too naive to serve as the basis for a theory of pattern recognition. For one thing, too many templates would be required. Consider, for example, the recognition of one single stimulus, the letter A. Our template hypothesis stipulates that there is in LTM a copy of the letter A that is compared to it whenever it occurs as a stimulus and that will match it better than any other template. But it follows that we would need a template for every kind of A. Change the size of the stimulus? A different template is needed. If it is rotated slightly (producing a still recognizable ⟨⟩), another template is needed. If we draw it in some peculiar manner, such as A̶, we need a peculiar template to match. If we didn't have templates for all these versions of the letter A, we could expect errors in pattern recognition. For example, a tilted A might fit a template for R better than A, so we would recognize R when A occurred. To avoid such errors, we would need an immense number of templates, undoubtedly more than LTM could hold.

It is possible to modify the template hypothesis so that it is more satisfying. One modification is to add a process to the model, one that occurs prior to comparisons and acts to "clean up" the stimulus input. Such a precomparison processor might act on the stimulus to bring it into a standard orientation and a standard size. This is called *normalizing* the stimulus, for it reduces the irregularities and brings the stimulus into a more normal form. For example, if the stimulus looked like *A̶*, normalizing would reorient it, reduce it in size, and straighten out the bend on the right, all *before* it was compared to a template. Such a process would greatly reduce the number of templates required to recognize an A.

However, a precomparison process that normalizes the stimulus will not solve all our template hypothesis's problems. A logical objection can be raised: In order to know the appropriate orientation and size, must you not *already* know what pattern the stimulus represents? For example, should a stimulus that looks like this: Q, be in this orientation: Ɒ, or this one: Q? In one case, it looks like a P; in the other, like a Q. In order to know which orientation is appropriate, you must first decide which letter it is. But that is what the pattern-recognition system, not the precomparison processor, is supposed to do. However, this logical problem is not difficult to deal with. For one thing, gross departures from standard orientation would probably result in a truly unrecognizable stimulus. That is, there is no need to postulate that the preprocessor must be able to deal with the stimulus Ɒ, when in fact it is the sort of stimulus that the recognition system could not handle. Moreover, as we have mentioned, stimuli to be recognized usually occur in some larger *context*, and the stimulus context could help the normalizing process by indicating what the proper orientation or size of a stimulus might be.

Prototypes

A normalizing process may help to deal with some of the difficulties with the template hypothesis, but it cannot completely solve the problem. The fact is that many stimuli we can recognize do not occur in a special context and we can still recognize them in spite of variations in size or orientation. It therefore seems necessary to have a template system that allows some variation, or slop, in patterns coming into it. In other words, the recognizer must be able to perform despite minor variations that might remain after some normalizing operation. When we introduce variable patterns into the recognizer, the literal template system becomes more like what is called a prototype, or schema, system.

A *schema* is simply a set of rules for producing or describing a *prototype*, which, as the term is used here, is an abstract form that represents the basic elements of a set of stimuli. For example, we might think of the prototypical airplane as a long tube with two wings attached, with all airplanes being some variant of the prototype. A prototypical representation, in other words, is an essence, a central or average tendency, even a Platonic ideal. According to the prototype hypothesis of pattern recognition, what are stored in LTM are prototypes—central, ideal representatives of sets of stimuli. In theory, any stimulus can be encoded as a prototype plus a list of variations, and incoming stimuli can then be compared to prototypes rather than templates. (Thus, the concept of prototypes replaces that of templates here.) What this suggests is that you have in LTM prototypes of all the categories you recognize—dogs, people's faces, or the letter A—enabling you to recognize unique members of those categories.

Do prototypes exist? There is some experimental evidence that they do; that is, that prototypes are formed for sets of stimuli. For example, Posner and Keele (1968) conducted an experiment in which subjects performed as if they had learned prototypes. First, Posner and Keele constructed prototypical patterns of nine dots each. In some instances, the nine dots formed a geometric pattern such as a triangle; in others, the dots formed a letter; and in still others, the dots were placed in a random pattern. Then Posner and Keele constructed new patterns, which were distortions of the prototypes, by moving some ofthe dots around a bit (Figure 4.2A). Sometimes the dots were moved in one direction, sometimes in the other, so that the original prototype was equivalent to the pattern that would be formed by placing each dot in the position it occupied on the average in the distortions. Having formed prototypes and several distortions of each, the authors had groups of subjects learn about them.

Let's consider the case where the prototypes were random collections of dots; the distortions would, of course, also be random sets. Subjects were first shown four distortions of each of three random-

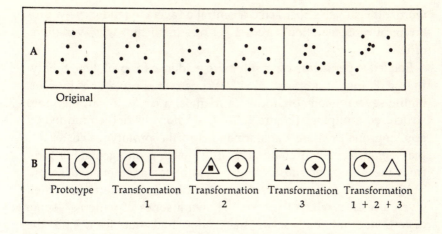

Figure 4.2 (A) A prototype pattern—a triangle composed of dots—and distortions of the pattern (increasing in distortion from left to right) as used by Posner and Keele (1968). [From Posner, Goldsmith, and Welton, 1967.] (B) Prototype form and transformations of that form. [From Franks and Bransford, 1971. Copyright 1967, 1971 by the American Psychological Association. Reprinted by permission.]

dot prototypes, one at a time. The subjects were supposed to classify each distortion; that is, indicate in which of three categories it belonged. All the distortions corresponding to a single prototype were to be put in the same category; however, the subjects were *not* shown any of the prototypes. Eventually the subjects learned to classify the patterns correctly, that is, they learned to classify all the distortions of one prototype into a common category, all distortions of another prototype in another common category, and so on. Next, the subjects were given a new classification task. They were shown a series of patterns and asked to classify each as a member of one of the three categories learned previously. Some of the patterns were those that the subjects had already seen (old distortions), some were new distortions of the same prototypes, and some were the prototypes themselves, which the subjects had not previously seen. The old distortions were, not surprisingly, classified quite well—with 87 percent accuracy. More surprisingly, the prototypes were classified about equally well, even though they had never been seen. But the new distortions, those the subjects were seeing for the first time but were not prototypical, were classified less well—with about 75 percent accuracy. Since the prototypes were classified so well, the authors suggested that in the course of learning to classify the first set of distortions, the subjects actually learned the prototypes. In other words, the subjects abstracted a central or average tendency—a prototypical representation—from a set of stimuli that were variations of it.

Related experiments offer still more evidence for prototype theory. In one, Franks and Bransford (1971) constructed prototypes by combining several geometric forms (a triangle, a circle, a star, etc.) into structured groupings (Figure 4.2B). Distortions were then formed by applying one or more transformations to the prototypes.For example, a transformation could consist of deleting one geometric form from the group, of substituting one form for another, and so on. Subjects were first shown some of the distorted patterns and then given a test, in which they were shown a series of patterns—some distortions they had seen, some they had not seen, and the prototypes—and asked to indicate for each how confident they were of having seen or not seen that particular pattern in the originally viewed set. The confidence ratings indicated that subjects were most "confident" of having seen the prototypes, even though they had *not* been shown them during the first part of the experiment. Moreover, the subject's rating for any pattern on the test was predictable from the degree of transformation from a prototype. The prototypes were most confidently rated as having been seen before, patterns differing from them by one transformation were next most confidently rated, and so on. The originally seen distortions were rated as previously seen with no more confidence than new (previously unseen) distortions with the same number of transformations of the prototype!

What these experiments seem to suggest is that experience with a set of related patterns leads to the development of a prototypical representation of that set. Subjects are said to abstract the prototype from the patterns they see. The Franks and Bransford experiment also suggests that subjects may use those prototypes when they identify new patterns, since the degree to which the prototype was distorted, or transformed, to produce a distortion determined whether or not it was designated as having been seen before.

Research of Rosch and her associates (Rosch, Mervis, Gray, Johnson, and Boyes-Braem, 1976) also supports the idea that prototypes exist. Their work was concerned with prototypes that might represent common objects like those we see around us. One characteristic of the objects they studied was that they could be given different names, and the names could be ordered to form a hierarchy. For example, the object we might call a *hack hand saw* can also be called just a plain *saw*; it can also be called a *tool*. These three names, hack hand saw, saw, and tool, are given in the order of increasing generality. This ordering is a hierarchy. Similar hierarchies are: four-door sedan/car/vehicle, and living-room chair/chair/furniture. In each hierarchy, there is a name that it seems most natural to apply to a given object in everyday discourse. In the examples above, it is the second name given. For example, we speak of sitting in "that chair," not in "that living-room chair" or "that article of furniture." This type of name was called by Rosch et al. the *basic-level* name. The more specific term (the first one given) was called the *subordinate-level* name, and the more general term (the last one) was the *superordinate-level* name.

Rosch et al. began their work on objects by giving people one of the three levels of name for an object and asking them to write down the things that were characteristic of objects with that name. For example, subjects were asked to write down common attributes of saws, tools, or hack hand saws. As you might suspect, how well people did at this task depended on the name they were given. Rosch et al. found that when people were given the superordinate level name (such as tool), they could agree on few common attributes (all tools are used to make or fix things and are made with metal, but they have little else in common). With the basic-level name, however, they were able to list quite a few common attributes (objects with the name *saw* have in common the attributes of tools, as well as such characteristics as blades, teeth, the ability to cut, and so on). When the name was at the more specific subordinate level, you might think that objects would be said to have even more in common. But this wasn't the case. The subjects could come up with very few attributes common to objects with the same subordinate-level name (hack hand saws) that were not also common to objects with the same basic-level name (saw). In other words, making the name more specific helped people to find common attributes when the move was from the superordinate level to the basic level but not when the move was from the basic to the subordinate level. This suggests that the "basic" level is in fact basic; it is the most general level of naming where the named objects have a great deal in common.

In short, the work of Rosch et al. suggests that certain collections of objects—those having the same basic-level name—are fundamental, in that the objects have many attributes in common. A collection of saws, for example, has this virtue, but a collection of tools does not (for hammers do not have much in common with saws). Nor does it help to make the collection even more specific (such as a set of hack hand saws), for items in this sort of set do not have much more in common than objects at the basic level.

The collection of objects having the same basic-level name seems ideally suited to be represented by a prototype. We could conceive of the prototype as having the very attributes that all the objects have in common. As we know, there are quite a few such attributes in a set of objects with the same basic name, so that the prototype would not lack for attributes. Moreover, Rosch and Mervis (1975) have shown that objects judged prototypical of a basic-level category (for example, a picture of a chair judged as a very typical chair) tend not to share attributes with other related basic-level categories. Not only does a prototypical chair have the attributes common to all chairs, but it tends not to have the attributes of stools, cushions, and sofas—other articles of furniture. This means that the prototype of a basic-level category is not only well defined (that is, it has a reasonable number of features that are common to category members), but it is also maximally distinct from the prototypes of other categories at that level.

A prototype of a basic-level category would seem to be very useful in pattern recognition. It would provide a good way of representing the members of a category, for it conveys the features they have in common. At the same time, it would be distinct from prototypes of other categories, which would reduce the potential for errors in recognition. If such a prototype were used in recognizing patterns, that is, if the LTM codes to which stimuli are compared were prototypes, then objects might first be recognized as members of a basic-level category. For example, a saw stimulus might be first recognized as a saw, not as a tool or a hack hand saw. Consistent with this idea, experimental work of Rosch et al. (1976) suggests that the basic level does have a special status in recognition. In one study, they found that when subjects were briefly shown a visual stimulus and asked to say whether it matched a name given beforehand, they were fastest when the name was at the basic level. For example, they could decide whether a picture represented a "lamp" faster than they could decide it was a piece of furniture or a floor lamp. This suggests that the basic level is where categorizing naturally occurs; it is the fastest level at which we relate things to their names. In fact, when people are shown pictures of objects and simply asked to provide a name, they commonly provide the basic-level name even when they know the other names. Still more support comes from a study in which people were shown "average" drawings, formed by putting two pictures of different objects with the same name on top of one another and essentially drawing a new object representing their overlap (the pictures were initially similar in size and position, of course). Subjects were able to identify the new, averaged, drawings if the original two objects came from the same basic category, such as chair, but they were unable to recognize the average of a chair and a table—both with the same name at the superordinate level (furniture). This finding indicates that members of the same basic category share a common, prototypical shape. We could speculate that something like this shape can be used as a memory code when the objects are recognized.

In summary, the prototype hypothesis of pattern recognition assumes that people store in LTM prototypical patterns, ideal examples for every class of information—prototypical letters, faces, or random dot patterns. When a new pattern is presented, it is compared with the prototypes, with the expectation not of an exact (template) match, but rather of an approximate match, one that allows for some variation in the stimulus. The most closely matching prototype determines what the pattern is recognized to be. Such a hypothesis, including the notion of precomparison processing, represents an improvement over the template proposal because it allows a pattern to be recognized even though it is not a close copy of some memory code.

Features

Up to this point, we have been discussing pattern recognition without defining the word *pattern*. According to one definition (Zusne, 1970), a pattern is a configuration of several elements that belong together. Such a definition implies that any pattern may be broken down into more basic subcomponents, or features, and that when those subcomponents are put back together, there is the pattern. For example, we might think of the letters of the alphabet as being composed of such basic features as vertical lines, horizontal lines, 45 degree lines, and curves. The letter A might thus be represented as / plus \ plus —; those features, appropriately combined, make up the pattern A. In general, the idea of basic features implies that a relatively small set of features, combined in various ways, can be used to construct all the patterns in some larger set (such as the printed letters of the alphabet). Some theories of pattern recognition propose that LTM codes for stimuli consist of lists of such features. According to this hypothesis, an incoming pattern is analyzed into a set of features, which is compared to memory codes that describe patterns in featural terms.

We have noted that letters might be describable in terms of components like lines and angles. Another example of a set of patterns that might be composed of features is human speech. Speech comprises basic units of sound, called phonemes, analogous to the letters that make up visually presented words. A phoneme can be defined as a sound that, by itself, can change the meaning of a word. For example, the sounds corresponding to *b*, *p*, and *g* in the following words—but, putt, and gut—are different phonemes because each sound changes the word that is spoken. On the other hand, a single phoneme corresponds to a wide range of sounds, for each speaker pronounces it just a bit differently; in fact, it changes from word to word (the sound of *b* in bill differs from *b* in bull). Yet we can recognize the same phoneme spoken by different people and in different words. In other words, we can think of the phoneme as a unit of speech, a concept that encompasses many "sloppy" examples. In that way, it is not unlike a hand-written letter, the shape of which varies from writer to writer and from one writing to another, but which is still recognizable.

Finding a set of features that can be used, in different combinations, to make up phonemes (as one might try to use lines, curves, and angles as the basis for printed letters) has proved to be difficult. One method examines the production of sounds, attempting to describe each speech sound according to the way people use their vocal apparatus in articulating or producing it (Jakobson, Fant, and Halle, 1961). That vocal apparatus includes the tongue, the nose, the teeth and lips, the vocal cords, and the muscles of the diaphragm.

For example, consider the sounds of *s* and *z*. Try saying each, and you may notice that, in saying *z*, your voice seems to emanate from your throat, whereas the sound of *s* is produced solely in your mouth. This difference in the sounds of *s* and *z* is called *voicing*. The *s* is unvoiced; the *z* is voiced, meaning that when you say a *z*, your vocal cords vibrate, whereas they do not when you say *s*. The two sounds are said to differ by a single articulatory feature (voicing). Of course, there are many other features of speech, including tongue position (forward in the mouth, in the middle, or in the back); whether air passes through the nose or does not; and so on. There is supposedly a unique combination of such features—a specific configuration of the vocal apparatus—that produces each phoneme. What the articulatory-feature analysis of speech attempts to do is to find the set of vocal components that describes each separate phoneme.

However, applying this analysis to pattern recognition raises another problem. People listening to speech have *sounds* to work with. They cannot see the articulatory apparatus of the speaker, so they cannot analyze an incoming speech pattern into articulatory components. How, then, can they use articulatory features to recognize speech? One solution to this problem assumes that listeners construct internal copies of the sounds they think they might be hearing and then compare those internal copies to the actual incoming sounds. This theory is called the *analysis-by-synthesis* model of speech perception (Halle and Stevens, 1959, 1964). Essentially, it assumes that what is stored in LTM for comparison with an incoming stimulus is not some copy of the stimulus or its features, but a set of rules for articulating the stimulus. These rules are used to synthesize, or construct, an internal pattern or set of patterns for comparison with the stimulus. However, one problem with this model is that it would seem to place an incredible burden on the pattern recognizer in terms of the number of patterns that would need to be synthesized. To reduce this number, the model assumes that the listener synthesizes patterns that are most likely to occur in the present context and does so only after the incoming sounds have been given a preliminary feature analysis. This brings us back to the problem of specifying the acoustic features of the sounds themselves, rather than the vocal apparatus used to produce them.

It appears that any model that assumes speech patterns are processed in terms of features (whether or not it assumes sounds are internally synthesized) must deal with the problem of specifying acoustic features of speech. Work on this problem has developed somewhat later than that on articulatory features, but candidates for acoustic features have indeed been found (for example, Cooper and Blumstein, 1974; Eimas and Corbit, 1973; Repp, Liberman, Eccardt, and Pesetsky, 1978), and the study of acoustic features of speech is a promising and exciting research area. Although no attempt to specify distinctive features for speech or the printed alphabet has been completely successful, the progress that has been achieved makes the idea that patterns can be described in terms of basic features an important and intriguing one.

Let us consider the hypothesis for pattern recognition based on this idea in more detail. The feature hypothesis holds that the stimulus to be recognized is first analyzed in terms of its features. A list of features is compiled as the result of the analysis—features which, if combined, would make up the stimulus. The list is compared to lists in LTM. Thus, this theory holds that the LTM code for a given stimulus is a list of features rather than a template or prototype. The best-matching list is obtained, and the pattern is recognized.

One version of the feature hypothesis is called *Pandemonium* (Selfridge, 1959). The Pandemonium model is depicted in Figure 4.3. Like our initial model (Figure 4.1), it shows that patterns are recog-

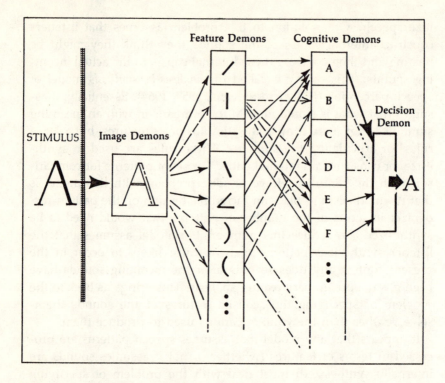

Figure 4.3 Selfridge's Pandemonium model of pattern recognition: The stimulus is registered by image demons. Feature demons analyze it to see what features are present. Cognitive demons compare the features to their patterns. A decision demon decides which pattern has occurred.

nized in stages, or levels. At each level are a set of "demons," who work on the pattern recognition in some way. At the very first level are image demons, who do what we have been calling sensory registration; that is, they record the stimulus as a sensory event. Then that event is analyzed by feature demons, who break down the pattern into its component features. Each such demon represents a single feature—such as a line at a certain angle, or a curve—and it responds if its feature is present. The feature demons are observed by cognitive demons, who correspond to feature lists. Each cognitive demon's list represents a certain pattern, and the demon's job is to "yell," or signal, as loudly as is justified by how well it is indicated by the feature analysis. That is, a cognitive demon looks at the number of responding feature demons that correspond to features in its list, and it yells loudly if it finds many such feature demons, less loudly if there are fewer. Sitting above all of this is a decision demon (the decision process), who decides which cognitive demon is yelling the loudest, and thereby recognizes the pattern.

If all this has a ring of familiarity it is not surprising, since the feature hypothesis is very similar to the template hypothesis. What is a feature, if not a template? Here, the template corresponds to some part of a stimulus rather than to the whole. The advantage of the feature hypothesis is that if a set of features can be obtained which describes a much larger set of patterns (as it could, for example, if we could describe speech in terms of a few basic features), there are many fewer templates to work with. On the other hand, the similarity of the feature hypothesis to the template hypothesis brings with it a host of similar problems.

For example, how would a feature system handle variations in the size of a visual feature? How would novel stimuli, never seen before, be recognizable? What would happen when two stimuli differ only by the presence or absence of a single feature? (An example is the lower line in E, which is absent in F. Here, two lists of features in LTM might match the stimulus F, because every feature of F would match features in lists corresponding to both E and F.) In the case of speech recognition, there are even greater complexities. For one thing, units of speech are not organized into distinct, nonoverlapping segments of time. A single acoustic feature can be distributed over a span of speech as long as about a half-second (Repp, 1976), and features from different phonemes overlap in time.

At this point, there is no definitive solution to all of these problems for a pattern recognizer. That does not mean that the feature hypothesis should be abandoned, however. After all, alternative hypotheses also have their limitations. Moreover, there is some experimental evidence that a feature-matching process is used for recognizing patterns.

Some of the evidence for the role of features in pattern recognition is physiological, stemming from research indicating that the visual system contains specialized cells whose function it is to recognize particular features. In the past decade or so, physiologists (Hubel and Weisel, 1962; Lettvin, Maturana, McCulloch, and Pitts, 1959) have discovered nerve cells in the visual systems of cats, frogs, and other animals that fire (respond) only when a particular pattern of visual stimulation occurs. Such patterns include horizontal lines, vertical lines, and moving lines. In the frog's brain, cells have been found that fire when moving black dots appear in the visual field; the suggestion has been made that these are bug-detector cells, firing so that the frog can catch its dinner! There is an obvious analogy between the patterns that set off specialized neurons and what we have been calling features. In humans, it might be surmised, there may be cells that fire when specific features appear and that serve as the feature analyzers for incoming visual stimuli. Moreover, some cells seem to fire independently of specific stimulus characteristics such as length. Thus, these cells seem to detect more abstract features (such as a line of any length at a particular angle) and may help to explain why patterns can be recognized despite transformations such as variations in size.

There is other evidence for the importance of features in pattern recognition. Young children, for example, often call printed *b* and *d* by the same name. This may reflect an inability to distinguish between two visual features—C and ⊃, say—differing only in their orientation. In adults, a similar effect is obtained if visual stimuli are presented so rapidly that perception may be incomplete. This kind of experiment leads to confusions similar to those found in experiments on the memory span. When a letter, for example, is presented very briefly and subjects are asked to report what it was, they may make a confusion error—the substitution of some other letter in their reports. Unlike memory-span confusions, which seem to follow patterns of acoustic similarity, the errors in the experiment just described follow visual patterns (Kinney, Marsetta, and Showman, 1966). Here, D is much more likely to be reported when Q is presented than when B is presented. The D and Q share visual features, whereas the B and D are acoustically similar but visually dissimilar. These confusions may be used to infer that the process of perceiving letters deals with visual features. Similarly, confusion errors made in identifying speech sounds heard in noise follow regular patterns. The closer two syllables are in terms of articulatory features, the more likely they will be confused (Miller and Nicely, 1955).

Thus, it seems that there is evidence both for the formation of prototypes and for the use of features. We have also seen that both prototype and feature hypotheses seem to explain many of the same things about pattern recognition and to leave many of the same problems unanswered. So which approach is better? There may be room for both hypotheses, for what we call prototypes and features may not be as different as they first appear. For one thing, the two ideas can be combined: We can consider a prototype to consist of the features common to all instances of a pattern; the idea of prototypes can thus be as consistent with features as it is with templates. It is also important to recognize that, at some level, a feature hypothesis is very like a template hypothesis. One problem in stating a feature hypothesis is that of describing how individual features, such as lines of a given angle, are recognized. The answer may call for a comparison process that matches the feature with an internal template. Thus, we would have a template theory of feature recognition! These considerations suggest that all three hypotheses about LTM codes we have discussed have something to offer; all may play a part in recognition.

THE COMPARISON PROCESS: SERIAL OR PARALLEL?

One topic that has not yet been discussed in any detail is the comparison process of pattern recognition. Consider the template hypothesis. A pattern must be compared with a great number of templates; then the template that best matches the pattern can be selected. It immediately becomes apparent that with all the templates there must be in memory, such a comparison process would be immense. Thousands and thousands of templates would have to be compared before a decision could be made—how could it be done? If the recognizer had to compare the pattern with one template at a time, one after another, it would surely take a very long time to recognize some stimuli; and the same argument applies if *prototypes* or *feature lists* is substituted for *templates*. Yet we know that pattern recognition proceeds very quickly.

One answer to this question may be that the recognizer does not compare LTM codes to new patterns one after another. The one-after-another process has a name; it is called a *serial* process. The label *serial* derives from series, because the process involves a series of comparisons. The alternative to serial comparisons is called a *parallel* process. The label *parallel* derives from the geometric meaning, referring to two or more separate lines that go on together side by side. That's just what parallel comparisons are like—many separate comparisons going on at once. What this means in pattern recognition is that a stimulus could be compared to many internal codes at the same time, the whole process taking no longer than a single such comparison. In this fashion, comparisons could proceed very quickly.

Parallel comparisons sound like a potential answer to the problem of saving time during the comparison stage, and we do know of such parallel processes in the physical world. One example (Neisser, 1967) is found in the use of tuning forks. If we take a tuning fork of unknown frequency and strike it (so that it hums) and hold it near a group of forks of known frequency, then one of the known forks will also begin to hum. The fork that hums matches the frequency of the unknown fork; no other fork will hum. In that way, we can determine the unknown frequency. That is a parallel-comparison process, for the unknown fork is tested against all the known forks simultaneously.

Experimental evidence for parallel activity in psychological processes has also been found. One example comes from Neisser's (1964) visual-search experiments, in which subjects were confronted with lists of letters 50 lines long. On each line were several letters, such as U F C J. Each subject was instructed to start at the top line and find some target letter, designated by the experimenter, as rapidly as possible. The target was placed at a randomly determined position in the list, and the subject pressed a button when he or she found it. The total search time, the time between first seeing the list and finding the target, was recorded. Neisser (Neisser, Novick, and Lazar, 1963) found that when well-practiced subjects were given *ten* targets and asked to respond when they found the one that was present, they responded just as quickly as when they had only one target to consider. That result argues against a serial-search process. For if the subjects looked for ten targets sequentially, scanning the entire list for one, then another, it should take them much longer (on the average) to find the target than it would take when they were looking for a single letter. Instead, it seems that the subjects could search the list for ten targets at once—a parallel search. Shiffrin and Schneider (1977; Schneider and Shiffrin, 1977) have conducted a related task, and they report that subjects who have received extensive training on certain target letters say that those letters seem to "jump out" of printed pages as they read. This is much like the sound of a test tuning fork "jumping out" of a matching tuning fork without a serial search.

Parallel processes are one way—but a good one—of confronting the problem we have proposed: how the comparison process can operate fast enough for patterns to be quickly recognized, given the size of the job it has to do. With parallel processes, recognition can be fast because many operations can go on simultaneously, saving time over a serial process. It is theoretically possible that an incoming pattern could be compared to every existing LTM code if the processing were parallel (and assuming the system has enough capacity to perform all those comparisons at once).

But there is evidence that people do not have to compare incoming patterns to every code in LTM. They can save time by restricting the comparisons to only some of the many codes there. At first, this may seem logically impossible. After all, how can we reduce the set of LTM codes to compare to a stimulus without knowing what the stimulus is? The answer to that question becomes clearer when we consider how the context in which a stimulus occurs can be important in determining its ultimate classification. As an example, suppose our task is to determine whether or not a predesignated object (such as a cup) is in a briefly presented scene. Suppose, too, that we recognize that the scene depicts a kitchen before we detect the cup (a likely possibility; see Navon, 1977). We now have a context for recognizing the objects in the scene. One result of this context might be that we restrict the number of possibilities for each object. One could be a cup, for example, but it is almost certainly not a shoe. Restricting the possibilities in this way would reduce the demands on the comparison process (the shoe code need not be compared); it could also aid in the decision (we know it is not a shoe). Not surprisingly, experiments demonstrate that we do better in such a task when the scene is a coherent picture than when it is disorganized (Biederman, Glass, and Stacy, 1973), for only in the former case is there likely to be a meaningful context. And probable objects (those consistent with the surrounding context) are identified better than improbable ones in a coherent scene (Biederman, 1977).

We have seen that knowledge about the context in which a to-be-recognized pattern occurs could act to reduce the demands on the comparison and decision components of recognition. But in order to incorporate such effects in our recognition model, we must go beyond the simplified version presented in Figure 4.1. That model assumes that pattern recognition is what has been called a *data-driven* or *bottom-up* process; that is, it works only with information (data) coming from the periphery (bottom) of the system through the senses. Context effects, however, are quite different. They involve knowledge in LTM, not from the immediate sensory world—for example, knowledge about objects that might be found in kitchens. This knowledge is used to guide the recognition process; it is as if hypotheses about what a pattern might be are formed and tested. Because this sort of processing uses conceptual information from within the system (from the top), it is called *conceptually driven* or *top-down*. (These terms derive from treelike diagrams used in linguistics and computer science, which put the specific details of a structure—in this case the peripheral input—on the bottom and the general concept—the recognized code—at the top.) Our simplified model describes the case where a single pattern occurs in isolation, with no prior information to induce expectancies about what will occur. This is a case where processing is predominantly bottom-up, because there is no stimulus context to use in a top-down manner. Because top-down processing plays an important role in recognition, however, we must expand the model to include it.

AN INTERACTIVE MODEL OF RECOGNITION

The expanded model of recognition is depicted in Figure 4.4. This model can be called an *interactive model*, because it depicts recognition as combining sensory information and hypotheses, both bottom-up and top-down processing. It has been called by Neisser (1976) the *perceptual cycle*, to suggest that activity cycles back and forth, between information picked up from the world and hypotheses (called by him *anticipatory schemata*), states of readiness for certain kinds of information to occur. We can see from the figure that our initial depiction of top-down processing as guiding the comparison and decision processes is overly restrictive. Hypotheses about what the current pattern might be could have more diverse effects. They could guide feature extraction during the analysis stage as well as enter into the comparison process and restrict postcomparison decisions. Hypotheses can take effect even before a to-be-recognized pattern enters the sensory register, to direct its initial registration; for example, eye movements that will pick up new visual events can be guided by information recognized during previous fixations of the eyes (Gould, 1976; Loftus and Mackworth, 1978). Nor need hypotheses be based only on contextual information separate from the to-be-recognized pattern itself. Partial recognition of the stimulus, for example, extraction of certain critical features, could activate knowledge in LTM and thus lead to hypothesis formation. Whatever component of recognition is directed by hypotheses, and however those hypotheses are derived, at the heart of the interactive model is the assumption that recognition is driven from both the bottom and the top; sensory input is only part of what is used.

Figure 4.4 suggests that several different sources of information in LTM can be used to form hypotheses. Knowledge about the physical characteristics of inputs might be used to form hypotheses about raw data found in the sensory register; knowledge about the concepts being processed might lead to hypotheses about the conceptual meaning of what is being presented. There is evidence that the recognition system makes use of just about every source of information possible. In the case of linguistic input, as in reading and speech, it has been found that people use knowledge about the spelling patterns of words, their sounds, the frequency with which

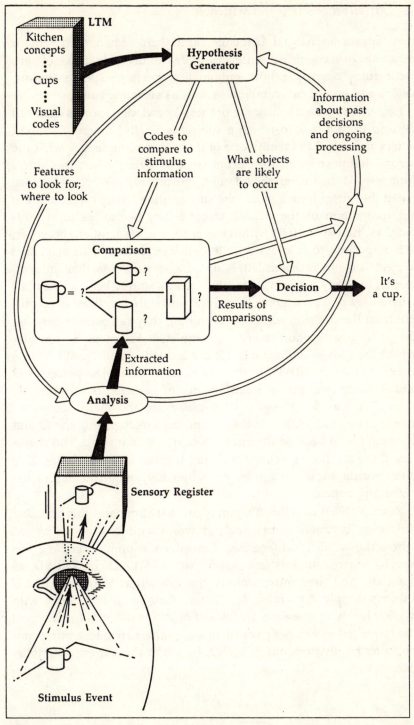

Figure 4.4 An expanded model of pattern recognition, depicting the roles of data extracted from the stimulus (bottom-up processing) and hypotheses based on knowledge in LTM (top-down processing).

they appear in natural language, and their semantic content or meaning. In recognizing sentences, they can take advantage of syntactic rules restricting how grammatical parts of speech (nouns, verbs, and so on) can combine as well as semantic rules.

Evidence for the use of some of these knowledge sources has been derived from a task in which a subject is briefly shown a string of letters and asked to identify one of them (for example, say what the second leftmost letter is). Performance is better when the letters form a word than when they do not. Presumably this occurs because when the letters form a word, the surrounding letters can be used to aid recognition of the critical, target letter. Before we locate this word vs. nonword effect within the process of recognition, however, it is important to rule out an alternative explanation; namely, that subjects do not *recognize* letters any better in words than in nonwords, but they perform better with words simply because on trials where they don't recognize the critical letter, that is, there is no output from the decision stage of recognition, they can *guess* better after the pattern-recognition stages are completed. For example, consider where the to-be-identified letter is the last letter, and the stimulus is either WORD or ORWD. In the first case, if the subject perceives O and R, there might be a decent chance of guessing the D correctly even if it was not recognized, because not too many four-letter words are spelled–OR–. In the second case, recognizing the O and R doesn't help because the string does not form a word, and therefore there are no restrictions on what the last letter might be. This gives words an advantage even though they might not be recognized any better.

Reicher (1969) developed a paradigm that eliminates this guessing difference between words and nonwords and enables us to tell where the word advantage lies. Consider the same example given above, where subjects are given either WORD or ORWD as stimulus, and they must identify the last letter. We know that if subjects simply report the last letter, they might do better with WORD by sheer guessing. So instead of letting subjects freely report the target letter, Reicher gave them a two-alternative test. For example, after briefly presenting WORD, he might show them a stimulus like:

D
––– or
K

This indicates there were three initial letters and forces them to choose one of the alternatives for the last letter. Subjects shown ORWD could be given the same test.

The critical aspect of this test is that both choices form a word in the first case. Thus, if a subject does not know the target letter, both choices are equally likely, and he or she has a 50 percent chance of guessing correctly. This is no better than the chance of the subject in the ORWD case, because both choices are equally likely in that case as well. If subjects do better with WORD than ORWD, then it cannot be due simply to their being able to guess better when words are presented. The source of the words' advantage must instead be within the pattern-recognition processes; the letters in words must truly be easier to identify than those in nonwords. Reicher found, as others have subsequently (Wheeler, 1970; Johnston, 1978) that letters are better perceived in words than in nonwords, even when guessing is made equally easy (or hard) for both. This suggests that knowledge about words is utilized in actually recognizing their letters.

Just what use is made of word information in letter recognition is a matter of debate. One suggestion, and the one most consistent with the interactive model of recognition, is that information about letters surrounding a critical to-be-recognized letter in a word reduces the set of patterns the target letter might match, thereby enabling the comparison and decision processes to arrive at a more accurate identification. However, more bottom-up mechanisms have also been suggested. For example, Johnston (1978) has argued that processing of individual letters in a word might activate an LTM code for the word itself, which would be more resistant to disruption such as masking. Yet another alternative is that words have their own features, which can be extracted in addition to features of letters, enhancing the pool of information provided by stimulus analysis. Although the extent to which top-down processing is used in these hypotheses varies, all assume that knowledge about higher-order units in which patterns appear aids their recognition.

As was mentioned above, the relevant knowledge has been shown to be of several types. For example, in a letter-identification task where all the strings are nonwords, performance is better when they follow the spelling rules of English (like BURK) than when they do not (BJHK) (Baron and Thurston, 1973). This suggests that the knowledge of spelling rules and pronunciation is applied to make the recognition process easier. The familiarity of words, as well as their spelling and pronounceability, has been shown to affect the perception of letters within them. For example, letters in words are better recognized than those in even pronounceable nonwords (McClelland and Johnston, 1977).

Evidence for the use of syntactic and semantic rules within spoken and written sentences has also been obtained. Miller and Isard (1963) asked subjects to identify words heard against a background of noise. The words could form completely random strings; strings that were syntactically correct but meaningless (all the nouns, verbs, and so on were in the right place but together they made no sense; for example, "Bears shoot work on the country"); or completely correct, meaningful sentences. Subjects were better at identifying the words from the syntactically correct but meaningless strings than those from the random strings. This indicates that syntactic context, even without conventional meaning, could facilitate recognition. They were also better with the meaningful sentences than with the nonmeaningful but syntactically correct strings. The fact that both types were syntactically correct indicates that meaning could also facilitate recognition, over and above the effects of syntax, to give meaningful sentences the advantage. Similar effects have been shown for visually presented sentences (Tulving, Mandler, and Baumal, 1964).

We have described a variety of sources for hypotheses that could be used in top-down processing, as well as a variety of ways these might be brought to bear in the recognition process. These ideas can be made more concrete by considering a computer simulation of recognition based on the interactive approach. This program, developed by Reddy and associates (Reddy, Erman, Fennell, and Neely, 1973; Reddy and Newell, 1974) is called HEARSAY. It attempts to recognize spoken language. At present it operates within rather restricted domains, a principal one being speeches about chess games. This restriction enables HEARSAY to use a small set of hypotheses that are bound to be useful in recognizing the speech it hears. But the principles it embodies can, in theory, be extended to broader areas as well.

Essentially, HEARSAY recognizes speech in chunks, or segments. It works on several segments simultaneously, so that decisions about one part of speech can affect decisions about other parts. Each speech segment is recognized through inputs from several sources. One source is the output of an acoustic analysis, which is used to generate hypotheses about what a sound might be, much as our initial simple model of recognition described such a process. At the same time, hypotheses about the segment may be generated from other sources: A syntactic hypothesis is formed on the basis of the parts of speech already recognized and the position of the current segment; for example, the fact that sentences about chess moves do not begin with actions indicates that the first segment of speech is not part of a verb. A semantic hypothesis is based on the meanings of other recognized segments as well as on general knowledge of chess; for example, if the current sentence is known to be about a king, only certain types of movements are possible. The hypotheses generated by these various knowledge sources are then combined. Some can be eliminated outright by one of the knowledge sources; for example, the acoustic processor can decide on the basis of its analysis that "rook" is not being said, even though the semantic processor hypothesizes the possible occurrence of that word. Those hypotheses that are not eliminated outright are rated in terms of their plausibility by each of the knowledge sources, with the hypothesis getting the highest joint rating being "recognized" (at least temporarily, for old recognitions are updated as new information comes in). If more than one hypothesis gets a high rating and no unequivocal decision can be made, both hypotheses can be carried until a later point, at which more is known about the speech and a decision can be made.

Perhaps the most important fact about HEARSAY is that it is quite successful at recognizing speech within its limited domain. One important reason for its success is that it has more than one knowledge source. Unlike our initial recognition model, where stimuli were presented in a rather impoverished environment, this model can take advantage of expectations generated by past and co-occurring recognitions and by knowledge about the general situation in which the stimulus appears. In an interactive system like HEARSAY, our initial model of Figure 4.1 fits as the data-driven process that analyzes the stimulus and generates hypotheses about its physical form. But this is just part of what turns out to be a more complex event.

The event of pattern recognition is rendered still more complex by the fact that we generally do not recognize and pass on for further processing all patterns presented to us. In that sense, recognition is what we have previously called a limited-capacity process. The limitation in capacity is called *attention*. Some theorists see attention and recognition as virtually synonymous; they assume that the capacity limitation resides in the fact that only a limited number of patterns can be recognized. Others see attention as a more general phenomenon. Let us turn now to a discussion of attention and its role in recognition.

ATTENTION

Suppose you are at a cocktail party and are listening to a conversation. Suddenly you hear your name mentioned in a conversation occurring nearby. Immediately you begin listening to that conversation, only to discover that you are no longer aware of what is happening in the first. You can only follow one conversation at a time; when you listen to it, you "lose" the others. This "cocktail-party phenomenon" has often been used to illustrate the concept of attention. It is said that we can only attend to one conversation. We can select which one we choose to attend to, but all the others will then be filtered out.

This sort of analogy helps to explain why the word *selective* has been applied to attention: The process of attending is seen as selecting some of the many inputs available. It is also seen as a filter or bottleneck, so that, once one channel of input has been selected for processing, others are not able to pass through. As we have mentioned, this is one concept of attention. There is also an alternative concept, in which attention is seen not as a fixed bottleneck at some point in the system, but rather as a general limitation on the capacity to process information in general. We will consider each of these concepts of attention in the following discussion.

Selective Attention: Data and Models

Selective attention has been extensively studied in experiments with dichotic listening and shadowing. *Dichotic listening* refers to hearing two channels of sound at once. You may recall, from Chapter 3, that a channel is a source of sound. In a typical dichotic listening and shadowing experiment, a subject listens to two spoken messages on two channels, one coming to each ear via headphones. The subject is asked to listen to one of the messages and to "shadow" it; that is, to repeat the words in the message as they occur. Surprisingly, subjects have little trouble shadowing one message while listening to two. They tune out the unshadowed message and attend to the one they are shadowing.

Dichotic listening and shadowing effects were extensively studied by Cherry (1953). One of his interests was to find out what became of the unattended, unshadowed message. It suffered from being tuned out, yet certain of its characteristics came through. For example, subjects did know something about the unattended message: that it occurred (some sound was there) and whether it was human speech or some nonspeech sound, like a buzz. Subjects also noticed when the unshadowed message changed from a male voice to a female voice. On the other hand, subjects could not report any of the specific meaningful content of the unshadowed message. They could not tell whether it was actual speech or nonsense speech sounds, what language was spoken, or whether the language changed in the course of the experiment. They did not know any of the words, even if one word was repeated over and over (Moray, 1959).

Dichotic listening and shadowing is an experimental version of the cocktail-party phenomenon. It is a useful procedure with which to study attention, for in order to perform the task, the subject must selectively attend to one channel, the one shadowed, and not the other. The experimental results have given rise to several models of attention, for they provide some of the critical data that such models have to explain. In particular, a theory of selective attention must explain *how* just one channel and not others can be focused on. It must also explain what happens to the information in the un- attended channel.

One of the best known theoretical models of attention is Broad- bent's (1958) filter model. It proposed that selective attention acts like a filter, blocking out some channels and letting only one through. The blocking-out process is made possible by an analysis of the incoming messages on all channels for their physical characteris- tics. A particular message can then be selected and attended to on a physical basis. For example (see Figure 4.5), in dichotic listening, the two messages can be discriminated on the basis of their origin in space (one on the left, one on the right). That discrimination forms the basis for the action of the filter, which selects and tunes in just one of the messages, for example, the one on the left. Similarly, a male or female voice could be selected on the basis of pitch. This also explains why subjects know some of the physical characteristics of the unshadowed message in a dichotic listening experiment. They know them because the physical analysis takes place prior to the filtering.

Broadbent's filter model was shown to be inadequate by experi- ments demonstrating that attention can jump back and forth be- tween channels to follow the meaning of a message. For example,

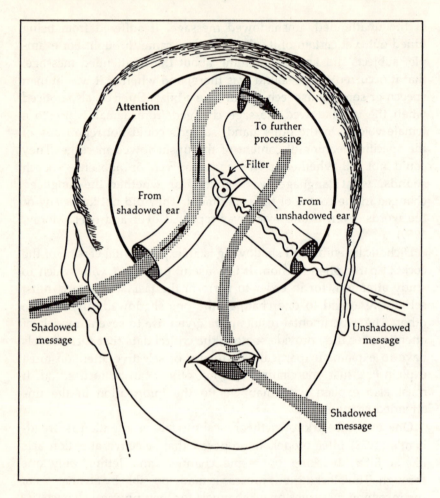

Figure 4.5   The dichotic listening and shadowing task as viewed by Broadbent's filter model. The filter selects one message for further processing on the basis of its location, filtering out the other message.

Treisman (1960) has shown that, in dichotic listening, the subject's shadowing sometimes follows something other than physical characteristics of the message. If a subject is shadowing a message—for example, a story—coming to the right ear, and if that message is suddenly switched to the left, changing ears with the unshadowed message—for example, a list of unrelated words—then the subject's response may also jump to the left ear. The subject may persist in shadowing the story when it jumps ears, even though he or she is instructed to continuously shadow the right-ear channel. Thus, the shadowing follows meaning rather than staying at a designated location.

Because of such results, an interpretation of attention as based solely on physical characteristics of the stimulus must be faulty. To compensate for such problems, Broadbent's model was subsequently modified by Treisman (1964), who proposed that attention acts more like an attenuator—something that turns down the volume on unattended channels without blocking them out. She proposed that all incoming signals undergo a series of preliminary tests. The tests first analyze the inputs on the basis of rather gross physical characteristics, but there are also more refined tests that can analyze an input in terms of its content. After these tests, attention can be directed to one of the channels. The tests determine what is attended to and what is not, because the particular channel that is selected for attention is determined by what the preliminary analysis has revealed. Thus, if I am listening to a message on one channel, and if that same message suddenly continues on a different channel, the preliminary tests will indicate that fact, enabling me to switch to the new channel to follow the message.

The problem with Treisman's model is that the preliminary, preattentional tests can require so much analysis that we find ourselves claiming that a message that has already been analyzed for its meaning has not yet been attended to. The question arises of just where in the system the attentional bottleneck lies, especially in relation to the pattern-recognition process. Is attention at a rather peripheral level, filtering after incoming patterns have undergone only an analysis of physical features, as in Broadbent's model? Is it as late as Treisman's model implies is possible, occurring after all incoming channels have been recognized and analyzed for meaning? The latter possibility makes it seem there is little for attention to do, for the system is capable of extracting meaning from all channels.

One model that attempts to explicitly define the relationship between pattern recognition and attention is that of Norman (1969), following a proposal of Deutsch and Deutsch (1963). Norman's model proposes that all channels impinging on the processing system get some analysis—enough to activate a representation in LTM. (In HEARSAY terms, we might say that the sensory analyzer comes up with a set of hypotheses about potential recognitions for all of the occurring patterns and activates the relevant codes.) At that point, selective attention takes effect; it corresponds to full recognition (an output from the decision process, in terms of our initial model) of the patterns on just one channel, the most highly activated one. Patterns on competing channels do not receive attention and are eliminated from further processing. Thus, according to Norman, recognizing a pattern corresponds to attending to it.

Context also plays an important role in the model; it assumes that recognition of previous patterns establishes a context for the current input. The patterns that are most probable, or *pertinent*, in this context receive activation independently from sensory analysis, which increases the probability they will be selected for full recognition.

The Norman model seems to attempt a compromise, putting the bottleneck neither too early—all incoming channels receiving a sensory or physical analysis and activating codes in LTM—nor too late—only recognized messages being given a full meaningful analysis. But clearly, locating the attentional filter has been problematic for theorists. Moreover, experiments that have attempted to verify or disconfirm the various locations have had contradictory results (Kahneman, 1973). Some of this work, such as Treisman's demonstration that subjects switch channels in shadowing to follow a switch in meaning, indicates that meaning from unattended messages does get through. For another example, MacKay (1973) had subjects shadow ambiguous sentences, with information that clarified the meaning coming in over the unshadowed ear. (The shadowed sentence might be about a bank, with the unshadowed ear presenting either "river" or "money.") In a later test on memory for the meaning of the shadowed sentences, subjects tended to remember whichever meaning was consistent with the input from the unshadowed message, even though they were unable to recall that message. Thus, the meaning of the unattended message apparently did "filter through." However, other experiments seem to show that unattended messages are not analyzed for meaning. Moray (1959) found that subjects could not remember words from an unattended channel even after they were repeated 30 times, suggesting that very little from that channel got through.

Bottleneck theories find it hard to deal with such inconsistent results, some studies suggesting that attention filters out messages before meaningful analysis and others suggesting that filtering occurs after meaning is processed. One possible explanation of the discrepancies cites differences among the experiments. For example, if a shadowing experiment does not fully occupy the subject, he or she may periodically analyze the message coming to the unshadowed ear without making shadowing errors, so that information from the unshadowed channel will be retained. In addition, as we shall see, stimuli vary in the extent to which they can be excluded from attention, and this may have affected results of previous studies. It is difficult, for example, to ignore the sound of one's name, even on an unattended channel (Moray, 1959).

There is another solution to the problem of determining where the attentional filter resides, however. That is to assume it has no permanent residence; to view attention as something other than a filter.

Attention as Limited Capacity

In discussing the Norman Deutsch model above, we considered the possibility that all incoming patterns "excite," or activate, corresponding codes in LTM to some extent, and that attention corresponds to the more robust, full activation or excitation of codes for just some patterns, those that are recognized. Neisser (1967) proposed a similar distinction, calling the initial processing *preattentive* and equating full recognition with attention. These models thus make a distinction between two kinds of activation—*automatic*, which can happen to all patterns at once (the initial excitation) and *attentional*, which can happen to just some patterns (full recognition). (More generally, the terms *automatic* and *attentional* have been applied to any processes that operate on information, not just the process of activating LTM codes.)

The view of recognition and attention as involving automatic and attentional activation of LTM codes has been presented in terms of a *logogen* model (Keele, 1973; Morton, 1970). This model assumes that various LTM codes for an item (particularly a letter or word), representing its meaning, sound, and visual form, are associated in LTM with a common site called a *logogen*, which combines information from the codes. When any one of these codes is excited, the excitation is registered in the logogen. When the excitation received from all sources passes a certain critical level, the logogen makes a recognition decision; it determines that its pattern has occurred. (This is much like HEARSAY's decision, where evidence about a hypothesis comes from various sources and is combined.) Moreover, both automatic and attentional activation can be registered in the logogen. The difference between the two types is that automatic activation can be applied to many logogens at once, but there is only a limited capacity to activate codes using attention. The activation of codes representing patterns on one channel uses up this capacity, so others cannot be activated and recognized.

An experimental distinction between these two types of processes has been demonstrated by work of Posner and Snyder (1975a; 1975b), using what is called a *priming* task. In this task, subjects were asked to perform a simple judgment—deciding whether two simultaneously presented letters were same or different. For some judgments, the subjects were given a prediction (0–½ seconds beforehand) about what the letters might be (but not what they would be with 100 percent certainty); the predictor was called the *prime*. Thus a *trial* of the task (that is, the occurrence of one judgment) might consist of a presentation of the letter A (the prime) followed by AA (the judged letters). Alternatively, a trial might consist of the letter A followed by BB, or the letter B followed by XY. In the first two cases, since the pair of letters match, the subject should respond "same"; in the third case, the response should be "different."

In the situation where the prime matches the subsequent pair of letters (for example, A followed by AA), the prime is said to be *correct* in its prediction. Alternatively, the prime might be *incorrect*; that is, it might name a letter other than the ones subsequently presented (such as A followed by BB). In the latter case, the subject must still respond that the judged letters are the same if they are; the prime does not enter into the judgment. Posner and Snyder also used primes that varied in their usefulness, that is, in the probability that they named letters that would actually be presented. Some primes were *high-probability*; they correctly predicted letters that would actually be presented 80 percent of the time; others were *low-probability* and made a correct prediction only 20 percent of the time. The subjects knew what the overall probabilities of correct prediction were, but of course they did not know at the time of the prime's occurrence whether its prediction would be correct for the current trial. Finally, there were no-prime trials, where only the judged letters appeared. The various types of trials are depicted in Figure 4.6A.

Posner and Snyder predicted that the primes in this task would produce two types of effects on trials where the response was "same." One type of effect is automatic: The prime is assumed to activate its corresponding LTM code quickly after its onset in an automatic fashion, without expenditure of attention. Consider what happens when the prime correctly predicts the judged stimuli (for example, the prime is A, the judged stimuli are AA). When the subjects receive the to-be-judged stimuli, they have just seen the same stimulus, as the prime. The automatic activation of the prime's memory code is assumed to facilitate the judging of the subsequently presented letter pair, because processing of that pair will use the very same code, and the code's already being active will speed the processing. Now consider the case of an incorrect prime (A as prime, BB as judged letters). Here the code activated by the prime's presentation does not match the codes of the judged letters, so no facilitation will occur. However, it is assumed that activation of some

A	Examples of Conditions			
Prime	Frequency of Occurrence of Predicted Letters with Prime	To-Be-Judged Stimuli	Type of Prime	Response
A	80%	AA	High-Probability, Correct	Same
		BB	High-Probability, Incorrect	Same
	20%	AA	Low-Probability, Correct	Same
		BB	Low-Probability, Incorrect	Same
	. . . .	BC	. . . .	Different
None	. . . .	AA	. . . .	Same
		BC	. . . .	Different

B	Type of Prime		Automatic Effects	Attentional Effects
High Probability	Correct		+	+
	Incorrect		0	−
Low Probability	Correct		+	0
	Incorrect		0	0

+: Lower response speed than no-prime condition
−: Higher response speed than no-prime condition
0: No effect

Figure 4.6 (A) Types of trials in the Posner/Snyder task. Prime can have a high or low probability of correct prediction and can be correct or incorrect on the current trial. There can also be no prime. Response can be same or different. (B) Predictions for various conditions in the Posner/Snyder task. Automatic facilitation is expected for correct primes of either probability. Attention to a high-probability prime should produce facilitation if it is correct, inhibition if it is incorrect.

other code is not a hindrance to the processing of the letter pair; that is, the automatic activation due to an incorrect prime does not produce any negative effects on performance.

The second type of priming effect is not automatic, but due to expenditure of attention. Here is where the effects of prime usefulness (that is, the probability with which the prime predicts the identity of the to-be-judged letters) come in. If the prime is high probability, and the subject knows it is very useful (accurate most of the time in its predictions), he or she should devote attention to activate the code of that prime. In this case, if the prime is correct, the attention-produced activation will facilitate responses. If the prime is incorrect, attention will be devoted to the wrong code, and this should actually impair responding to the judged letters. That is, if the subject is expending attention on A's code, there will be less available for BB, the judged stimuli. Note that this is different from automatic effects, which are assumed not to impair processing on incorrect-prime trials. Finally, if the prime is low-probabiltiy, the subject will probably choose to ignore it, and no attention will be devoted to it. In this case, there will be only automatic effects.

The various possibilities for this situation are depicted in Figure 4.6B. In the case of low-probability primes, no attention is used, so only automatic effects occur—facilitation in the case of correct primes, no effect in the case of incorrect primes. In the case of high-probability primes, added to the automatic effects are the effects of the subject's expenditure of attention. This helps in the case of correct primes and hinders in the incorrect-prime case.

To test these predictions, Posner and Snyder measured the time it took the subject to respond to the to-be-judged letters. A prime's facilitation of responses, through either automatic or attentional processes, should make response times shorter than when there is no prime. Inhibition of responses by an incorrect prime should make the time longer than when there was no prime. The actual results are shown in Figure 4.7, which presents, for each priming condition, the response time for trials with identical stimuli in that condition, subtracted from the time for the corresponding trials with no prime. If this measure is greater than zero, the prime was beneficial; it produced faster responses than the no-prime case. If the measure is less than zero, the prime impaired responding; it lengthened the time over the no-prime trials. These measures are shown as a function of the interval between the prime and the to-be-judged stimuli. The figure shows results very consistent with the predictions. In the case of a low-probability prime, where only automatic effects are as-

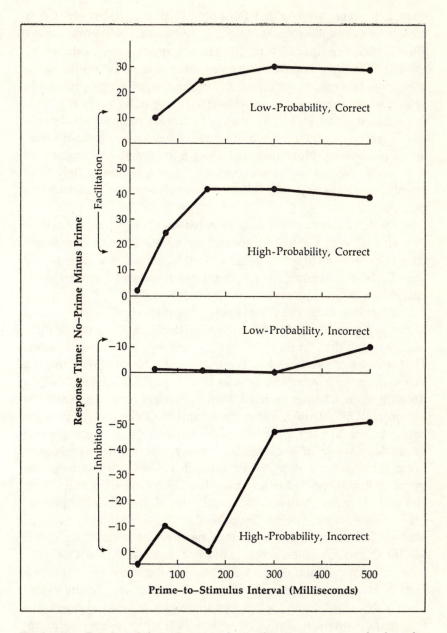

Figure 4.7 Results of the priming task. Facilitation is measured when the prime predicts correctly and response time is faster than the no-prime case; inhibition is measured when the prime predicts incorrectly and response time is slower than the no-prime case. The data are shown for each type of prime (high versus low probability of correct prediction) and for several prime-to-stimulus intervals. [After Posner and Snyder, 1975b.]

sumed to occur, we see that the prime facilitates responses if it is correct but does not impair them if it is incorrect. Moreover, these effects occur very quickly after the prime's appearance, as shown by the fact that there is facilitation even when the prime comes just a short time before the judged letters. In the case of a high-probability prime, where we expect attentional effects as well as automatic ones, we see facilitation rapidly occurring to correct primes. But there is also inhibition in the incorrect-prime case, which arises from attentional processing. Note that inhibition does not rise as quickly as facilitation. Presumably this is because inhibition arises solely from attentional processing, which begins more slowly than automatic activation.

In short, Posner and Snyder's research shows two kinds of activation effects. When a letter appears, automatic activation facilitates later responses to identical letters. To this activation can be added the effects of attention, which facilitates responses to attended-to letters and inhibits responses to other letters.

The fact that facilitation arises when the prime and judged stimuli in this task are identical might seem to imply that the prime must exactly match the stimuli it activates in order for facilitation to occur. That is not necessary, as has been shown by Neely (1977), using a variation of the Posner and Snyder task. Neely had subjects make a decision as to whether or not a string of letters formed a word (for example, ROBIN would lead to "yes" and BRONI to "no"). In some cases, before the string of letters occurred, subjects were given a prime—the name of a category in which the word was likely to occur if the letter string indeed formed a word (for example, the prime is BIRD, and the letter string is ROBIN). Neely found effects similar to those of Posner and Snyder with high-probability primes. (There were no low-probability primes in this experiment.) Subjects showed facilitation when the prime matched the letter string (BIRD–ROBIN) and inhibition when it did not match (BIRD–ARM).

In another variation of the task, Neely isolated the facilitating effects of attention from those of automatic processing. In the experiments described so far, whenever there is a facilitating effect due to attention, there is simultaneously a facilitating effect due to automatic processing. That is because facilitation due to attention occurs when the prime correctly predicts the stimulus (and is high-probability). In this situation the prime also matches the stimulus (in form or meaning), so we also get automatic facilitation. Neely was able to separate the effects of correctly predicting a stimulus from those of matching it, and thus was able to separate attention from automatic effects. He did so by first teaching subjects that a certain prime word actually implied some meaning other than its own. For example, subjects were told that if the prime word was BUILDING, then there was a high (67 percent) chance that a subsequent word string would be not the name of a building part, but the name of some part of the body.

The effects of the BUILDING prime were found to vary with how recently it had been presented when the letter string appeared. If the interval from prime to letters was short, then subjects were faster to respond "yes" to building part names (e.g., DOOR) than they were with no prime. This indicates that the word BUILDING as a prime automatically activated the LTM codes for building parts. But with a longer interval between the prime and the letter string, the BUILDING prime no longer facilitated, but inhibited, responses to building parts. Instead, it now facilitated responses to body parts. This shows the effects of attention kicking in. Subjects were intentionally using the BUILDING prime to activate their codes for body parts, and this overrode the automatic effects of the prime on buildings.

Automatic processing is obviously very handy. It makes possible the consideration of many sources of information simultaneously: We are not forced to disregard one in order to process another. It is therefore exciting to find evidence that we can learn to process automatically. In fact, the experiments just described indicate that learning is involved. The presentation of a word, we have said, automatically activates codes for members of its category (as BIRD activates ROBIN). Clearly this involves reading skills developed through learning, for a word is a rather arbitrary symbol for a category.

Research of Shiffrin and Schneider (1977; Schneider and Shiffrin, 1977) provides a rather direct means of examining the learning of automatic processing. Their research uses a task in which subjects are asked to detect when a *target* item (for example, the letter M) occurs in a series of rapidly flashing visual arrays (see Figure 4.8). Each detection problem constitutes a trial of the task. On each such trial, subjects are first given a set of potential target items that might occur, called the *memory set* (since it is to be held in memory). The memory set can include from one to several items. Subjects then view the series of visual arrays. Each visual array that is flashed can also include from one to several items. At most one item—and possibly none—in all the arrays can be a target from the memory set. All other array items are not from the current trial's memory set; they are called *nontargets*, or *distractors*.

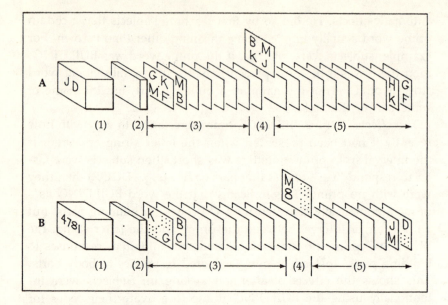

Figure 4.8 Examples of trials in the detection task where target occurs. (A) Subject looks for J or D (the memory set) in arrays of four letters each (J occurs). (B) Subject looks for 4, 7, 8, or 1 (the memory set) in arrays of two letters each (except for the array in which 8 occurs). Events on each trial include: (1) presentation of memory set; (2) fixation dot; (3) arrays of distractors prior to target; (4) occurrence of array with target; (5) arrays of distractors following target. [After Schneider and Shiffrin, 1977. Copyright 1977 by the American Psychological Association. Reprinted by permission.]

This task is similar to that of Neisser (1964), which was described previously as producing evidence for parallel processing. In particular, if performance does not increase with the size of subjects' memory sets—that is, with the number of targets they must keep in mind as they view the arrays—we can assume all the targets were searched for "in parallel."

Two versions of this task were designed, one intended to induce automatic processing and the other to induce attentional processing. The two versions differ in the relationship between subjects' memory-set items and the nontarget distractor items in the arrays. In one version, these two sets of items are nonoverlapping; that is, target items, those occurring in memory sets from trial to trial, *never* are seen as nontarget items in an array. For example, the subjects' memory sets might always be taken from letters of the alphabet, and nontargets in the stimulus arrays might always be digits. Because the set of potential target items are used consistently as target items and in no other way, this is called the *consistent* version of the task. The second version mixes up the memory set and array items. A memory-set item on one trial might not be in the memory set on the next trial but might occur instead as a nontarget item in one of the arrays. (For example, all items might be digits, with 1 occurring as a member of the memory set on one trial and as a nontarget on another trial.) Because a given item has no consistent role in the task but varies from trial to trial, this is called the *varied* task.

Shiffrin and Schneider found that these two tasks gave rise to very different performances. After several hours of practice, subjects performing in the consistent condition were able to search for several memory-set items as rapidly as for one (see Figure 4.9). This is termed *automatic detection*, because no attentional capacity is used. If attentional capacity were used, then searching for more items would use up more capacity and impair performance. This is precisely what occurred in the varied condition, as the figure shows. Processing in the varied task is called *controlled search*. It is as if the subjects have to seek out target items in the displays instead of automatically responding to them, and this seeking is a relatively arduous task that

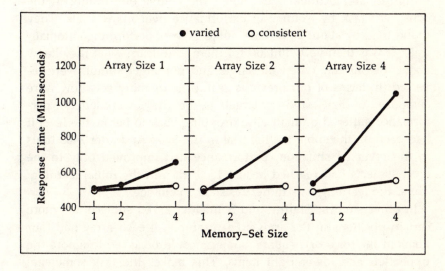

Figure 4.9 Results from a version of the target-detection task in which only one array contained digits or letters, and the time for the subject to respond "yes" (there was a target in the array) or "no" (there was not) was recorded. Data (for correct responses) are shown for arrays containing 1, 2, and 4 items, and memory sets of 1, 2, and 4 items, for the varied and consistent conditions. [After Schneider and Shiffrin, 1977. Copyright 1977 by the American Psychological Association. Reprinted by permission.]

demands attention. Another difference between the two versions of the task is in accuracy: Subjects performing the consistent task performed with almost no errors (they knew when a target had been in the arrays and didn't think one was there if it had not been presented) when the arrays flashed by at speeds of 120 msec. each, under conditions where subjects in the varied condition performed at only about 75 percent accuracy with even more time to view each array (400 msec. per array).

The difference between the varied and consistent tasks lies in what subjects have learned about the stimuli. In the consistent situation, an item from the pool of potential targets is never seen in the series of visual arrays on any trial, unless it is a member of the current trial's memory set and should receive a "yes, I see it" response. In this condition, therefore, subjects can form a strong connection between the item and the response. Thus "targets develop the ability to . . . initiate responses automatically, immediately, and regardless of . . . memory load" (Schneider and Schiffrin, 1977, p. 51). But in the varied condition, as there is no one pool of stimuli always used as targets, no learning can occur.

Shiffrin and Schneider examined the course of learning in the consistent task by examining performance over many trials. They found that, by about 2000 trials, subjects were performing automatically. It was then very difficult for them to unlearn what they knew about the stimuli. When the target and nontarget stimuli were reversed (in terms of our previous examples, memory sets now were composed of digits, and nontargets in the arrays were letters), performance suffered dramatically, dropping back to below the level it had been on the subjects' first trial in the task. And after 2400 trials in the reversed situation, performance had improved only to the level subjects had reached in just 1500 trials in the initial learning. Thus, the learning was rather resistant to change.

In other studies, Shiffrin and Schneider asked subjects to ignore certain positions in the arrays. For example, if each array had four items in the form of a square, subjects could be asked to ignore the upper left and lower right items. This makes the task somewhat analogous to dichotic listening and shadowing, where one of two channels comes in but is to be ignored. The effects of the irrelevant, to-be-ignored items were rather different, according to what had previously been learned about those items; that is, whether there had been training on those items that would lead to automatic detection. Consider the following scenario: A subject is first trained in the consistent task, with letters as memory-set items and digits as distractor items, for many trials. This subject is then put in the varied condition, with digits serving as both target items and nontargets. That is, on each trial, he or she receives a memory set of digits, then sees arrays in which digits occur as the relevant (*not*-to-be-ignored) items, and responds when one of the memory-set digits appears. Suppose now that one of the irrelevant, to-be-ignored items is a memory of the current memory set. What happens? Very little, apparently. Subjects are able to ignore these items so well that it does not matter whether they are present or not; and if they are present, it matters little whether they are in the current memory set. Now suppose that one of the irrelevant items is a member of the subject's previously learned letter targets from the consistent condition, which should be detected automatically. In this case, there is a big effect. When the irrelevant letter appears in the same array as one of the current memory-set digits, detection of the digit suffers. Apparently the presence of the letter causes attention to swerve from the processing of relevant items in the array to the irrelevant ones. Subjects cannot ignore such an item; it is as if its automatic detection acts to draw attentional processing toward it, robbing capacity needed by the digit-detection task.

The distinction between automatic and attentional processes is an important one that is bound to be a focus of future research. One obvious application is to the area of reading, which progresses from a laborious, attention-demanding process in the novice to an automatic operation in the skilled reader (LaBerge and Samuels, 1974). One early demonstration of the automatic way words evoke responses is the Stroop (1935) color-word phenomenon. In this task, a subject is simply asked to name the color of a stimulus. The stimulus might be the word seven, for example, printed in brown, and the subject is to say "brown." There is no trouble in naming the word's color unless the word itself is the name of some other color. When subjects try to say "brown" to the word *orange* printed in brown ink, they take much longer than to say the color of a neutral word. They may even try to squint to prevent themselves from reading the word, but to little avail. The word can be said to automatically evoke its own meaning before the color can be named, and it then interferes with the ability to name the color.

Although the distinction between attentional and automatic processing represents a promising theoretical advance, one question it raises is how we should view the relationship between pattern recognition and attention. It would seem impossible to place attention at some fixed point in the pattern-recognition system, given the difficulties in locating that point and the indication (in Schneider and Shiffrin's work) that the point at which attention is needed changes as a result of learning. Perhaps we are limited to a rough generalization implied by Neisser's term *preattentive processes*, that early stimulus analysis is more likely to be automatic than later thinking about what a stimulus means. But even this generalization must be regarded as limited, given that a category name like BIRD seems to automatically access the meanings of related words like ROBIN, which indicates that at least some meaningful processing is not attentional. On the other hand, complex cognitive processes like solving problems undoubtedly use attentional capacity (e.g., Baddeley and Hitch, 1974).

Though we must leave many problems unsolved, our discussion of pattern recognition has furthered our understanding of the information-processing system. So far, we have considered the operations that intervene between external stimulus events and the point at which stimuli make contact with LTM and can be further processed. In the next chapter, we will discuss the nature of active processing.

5

Short-Term Memory: Verbal Storage System and Working Memory

We have followed the course of a stimulus from its external presentation to its sensory registration and recognition. We will now consider what happens to recognized memory codes. According to the general model presented in Chapter 2, at least some of them are transferred to short-term memory (STM). Most research on STM has been conducted with verbal material, so that we know much more about STM as a storehouse for words than about its other characteristics. The general picture that has emerged from such research is an STM that holds a few words in acoustic form, that is, as sounds. However, there is evidence that STM can hold words nonacoustically—visually and meaningfully—as well. In addition to its function of storing words, STM is depicted as "working" memory, the site of ongoing cognitive activities—for instance, meaningful elaboration of words, symbol manipulation such as that involved in mental arithmetic, and reasoning. It is these roles of STM, storing and "working on" verbally coded material, that we will consider in this chapter. In Chapter 6, we will consider how verbal material is forgotten from STM, and in Chapter 7 we will expand the picture to include short-term storage and processing of visually coded items, or "mental images."

THE WORKBENCH ANALOGY

It may be helpful to think of STM as a workbench in a workroom where a carpenter is building a cabinet. All her materials are neatly organized on shelves around the walls of the room. Those materials that she is immediately working with—tools, boards ready to be put into place, and so on—she brings from a shelf and places on the bench, leaving a space on the bench where she can work. When the bench gets too messy, she may stack material in orderly piles, so that more can be fit onto the bench. If the number of stacks increases, some may even fall off, or the carpenter may replace some things on a shelf.

Now, how does this analogy fit our notion of STM as one of two stores in a duplex system? We can think of the shelves in the workroom as LTM, the repository for the large set of material available for the carpenter's work. The bench—divided into the carpenter's work space and a limited-capacity storage area—is STM. The carpenter's operations are like the work that goes on in STM. When the carpenter stacks things in order to create more space, she is performing a process analogous to one associated with STM: chunking. (We shall see that in the process of memorizing a short list, chunking is often used to combine several items into one, which takes up the space of a single unit in STM.) Things that fall off the bench correspond to the items forgotten from STM, just as bringing things from the shelves and replacing them there is akin to transfer of information from and to LTM. In order to accommodate the idea that LTM is permanent and that material is not actually *removed* from LTM when it is put into STM, we might stretch the analogy a bit and assume that the LTM shelves contain an essentially unlimited supply of any given material, so that when the set or copy of some material is transferred to the workbench, another set still remains on the shelf.

Although it should not be pushed too far, the workbench analogy is useful. From it, we get an idea of STM as a rather changeable entity, in which various things may be stored and worked on. Also, we see that there is a trade-off between work space and storage space, so that more of one means less of the other. However, the complexities of STM involve more than placing things in stacks or on shelves.

STORAGE IN STM

The idea of STM as a memory capable of holding only a few items for a short time is derived in part from the memory-span task previously discussed. This task has been with us for almost a century, since Hermann Ebbinghaus began the first systematic study of learning and memory in 1885. Ebbinghaus developed a procedure called *serial learning*, in which a subject (usually Ebbinghaus himself) was presented with a list of verbal items and then attempted to recall them in the order of presentation; then was presented with them again and recalled again, and so on until the list was learned. (The items Ebbinghaus used were often "nonsense syllables" that have the form consonant-vowel-consonant, such as RUK or DAF.) Ebbinghaus discovered that if a list was short enough—say, seven or fewer items—he could recall it perfectly after just one reading. If the list increased to eight or more items, however, the learning time increased dramatically. There seemed to be an abrupt discontinuity at around seven items; below it, there was immediate learning; above it, learning took several readings, the number of readings increasing with the number of items. The seven-item limit is called the memory span, and, as we have previously noted, it is viewed as a limit on the storage capacity in STM. It is as if STM has a certain number of slots—about seven—and once the slots are filled, people begin to make errors in remembering.

The memory span is not the only means of measuring STM; another method is to use the list-learning procedure called free recall, described in Chapter 2. A subject gets a fairly lengthy list (20 items or so; in any case, greater than the memory span) and is asked to recall the items in any order. We have described the serial-position function for this task, where the proportion of the time a word is recalled is plotted against the serial position of that word in the list. In general, there is a recency effect: Recall of words in the last few positions is viewed as measuring recall from STM, and it can be used to measure its capacity.

There are problems with the use of both memory span and the recency effect as STM measures, however. There is some evidence that they arise from different sources. For one thing, in experiments that manipulate the nature of the to-be-remembered list, many variables that affect the memory span do *not* change performance on recency items in free recall. For example, when items in a memory-span task sound alike, performance suffers and the measured span is less than when items do not sound alike (Conrad and Hull, 1964). In contrast, the acoustic similarity of items in a free-recall list has little effect on the recency region of that list (Watkins, Watkins, and Crowder, 1974). Yet another problem is that memory span estimates are usually greater than the number of items producing the recency effect in free recall (5 to 9 items vs. 2 to 4), suggesting that we need two measures of STM's capacity, one for each task.

Given these discrepancies, it is clear that the concept of STM will depend on the task used to measure it. Proponents of the recency measure argue that the memory span is too variable to be equated with STM's presumably fixed capacity. It has also been demonstrated that the memory span shows something analogous to a serial position effect, indicating that not all "slots" in the STM storage space—as measured by the memory-span task—are equivalent. Watkins (1977) showed this by using two kinds of items in a span task: words that occur frequently in natural language, and words that occur infrequently. It is well known that frequent words are easier to recall in tasks that tap LTM. In the memory-span task, Watkins found that the difference between frequent and infrequent words depended on their relative positions in the list. When a list was constructed half of frequent and half of infrequent words, performance was better when the frequent words were in the first half of the list and the infrequent words in the second half than with the reverse order. This suggests that only the first few slots could take advantage of frequency. In fact, Watkins's results suggest that the initial items in a list about the size of the span may be recalled from LTM, at least in part, and only the recent items from STM.

But there are also arguments against the use of recency effects to measure STM. Proponents of the memory span argue that the recency effect is affected by too few manipulations. Not only acoustic similarity, but other characteristics of items in the free-recall list, such as frequency, fail to alter the recency effect. A related phenomenon was pointed out in Chapter 2. When subjects are required to perform in memory-span tasks at the same time that they listen to a list of items for later free recall, the recency region of the serial-position curve is unaffected (Baddeley and Hitch, 1974). Just as many items from the last positions in the list are recalled when the memory-span task is required as when it is not. This result does not jibe very well with the view of the recency effect as tapping an STM of limited storage capacity, for if the effect did so, then performing the memory-span task should use the same capacity and impair performance on the recent items in free recall.

It is not clear how to resolve the problem of measuring STM. A number of suggestions have been offered to reconcile the discrepant results from the two tasks we have discussed. Given the general resistance of the recency effect in free recall to experimental manipulations, some theorists have proposed that it arises from LTM; that very recent items have a special status there which enhances recall, whatever their frequency, sound, or semantic properties. On the other hand, some theorists view the recency effect as tapping STM and the memory-span task as relying not only on the same STM component but also on LTM storage. Still another suggestion is that both tasks measure STM, but they draw on different types of stored information. In any case, we shall continue to evaluate data from both of the tasks in our discussions of STM. Because the memory-span task appears to be more relevant to the concept of STM as working memory, we shall consider it in more detail.

Chunking to Increase STM Storage Capacity

Although the span of immediate memory can be said to be about seven words, it is also seven letters (if the letters do not form words) or seven nonsense syllables. That is, the memory span is not defined in terms of any particular unit—word, letter, or syllable—but instead seems to be about seven of whatever units are presented. Thus, subjects can remember seven letters if they do not form any particular pattern (X, P, A, F, M, K, I), but they can remember many more letters if they form seven words. That is because they are able to *recode* multiple-letter sequences into single units when the sequences form meaningful words. The ability to recode in this way, to combine single stimuli (the letters) into larger units (the words) is called *chunking*. The units that result are, not surprisingly, called *chunks*. This term was used by Miller (1956), who coined a now-famous phrase when he claimed that the memory span, as measured in chunks, was "the Magical Number Seven, plus or minus two."

Miller discussed some other spans that fit this magical number range of five to nine, but what is particularly important for our present discussion is his view of STM: The short-term memory span is measured in units that can vary quite widely in their internal structure. A unit of STM's capacity corresponds to a chunk, and a chunk is a rather variable entity, containing more or less information as circumstances permit.

One problem with the concept of the chunk is that its definition is circular. On the one hand, we define a chunk as whatever STM holds seven of; on the other, we claim that the span of STM is seven chunks. That means that the span of STM is seven of whatever STM holds seven of. The claim that STM has a capacity of seven chunks is thus not very meaningful unless there is some way of defining chunk other than as "that which STM holds seven of." Quite often, of course, there is some other way to determine the nature of a chunk. For example, suppose we present to a subject the letters of several three-letter words, in sequence (e.g., C, A, T, D, O, G, F, A, R). We may find that a subject can remember about twenty-one letters—those of seven words—for immediate recall. In that case, a chunk corresponds to a word, if we define a chunk as that which one can recall seven of. But a chunk also corresponds to a word on the basis of our knowledge of words. That is, we could have predicted in advance that the subject could remember twenty-one (not seven) letters, because a chunk should be a word in this case. Thus, there is agreement between two ways of estimating what a chunk might be—the memory span, and our knowledge of what corresponds to a unit.

In addition, it has been found that chunks can be estimated from one type of task and then used to predict performance on another (Simon, 1974). For example, assuming that the number of syllables that can be learned in a given time depends on how those syllables combine to form chunks, we can use a syllable-learning task to estimate chunk sizes for different kinds of items. We can then use the estimates to predict performance on memory-span tasks with these items. The success of such predictions provides another means of validation for the chunk concept.

In general, chunking is any sort of operation that combines many individual units of information into one. We might ask what sorts of operations are used to integrate these units. We can divide chunking operations into two, somewhat related, classes. First, there is the case where each chunk combines a cluster of items occurring closely in time or space, and where the grouped items need not form a meaningful unit. It has often been demonstrated, for example, that immediate recall of items (that is, recall immediately after presentation) is better when the items are presented rhythmically than when they are presented at a fixed rate (e.g., Bower and Winzenz, 1969; Huttenlocher and Burke, 1976). Apparently, it is easier to combine several items into one unit when those items stand as a temporal (or spatial) group, and the rhythmic presentation serves this function. This sort of chunking is often called *grouping*, for just that reason.

Grouping does not demand that items in a chunk be meaningfully related to one another. In contrast, the second sort of chunking utilizes information from LTM to meaningfully relate many incoming items to a single known item. For example, the single letters C, A, T, might be combined into *cat*. This sort of chunking should be facilitated to the degree that to-be-chunked items have some inherent relationship that permits them to form a unit. In particular, if a group of stimuli has a structure that matches some code in LTM, we might expect the stimuli to form a chunk that corresponds to that code.

Bower (1970; 1972a; Bower and Springston, 1970) demonstrated this aspect of chunking by manipulating the extent to which items in a list matched known units in LTM. Subjects in his studies performed a memory-span task in which letters were spoken aloud to them. The experimenter separated the letters by brief pauses, and the positions and durations of the pauses varied selectively. For example, the experimenter might read a letter sequence as: TVF . . . BIJF . . . KY . . . MCA. Subjects hearing that sequence could not remember as many letters as subjects who heard: TV . . . FBI . . . JFK . . . YMCA, even though the number of letters as well as the number of two-, three-, and four-letter groups, was identical in both conditions. Bower found very similar effects when he presented the letters visually and manipulated the letter groups by varying the color of adjacent letters (here, capital and lower-case letters signify two different colors): TVFbijfKYmca versus TVfbiJFKymca.

Bower's experiments indicate that previously learned letter sequences such as acronyms can be the basis for chunking, particularly when the inputs are grouped so as to be readily perceived as corresponding to those patterns. Chunks can also be formed with material more complex than letter sequences, although the principles of chunking remain the same. This is illustrated by work on the verbatim recall of lists of words that vary in how closely they resemble sentences. Such lists are said to vary in their "order of approximation to English." The concept of order of approximation, developed by Miller and Selfridge (1950), refers to a property of a list that characterizes its relationship to English text. The order furthest removed from English, called a zero-order approximation to English, is simply a list of randomly selected English words. A first-order approximation is similar to the zero-order, except that the words are drawn from text. Thus, the frequency with which words occur in first-order lists reflects their frequency of use in the language. Second-order lists are generated by particular human subjects. First, one subject is given a common word such as *the* and asked to use it in a sentence. His response might be, "The sky is falling." The word that follows the given word in his sentence (*sky*) is then passed on to another subject, who uses *that* word in a sentence. The second subject's sentence might be, "In the sky are birds." The word following the given word in her sentence (*are*) is given to another subject, and so on, until a list of words of some chosen length has been generated ("sky are . . ."). For third- and higher-order approximations to English, the same procedure is used, except that each subject is given *two* or more consecutive words to use in forming a sentence. Thus, as the order of approximation increases, the amount of context present when a new word is added to the list increases, and the list increasingly resembles English prose. The highest order, following seventh-order approximation, is text itself. An example of a first-order list is "abilities with that beside I for waltz you the sewing"; a fourth-order list, "saw the football game will end at midnight on January"; and a seventh-order list, "recognize her abilities in music after he scolded him before" (Miller and Selfridge, 1950).

The development of word lists with measurable resemblances to English sentences is useful in the investigation of chunking. Miller and Selfridge found that immediate recall of a word list improved as the list increased in order of approximation to English. The improvement was greatest in the range of zero-order to about third-order. This suggests that subjects could use their knowledge of English to facilitate their immediate memory, which suggests in turn that the subjects were using chunking to do so.

That the subjects were in fact chunking is supported by an experiment by Tulving and Patkau (1962). They generated lists of 24 words, varying in approximation to English, and presented the lists to subjects for immediate recall. In examining the subjects' recall performance, Tulving and Patkau defined a unit called the *adopted chunk*. This was a grouping of items in output (the subject's recall) that matched a sequence of the input (the list as presented). For example, if an input list included "saw the football game will end at midnight on January," and the subject recalled "the football game saw at midnight will end," he or she would be judged to be using the adopted chunks: (1) "the football game" (2) "saw" (3) "at midnight" (4) "will end." Such units were labeled chunks because the fact that each was grouped at recall in the same order as it had been presented suggested that the words within the adopted chunk were grouped together (chunked) by the subject at the time of presentation.

The results of the Tulving and Patkau study provided some interesting evidence for the use of chunking in remembering the word lists. First, they found, just as Miller and Selfridge did, that the order of approximation to English was positively related to the number of words recalled. In addition, they found that the subjects almost invariably recalled about five or six adopted chunks, regardless of the order of approximation. Thus, the observed improvement in recall (the increase in the number of words recalled) as the order of approximation increased was not due to the subject's recalling more chunks. Instead, it reflected the fact that the more the list approximated English prose, the more words were included in the average chunk. That is, it seemed that the more the word list resembled English sentences, the larger a chunk the subjects could form and later recall. Since they always recalled about the same number of chunks (a number equalling the typical memory span), their ability to form larger chunks led to better recall performance. In short, it appears that something about the structure of English leads to chunk formation.

Just what might be the factor in English sentences that leads to increased chunk size is not clear. One possibility is that chunking is based on the rules of English syntax, rules that specify how words can be arranged to form sentences. For example, one rule of syntax says that a sentence contains a noun phrase (the subject) followed by a verb phrase (the predicate). Thus we learn that "the boy ran" is proper English syntax, but "ran the boy" is not. All speakers of English learn to apply the rules of syntax, and it may be the knowledge of those rules that leads to the chunking of English text. As lists of words increase in their approximation to English, they increasingly comply with English syntax, and on that basis chunking could be facilitated.

One set of evidence favoring the view that syntactic rules lead to chunking comes from experiments by Aaronson and Scarborough (1976; 1977). They had subjects read sentences presented one word at a time on a computer scope. The subjects themselves could control how long each word remained on the scope, pressing a button whenever they wanted the next word to appear. The experimenter could therefore measure how long a subject looked at each word, and these word-by-word reading times were plotted against the positions of words in the sentence, as in Figure 5.1. This figure shows reading times for two groups of subjects, a "memory" group, who had to recall each sentence immediately after its presentation, and a "comprehension" group, who had to answer a simple true-false question about the sentence content immediately after reading it.

The data in Figure 5.1 show clear evidence of chunking by syntax-defined units on the part of the memory group. The peaks in the graph, where particularly long reading times occur, tend to fall at the beginning or end of these units. In 90 percent of the sentences used, all major breaks between syntactical units were accompanied

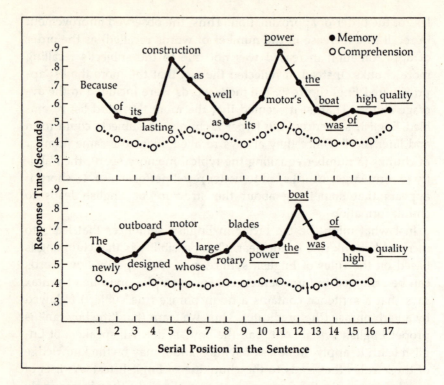

Figure 5.1 Word-by-word reading times for two sentences, as produced by a memory group and a comprehension group. The intersecting short lines indicate boundaries between sentence units. Note that the last seven words are identical for both sentences, but the unit boundaries differ, and the memory group's reading times differ accordingly. [After Aaronson and Scarborough, 1976. Copyright 1976 by the American Psychological Association. Reprinted by permission.]

by such peaks. The authors hypothesize that a peak in reading time occurs at the end of a unit because subjects are processing all the material from the unit at once; that is, they are chunking that material. They may chunk material not only from the immediately preceding unit, but also from units before that. This is suggested by the fact that the later in the sentence a syntactic unit occurs, the higher the peak that measures processing time for that unit.

The relationship between reading time and syntactic units clearly depends on the fact that the subjects in the memory group knew they would have to recall the sentence. When subjects knew they merely had to comprehend it well enough to answer a question, they did not show a similar pattern of peaks, and they also read faster, as the figure shows. The contrast between groups supports the idea that, for subjects in the memory group, the peaks at boundaries between syntactic units reflect a mode of processing specialized for encoding with the goal of later recall. Presumably, this processing consists of forming chunks on the basis of syntactic information.

Aaronson and Scarborough's results are clearly consistent with the idea that chunking can be based on syntactic rules. There is also another source of LTM data for use in chunking sentences—meaning. Words that form units according to the rules of English syntax also tend to form units of meaning. Thus, the data on reading time could reflect chunking by meaning as well as, or instead of, by purely syntactic units. Similarly, the beneficial effects on memory of increased order of approximation to English could be semantic as well as syntactic. For as order of approximation increases, sentences become both more grammatical (syntactically proper) and more meaningful.

In fact, there is evidence that subjects chunk sentences into higher-order units by using knowledge of both meaning and syntax (e.g., Johnson, 1968; Salzinger, Portnoy, and Feldman, 1962; Tejirian, 1968). Semantic effects appear to be particularly important in the approximation-to-English studies for orders of approximation above the third. Tejirian generated new lists of words from approximations to English by substituting, for words in the original lists, new words of the same grammatical class (noun, verb, adjective, and so on). The substitution of a new word changed the semantic structure of the list but left the syntax unchanged. Tejirian's results indicated that such changes had no effect on the number of words recalled for orders of three and below. This indicates that semantic content of first- to third-order lists is not an important factor in recall. However, above the third order, semantics were much more important, and word substitutions led to decreases in recall.

The effects of spelling patterns, grammatical rules, and meaning all demonstrate how chunking can utilize previously acquired knowledge.* Chunking can also be facilitated when people learn particular rules designed for just that purpose. For example, Miller (1956) reported that subjects learned to recode long strings of zeros

---

*In discussing those effects, we have examined experiments that might be thought of as long-term retention studies rather than as experiments with short-term storage. In particular, the Tulving and Patkau study used lists of 24 items, which exceed the memory span, so that LTM storage appears to be involved. However, since the processing involved in chunking material to be stored in STM is also assumed to enhance the material's representation in LTM, experiments that measure long-term recall can provide valuable insights into short-term storage and processes as well.

and ones into short strings of numerals by first learning to translate three-digit patterns into single numerals as follows: 000 = 0; 001 = 1; 010 = 2; 011 = 3; 100 = 4; 101 = 5; 110 = 6; 111 = 7. Then, given a sequence like 001000110001110, they converted it into three-digit patterns (001,000,110,001,110) and used the above system to convert those into single digits, resulting in 10616. A well-practiced subject could, in this manner, remember sequences of twenty-one or so zeros and ones!

The process of chunking is important because it provides a means of circumventing the limited space in STM. Successful chunking means that more can be packed into each storage "slot," and more total information can be held. Of course, we will be successful in increasing our immediate memory performance only to the extent that we can subsequently *decode* our chunks and recall their components. For example, a subject given the four-letter series R N C T in a memory-span task might recode it into the one-word chunk *raincoat*. If, at the time of recall, the items were reported as R A C T, the attempt to chunk would not have succeeded in producing accurate performance, and the estimate of that subject's STM capacity would have to reflect the fact.

Individual Differences in STM Capacity

Not all people have the same memory span; yours may be seven, someone else's may be five. Memory span varies with age as well as among individuals of the same age. These differences among individuals led to the early use of memory span as a measure of mental abilities (Jacobs, 1887). Typically, when the task is used in this way, the items that compose lists are single digits, and the subject is required to recall the digits in order. (Note, however, that free recall can also be used in a memory-span task. The difference between such a task and the standard free-recall task is that the lists are longer in standard free recall.) The subject is given a series of lists, at first rather short ones but gradually increasing in length until the point at which mistakes are made. The memory span can be taken to be the number of items in the list *prior* to the list on which the first mistake is made (although there are other formulas for the measure as well).

The use of memory span as a component of intelligence scores is somewhat questionable. It has been found, for example, that in a group of tests commonly used to measure IQ, the span is the *worst* test when it comes to predicting performance in college (Conry and Plant, 1965). However, the fact that individuals do differ in span has led psychologists to wonder why the differences arise. One possibility is that children and low-IQ individuals have smaller STM capacities, fewer "slots" in STM. Unfortunately, this hypothesis is somewhat difficult to test, as Chi (1976) has pointed out in a recent review. For one thing, the span varies even within an individual as the type of material used to measure it is varied, suggesting that there is no fixed set of slots. For another, it is difficult to separate effects of the number of slots from the ability to chunk information. If a child remembers fewer letters than an adult, is it because there are fewer spaces for the letters in the child's STM or because adults are better at chunking letters so that more of them fit into a single slot? (As we have seen, some adults practice at chunking with special tricks and, as a result, remember extremely large numbers of items in span tasks. We do not assume, however, that each of these items counts as a slot.) There is evidence that children do not use chunking strategies as much as adults, so they would certainly be expected to produce poorer performance in span tasks (e.g., Belmont and Butterfield, 1971). Perhaps children have less information in LTM that can be used as the basis for a chunk; they know fewer words, for example.

The hypothesis that individual differences in chunking ability underlie the observed differences in memory-span tasks has been tested. One would predict, on the basis of this idea, that if subjects were given assistance in grouping (such as instructions as to how to group items, or rhythmic grouping on the part of the experimenter), the differences among individuals should be reduced. That is because good chunkers would be able to perform well without any help and would not be aided very much, but poor chunkers would be helped a lot by the assistance and would therefore gain relative to the good chunkers. However, this prediction has not been supported. Telling adult subjects how to chunk did not help a group with low span any more than a group with high span (Lyon, 1977), nor did it help younger children more than older (Huttenlocher and Burke, 1976).

Another possibility, that people with better spans can rehearse items better, has similarly lacked support. Presenting items at a rate fast enough to preclude their being subvocally repeated (rehearsed) did not reduce differences between a high-span and a low-span group, as is shown in Figure 5.2. This is contrary to the rehearsal

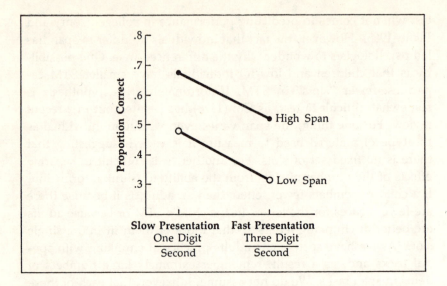

Figure 5.2 Proportion of digits recalled from ten-digit lists (immediately after presentation) by subjects with high and low memory spans for digits. Data are shown for two presentation rates. [From Lyon, 1977.]

hypothesis, which would assume that because rehearsal would be eliminated by a fast presentation rate, differences in span should be eliminated (Lyon, 1977; Cohen and Sandberg, 1977).

It is easier to find hypotheses about memory-span differences that have *not* been supported than it is to find those that have been. One still viable possibility is that children and low-IQ adults suffer in pre-STM processing, such as pattern recognition or sensory registration, although the case is not clear (Chi, 1976; Cohen and Sandberg, 1977; Huttenlocher and Burke, 1976). Perhaps the best conclusion is that STM storage space is clearly more complex than its depiction as a set of slots would suggest. The memory-span task used to measure it quite possibly measures other capabilities as well, so that individual differences in the task should not be taken as incontrovertible evidence for differences in STM storage space. Although the memory-span task remains a useful device to investigate STM, it cannot be considered to measure some absolute limit, such as the number of internal slots.

RETRIEVAL FROM STM

Successful performance in a memory-span task requires more than storage space to hold the items. When the time comes to recall, the items must be retrieved from storage. You may think that this retrieval process is trivial; that we just examine the storage space, and if an item is there, we report it. However, things are not that simple.

Retrieval from STM has been studied primarily with an experimental procedure called *memory scanning*, developed by Sternberg (1966; 1969). Memory scanning is similar to the task used by Shiffrin and Schneider (1977; Schneider and Shiffrin, 1977) to study automatic and attentional processing (see Chapter 4). Subjects take part in a series of trials. On each trial, they are given a *memory set*, a brief list of items (for example, a set of one to five digits, such as 2, 4, 7, 3). The number of items in the set is below the span of STM, and the subject commits them to memory. So far, the task is much like the typical memory-span task. But instead of asking the subject to recall all the items from the memory set, the experimenter next shows a single item, a test stimulus, that might or might not be a member of the set. The subject is to respond "yes" if the test stimulus matches one of the memory set items, and "no" if it does not. The responses are usually made by pushing one of two buttons.

Unlike most tasks we have discussed, this task is one a subject can do without making any mistakes; thus, the data collected by the experimenter cannot be merely percentage correct or incorrect. Instead, the dependent variable is the subject's reaction time (RT)— the time it takes to respond "yes" or "no" after seeing the test stimulus. Specifically, RT is the time that elapses between the onset of the test stimulus and the subject's response.

In theory, using RT in this way will give an indication of how long it takes for internal events to occur. In Sternberg's task, the RT includes the time required for the subject to perform such processes as perceiving the test stimulus and comparing it to the memory set. The RT should be longer or shorter as the subject takes more or less time to perform these actions. The use of RT in psychological experimentation is not restricted to just one task. In fact, it has a rather long history. It developed from the work of Donders (1862), who devised a "subtractive procedure" for using RT to investigate psychological processes. The technique is quite simple: Suppose we have two tasks, X and Y, and suppose that task Y includes all of task X plus some other component, Q (that is, $Y = X + Q$). If we measure RT for the completion of tasks X and Y, then we can subtract the RT for task X from that for Y and derive the time it took for component Q. By this means, we can investigate the nature of Q, even though it may not be directly observable in isolation. More generally, by using RT, we can isolate task components and discover some of the properties of mental performance.

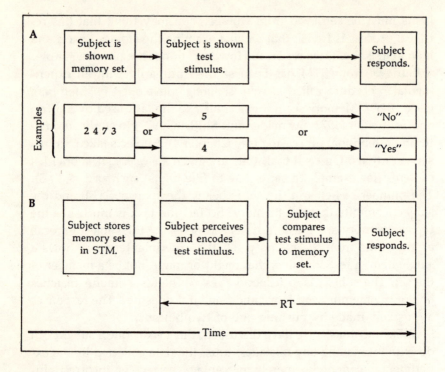

Figure 5.3 Sternberg's memory-scanning task: (A) Events of a typical trial. (B) Proposed mental events during the trial.

What kind of processing goes on during the RT interval in Sternberg's task? As we have indicated, the task can be broken up into component processes (see Figure 5.3). We assume that when the test stimulus appears, the subject has the memory set stored in STM. Let us say that the subsequent processing includes three stages. First, the subject perceives and encodes the test stimulus— gets it into some appropriate mental form. Then that test stimulus is compared to the members of the memory set. Finally, a response is made on the basis of those comparisons. The total time taken by these stages is the RT.

Sternberg was particularly interested in the variations in RT that correspond to variations in the memory-set size, that is, the number of items in the set. From those RT variations, we can make inferences about the comparison process the subject goes through in the second stage of the task. To see this, consider what happens if we increase the memory set by one digit. This means that the subject will have more comparing to do, because the test stimulus must be compared to the elements in the memory set. The effects on RT of adding a single digit will vary according to how the subject does the task. Therefore, finding out what those effects are gives us a tool to find out how he or she is processing this information.

As an example, suppose we had a simple *parallel* hypothesis about the STM comparison process; namely, that the subject has a limitless processing capacity and can examine everything in STM at one time with no more effort than it takes to look at some part of it. This would be like the automatic processing of subjects in the consistent condition of the Shiffrin and Schneider studies. This hypothesis enables us to make certain predictions about the pattern of RT to be obtained. Specifically, we can predict that adding a single digit to the memory set will have no effect on RT. Whether the memory items number two, or three, or four, RT in the task should not vary, because it takes the subject no more time to compare one element of the memory set to the test stimulus than to compare several. This prediction is illustrated in Figure 5.4A, showing RT plotted against the number of items in the memory set.

Alternatively, suppose *serial* scanning occurs, that is, the subject can examine only one item in the memory set at a time. In this case, each item added to the set should increase the time it takes to perform the task. We would predict an increase in RT with memory-set size, the amount of increase depending on just how long it takes to scan an additional digit and compare it to the test stimulus. We would expect to find data like those shown in Figure 5.4B.

Now let us look at this serial-scanning hypothesis in more detail. We have proposed that the subject's task has three stages, each taking up part of the total amount of time. Let us now assign times to these stages. Suppose it takes the subject e milliseconds to encode the test stimulus; c milliseconds to compare a single item in the memory set with the test stimulus; and r milliseconds to perform the third (response) stage. If the memory set had only one digit, the subject could perform the task in $e + c + r$ milliseconds—that would be the RT. Now, suppose there were five elements in the memory set and none of them matched the test stimulus. The subject would make a negative response and would have an RT of $e + c + c + c + c + c + r$ milliseconds. In general, the time it would take the subject to say "no" in the negative-response situation would be $e + s \times c + r$, where s is the memory-set size. The data would thus form a straight line on our graph plotting RT against s. The line could be expressed as $RT = (e + r) + (s \times c)$. Thus, the slope of that line would be c. What this means is that if we had a subject perform the task, and we plotted his or her RTs for negative responses against the size of the

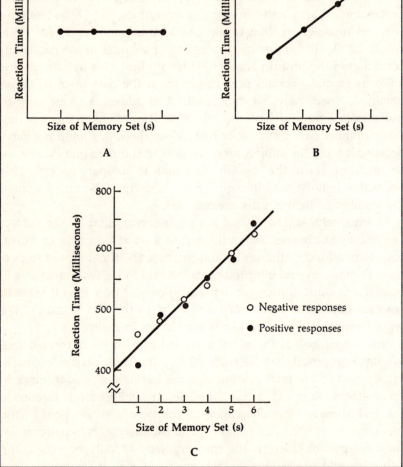

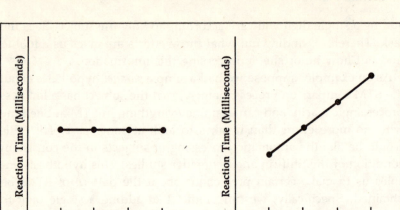

Figure 5.4 Sternberg's memory-scanning task: (A) Results, showing reaction time as a function of size of memory set, as predicted by the parallel model. (B) Results as in A, but as predicted by the serial model. (C) Actual results of the scanning task. [After Sternberg, 1966. Copyright 1966 by the American Association for the Advancement of Science.]

memory sets, we would get a straight line. The slope of that line would correspond, in theory, to the time (*c*) it took the subject to make a single comparison. The zero-intercept of that line (that is, the point on the line corresponding to s = 0) would include the time required to encode the stimulus (*e*) and respond (*r*).

At this point you might be wondering why we have been focusing on negative responses. The reason is that the negative response can be made only after the subject has compared every member of the memory set to the test stimulus; otherwise, how would he or she know the test stimulus was not in the set? The picture is more complicated for positive responses, because the subject might stop after finding a match between some memory-set item and the test item, not necessarily making all the possible comparisons. This particular hypothesis of what the subject might do is called the *self-terminating* hypothesis, because it implies that the subject terminates scanning whenever a match is found. Alternatively, we could propose what is called the *exhaustive* hypothesis, which says that whether or not the subject has found a match, he or she exhausts the memory set in the comparison stage. The comparisons do not stop with the match; the subject goes on to finish them. The latter hypothesis may not even seem reasonable intuitively, but it should be tested.

The crucial test of the self-terminating hypothesis versus the exhaustive hypothesis lies in the value of the slope of the RT function (which plots RT against memory-set size) for positive responses. Whenever the subject does find a match between the test stimulus and some item in the memory set, that matching item will be found, on the average, half-way through examination of the set. According to the self-terminating theory, this means the subject will stop (on the average) half-way through the set when a positive response is made, but will go all the way through when a negative response is made. On the average, the subject will make $(s + 1)/2$ comparisons for positive responses if he or she self-terminates. The RT for positive responses will include $e + r + ([s + 1]/2) \times c$. If we rearrange these terms to show RT as a function of s (obtaining: $RT = (e + r + c/2) + (c/2)s$), we find that the slope of the function will be half as great for positives as negatives ($c/2$ for positives, c for negatives). The exhaustive hypothesis, however, says that the comparison stage does not differ for positives and negatives—both involve all possible comparisons—and therefore implies no such difference in the slopes of their RT functions (both slopes should be c).

We now have three hypotheses. One is the parallel-scanning hypothesis, which predicts that the RT function (relating RT to s) will be flat for both positives and negatives (Figure 5.4A). The other two are versions of the serial hypothesis, which says that comparisons go on one by one and predicts RT will increase with memory-set size (Figure 5.4B). One version says that scanning is self-terminating. It predicts that the RT function for positive responses will have a slope half as great as the function for negative responses.

The other version says that scanning is exhaustive, and predicts no difference in the RT functions for positives and negatives.

In order to assess the validity of the hypotheses, we must conduct an experiment. We must collect RT data from several subjects, each performing many trials. We must include both positive and negative trials with several memory-set sizes. We must then obtain the average RT for each type of trial—positive and negative—and each memory-set size. Then we must plot graphs of the RT functions, RT versus s. This is what Sternberg did, and his results are plotted in Figure 5.4C. According to the arguments just presented, these data support the serial, exhaustive hypothesis.

We might have predicted that Sternberg's data would not support the parallel-scanning hypothesis on the basis of what we know about automatic and attentional processing. Subjects in his studies were similar to those in Shiffrin and Schneider's varied condition (since an item in the memory set on one trial could be a nontarget item, serving as a negative-trial test stimulus, on another trial), and they therefore performed an attention-demanding, controlled search like that described by the serial model. That Sternberg's results support the exhaustive version of serial scanning is of special interest because, as we have noted, the exhaustive hypothesis runs counter to our intuition.

The exhaustive hypothesis seems to imply that in the case of positive responses, those where a match is made, the subject makes many unnecessary comparisons. However, it is possible to explain why exhaustive scans might occur. To do so, we first divide the comparison process of the scanning task into two components. One is the act of *comparison* itself; the other is *deciding* what the results of the comparison are. If the comparison shows correspondence between a memory-set item and the test stimulus, that decision will be positive, leading to a positive response. Otherwise, the response will be negative. Now consider what would happen if the time for the subject to compare the test stimulus to a memory item were very fast, and the time to decide whether or not that comparison was positive (a match) relatively slow. If the process were self-terminating, progress through the memory set would go: compare, decide, compare, decide, and so on, until a match was made (the decision would be "yes") or the set was completed. On the other hand, the subject could perform exhaustively, and his or her progress might be: compare, compare, compare, and so on, and—when the memory set was exhausted—decide. It is easy to see that if decisions took a long time relative to comparisons, an exhaustive search could be more expedient: It would require only one decision. In short, an exhaustive search would be efficient if the subject could compare at an extremely fast rate, so fast it would be difficult to stop for decisions. Instead, the subject would just "shoot on through" all the comparisons, and only then decide and respond.

If the above explanation of exhaustive scanning is accurate, we should find that the comparison time is very fast. We can learn this from the RT data by computing the slope of the function plotting RT against memory-set size, which in theory represents the time it takes to compare the test stimulus to one item in the memory set. Such computation shows the rapid-comparison notion to be supported by the data. From the data in Figure 5.4C, we find that the value of our variable c, the slope of the RT function for negative responses, is about 35 milliseconds (.035 seconds). We infer that it takes the subject .035 seconds to compare the test stimulus to one memory-set element. Converting .035 seconds per comparison to the number of comparisons per second, we find out the subject can make about thirty such comparisons in a single second. That's surprisingly fast, and the rate helps to explain why exhaustive scans might occur.*

In summary, Sternberg's data are consistent with the idea that STM retrieval is a serial, exhaustive process that demands attentional capacity. On the other hand, the results of Shiffrin and Schneider previously described indicate that subjects who are highly practiced at retrieving selected items can do so without attentional capacity. Which really describes STM retrieval? Apparently, both types of processes can occur. The Schneider/Shiffrin work tells us that when a stimulus that consistently elicits a certain response occurs, it can trigger that response automatically. If the item is currently in STM, that can be called automatic retrieval from STM. However, another of these author's findings is noteworthy: When a subject in the consistent condition has been trained

---

*It is important to note that the presentation of Sternberg's task has of necessity been simplified. One simplification deserves mention here; it is that the serial exhaustive model is not the only model that can explain the classic results—RT increases linearly with memory-set size. It is possible to devise a parallel model that will do the same (Townsend, 1972). Such a model *differs* from the simple parallel model we first discussed (the one that predicts no effect of memory-set size on RT) in that it proposes that the subject has available only a limited amount of processing capacity. This is to be distributed over all the items to be processed. When there are a small number, then each item gets relatively more capacity and can be processed quickly. When the number of items in the memory set is greater, then the processing capacity must be distributed more "thinly"; each item receives less and thus takes longer to process. This sort of model is parallel, because it assumes that all the items can be scanned at the same time. Yet it predicts that RT will increase with memory-set size because it assumes that memory scanning uses limited attentional capacity.

to detect a certain item, that item could attract processing even when it was not in the current memory set and thus not in STM at the time. It would seem that automatic responses do not always correspond to retrieval from STM. It could also be argued that Sternberg's task represents a more general case of STM retrieval, since it does not demand extensive training. Yet, as we shall see in Chapter 6, retrieval from STM may not always be the fast and accurate process depicted by data from the Sternberg task. In any case, the study of that task enhances our knowledge of the way that information in STM is accessed and utilized.

ENCODING IN STM: THE FORMAT OF INFORMATION

Having considered the amount that STM can hold and the way items are retrieved from it in Sternberg's task, we turn now to the form in which verbal information is held there. As we have noted, the principal form in which words are held in STM appears to be acoustic, that is, in terms of the way they sound. This idea has several sources of support. One comes from the acoustic confusions that occur when subjects are given an immediate-memory task (Conrad, 1964; Wickelgren, 1966). Essentially, items that sound alike are likely to be confused, independently of whether they are visually similar or similar in meaning and whether they are presented auditorily or visually. Similarly, the number of errors that people make in immediate-memory tasks is greater when the to-be-remembered items sound alike than when they do not (Conrad and Hull, 1964).

Sperling and Speelman (1970) suggest that these data result because items stored in STM are in acoustic form and may be lost phoneme (individual sound) by phoneme. At the time of recall, the subject attempts to reconstruct the items from whatever sounds remain. If a mistake is made, it tends to share sounds with the items actually presented, leading to the acoustic pattern of confusions. The detrimental effects of the acoustic similarity among list items on the number of errors in recall can also be explained. If the list items are drawn from a pool that differs in relatively few phonemes (i.e., they are acoustically similar), then the loss of just one phoneme can make an item unidentifiable; if, on the other hand, list items are quite dissimilar, an item could still be identified even if it were missing a phoneme.

Not all storage in STM is in an acoustic format. As we shall see in Chapter 7, there is ample indication that verbal information is retained, at least to some extent, in visual form. In addition, there is evidence (reviewed in Shulman, 1971) for the presence of semantic information in STM. One demonstration of this format is based on confusion errors, much as such errors were used to infer acoustic storage. Shulman (1972) demonstrated that STM confusions could follow a pattern predictable on the basis of meaning. In his experiments, subjects performed in a series of trials, during each of which they first received a ten-word list. The tenth word was followed by a probe word, and the subject was instructed to say whether or not the probe "matched" a word that was in the list. On some trials, "match" meant "is identical to"; on others it meant "means the same as" (or "is a synonym of"). Just before the probe occurred during each trial, the subject was signaled as to which meaning of "match" applied for that trial.

The conditions of particular interest are those in which the probe was a synonym of a word that had been in the list and the subject was instructed to match on the basis of identity. If the subject says the words match under these conditions, even though the probe is not identical with a word in the list, it indicates semantic confusion. That is, we suspect that the subject made this particular error (mistakenly identifying a word as having been in the list when it is actually a synonym of a list word) because he or she confused the two words—the one in the list and the probe—on the basis of semantic similarity. Thus, there must have been in STM some knowledge about the semantic content of the list words. The reason that Shulman included trials in which a match was defined in terms of synonymy was to induce the subject to make such semantic information available if that were possible.

Shulman found that a subject mistakenly identified a probe word as a member of the list more often when the probe word was a synonym of a list word than when it was unrelated to the list words. This effect was manifest even when the probe was a synonym of one of the most recently presented words (for example, a word in one of the last three serial positions), the words that are most likely to be in STM (as is assumed for the free-recall serial-position curve). Thus, he found short-term confusions that follow semantic patterns, indicating STM storage of semantic information.

It is interesting to note that in order to demonstrate semantic confusion errors in an STM task, it was necessary for Shulman to induce semantic coding by using synonymy as the basis for a match on some trials. Why are such machinations necessary? Coding items by sound appears to be a more usual means of STM storage than coding by meaning, at least as measured by tasks like those we have been discussing. A possible explanation is that coding by sound uses less capacity than coding by meaning, so that if acoustic codes are sufficient for task performance, they will be used. This is consistent with the idea that acoustic coding represents a relatively "shallow" level of processing (see Chapter 2), requiring less encoding effort.

One question that comes to mind is how STM stores material in nonhearing people, especially the congenitally deaf. Lacking information about sounds, do they lose STM and have a memory span of zero? The answer is clearly negative; instead of losing their STM capacity they seem to code in a different format. In contrast to the deleterious effects of acoustic similarity on immediate-memory performance by hearing subjects, deaf subjects are negatively affected by *visual* similarity of letter stimuli (e.g., of X to Y, rather than X to S). This suggests that they retain items in terms of their visual printed shapes (Conrad, 1972). That deaf subjects can retain verbal items in a code representing their sign-language symbols has also been demonstrated. Bellugi, Klima, and Siple (1975) gave deaf subjects a short series of signs on videotape and required them to immediately write down the corresponding English terms. This is essentially a memory-span task with signs replacing spoken or printed items. The confusion errors made by deaf subjects tended to be based on manual similarity, suggesting that the items were coded by their signed form. A similar result is obtained when to-be-recalled items are presented in printed form rather than as signs (Locke and Locke, 1971), just as hearing subjects make acoustic errors whether presentation is auditory or visual.

Patterns of confusion based on orthographic (visual print) and sign similarity suggest that the deaf have alternatives to the usual acoustic STM coding. There is some evidence, however, that their STM is not quite the same as that of hearing persons in another respect. Specifically, the tendency to encode items semantically appears to be greater in the deaf. This was found by Frumkin and Anisfeld (1977), who used a "continuous recognition task" in which subjects (children aged 6 to 15) received a series of words and indicated whether each was "old" or "new." The first time a word appears on the list, a subject is supposed to say "new"; with its second appearance, the correct response is "old." Frumkin and Anisfeld introduced into the sequence "distractor" words (always new items) that were similar but not identical to previous items in the list. The distractor for a given list word could be semantically similar (for example, the original word was *boy* and the distractor was *girl*) or orthographically similar (for example, *boy* vs. *toy*). When the list was given in sign language rather than printed form, distractors could be either semantically similar to a previous word or similar in terms of sign formation.

If a subject makes more errors in this task by saying "old" to similar distractors than by saying "old" to dissimilar distractors, we can infer that the original words paired with the similar distractors were encoded so as to convey the similarity. Since the distractors followed soon (24–65 sec.) after the corresponding original item, the encoding being studied can be assumed to be in STM. The nature of the similarity that produces errors therefore tells us about the nature of the short-term code (as in Shulman's experiment, semantically based errors were used to deduce that coding was semantic). The data from these experiments revealed certain differences in the pattern of errors made by deaf and hearing subjects. When the list was in printed form, deaf subjects made predominantly semantic confusions (saying "yes" to *girl* when *boy* had been presented earlier) and some orthographic confusions ("yes" to *toy* after presentation of *boy*). Hearing subjects made some orthographic confusions but did not make semantic confusions. Thus, the deaf subjects seemed to rely more on a semantic code than the hearing subjects did. Similar results were found for deaf subjects when the lists were presented as signs. They showed not only confusions based on sign similarity, but also effects of semantic similarity.

Frumkin and Anisfeld attribute the semantic-similarity effects in deaf subjects to their inability to rely on acoustic coding. Acoustic coding, as utilized by hearing subjects, appears to be a very effective way to retain verbal information for a short time. Hearing persons therefore have relatively little need for alternative forms of coding, and evidence for the acoustic format predominates. But deaf persons, particularly those who are poor at oral communication, lack the acoustic basis for coding, and the visual forms of short-term coding they develop may not substitute completely for the acoustic codes of hearing persons. As a result, they appear to rely more on semantic coding.

The view that hearing persons usually do little semantic coding of items in STM is derived from studies of the STM storage space, where a brief list of items is passively held for a short time. But recall that STM is also called "working" memory. If we consider the work space, where activities such as chunking are assumed to be performed, it is clear that semantic knowledge stored in LTM plays an important part in the operation of hearing persons' STM. We can assume that passive storage in STM is usually acoustic, but we must also recognize the importance of meaning in STM "work." It is to the nature of that work we now turn.

WORKING MEMORY

Rehearsal

One type of work associated with STM is rehearsal—the cycling of information through the memory store. We have previously considered what are hypothesized to be the two main functions of rehearsal: to maintain information in STM so that it is not forgotten, and to transfer information about the rehearsed items to LTM. Nevertheless, it is not at all clear just how rehearsal works and precisely what is rehearsed.

One notion about the rehearsal process is that it is some kind of speech—implicit or subvocal. This idea is supported by the observations of Sperling (1967), who noted that subjects writing letters in an immediate-memory task often spoke the letters to themselves. This tendency, noted Sperling, might reflect a more general process in STM, that of rehearsal. He suggested that, in the course of rehearsing, the subjects *said* items to themselves, *heard* what was said, and then *stored* what was heard in STM—thereby restoring the items to their original strength. The "to themselves" part of this description is what is called implicit or subvocal. Though no sounds may actually be present, rehearsal may use *mental* representations of sounds, which remain unspoken.

One bit of evidence for this idea comes from estimates of the rate at which rehearsal takes place. If subjects are asked to rehearse a series of letters to themselves ten times, and we measure how long it takes them, we can get an idea of how fast they can rehearse, say, in terms of letters per second. If we compare this rehearsal rate to the rate of vocal, overt speech, we find that the two rates are about the same; usually about three to six letters per second (Landauer, 1962). Thus, rehearsal and speech are alike in that they take about the same amount of time to perform.

The notion that rehearsal is a form of speech also fits in with the pattern of confusions in memory-span tasks, which reflect the similarity of items as they are produced by speech. In the Sperling and Speelman (1970) model that accounts for such confusions, rehearsal is seen as implicit speech that results in the reentry of the sounds into STM. The model assumes that if they were not rehearsed, items in a to-be-remembered list would lose some of their component sounds. Rehearsal renews them, bringing them back to a form equivalent to that of their original encoding and storage there.

Maintenance Rehearsal and Elaborative Rehearsal. Rehearsal includes more than the maintenance, or renewal, function apparently served by internal speech. It is also assumed to transfer information to LTM, so that items rehearsed longer will be remembered better after relatively long periods of time. It is often said that rehearsal results in the buildup of "strength" of rehearsed items in LTM.

One demonstration of the relationship between rehearsal and recall from LTM was that of Rundus (1971; Rundus and Atkinson, 1970), who had his subjects rehearse out loud. In one of his experiments, subjects performed a free-recall task in which a list of words was presented at a rate of one word every 5 seconds. The subjects were instructed to study the list by repeating some of the words aloud during the 5-second interval between words. They were not told any particular words to recite; they were free to choose whichever words they liked. The set of words a subject chose to speak during a particular 5-second period was called the *rehearsal set* for that period (Figure 5.5A). Rundus was concerned with the relationship between the nature of the rehearsal sets and performance on the recall test that followed the list's presentation. Not surprisingly, Rundus found a strong relationship (Figure 5.5B): The more overt rehearsals (recitations) of a word, and the more rehearsal sets it appeared in, the greater the probability that the word would be recalled.

Rundus also found that which items subjects chose to rehearse tended to depend on knowledge about their meanings. In particular, a newly presented word was more likely to be rehearsed if its meaning fit in with the current rehearsal set. An incoming word like *sparrow* would be likely to be included in a rehearsal set already containing *robin, canary, wren*, but it would probably not be rehearsed if the current rehearsal set was *bread, eggs, cheese*. Thus, Rundus's work suggests that rehearsal does indeed serve the function of increasing the strength of particular items in LTM (as indicated by the positive relationship between rehearsals and recall), and that organizing processes use information in LTM to determine what is to be rehearsed in STM.

A criticism of Rundus's experiments on rehearsal is that they are essentially correlational, because the number of rehearsals is controlled by the subject and not the experimenter. That is, although they show a relationship between number of rehearsals and recall, the direction of the relationship is uncertain: They do not prove that rehearsals determine recall. Instead, it is possible that subjects re-

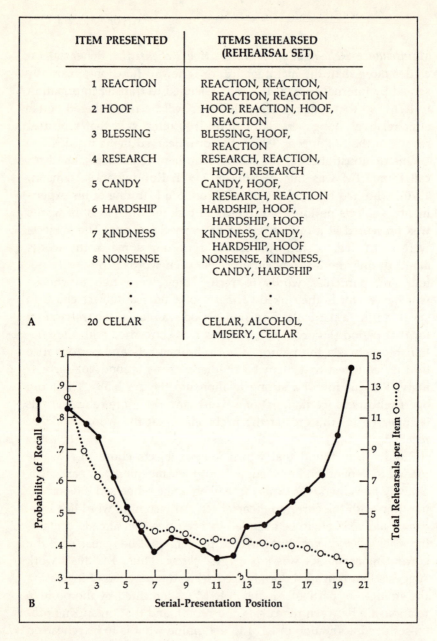

ITEM PRESENTED	ITEMS REHEARSED (REHEARSAL SET)
1 REACTION	REACTION, REACTION, REACTION, REACTION
2 HOOF	HOOF, REACTION, HOOF, REACTION
3 BLESSING	BLESSING, HOOF, REACTION
4 RESEARCH	RESEARCH, REACTION, HOOF, RESEARCH
5 CANDY	CANDY, HOOF, RESEARCH, REACTION
6 HARDSHIP	HARDSHIP, HOOF, HARDSHIP, HOOF
7 KINDNESS	KINDNESS, CANDY, HARDSHIP, HOOF
8 NONSENSE	NONSENSE, KINDNESS, CANDY, HARDSHIP
. . .	. . .
20 CELLAR	CELLAR, ALCOHOL, MISERY, CELLAR

A

B

Figure 5.5 (A) Examples of rehearsal sets in Rundus's experiment. The figure shows sets of items that were rehearsed as each new item was presented. (B) The relationship between rehearsal and recall for each position in the recalled list. In general, the more an item is rehearsed, the higher its probability of recall. Items in the recency portion of the list are assumed to be recalled from short-term memory and thus not to depend on rehearsal for recall. [From R. C. Atkinson and R. M. Shiffrin, "The Control of Short-Term Memory." Copyright © 1971 by Scientific American, Inc. All rights reserved.]

hearse those items that they recall most readily and that they would recall later in any case, rather than that rehearsal is the *cause* of recall.

The possibility of drawing an alternative conclusion from Rundus's evidence does not, by itself, invalidate the idea that rehearsal strengthens recall. However, there is other evidence against the notion that rehearsal necessarily results in the transfer of information to LTM, from experiments showing that the amount of rehearsal an item gets does not always affect later recall (Craik and Watkins, 1973; Woodward, Bjork, and Jongeward, 1973; Glenberg, Smith, and Green, 1977; Rundus, 1977). Craik and Watkins induced subjects to hold single words in STM for varying amounts of time. In one experiment, they told the subjects they should report the last word that began with a given letter in a 21-word list. For example, the critical letter might be G, and the list might begin: *daughter, oil, rifle, garden, grain, table, football, anchor, giraffe. . . .* As they listened, the subjects would hold *garden* in memory until *grain* appeared, then hold *grain* until they heard *giraffe*, and so on until the last G-word in the list, which they would report when the list ended. Thus, the period of time a word was retained in STM varied—*garden* was held much less time than *grain*, for example. After 27 such lists, the subjects were unexpectedly asked to recall as many of the words as possible, from all lists. Craik and Watkins found that the amount of time a word beginning with the critical letter was held in STM, defined by the number of words beginning with noncritical letters that intervened between that word and the next critical word, did not affect performance on the unexpected recall test. Thus, the amount of time a critical word was held in STM—which gives a measure of rehearsal time—did not appear to affect its LTM strength.

Results like these have led some theorists (Bjork, 1975; Craik and Watkins, 1973) to make a distinction between two types of rehearsal, differing in their effects on LTM storage. *Maintenance rehearsal* (also called *Type I, primary,* or *rote* rehearsal) is used only to maintain items in STM, presumably by renewing them before they can be forgotten. It has no effect on LTM storage, however. *Elaborative rehearsal* (also called *secondary* or *Type II*) not only maintains items in STM but enhances their storage in LTM. According to the levels-of-processing theory described in Chapter 2, the two types of rehearsal represent processing at different levels. Maintenance rehearsal represents continued processing at a shallow, acoustic level. Such same-level processing, you may recall, is not supposed to increase items' recallability. Elaborative rehearsal merits its name, because it corresponds to deep, meaningful processing, where the rehearsed items are associated with one another and generally enriched through contact with meaningful knowledge. According to this theory, when seemingly rote rehearsal results in better recall, it is because it is not really rote at all. Rundus's experiments, showing that subjects do use LTM information in constructing rehearsal sets, suggest that purely rote rehearsal is relatively rare. Instead, subjects may elaborate on rehearsed material as a matter of course, giving rise to the usual finding, that rehearsal does increase recall.

The distinction between maintenance and elaborative rehearsal readily accommodates both types of results we have described so far—positive effects of rehearsal on performance in LTM tasks and no effects at all. Yet the distinction rests on a relatively small number of studies showing evidence for purely maintenance rehearsal. In contrast, many studies support the concept of elaborative rehearsal, since it is commonly found that the longer subjects have to study an item, or the more times it is presented for study, the better it is remembered (see Chapter 2). Part of the problem of demonstrating maintenance rehearsal is the general tendency of subjects in memory tasks to elaborate on presented items. It is rather difficult to induce them to rehearse items purely by rote, as the Craik and Watkins (1973) experiment with the G-words appears to do.

Another procedure for inducing maintenance rehearsal has been developed by Glenberg, Smith, and Green (1977) and Rundus (1977). In this task, rote rehearsal of words is elicited by making subjects think that memory for other items is more important and that the words are to be rehearsed only as a secondary, distracting task. On each of a series of trials in this situation, subjects are given a small number of digits (up to four) to remember for a short time, as in a memory-span task. They are told that they must hold the digits over a brief retention interval (less than a half minute), during which time they must repeat a word (or words) aloud. The subjects do not realize that, after a series of such trials, they will be asked to recall as many of the words as possible.

Glenberg et al. point out that the repetition of the words in this task fulfills the requirements for producing and observing maintenance rehearsal. First, subjects should process the words at the minimum level needed to maintain them, since they think that their real task is to remember the numbers, and elaborating on the words could distract them from that task. Second, the experimenter can observe that the maintenance function is in fact fulfilled, because the subjects say the words aloud during the retention interval. Third, the experimenter can vary the length of the retention interval, that is, how long the subjects must keep repeating the word on each trial, and can look at the effects on later word recall. Assuming that the rehearsal really is rote in this task, there should be no effect of rehearsal time. That is, subjects should recall the same number of words after just a couple of seconds of repetition as after a longer period of rehearsal.

A number of interesting results have been obtained with this procedure. First and most importantly, the prediction is confirmed: The length of time words are repeated (from 2 to 18 seconds) generally does not affect recall, which is usually quite low. (For example, Glenberg et al. found that an average of only about 7 percent of the words were recalled, despite the fact the average number of repetitions was nine per trial.) This is what we would expect if the rehearsal were performed at a shallow level, with little information sent to LTM.

On the other hand, if the same word is presented in more than one trial, its recall increases (Rundus, 1977), suggesting that we should make a distinction between the number of times a word is rehearsed after a single presentation and the number of presentations it receives (even if all presentations occur in the same circumstances and are accompanied by the same type of processing). Repeated presentation had similar effects in the Nelson (1977) experiment described in Chapter 2. Apparently, each new presentation of a word can result in slightly different processing of it, even if the difference is merely encoding the fact that this is a new presentation! The processing that accompanies a new presentation could be said to constitute elaboration of the word rather than purely maintenance. Thus, it seems we should restrict the concept of maintenance rehearsal to the continued processing that goes on after an item's presentation, without any other presentations intervening. And the data described so far indicate that, with this restriction, maintenance rehearsal does not lead to better recall from LTM.

But a result of Glenberg et al. adds a complication to the maintenance-rehearsal concept. Although they found, as predicted, that rehearsal time did not affect recall, they did find it had an effect on performance in a *recognition* test. The difference between recognition and recall is like the difference between a true-false exam and a fill-in-the-blanks exam. In recognition, you are shown a potential to-be-recalled item and asked if it was one of the items seen in a previous set. (For example, a subject might be asked, "Is the word *house* one that you repeated during the series of trials?") In recall, you have to do the whole thing yourself, reporting the item from scratch. ("Tell me all the words that you repeated during the series of trials.") The requirements of these two types of task for the process of retrieval from LTM are different, as we will discuss further in Chapter 10. For now, however, the noteworthy point is that performance on the recognition test in Glenberg et al.'s experiment, unlike the recall test, did show small improvement with increases in rehearsal time. Why the difference between recall and recognition? Maintenance rehearsal's effects on LTM may be of a sort that recognition-test processing uses but recall-test processing does not. Alternatively, it may be that recognition testing is more sensitive, picking up differences in LTM knowledge too small to show in recall scores. Whatever the reason for the difference, however, it forces some modification in the maintenance-rehearsal concept, for it shows that the length of such rehearsal can influence LTM.

Maintenance and elaborative rehearsal may represent points on a continuum, not so much being two different processing modes as producing differing amounts of LTM transfer. Although it would present a neater theory to show that the two types of rehearsal are completely separate, the differences between them seem substantial enough in any case to merit giving them different names and making a distinction between them. One thing the distinction tells us is that rehearsal is flexible enough to change with the goal of the rehearser. If the goal is to remember items for later mental activity, elaborative rehearsal is likely to be used; if the goal is to maintain items for the shortest possible time, only rote rehearsing—repetition without elaboration—will be performed. In fact, this sort of flexibility seems desirable. It is just the sort of goal-oriented processing we would expect of a memory system designed for mental work.

Elaborative Rehearsal as Mental Work.   Of the two types of rehearsal, elaborative seems to best fit the concept of working memory. Whereas maintenance rehearsal simply holds items in STM, supporting its storage function, elaborative rehearsal requires thinking about items, interpreting them, and relating them to other information in LTM. As we shall see in Chapter 9, these processes prove remarkably effective at enhancing later recall of information from LTM. In the present discussion, we will consider some of the forms that elaboration can take.

Elaborative rehearsal is assumed to go beyond the physical form of the items presented or their sound, to interpret them with respect to knowledge in LTM. One label for the process of relating input items to knowledge is *mediation*. More generally, mediation refers to processes that intervene between the presentation of a stimulus and overt responses to it; these processes are not necessarily predictable from the stimulus by itself (Hebb, 1958). In S–R theory, the concept of mediation is essential if one is to explain why a given stimulus can elicit a response to which it has not been directly connected in the past. For example, a subject in a free-association task might respond *lakes* to the stimulus word *seven*. The response becomes understandable if we know that there has been a mediating link in between the stimulus and response. The word *seven* elicited the internal response *seas*, which in turn elicited *lakes*, which became the overt response. In short, the internal response was mediational: It transformed the stimulus in a way that enabled it to elicit indirect associative connections.

The use of mediation to enhance memory is particularly apparent in experiments using nonsense syllables, consonant-vowel-consonant sequences of the sort developed by Ebbinghaus. He wished these syllables to be truly meaningless items. His wish notwithstanding, mediation enables subjects to give these items meaning, and the more meaningful they are made, the better they are remembered. For example, subjects presented with the items FEL, GOH, and HOZ might encode them in the elaborated versions: *fell*, *go*, and *hose*. Later, the subjects would recall by retrieving the mediated form of each stimulus and the device used to transform it. The mediated form would be decoded back into its original version and recalled. This is much like the process used when input items are formed into chunks and decoded at the time of recall. In particular, this example illustrates the use of an NLM—natural-language mediator.

Prytulak (1971) made a detailed study of the sorts of devices subjects use to mediate nonsense syllables. He was able to classify these devices and rate them for their usefulness and then, on the basis of these ratings, predict performance on memory tasks. There were clearly good and bad mediators, leading to good and bad retention. In particular, simple encoding operations were better than complex ones. For example, mediating by inserting an internal letter (as in converting FEL to *fuel*) would be superior to a more complex sequence that included both inserting a letter and adding a suffix (as in converting PEC to *peach*).

Chunking too involves mediation, used to integrate several input items rather than to encode a single item meaningfully like the NLM formation just discussed. We have considered one case in which a special system was used to chunk sequences of the digits zero and one. This system is one of a special category of mediating procedures called *mnemonic devices*. In general, a mnemonic device is a rule or system of rules that has been developed to improve our ability to recall items. Many of these devices are ancient, and some, like the system of recoding zeros and ones, are rather new. Some mnemonic devices are designed for remembering specific information ("Thirty days hath September . . ."), and some are intended for use with any list of items. An example of the latter is an ancient mnemonic device called the *method of loci*. With this method, you first learn to think of a sequence of places; for example, ten positions in your living room (at the TV, at the clock, and so on). Then the positions can be used to remember lists. If I give you a list of ten items, you imagine each item as if it were positioned in one of these places, matching the sequence of items with the sequence of locations. For example, given a list of *dog, fire, pot* . . . , you imagine the dog on the TV, a fire in the clock, and so forth. When recalling, you—the mnemonist—merely travel mentally around the room and think of each location. As you imagine the TV, you will recall the dog; next on to the clock, where you recall the fire; and so on. Thus, you can remember each of the objects as you come to its position.

The variety of elaborative-rehearsal devices that can be used to enhance memory is as great as the variety of people who use them. Almost everyone has a trick or two. In Chapter 9, we will consider the effects of elaboration on recall from LTM in more detail. And in a later chapter, we shall look at some exceptional individual mnemonists, who specialize in developing very useful tricks. Clearly, the memory system has an astounding facility for this sort of mental work.

Working Memory and Limited Capacity

The workbench model of STM with which we began this chapter not only describes the storage space and work space but postulates that the two must fit within the same limited STM capacity. This concept makes a rather straightforward prediction: The more information is to be passively stored in the storage "slots," the less work can be done. Baddeley and Hitch (1974) have tested this assumption in a series of experiments, where subjects were required to store items from a short list while simultaneously mentally working.

One type of work required of the subjects was to perform a very simple reasoning task. On each trial of the task, subjects were given a pair of letters and a sentence about them and were required to indicate whether the sentence was true or false. For example:

Sentence	Letters	Answer
A is not preceded by B.	AB	True

Just before receiving the problem, the subjects in one condition of the experiment were given a set of six randomly ordered digits, which they were to repeat aloud rapidly throughout the problem-solving interval until the true or false response had been given. Another group of subjects simply repeated the digits one to six in order during the problem-solving interval; this was assumed to impose little demand on STM storage space because the digit sequence was so well known. As expected, repeating the random series of digits had a pronounced negative effect on performance in the reasoning problems. Subjects who had to remember those digits performed more than 30 percent slower than subjects who simply repeated the digits one through six. This is consistent with the idea that the memory task with random digits used up storage space that would otherwise be used for problem-solving work.

In another of Baddeley and Hitch's (1974) studies, subjects listened to a prose passage while performing a series of memory-span tasks. The memory tasks consisted of viewing a set of six digits on a screen, then writing them down after they had been removed, then viewing another set, and so on until the prose passage was completed. Other subjects simply copied the digits as they appeared and did not have to remember them. At the end of the passage, all subjects were given a prose comprehension test. Scores on this test were lower for the subjects who had to remember the digits than for those who merely copied them, as we would expect if the memory task used up space that was needed for comprehending the passage.

These results clearly indicate that mental work, such as reasoning and comprehension, competes for a limited capacity with the task of remembering short lists. Such a memory task is commonly used to assess STM, so it seems reasonable to assume that STM is the site of the competition. Still other evidence for the involvement of STM comes from manipulations of the auditory similarity of items in the reasoning and comprehension tasks. We know that when the items in a memory-span list sound alike, performance suffers. Similarly, Baddeley and Hitch found that performance on the reasoning problems took longer with letters that sounded alike (T is not followed by D: TD—true or false?) than with those that were acoustically dissimilar. And comprehension performance suffered when the to-be-comprehended prose used words that sounded similar. These findings support the idea that STM is the limited capacity involved, as STM is the store in which items are commonly coded by sound.

The idea of a limited capacity for mental work bears some obvious similarities to the concept of attention as limited capacity. In fact, some theorists treat the work-space concept as synonymous with attention (e.g., Hunt, 1978). In this view, maintaining items (as in the storage space) is an attentional process, and it will compete for capacity with **any** other attentional process. Reasoning problems and comprehension of prose appear to be two such processes. (But it is noteworthy that the processing that leads to the recency effect in the free-recall task is apparently not attentional. At least, it does not compete for capacity with a memory-span list, according to Baddeley and Hitch.)

CONSCIOUSNESS AND STM

A final consideration in our discussion of STM is the relationship between short-term storage and consciousness. We have discussed STM as a working memory, because it seems to be the place where items are held while they are worked on—chunked, mediated, or rehearsed. A logical question is whether that kind of work might be synonymous with consciousness, or awareness; that is, whether "working on" is the same as "thinking about."

At present, there seems to be no definite answer to such a question. If it is true that when we are conscious of something we are working on it, we may conclude that consciousness is included in STM. But STM may include more than conscious activity; we may be working on things without being conscious of them. Many complex activities, such as driving a car, seem to require mental work, but we often drive while conducting a conversation with someone else in the car. We are unaware of driving; does that mean it is done without STM involvement? Part of this problem is the relation of consciousness to attention. It may be that we are not conscious of automatic processes but we are of attentional ones. Depending on the view of the attention-STM relationship, then, consciousness could be equated with STM or could not. Consciousness is rather difficult to define; we might call it a "mystical" aspect of STM.

Because of that mystical quality, it seems appropriate to consider here some remarks Freud (1940) made on the nature of consciousness and short- and long-term memories, in connection with something called the Mystic Writing Pad. This writing pad is a sort of apparatus you may have played with as a child. It consists of a dark waxy pad, covered by a transparent layer of celluloid, and between the two is a translucent thin sheet of waxed paper. One writes on such a pad with a pointed stylus, pressing it down on the celluloid. The celluloid in turn presses onto the thin sheet, which adheres to the wax below, causing the writing to appear on the surface of the pad. The writing can be erased by merely lifting the upper layers of celluloid and waxed paper, leaving the pad available for new writing. Sometimes, if one carefully lifts the upper layers, one can see that the wax below still holds what has just been written, even though it has disappeared from the upper surface.

Such a pad, said Freud, was like the human memory. He proposed a two-part memory: a permanent memory like the wax pad, and a memory that received and held information only briefly, like the middle layer. That renewable, impermanent memory was the locus of consciousness, and as information appeared on it and was erased, consciousness would come and go. All this sounds much like what we call STM and LTM. If so, it seems that Freud felt that transient, short-term memories were part of consciousness. And just as lifting the upper sheets on the Mystic Writing Pad caused information there to vanish, so too might the departure of information from STM cause it to leave our consciousness. Freud may have been right; at least, we cannot prove that he was wrong.

6

Short-Term Memory: Forgetting

When information is first encoded into STM, we may be able to report it perfectly, but as time passes, our ability to remember it declines. This loss of ability to remember initially encoded information is what we call forgetting. For an everyday example, suppose that you ask a telephone operator for a phone number. You repeat the number to yourself as you reach for the phone, but at that moment a friend enters the room, and you say hello. When you turn back to the phone, the number seems to have vanished; you can no longer remember it. Information about the number was being held in STM, and it was forgotten when another event prevented you from rehearsing it.

Forgetting is familiar to all of us, but what is less well known is why it occurs. This chapter addresses the problem of what causes forgetting. This question has quite a history, and there is some debate about it. The chapter also explores the locus of forgetting. That is, we will consider whether an item is forgotten from STM because information is lost from storage or because, although information is stored, it cannot be retrieved.

THEORIES OF FORGETTING

The problem of what causes forgetting is often set up as a dichotomy; forgetting is said to be result of either *passive decay* or *interference.* To make sense out of these terms, let us consider an item that resides in STM. When this item is fresh and new and we can retrieve it readily, we will say that it is at full strength. (The concept of memory strength can be a controversial one, but we will use it at present in the sense of "amount of information available.") We can say that forgetting occurs when the item is no longer at full strength. This might occur, for example, if some information about its sound is gone. In general, this will occur only when the item is not being rehearsed, because we assume that rehearsal maintains the item at full strength. Forgetting occurs because the item's strength has so declined that it cannot be reported. Our basic question is: What is the cause of the item's decline in strength?

To say that the item decays means that the item's strength simply decreases with the passage of time. Only time's passing is necessary for recall of the item to deline—no other causal factor is specified. Because there is no other specified cause, we say that the decay is passive. In contrast, the interference hypothesis suggests a more active cause of forgetting. It holds that an item declines in strength because new items enter STM. It is the presence of other items, then, that impairs recall for a given item.

It would be easy to determine which of these two hypotheses is correct if only we could perform the following experiment. First, we would present an item to a subject. Then, we would have the subject do nothing for some period of time (this is called the retention interval)—30 seconds or so. That's absolutely *nothing*—no rehearsal (so that the item cannot be maintained at full strength by that means) and no thinking about other things (for that could bring information into STM and cause interference). Then, after the 30-second period, we would ask the subject what the item was. If he or she could not remember, it would be evidence for passive decay, because the only occurrence during the retention interval would have been the passage of time. Nothing could have produced interference during the interval. On the other hand, if forgetting had *not* occurred in this interval, we could consider it evidence against the decay hypothesis and consistent with the idea of interference.

Unfortunately, we cannot do this "perfect" experiment, because there is no situation in which a subject does absolutely nothing. However, attempts have been made to approximate this experiment, and the results have been rather controversial.

Before we discuss the experiments, let's take a closer look at the alternative hypotheses. First, the interference hypothesis. One version of this hypothesis is what might be called the *simple slot*, or *displacement* model. According to this model, STM has a certain number of slots—about seven plus or minus two. Each slot holds a chunk of information. When items come into STM, each item (chunk) occupies a slot. When there are no more empty slots left for incoming items, old items must be moved out to make room for the new. According to this model, each new item that enters a filled STM displaces an item already there, resulting in the latter's being forgotten. Each of the old items in STM has some chance of being displaced.

The displacement model is of interest because it helps to clarify the more general hypothesis that says that STM forgetting is caused by interference. One implication of the model is that the first few items to enter STM should not interfere with each other. There should be no forgetting until enough items come into STM to fill up the slots. This means that forgetting occurs only when the number of items is greater than the capacity of STM. Another implication of the simple slot idea is this: Because each item, or chunk, occupies a single slot, and the slot either contains the item or does not, then an item should be either all gone (the slot does not contain it) or all there. But we know this is not true. The fact that we get acoustic confusions among syllables (for example, letter names) held in STM can be explained by partial forgetting of the syllables, one phoneme at a time. If a syllable is a chunk, this sort of partial forgetting is inconsistent with the simple slot model.

It is not difficult to modify the simple slot model of STM forgetting so that it is consistent with partial forgetting. We just allow an item in STM to vary in its completeness—to take on several values like all there, mostly there, just a little left, and all gone. When we modify the model in this way, we are essentially assuming that the item can vary in strength, equating strength with completeness. Our displacement hypothesis now states that new items entering STM can partially displace other items, that is, can cause the strength of those items to decrease.

The other implication of simple slots—namely, that there should be forgetting in STM only if the number of items to be stored there exceeds its span—also demands modification. That is because the claim that forgetting can occur only when STM is full makes the decay and interference hypotheses compatible. To understand this, consider what it means to a duplex theorist to speculate about forgetting by decay: The decay hypothesis is relevant only to an *unfilled* STM, for implicit in the idea of a limited-capacity STM is the idea that forgetting will occur when more information enters STM than it can hold. Such forgetting cannot be attributed to passive decay; thus to consider forgetting by decay, we must look at forgetting that occurs when the information in STM does not exceed the memory span.* But if the decay hypothesis is most meaningful when it is applied to below-span forgetting, then the interference hypothesis should be similarly restricted. That is, the interference hypothesis cannot assume that there should be forgetting in STM only if its capacity is exceeded. Otherwise, the source of controversy between the two hypotheses would be eliminated: Decay could apply to below-span forgetting and interference to forgetting that occurs when the span of STM is exceeded. In short, the displacement model needs a second modification. Let us say that interference can lead to forgetting in STM even when its capacity is not exceeded. That is, the entry of other items in STM can interfere with a given item even if there is room in STM for all the items to be held. Such an interference hypothesis contrasts with a decay hypothesis that says the strength of an item in STM gradually declines even if there is room in STM to hold the item and if no other items enter.

It is possible to modify the interference hypothesis still further. Some theorists assume that interference is a function of similarity; that is, that new items will interfere with old items to the extent that they are similar. This version of the interference hypothesis we might term "interference by similarity" to contrast it to interference by displacement, which does not assume that similarity determines the extent of forgetting.

Our new, revised interference hypothesis might go like this: Each item in STM has a certain strength. When the item is newly entered or just rehearsed, it will be at full strength. Forgetting occurs when strength declines sufficiently so that the item cannot be recovered and reported. The cause of forgetting is the entry of other items into STM. We may also assume that the extent of the forgetting depends on the similarity of those new items to the original items. Gradually, as more items enter STM, the strength of those already there fades

---

*This limitation on the decay hypothesis, which is dictated by the concept of a short-term store with a limited capacity, differs somewhat from traditional views on decay. That is, outside of the context of the duplex theory, the decay hypothesis can be applied whether the information being forgotten is greater or less than the span of immediate memory. In fact, the memory span can be viewed as the *result* of decay, as follows: When the number of items presented is small, all of the items can be rehearsed before any of them has a chance to decay completely. As a result, there are no errors in recall. When the number of items presented is large, there are too many items to allow for rehearsal of each one before it can decay. Thus, some do decay, and there are errors in recall. The memory span is thus viewed as the point at which the number of items becomes too great to permit rehearsal of all of them in less time than it takes for any one to decay completely.

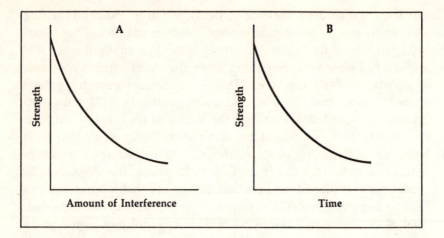

Figure 6.1   Theoretical curves predicted by (A) the interference hypothesis, and (B) the decay hypothesis.

away, as shown in Figure 6.1A. In contrast, the passive-decay hypothesis, which says that forgetting occurs because time passes and not because of item interference, would predict a strength function like that shown in Figure 6.1B.

The two strength functions illustrated in Figure 6.1 clearly differ. For one, the *x*-axis measures amount of interference; for the other, it represents time. The way to determine which theory is correct is to translate the theoretical (and internal, unobservable) variable of strength into something external and measurable. Then we can determine what affects our strength measure. If the measure is affected by time, we have evidence supporting decay theory; if it is affected by interfering items, interference theory is supported. For example, one measure that would presumably reflect strength is the percentage of correct responses on a recall task. Suppose we were to present a small set of items, then generate a series of items specifically designed to interfere, and then ask the subject to recall the initial set. If recall decreases as a function of the number of interfering items, we have evidence for interference.

Unfortunately, this sort of procedure presents a problem. Assuming that the generation of interfering items takes time, as more interfering items are presented, more time passes. The two variables, number of items and amount of time, are confounded; as one increases, so does the other. Thus it would be impossible to tell just what caused the decline in recall—time or interfering items. It is because of this sort of confounding that we need some other procedure to test the two hypotheses. That other procedure is the perfect experiment previously described, in which time passes and nothing interferes.

DISTRACTOR TASKS

Although we cannot perform the perfect experiment, that does not mean it cannot be approximated. Experiments that attempt to do this typically use what are called distractor procedures. These procedures were first used by Brown (1958) and Peterson and Peterson (1959). The latter researchers are usually credited with giving the impetus to experiments on decay versus interference in STM, as well as giving research on STM an immense boost.

What the Petersons did was quite simple. They had subjects perform in a series of trials like this: First, the subjects hear a three-consonant sequence (a trigram), such as PSQ. Then, they hear a three-digit number, say 167. They count backward from that number by threes: 167, 164, 161, 158 . . . , keeping time to the beat of a metronome, for a certain period of time—called the retention interval. Then, a recall cue occurs, indicating that the subjects are to recall the three letters.

This task is called a distractor task because the counting backward is supposed to distract the subjects, preventing them from rehearsing the letters in the trigram. The counting is assumed not to interfere with the letters of the trigram, presumably held in STM, because the numbers do not have to be stored for later recall. Thus, we have an approximation of the case where time passes, in the form of the retention interval, while the subjects do nothing—except count backward, which is presumed to be noninterfering. If the subjects forget the letters, we have support for a theory of decay.

The results of the Petersons' experiment are shown in Figure 6.2. In the range of retention intervals they used, from 3 to 18 seconds, there was a marked decline in the subjects' ability to remember the trigram. This was astonishing—such rapid forgetting had not previously been obtained in research on memory. For one thing, most of the then-current research concerned long lists. For another thing, with those long lists, forgetting functions were plotted in terms of hours or days. Most astonishing, the results of this experiment were readily interpretable as the result of passive decay in STM.

That the Petersons found experimental evidence favoring the passive decay hypothesis was an important event in the world of memory. It came at a time when a duplex theory of memory had been

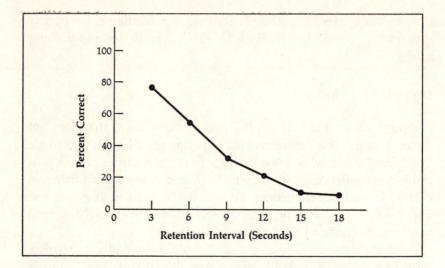

Figure 6.2   Results of the experiment on forgetting in short-term memory, showing that recall decreases as a function of the retention interval. [From Peterson and Peterson, 1959. Copyright 1959 by the American Psychological Association. Reprinted by permission.]

proposed (Hebb, 1949) but was by no means popular. Moreover, a large body of evidence then in existence pointed to interference as the primary causal factor in long-term forgetting; that is, material appeared to be forgotten over long intervals because of the occurrence of other information. Thus, the distractor experiment suggested that two kinds of forgetting mechanisms were operative—passive decay *and* LTM interference—strongly suggesting that there might be two kinds of forgetting because there were two systems of memory. In other words, (1) the finding by the Petersons that decay is operative in the short run and (2) the findings of others that interference is operative in the long run could be attributed to forgetting taking place in two different stores, an STM and an LTM.

Thus, a goal was set for theorists who felt more comfortable with one kind of memory: to somehow show that the Peterson experiment did not necessarily demonstrate the existence of a previously unknown short-term memory where forgetting occurred through decay. The most likely means of disproving the STM notion was to show that interference was actually responsible for the short-term forgetting. To understand how this might be accomplished, it is necessary that we have an idea of what was known about interference as the cause of forgetting in LTM. Most of the knowledge came

RETROACTIVE INHIBITION

Experimental Group	Learn List A	Learn List B	Retention Interval	Test List A
Control Group	Learn List A	———	Retention Interval	Test List A

Time →

PROACTIVE INHIBITION

Experimental Group	Learn List A	Learn List B	Retention Interval	Test List B
Control Group	———	Learn List B	Retention Interval	Test List B

Time →

Figure 6.3 Diagram of RI and PI procedures. When learning of List B interferes with List A, RI exists. When learning of List A interferes with List B, PI exists.

from work with what are called *proactive-inhibition* (PI) experiments and *retroactive-inhibition* (RI) experiments.

The two types of procedure—PI and RI—are diagrammed in Figure 6.3. Of the two, RI is the most closely related to what we have been calling interference. RI refers to the detrimental effect of recently acquired information on previously learned material. It is retroactive because the new information affects the material previously learned. When we measure RI, we usually use several lists of items rather than one, as we might do in an STM experiment. We conduct an RI experiment with two groups of subjects, an experimental group and a control group. The experimental group learns two lists of items: first a List A, and then a List B. (The items are generally paired associates—consisting of two parts—and the subjects' task is to produce the second part of an item when given the first.) They learn each list to some criterion level of performance—say, three repetitions of the list without an error. Then they wait during a retention interval, after which they are tested on the first list they learned, List A. The control group is treated in the same way as the experimental group, except that they do not learn a List B. What is usually found is that the control group performs better than the experimental group. Presumably this is because the learning of List B, which was done only by the experimental group, had a detrimental —interfering—effect on the memory for List A.

Could RI have been operating in the Petersons' experiment? Yes, if the counting backward interfered with the trigram stored in memory. This seemed unlikely to investigators at the time, since the counting did not require the storage of new information in memory. Moreover, the numbers used in counting were much different from the letters that were to be remembered. One well-known fact about RI at the time of the Petersons' work was that its effect was large when the to-be-remembered material (List A) and the interfering material (List B) were similar and small if they were not. Therefore, because the numbers and letters did not seem to be similar, the interference theorists did not try to show that the stored trigram was forgotten because of RI from the counting.

We have mentioned proactive inhibition as another possible way that interference might account for short-term forgetting. The PI procedure is much like the RI procedure, with one crucial difference. In PI, the concern is with forward-acting interference—the detrimental effect of learning a List A on remembering a subsequently learned List B. Thus, the experimental procedure tests the second list learned, List B, after the retention interval (see Figure 6.3). Typically, the experimental group, which has learned a List A before learning List B, does worse on recall of List B than a control group, which did not learn List A. In this case, the experimental group can be said to exhibit PI.

Could PI have been the cause of forgetting in the Petersons' experiment? There is no obvious source of PI, since apparently nothing was learned prior to the presentation of the trigram on each trial. But wait—because each trial did not occur all by itself, but in the context of a long series of trials, it is possible that early trials could interfere with later trials. Such a PI effect would not be readily apparent in the Petersons' data, because their experimental design would obscure it.

The reasoning is this: The Petersons had subjects take part in two practice trials, followed by forty-eight trials (eight trials with each of the six retention intervals used). It is known that PI is something that rapidly builds up to a peak. Thus, although the detrimental effect of learning one prior list on learning and recalling a second may be great, the effect of learning two lists prior to learning and recalling a given list is not that much greater than the effect of learning just one, and the effect of learning five prior lists is not much greater than the effect of learning just four. On this basis, we would expect that PI might have rapidly grown to a maximum in the course of the first few trials of the Petersons' experiment. Thus, most of the

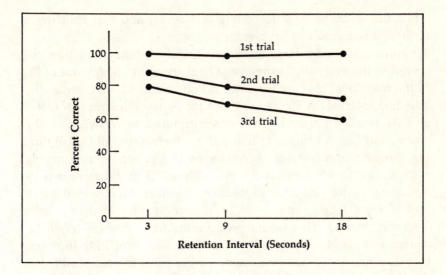

Figure 6.4 Results of the experiment on short-term retention by trial number, showing that correct recall depends not only on the retention interval but also on the number of prior trials. [From Keppel and Underwood, 1962.]

forty-eight trials would occur with PI at its maximum level, since PI could be expected to be strong after the first few trials (which would include the two practice trials). To see whether PI was operating here, it would be necessary to look at only the first few trials for each subject, making sure that all the retention intervals were represented equally often at each of the trial numbers.

The above analysis is that of Keppel and Underwood (1962), who went on to perform the experiment it suggests. They attempted to find out whether PI worked in the distractor experiments. To do so, they had to have each subject participate in only a few trials; also, they had to make sure that each retention interval they used was associated equally often (distributed over subjects) with a first trial, a second trial, and so on. This they did by using three retention intervals, three trials per subject (one for each interval), and a large number of subjects. Their results are shown in Figure 6.4.

The results of the Keppel and Underwood study were important to the one-kind-of-memory theorists. The data show that, on the first trial, there is no forgetting during an 18-second interval. However, on the subsequent trials, when PI has had a chance to build up, the rapid forgetting observed originally by the Petersons occurs. It seems that laws of LTM forgetting, notably laws of PI, determine when the so-called STM forgetting will occur, and that short-term forgetting is a result of interference.

Keppel and Underwood attributed the short-term forgetting observed in the Petersons' experiment to changes in the amount of PI. In the traditional PI procedure, it was known that PI increased as the retention interval (in Figure 6.3, the time between learning of List B and its recall) increased. This was attributed to recovery of the strength of List A (originally reduced by the learning of List B) during the retention interval. Recovery of List A would presumably allow it to interfere more and more with List B. In terms of experiments using the distractor procedure, a similar effect would mean that PI should be greater after an 18-second interval than after a 3-second interval. This would produce the forgetting observed. Of course, this could happen only when there was some PI to increase, that is, when there had been some earlier trials to produce PI. We therefore arrive at the prediction that the amount recalled should decrease as the retention interval increases, but only after the first few trials—exactly the results observed by Keppel and Underwood.

Keppel and Underwood wished to interpret their results in accordance with a unitary theory of memory; they were not duplex theorists. But since we know that other bases for separating STM and LTM exist, for purposes of the present discussion we can interpret their results as favoring the interference hypothesis of short-term forgetting; forgetting in STM is seen to be predictable on the basis of PI.

THE PROBE EXPERIMENT

The next study we shall discuss (Waugh and Norman, 1965) offered a different kind of evidence for interference in STM. It examined the interfering effects of subsequent information on information previously stored in STM. The experiments were not approximations to the perfect experiment discussed above, in that they did not use the distractor technique. Instead, their attack on the problem attempted to unconfound the effect of time and number of intervening items, which, as we have noted, usually vary together. The experiments used what is called the probe technique to accomplish the unconfounding. The subject gets a list of digits, say, sixteen, to remember. The sixteenth digit is a special one, in that it has occurred somewhere in the previous fifteen, and it is used to probe the list. The subject is told to recall the digit that followed the first appearance of the probe digit. (The probe digit is accompanied by a tone to signal that it is the last in the list, so that the subject need not count the digits.)

For example, a subject might hear the following list:

1 4 7 9 5 1 2 6 4 3 8 7 2 9 0 5*

(The asterisk denotes the tone.) He or she is being asked: "What is the digit that followed the first appearance of the digit five?" The correct answer would be "one." The crucial data here concern the percentage of recall (that is, the mean percentage of the time the digit following the first appearance of the probe is correctly recalled, averaged over many trials and subjects) as a function of the number of digits intervening between the initial presentation of the recalled digit and its recall (the appearance of the probe digit). In the above example, there are ten intervening digits (counting the probe). This gives us a way to look at recall as a direct function of intervening digits, which are considered interfering units.

In order to examine the effect of the passage of time, an additional variation can be introduced: We can vary the rate of presentation of the digits from fast (four digits per second) to slow (one per second). By this means, we can factorially vary time and number of interfering units. That is, we can separate their effects in such a way that we can look at the amount of *time* between the first and second appearances of the probe digit independent of *number of interfering units*, and vice versa.

This becomes clearer if we consider what the data from this experiment might look like according to the predictions of the two theories—decay and interference. First, if decay were acting, we would predict that recall would depend on elapsed time, regardless of the number of intervening digits. This would mean that the two different rates of presentation would lead to different recall for a given number of intervening items, because the rate would determine the elapsed time between the first and second appearance of the probe. Plotting the percentage of recall as a function of intervening time between the first and second appearance of the probe, we would get the curve in Figure 6.5A. It shows hypothetical data based on the assumption that forgetting occurs gradually as a function of time, regardless of the number of intervening digits that occur within the time. (This is evidenced by the fact that both rates yield the same result, although the fast rate corresponds to more interfering items than the slow for any given time interval.) The same data are plotted a little differently in Figure 6.5B, which uses intervening items on the *x*-axis and shows that the number of items alone does

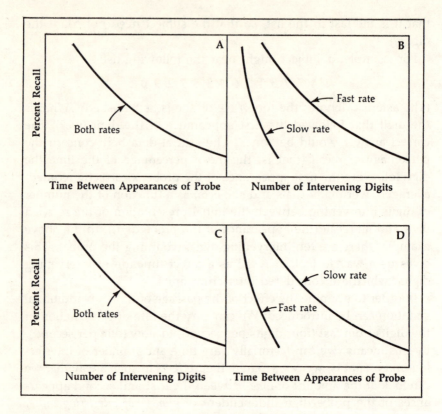

Figure 6.5 Possible results of the probe experiment, as predicted by the decay hypothesis (A and B) and the interference hypothesis (C and D).

not predict forgetting. It is still the elapsed time corresponding to a given number of items, as dictated by the presentation rate, that is the predictor when the graph is plotted in this way.

Alternatively, we can look at the predictions of interference theory, which says that the important determinant of forgetting is the number of digits intervening between the first and second appearances of the probe. We could plot its predictions in two ways, as in Figures 6.5C and 6.5D. Figure 6.5C shows hypothetical data based on the assumption that, regardless of rate, it is number of intervening items that determines recall. Figure 6.5D shows that if we plot the same forgetting data as a function of time, we get different functions for the two rates, because each rate corresponds to a different number of intervening items for a given time (the fast rate leads to more items than the slow rate within any time period).

Now, to see which theory is correct, we compare the predictions to the experimental results obtained by Waugh and Norman (1965),

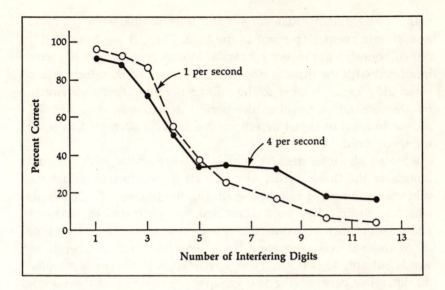

Figure 6.6 Results of the probe experiment, consistent with predictions of interference theory, showing that correct recall decreases as a function of the number of intervening digits. [From Waugh and Norman, 1965. Copyright 1965 by the American Psychological Association. Reprinted by permission.]

which are shown in Figure 6.6. The results support the interference theory. For both presentation rates, forgetting is determined by the number of digits that occur between the first appearance of the re-called digit and its recall.

DISTRACTOR TASKS, REVISITED

The results of the Waugh and Norman probe-digit experiment support the idea that interference is the causal factor in STM forgetting. Adding these results to those obtained by Keppel and Underwood (1962), which show that PI is also related to the rapid forgetting in the Peterson and Peterson task, there seems to be a strong case for interference theory. Keeping this in mind, we shall go on to an approximation to our perfect experiment conducted by Judith Reitman in 1971—the best approximation we have considered up to this point. She performed a distractor experiment in which the distracting task, instead of counting backward, was a signal-detection task. Subjects in the experiment first were presented with three words to be remembered. Then, for a 15-second period, they listened for the sound of a tone in a background of white noise (the signal detection). They were to press a button when a tone occurred. This task was rather difficult—Reitman set the tone so that subjects could hear it only about 50 percent of the time. Thus, it was presumably difficult enough to prevent rehearsal. Moreover, it should not have interfered with the three words in STM. It seemed therefore to be a reasonable approximation to the "doing nothing" that we demand for the retention interval in the perfect experiment. After the 15-second interval of signal detection, the subjects attempted to recall the three words.

Reitman was interested, of course, in whether the subjects could remember the three words. She also attempted to insure that the subjects were unable to rehearse during the interval. To determine whether rehearsal had been eliminated, she compared the accuracy and speed of their signal-detection performance to the performance of control subjects who were not attempting to remember three words but only to perform the signal detection. This check revealed no difference between the two groups, suggesting that the experimental subjects were really working at signal detection and not rehearsing. Thus, she believed that the results of her experiment truly could address the question of what happens to information in STM when rehearsal is prevented. The results were quite clear: There was no forgetting during the 15 seconds. That is, unlike the Petersons, Reitman found almost perfect retention of the words after 15 seconds had passed. There was no evidence that decay had occurred during the interval. Reitman's findings were extended and confirmed by Shiffrin (1973), who used signal-detection periods from 1 to 40 seconds long and found recall was almost perfect following any of the intervals.

In another version of her experiment, Reitman obtained some rather different results, more like the original findings of the Petersons. The results occurred when, instead of signal detection, the distractor task was *syllable* detection. Subjects tried to detect when the spoken syllable TOH occurred in a series of DOHs. With this task filling the retention interval, recall of the initially presented words did indeed drop below 100 percent, to about 75 percent. It seemed that the nature of the distractor task plays a rather important role in short-term forgetting, a phenomenon we will consider further below.

These experiments indicate no evidence for decay-induced forgetting in STM; all forgetting appeared to be the result of interference. However, this state of affairs was subsequently altered when Reitman replicated her original experiment with new controls for what are called ceiling effects and rehearsal. The term ceiling effects refers to the fact that task performance might be too good to show differences in memory strength. That is, subjects might have forgotten some of the information over the retention interval, but not enough to make them unable to retrieve the three words and show forgetting. Performance would stay at the 100 percent level despite the fact that the items' strengths declined over the retention interval. Reitman also felt that her original tests for the possibility that subjects were rehearsing during the retention interval might have been inadequate. And if subjects were surreptitiously rehearsing, that could have been the reason they showed no forgetting during the retention interval.

For these reasons, Reitman (1974) conducted experiments designed to eliminate ceiling effects and accurately assess the possibility of rehearsal. To accomplish the former, she made the task harder, requiring the subject to retain five words during the retention interval rather than three, as in her original experiment. To accomplish the latter, she instituted an extensive analysis of seven measures of recall and detection performance, and she applied them to data from subjects who were told to rehearse as well as those who were not. These measures were designed to indicate whether a subject rehearsed, which of several rehearsal strategies he or she might have adopted, and how strongly he or she rehearsed.

Reitman's results confirmed her fears; she found evidence that there had been a ceiling effect in her original data. She also found evidence that subjects were surreptitiously rehearsing during her original experiment and that her tests for rehearsal had not been strong enough to indicate that fact. In fact, in her new experiments, only 10 out of 52 subjects appeared actually to avoid rehearsal when told to do so. These 10 subjects then formed a critical group for testing the decay-versus-interference question. Did they forget information over a 15-second retention interval during which they performed a detection task *and* avoided rehearsal? The answer is yes: An average of about 25 percent of the original information was lost during a 15-second tone-detection task, indicating that the information decayed over that interval. Reitman concluded that ceiling effects and surreptitious rehearsal had given rise to misleading evidence against decay theory, and that forgetting in STM was actually affected by decay.

Subsequent evidence for decay was offered by Shiffrin and Cook (1978). They devised a situation in which subjects should be strongly motivated not to rehearse: They told subjects to try to *forget* the usual to-be-remembered items! In their task, subjects performed auditory signal detection (listening for a tone amid noise), during which consonants appeared visually. The subjects were told to say the consonants as they appeared (thus they could not ignore them) but then to try to forget them. After the detection interval, they were tested on the consonants, but the test was called a test of their ability to forget. These instructions were intended to motivate the subjects to encode the items superficially and not to rehearse. And apparently the instructions to forget worked, because forgetting was observed. The longer the period of detection that intervened between the letter presentations and the test, the worse subjects were at recalling the letters. Since only detection occurred during this interval, this result is evidence for passive forgetting over time—decay.

But Shiffrin and Cook also found evidence for forgetting by interference in their experiment. One result was that performance at any detection interval was worse when five letters were presented than when four were presented, suggesting that the extra letter had some sort of interfering effect. Moreover, they found that if subjects performed a period of mental arithmetic after the signal detection ended and before recalling the letters, performance dropped drastically, to virtually the level obtainable by sheer guessing. Apparently, the arithmetic task greatly interfered with memory for the letters. Shiffrin (1973) found similar detrimental effects of an arithmetic task in an experiment that used the typical distractor procedure, where subjects were given instructions to remember items rather than to forget them. In this case, subjects were given items to remember and then performed either signal detection alone or detection followed by a period of arithmetic. The arithmetic task caused recall to drop, even though the signal-detection task by itself did not affect recall. Similarly, in Reitman's experiments, there was evidence for forgetting from interference as well as decay, in this case interference from the syllable-detection task (detecting the syllable TOH in a series of DOHs and TOHs). In Reitman's 1974 experiments, this task produced an additional 44 percent more forgetting than tone detection. In short, both decay and interference seem to be operating in STM forgetting. And although distractor tasks were originally intended to prevent rehearsal without interfering with the items to be remembered, such tasks appear to be an important source of interference.

In general, two aspects of the distractor task appear to determine the extent to which it interferes and produces forgetting in STM. One is the degree to which the material to be remembered and the distractor material are similar. The idea is that of interference by similarity: More similar distractor material generates more interference with the to-be-remembered material, so that it cannot be recovered after the retention interval. The experiments discussed here support this hypothesis. For example, in the Reitman and Shiffrin experiments, it was found that distractor tasks involving verbal skills (skills that require word or syllable manipulation) were more likely to disrupt retention of verbal forms (syllables or words) than were nonverbal distractor tasks such as signal detection. Other experiments also indicate interference by similarity. Wickelgren (1965) found that if the distractor material sounded like the material to be remembered, more forgetting occurred than if it did not. Deutsch (1970) found that retaining a set of tones was more difficult if the tones were followed by an interpolated sequence of tones than if there was an interpolated sequence of numbers. All this suggests that the information in the distractor task can make contact and interfere with the to-be-remembered material in STM, the degree of interference depending on the similarity of the two sets of material.

The second factor to determine short-term forgetting is the general difficulty of the distractor task. To the extent that the distractor task uses processing capacity (or attention, in the sense of capacity), it should create interference by reducing the storage capacity available for the to-be-remembered items. A difficult task can interfere with verbal material even if it does not involve verbal items. Watkins, Watkins, Craik, and Mazuryk (1973) used a distractor task in which subjects listened to a sequence of piano tones and shadowed them by pressing a designated button corresponding to each tone after it occurred. This produced some forgetting of a to-be-remembered set of five words over a 20-second retention interval. The interference-by-difficulty idea also receives direct support from experiments showing that the difficulty of the distractor task does affect short-term retention (for example, Posner and Konick, 1966; Posner and Rossman, 1965).

LOCUS OF FORGETTING: STORAGE LOSS OR RETRIEVAL FAILURE?

So far, we have characterized forgetting as the loss of strength of items stored in STM, as measured by a decline in memory-task performance. Our principal concern was the cause of that loss—interference or decay. We concluded that although decay appears to effect the loss of some information, interference plays a major role. But another question about forgetting in STM concerns the components of memory that underlie the decline in the information's strength. When we consider this question, we see that forgetting can be characterized in more detail than as a loss of strength. As Bennett (1975) has pointed out, the ability to remember information could decrease for more than one reason. Information about to-be-remembered items could be lost from storage, or the items themselves could remain intact but the ability to retrieve them could decline.

The idea that forgetting represents a loss of information about items while they are stored works like this: Suppose that items in STM lose information during the period they reside there, and that forgetting occurs when an item is so lacking in information that it cannot be reconstructed and reported, even though we know where it resides. Reporting such an item from the information in STM is like trying to read the address on an old letter whose ink has faded. We know where the address is, but we can't make it out. This is forgetting through storage loss. The important point to note is that the inability to report the item is not due to an inability to locate it in STM.

Storage loss will inevitably lead to an inability to retrieve an item, but the failure is not in the retrieval process itself so much as in the item it is given to work with. In contrast, if we were to say that forgetting in STM was due solely to a failure to retrieve, we would be talking about a situation in which the item was intact but could not be located. If it could be located, in this view, there would be no trouble in reporting it; it would not be hard to decipher. Retrieval can actually be divided into two subprocesses—searching for items, and deciding which of several items that are found is the one to be reported. Even if an item were stored adequately, the ability to remember could be lost if either of these subprocesses failed. The item might never be found in a search, or if several others were found as well, the decision might be incorrect and the wrong item might be reported.

How does this storage/retrieval distinction fit in with the original dichotomy between interference and decay? The concept of decay, in the sense of the passive erosion of information about a stored item, seems to assume that forgetting is a storage problem. Interference, on the other hand, could be consistent with either a storage or a retrieval hypothesis. For example, similarity among items could have an abrasive effect on their stored representations. Or the interfering effect of an item could be due to its obscuring a to-be-remembered input and hindering the search subprocess of retrieval.

A number of experiments relevant to the storage/retrieval question have used a procedure in which performance on the Peterson task is examined over a series of trials. Keppel and Underwood (1962) demonstrated that performance declines from trial to trial in the task, as PI develops. The storage-loss hypothesis has no trouble explaining this phenomenon; it simply assumes that PI is observed because previously presented items erode the stored representations of current items. However, PI can also be interpreted as a retrieval failure, as follows: On a given trial, the subject is trying to recall the most recent items in a series (the last set of items to be presented). The problem is that in order for these items to be retrieved, they must be discriminated from items presented on previous trials. If there were no previous trials, then retrieval is easy; the current trial's items stand out. But if there were trials before the current one, the decision as to which are the current trial's items must be made on the basis of knowledge about the order or time at which items were presented. And the more previous items that were presented and are still in STM, the more complex this decision task is. Thus performance declines as more and more trials are given.

By this reasoning, if we do something to make items from the current trial easy to distinguish from items on previous trials, we should boost performance. This sort of manipulation has been done in a series of studies by Wickens and his associates (reviewed in Wickens, 1972), using a "release-from-PI" paradigm. Wickens, Born, and Allen (1963) conducted an experiment like the following: Suppose we have a subject perform three trials of a Peterson task, using various consonant trigrams as the to-be-remembered items and an 11-second retention interval, during which the subject performs a distractor task. During this time, PI builds up, and, as the trials progress, the subject remembers fewer and fewer consonants on each trial. On the fourth trial, called the *release* trial, we switch the material to be remembered. Instead of three consonants, we use three digits as the memory items. The typical results of such an experiment are shown in Figure 6.7. Relative to subjects in a control group, who have no switch in the material to be remembered, subjects in the experimental group, who switched to digits, show a sudden increase in their ability to remember. In fact, their performance on this fourth trial resembles their performance with the consonants on the first trial. It seems that the PI that had built up during the first trials is specific to the particular class of material to be remembered (here, consonants) and does not affect the new material (digits). Thus, the

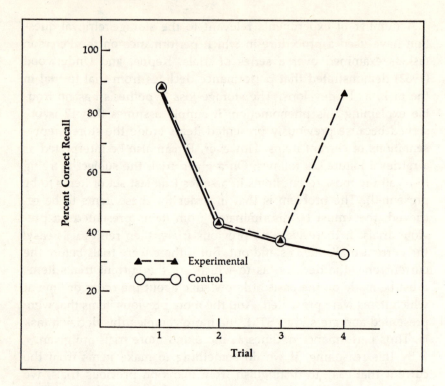

Figure 6.7 Release from PI: The graph shows idealized data for the percentage of items correctly recalled as a function of trial number. The fourth trial corresponds to the release trial (where, for the experimental group, the category of the to-be-remembered items differs from that of previous trials). [After Wickens, 1972.]

switch to digits is a switch to PI-free performance—performance notably higher than that with PI present. We say that performance is released from PI.

The release from PI with a switch in the class of to-be-remembered items in the Peterson task is readily explained by the retrieval theory. When the subject is performing on the third trial in a series, before the release trial, the decision component of his or her retrieval is very difficult. It consists of picking out the particular items presented on the current trial from similar items presented on two prior trials. On the fourth, release trial, however, the items are quite distinct. They may be the only digits in STM among a bunch of consonants. Thus, they stand out and are easy to retrieve, and performance goes up dramatically. After two trials with digits, of course, retrieval of digits becomes difficult, and performance on a third trial is poor. If, at that point, we switch to new items, such as common nouns, we will get release again.

The retrieval model makes further predictions about a variant of the release-from-PI procedure. Suppose we have subjects go through a series of three-trial sequences. That is, subjects have three Peterson-task trials with one type of item, for instance, words that name kitchen utensils. They then switch to another type of item, such as animal names, and have three trials with that type, and so on. Performance should go down in each sequence and then pop up at the start of the next as release from PI occurs. Now suppose that at the end of all these sequences of trials, we give subjects a surprise recall test. They are asked to report as many items as possible, from any trial. The storage and retrieval theories offer different predictions about performance on the final recall test. In particular, the theories differ with respect to how recall of items on the final test should be affected by their position in the initial three-trial sequence in which they appeared.

We know that, in initial recall of items, during the distractor-procedure trials themselves, performance declines from trial one to two, and from trial two to three, within a sequence. The storage theory says that this decline in performance occurs because items were stored increasingly badly in STM as the trials progressed, as a result of the buildup of PI from one trial to the next. Although we have been referring to STM, we could expect these storage effects to carry over to LTM as well. Compared to the item presented in the second trial of a sequence, the item presented during the third trial should be stored less completely and forgotten more quickly from STM, which means that there would be less information about it passed on to LTM. This poor LTM storage should show up on the final recall test given at the end of the distractor trials, for that is a test of long-term retention. Thus, the storage theory says that performance on the final recall test should mimic performance on the initial distractor-procedure trials; that is, the percentage of times an item is recalled on the final test should go down, the later in its three-trial sequence the item was initially presented.

The retrieval theory, on the other hand, assumes that the buildup of PI over the initial trials corresponds to increasing retrieval difficulty, not poor storage. When item X is presented on the first trial of its sequence, it stands out as the only item of its type and is easily retrieved. When item Z is presented on the third trial, it is too similar to X and Y (presented on the second trial) to be readily retrieved. But, at the time of final recall, items X, Y, and Z are all sharing the same fate. They are all in LTM together, where X no longer stands out and Z is no longer more obscured than X or Y. That is, the initial advantage of X, its being the only item of its type in memory (STM), has vanished. It now is in LTM along with Y and Z. The retrieval advantage was a transient phenomenon. The retrieval theory therefore makes the prediction that final recall performance should not vary with the position of the recalled item in the initial input sequence of trials. And the retrieval theory's prediction is confirmed (Loftus and Patterson, 1975; Watkins and Watkins, 1975). This suggests that the decline in performance over the successive trials in the initial Peterson task was due to a temporary inability to retrieve, not a storage deficit that carries its effects over to LTM.

From the phenomena discussed so far—the buildup and release from PI and the contrast between PI effects on STM and LTM—the retrieval hypothesis seems to provide the best account of PI in STM. More precisely, the effects we have described could be attributed to the decision subprocess of retrieval. These effects suggest that as more and more similar items are stored in STM over several trials, the decision as to which are the current to-be-reported items becomes more difficult, leading to errors in recall. This explanation further predicts the form of those errors: Since subjects are deciding (incorrectly) that items from previous trials are the to-be-reported items from the current trial, their errors should predominantly be "intrusions" from previous trials. That is, subjects will err on trial *n* by reporting items from trials prior to *n*. In fact, such intrusions are commonly observed, with the majority coming from trials just before the current one (Noyd, 1965; Peterson and James, 1967).

However, not all of STM forgetting can be accounted for by such failures in the decision subprocess of retrieval. Dillon and associates (Dillon, 1973; Dillon and Bittner, 1975; Dillon and Thomas, 1975) have argued that the loss in *accessibility* of items is an extremely important component of PI. One of their arguments (Dillon, 1973; Dillon and Thomas, 1975) focuses on the intrusion errors we have just discussed, where subjects tend to err in the distractor procedure by reporting an item from a previous trial rather than the current to-be-remembered item. If such intrusions reflect an error in the decision process, subjects should be greatly aided if they are told, at the time of recall on each trial, the identities of the *previous* trial's items. This would enable them to reject those items as incorrect and would help them to decide which are the current trial's items. However, this procedure does not improve recall (Dillon, 1973). The failure to enhance recall performance on a given trial by showing subjects previous trials' items suggests that PI is not simply due to errors in the decision process, but reflects an actual inability to generate items as candidates for that decision.

In another experiment, Dillon and Thomas (1975) instructed subjects to report all the items they remembered from any trial, at the time of recall during each trial. If subjects can find all the current trial's items but have trouble deciding which items are current, this procedure should greatly facilitate their performance, for it will eliminate the need for such a decision. Any items that are found can now be reported. However, instructing subjects to report everything they remember does not help them much in correctly reporting items from the current trial. The unreported items appear to be inaccessible; the failure is not merely in deciding which of many available items to report. On the other hand, the decision process in this experiment was also fallible. When subjects were instructed to indicate which of the items they reported were from the current trial, they sometimes indicated items that were actually from previous trials.

Dillon's research clearly implicates processes other than the decision component of retrieval in short-term forgetting. It appears instead that the PI phenomenon is due at least partly to a progressive decrease in the ability to obtain items for a decision process to operate on, as more and more trials are performed. This decrease could be due to a failure in the search subprocess of retrieval; that is, the presence of more and more items from previous trials could make finding the current items more difficult. However, Dillon points out that the results are not incompatible with a storage-loss hypothesis, either. That is, items could become more inaccessible over trials because less and less information about them remains in storage.

One argument in favor of the retrieval hypothesis over the storage-loss explanation is offered by experiments described above, in which subjects were given a long-term test on items from previous trials with the distractor procedure as well as tests of STM on each trial. Since the long-term test did not reveal effects of PI like those observed in the distractor trials themselves, it appears that the phenomenon was more transient than a storage loss.

The idea that items become inaccessible because of retrieval difficulties, rather than storage loss, is also supported by another version of the release-from-PI procedure. In this version, subjects are given a series of trials with the distractor procedure where all of the to-be-remembered items are from the same category (such as flowers) but may be drawn from different subcategories (such as wild flowers vs. garden flowers). After three trials with items from one subcategory (wild flowers), the subjects can be shifted to a new subcategory (garden flowers). Performance in this situation will decline over the first three trials as PI develops, but the question of interest is whether subjects will show release on the fourth trial, when the shift in the subcategories is rather subtle. If subjects are informed about the subcategory shift, their performance does improve, relative to that of subjects who are not told about the current items' subcategory following a shift, or who are told about the current items' subcategory but who were not given a shift in subcategory on the current trial (Dillon and Bittner, 1975; Gardiner, Craik, and Birtwistle, 1972; O'Neill, Sutcliffe, and Tulving, 1976). This occurs even when the subjects are told about a subcategory shift only at the time of recall, not when the items were first presented and encoded.

The fact that giving subjects the name of the current items' subcategory can take effect at the time of recall, after items have been encoded and stored, suggests that the subcategory-name cue aids the retrieval process. It is still possible that part of the subcategory name's effect is to counteract storage-loss effects. For example, subjects might use the name to guess members of the category, and a correct guess might act as a rehearsal, to renew an item that has lost information and make it easier to decipher. However, if this were the only effect of the subcategory name, it should not matter if there were a shift of subcategories before the current trial or not. For example, four trials could all use garden flowers, and giving subjects the name "garden flowers" at recall during the fourth trial could still help them to guess the names of such flowers and renew the current items. But, in fact, on trials where the subcategory name is given, recall is higher when there has been a shift (Dillon and Bittner, 1975; O'Neill et al., 1976). This suggests that the name's effect is on more than storage; it also helps subjects to retrieve items.

From the experiments discussed so far, it seems that at least a major component of STM forgetting, in the form of PI, consists of failures in the search and decision subprocesses of retrieval, although storage loss may also play a role. One problem raised by the retrieval theory, however, is that the nature of retrieval as inferred from work with the distractor procedure is quite different from STM retrieval as it appears in the Sternberg task (discussed in Chapter 5). In the latter situation, retrieval seems to be error-free and quite straightforward; STM is scanned until the desired item is found. The view of retrieval from the distractor procedure is quite different; it seems to be more like a problem-solving process, in which a to-be-remembered item is searched for and then discriminated from competing information on the basis of its unique characteristics. Sometimes these characteristics can be quite subtle, as the studies obtaining release after subcategory shifts tell us. Wickens (1972) has similarly found that retrieval in the release-from-PI situation can be facilitated by a shift from masculine nouns (butler, rooster, tuxedo) on the prerelease trials to feminine nouns (queens, nylons, cow) on the release trial, or from abstract nouns (advantage, boredom, position) to concrete nouns (palace, acrobat, factory). These are refined semantic distinctions, and that they affect recall indicates that the retrieval process can utilize nuances of meaning.

There are several possible ways to reconcile these two rather discrepant views of STM retrieval. One resolution can be offered on the basis of the difficulty involved in the tasks. In the Sternberg task, the subject is retrieving items from a list shorter than the memory span, under circumstances where list items should not be forgotten. Thus retrieval is not difficult; it would be possible to retrieve without having to discriminate among items on the basis of semantic content or time of presentation. The distractor procedure, in contrast, is designed to produce forgetting, and retrieval in this situation is bound to be more problematic. It is not surprising that more complex search processes are brought to bear in the latter situation.

Another approach is to assume that retrieval in the distractor procedure with PI present is from LTM rather than STM. The fact that such retrieval appears to use semantic information to discriminate the current to-be-recalled items from others has led Baddeley (1972) to postulate that it reflects LTM processing. He has pointed out that the retention interval involved in the distractor-task situation is often long enough so that the information might not be in STM. Moreover, the source of interference is the material presented over several earlier trials. This was shown in a study by Bennett (1975), who used a distractor procedure where a recognition test was given at the end of each trial. That is, subjects had to say which of two given items was from the current trial. The false choice on this test (the noncurrent item) could be from a trial one to twelve trials before the current one, or it could be a brand new item not seen before on any trial. Bennett found that discriminating the current item from a brand new one was easier than discriminating it from a previous trial's item, even one from twelve trials earlier. This suggests that items from trials long before the current one are still present in the current trial's retrieval situation. As an item presented so much earlier is likely to be in LTM, the entire retrieval process may be one of finding items in LTM. An argument against this, however, comes from the experiments by Loftus and Patterson and Watkins and Watkins. In those studies, after a long series of distractor trials, subjects were given a final recall test, which should certainly have been tapping information in LTM. It was found that the retrieval problems evident in the initial distractor trials were no longer manifested in the final test. This supports the idea that despite its difference from the Sternberg-task processing, the retrieval being tapped with the distractor procedure was from a less permanent store, presumably STM.

In summary, at this point it appears that forgetting in STM stems from a number of sources. At least a portion is due to decay. This occurs when rehearsal of to-be-remembered items is prevented, for example, by a distractor task. Decay's effects are usually assumed to weaken the strength of stored items. Forgetting in STM is also attributable to interference, however. One source of interference is material from previous events, which produces PI. It seems, from experiments we have reviewed, that the presence of this material interferes with the process of retrieving the current to-be-remembered items—locating them in STM and discriminating them from other items. It may also cause a loss of information from storage. Distracting activity following items' presentation may be another source of interference, with its effect on the to-be-remembered items dependent on similarity and difficulty. In this case, the interference is RI, and whether its effects are on storage—eroding items while they reside in STM—or retrieval—obscuring to-be-recalled items so they cannot be found—is unclear. The studies addressed to the storage/retrieval question have largely been concerned with PI, not RI. However, the fact that errors in STM recall take the form of acoustic confusions suggests that storage loss is a factor. You may recall that Sperling and Speelman (1970) accounted for such confusions by a model that assumed partial loss of items from storage.

7

Visual Codes in Short-Term Memory

Our discussion thus far has emphasized the properties of STM as a verbal memory—one that encodes, stores, retrieves, and works on information represented by words. We have considered experiments that used words and letters as the stimulus material of interest, rather than smells or sights or sounds that would be difficult to describe verbally. We have depicted the form of these verbal items in STM, the memory code, as acoustic (thus, A is stored as the sound "ay") or sometimes semantic (in terms of meaning rather than sound). In this chapter we will change this emphasis and focus on visually coded material in STM.

EVIDENCE FOR VISUAL CODES

To begin, it is important to clarify just what it means to say that information is represented visually in STM. We will say that a given situation constitutes visual coding in STM when certain conditions are satisfied: First, it should be a situation in which characteristics of STM are evident (other than the characteristic of acoustic coding). For example, the situation could be one like the memory-span task, in which a small amount of information is being held over a short term—on the order of seconds, if there is no renewing process such as rehearsal. Or we could say STM is involved if it is clear that the information is actively being worked on, currently being processed rather than merely residing in LTM. Another criterion for visual STM coding is evidence that the information being processed is in fact visual, that is, that it represents physical properties of an item's appearance rather than sounds or meaning. At the same time, however, it is important to rule out the possibility that the visual information is in the sensory register and not in STM. The visual register could clearly hold a stimulus in visual form for a brief time, so we must have evidence that the items are not held as "raw" sensory information, but rather that they have undergone pattern recognition and made contact with LTM. They must be postcategorical, in other words. In this chapter, then, we will consider the active processing or storage of information for short periods of time, as a nonsensory, visual code.

We will somtimes speak of the processing system under investigation as *visual STM*, although this term is not meant to imply that it is a completely different store from the STM we have studied thus far, which we will call *verbal STM*. Using the label *verbal* as a contrast to visual is somewhat inappropriate, for as we shall see, verbal stimuli such as letters can be represented in memory as visual codes. However, for the present, *verbal* will imply the acoustic (or possibly semantic) alternatives to visual coding.

Posner's Letter-Matching Experiments

One body of evidence for the existence of visual STM codes comes from a procedure developed by Posner (1969; Posner, Boies, Eichelman, and Taylor, 1969; Posner and Mitchell, 1967). Posner's work strongly supports the ideas that (1) visual information can persist after a visual stimulus has occurred, under conditions incompatible with iconic storage; and (2) visual information can also be "generated," or activated, from LTM. His basic procedure is as follows: Subjects take part in a long series of trials, each lasting for a brief time. On each trial, the subjects see two letters, and they are to indicate whether the letters have the same name (for example A and A or B and b) or different names (such as A and B). They do this by pressing one of two buttons, designated the "same" button and the "different" button.

Like the Sternberg task discussed in Chapter 5, this task is one subjects can perform without making any mistakes. Thus, the variable measured by the experimenter is the subject's reaction time

Type of Trial	Example of What Subject Sees	Subject's Correct Response
Identity match	A A	"Same"
Name match	A a	"Same"
Negative trial	A b	"Different"

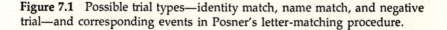

←————————————————— RT interval —————————————————→

Figure 7.1 Possible trial types—identity match, name match, and negative trial—and corresponding events in Posner's letter-matching procedure.

(RT)—the time it takes to respond "same" or "different," once the letters are presented. Recall that RT is assumed to give an indication of how long it takes for internal processing to occur.

As shown in Figure 7.1, there are different types of trials in Posner's task. In particular, there is more than one situation where the subjects say "same." They do so if the two letters are physically identical (say, A and A); this will be called an identity match. They also say "same" if the letters are not identical but have the same name (as in A and a); this is called a name match. When either of these conditions is violated, subjects are to say "different." ("Same" and "different" responses are also called *positive* and *negative* responses, respectively.) Typically, the various types of responses—identity match, name match, and negative—lead to different RTs. Subjects are able to respond faster by about .1 second (which is quite a lot of time in a RT experiment) in making an identity match than in making a name match or a negative response. This suggests that there is some difference in how the subjects are internally performing the task.

In order to find out what the difference might be, we must break down the task into components, each of which takes part of the total amount of time. In doing so, we attempt to isolate the component or components that contribute to the added time in those conditions that take longer than identity matching. We might tentatively break down the task as follows: First a subject must perceive the letters (visually encode them). Then, he or she must name the letters. Then, the subject decides whether or not they have the same name. Finally, a response is made by pressing the button. These activities use up the entire RT from the onset of the letters to the response. There is no compelling reason to suppose that the time it takes to perceive the letters varies from one condition to another, nor does it seem reasonable to suppose that the time it takes to push the button varies. The most likely source of the difference in RT lies in the naming and comparison processes. It must take less time to perform these components of the task when the letters are identical than when they are not.

In fact, Posner suggested that the difference in the RTs arose because there was no reason to name the two letters when they were identical. He suggested that two identical letters could be judged the same on the basis of their physical, visual forms. Only when the letters were not identical would it be necessary to name them and compare names. In short, for identity matches (A A), the task was to perceive and encode visually, compare physical images, and respond; whereas for name matches (A a) and negative responses (A B), the task was to perceive and encode visually, encode verbally (name), compare names, and respond. Name matches, having more components, would take more time, thus leading to the observed differences in RT. In short, Posner suggested that identity matches were based on visual information and name matches were based on verbal labels (see Figure 7.2).

To suggest that visual information is used for comparisons in the case of identity matches implies that the information must be available. This implication is unequivocal when two letters are simultaneously presented and stay in view until the subject responds—precisely the case we have been discussing. What we seek is evidence that there is visual information available in memory after the stimulus has vanished. Moreover, we want to demonstrate that the information is not in the icon but beyond it, in STM.

In order to show that this visual information exists in memory, the Posner task can be modified so that the two letters are presented not simultaneously, but sequentially. The typical trial goes like this: First, a letter appears for a half-second or so. Then there is an interstimulus interval (ISI) in which the subject sees a blank field. Next, a second letter appears. As before, the subject indicates whether the two letters are the "same" or "different." Reaction time is here defined as the interval between the onset of the second letter and the subject's response.

In this task, the first letter must be in memory when the subject makes the response because it vanishes from the display before the ISI. Thus, the comparison of the two letters must use information in

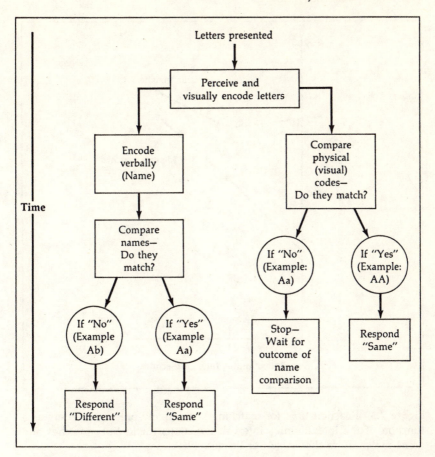

Figure 7.2 Possible mental events in the letter-matching task.

memory. Is there still evidence that visual information is used in the comparison; that is, do identity matches still take less time than name matches? The answer is yes—at least under some conditions. If the ISI is less than a second or so, the identity matches take less time, but as the ISI approaches 2 seconds, there is no longer a difference in RT (see Figure 7.3). Using the same reasoning as before, we can infer that when RT for identity matches is less than that for name matches, visual information is being used for identity matching. But in this case, since the first letter is not physically present when the match is made, the visual information being used must be in memory. Thus, we have evidence that visual information about the first letter persists for a period of about 2 seconds after the letter has vanished. The gradual decrease in the advantage (shorter RT) of

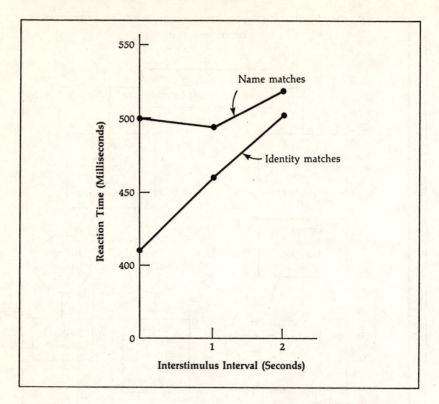

Figure 7.3 Reaction time for matching successively presented letters as a function of the interstimulus interval. Functions for identity matches and name matches are shown. [After Posner, 1969.]

identity matches over name matches can be interpreted as a gradual decay of the visual information about the first letter in memory.

In summary, we now have evidence that visual information can persist in memory for a brief time after the stimulus has vanished. However, that leaves an important problem: How do we know that the visual information is in STM, rather than in the icon? From the experiments that have been described, we cannot be sure that it is not iconic information that contributes to matching two identical letters. However, there is evidence that the information is not in the sensory register, but is more appropriately labeled short-term (according to the criteria we set out at the beginning of this discussion).

One bit of evidence for the nonsensory nature of this visual memory is that it seems to exist even when the iconic representation is erased (Posner et al, 1969). For example, suppose the two letters are separated by an ISI that is filled with a masking field, like a random black-and-white pattern. Under those conditions, we would expect the random pattern to erase the iconic representation of the first letter. In this case, identity matches are still made faster than name matches (although both take longer than when there is no pattern during the ISI). Thus, it seems that visual information about the first letter is present even after presentation of a masking pattern, which means that the visual information is held in some store other than the sensory register.

Another indication that this visual memory we are discussing is not sensory comes from evidence that it can be generated from LTM (Posner et al., 1969). Suppose that instead of giving the first letter visually, we say to the subject, "It is a capital A." Then we have a blank ISI, followed either by a capital A or some other letter. Under these conditions, RT for positive responses (those in which the second letter is what has been announced) is comparable to RT for identity matches (under the usual, both-letters-visual conditions) for ISIs of about 1 second and greater. For ISIs of less than 1 second, the identity matches are made a bit faster. What these results suggest is that the subject uses the spoken announcement to produce an internal visual copy of the announced letter. (He or she uses rules about letter sounds and appearance to do so.) This internal copy is compared to the second letter, when it appears. When the subject has a second or more to generate the internal copy, the copy is roughly comparable to what would then exist if the first letter had been presented visually. With less than a second to do so, he or she produces a generated copy that is inferior to the memory of a visually presented letter. Thus, the subject can either generate a visual representation from LTM rules or retain a comparable representation after a stimulus has actually been presented. This seems to be strong evidence that the visual memory that persists after the stimulus is not sensory, for it can also be produced from LTM, not just received directly via the senses.

"Mental Rotation" Experiments

More is known about visual representations in STM through the work of Roger Shepard, Lynn Cooper, and their co-workers (Cooper and Shepard, 1973; Shepard and Metzler, 1971; reviewed in Shepard, 1978). Their research is concerned with something called *mental rotation*—the rotation of visual codes like those we have been discussing. They had subjects perform tasks similar to Posner's. In one experiment, subjects were instructed to press one button if a letter stimulus was normal and another button if it was a mirror image. Particularly interesting is the fact that the stimulus could differ from its upright position by a rotation in the plane of presentation. For example, ⊬ was to be considered normal (for it is, within a rotation), whereas ⊬ was to be considered a mirror image. The degrees of rotation separating the stimulus from its upright position varied from 0 to 360. The researchers found that the RT for deciding if a letter was normal or mirror-reversed was a regular function of the amount (in degrees) of angular separation of the letter from the upright (Figure 7.4). As the letter was rotated more degrees from 0 to 180, RT increased; then from 180 to 360 degrees of rotation (which is 0 to 180 in the opposite direction), it decreased just as regularly. This RT pattern suggests that the subject was mentally rotating the stimulus into its normal orientation (clockwise or counterclockwise, whichever direction was closer to upright; for example, rotating ʚ clockwise into B) and then deciding on a visual basis whether it was normal. Each degree the stimulus had to be rotated would add to the RT, thus giving a regular increase in RT with degrees of separation from normal. Thus, these results suggest that subjects could rotate some mental representation of the stimulus. Since mental rotation is an active process, we will assume that the rotated representation is in STM.

The concept of a rotatable memory code has certain implications for the nature of that code. Could a sound be rotated? It certainly seems unlikely. Instead, the idea that the code can be transformed over space suggests that it itself is a spatial entity—a visual code. Moreover, the regular increase in RT with degrees of rotation suggests that the code has properties analogous to those of a physically present stimulus, which would also take longer to rotate into normal orientation the further its initial position from the upright. It is tempting to think of mental rotation as an internal equivalent of physical rotation, performed on a code that is like a template of the corresponding stimulus. If the code were a less faithful stimulus representation, such as a list of features, it is not obvious how it could be rotated, nor how rotation would produce such a regular effect on RT. However, as Shepard, Cooper, and associates have pointed out (and as we shall discuss further below), it is not necessary to assume that the visual code of a stimulus is like a template in order for it to be mentally rotated.

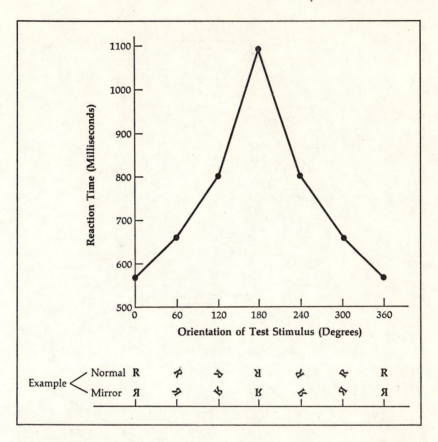

Figure 7.4   Reaction time for deciding whether a letter is presented in its normal form or as a mirror image of its normal form, as a function of the degrees of rotation of the letter in the plane of presentation. Below the graph are examples of letters at each rotation value [After Cooper and Shepard, 1973.]

Scanning over Visual Codes

The data on mental rotation suggest that a visual code is rather faithful to the stimulus it represents, in that it is processed analogously to a physical object. Further evidence for such a faithful stimulus representation, sometimes called a *mental image*, comes from studies of Kosslyn, Ball, and Reiser (1978), suggesting that subjects mentally peruse, or scan over, visual codes much as they would scan over pictures. In one such study, subjects began by memorizing the map shown in Figure 7.5A. Then the subjects took part in a series of trials where RT was measured. On each trial, they first heard the name of

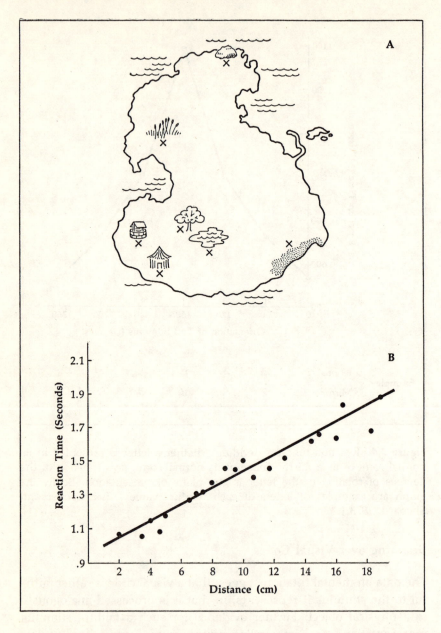

Figure 7.5 (A) Fictional map used in image-scanning study. (B) Time to scan between points on the imagined map, as a function of the distance between the points (marked by Xs) on the original map. [After Kosslyn, Ball, and Reiser, 1978. Copyright 1978 by the American Psychological Association. Reprinted by permission.]

an object on the map. They were asked to form a mental picture of the map (in other words, generate a short-term visual code for it from information in LTM) and focus on the named object. A few seconds later, another word was presented. On some trials, this word named another object on the map. In this case, the subjects were to mentally scan across the map to the named object, pressing a button when they reached it. (They were told to scan by imagining a black dot traveling quickly across the map from the originally focused object to the subsequently named one.) If the second word did not name an object on the map, the subjects were to press another button, without any scanning. (Trials of this type were included simply to prevent the subjects from pressing a button as soon as they heard the second word, without processing it.)

Kosslyn et al. were concerned with RT on trials where the second word named an object on the map, and the subject had to scan across the map image. They reasoned that if the subject's mental picture was like a real map, it would take longer to scan across it, the greater the distance to be scanned (that is, the greater the distance between the two objects named on the trial). The results of this study, shown in Figure 7.5B, confirmed this prediction. Mental scanning time, as measured by RT, increased with the to-be-scanned distance. And RT increased by a constant amount with each increase in distance; that is, the function in Figure 7.5B is linear. This suggests that the scanning of the mental picture occurred at a constant rate.

In another version of this task, where subjects did not scan their mental image of the map, very different results were obtained. In this case, as in the original study, subjects were to form the map image when they heard the first word during a trial. When they heard the second word, however, they were simply to press a button indicating whether or not it named an object on the map. They were not told to use their image in making this response. Under these conditions, on trials where the second word named an object from the map, RT did not change with the distance between the two named objects. This contrasts with the data of Figure 7.5B, where subjects had to scan. Thus, the results indicate that it is scanning of the map, not just forming a mental picture, and not just the presentation of the two words, that causes RT to increase. Without such scanning, RT remains constant; with such scanning, RT increases with the distance to be scanned.

Other studies by Kosslyn et al. give further support to the inference that visual codes can be scanned. When subjects were instructed to generate large mental pictures and then to scan across them, they took longer than subjects who were told to generate and scan the same pictures, but in a smaller size. It is as if the generation of a large image caused the distances within it to become large, and this increased the time to scan across it, just as would happen with a real picture. Again, we find results suggesting a similarity between operations on visual codes and on physical objects.

PROPERTIES OF VISUAL CODING IN STM

So far, we have considered several studies that offer evidence for visual codes in STM. These codes meet the criteria we initially set up: They are being retained in STM or actively processed; they are not in the icon, for they are present under conditions that preclude sensory storage; and they apparently represent visual properties of the corresponding item, for they can be mentally rotated and scanned in ways analogous to such operations on physical objects. We turn now to the properties of the STM that stores and processes these codes. Of particular interest is the correspondence between this visual STM and STM as we have studied it in previous chapters. As we shall see, the two views of STM reveal much in common.

Capacity for Visual Codes in STM

In our previous discussion of memory-span tasks, we portrayed STM for verbal items as having a limited storage space, as if there were a limited number of slots for acoustic codes. Is there an analogous limit on storage space for visual codes? One limitation is suggested by Kosslyn (1975), who has compared visual STM to a TV screen, which is limited in spatial size. If a visual code is large, in this view, it fills the screen, limiting the space available for other codes. A large code would have the advantage of conveying more detail of the represented object, however, just as a large TV screen shows more detail than a small one.

Kosslyn carried this TV-screen metaphor into experimental work designed to manipulate the size and detail of mental images. In one experiment, subjects took part in a series of trials, on each of which they first heard either the word *elephant* or the word *fly*, then the name of another object. They were to form a mental image of the two named objects, next to one another in relative sizes. For example, hearing *fly, goose*, they would imagine a fly next to a goose. At that point, the subjects were given a test word. They were told to examine their mental image of the *second* named object (goose, in this example) and to respond according to whether or not the test word named one of its parts. For example, if the test word was *legs*, the subjects would respond "yes," because legs are part of a goose. If the test word was *hand*, the response would be "no."

Kosslyn reasoned that if visual STM were limited in spatial size like a TV screen, then objects imagined next to an elephant would have to be rather small, because the elephant would take up a lot of space; those imagined next to a fly could be larger. Thus, an object imagined next to a fly could be more detailed than one imagined next to an elephant, and subjects should be faster to find parts in the fly case. This prediction was confirmed: Subjects were slower to find parts of an object imagined next to an elephant than one imagined next to a fly. This supports the idea that subjects have only so much "mental space" to imagine objects in, and the larger their image, the more detail it can convey.

The concept of limited space in visual STM seems analogous to the limited storage for acoustic codes revealed by memory-span experiments. But we know there is a more general limit on verbal STM—what we have called a limited work space (which can also be treated as an attentional capacity). This is a restriction not just on the amount of information that can be stored, but on the amount of processing—mental work—that can be performed. Like STM for acoustic codes, visual STM appears also to have a processing limitation. Kosslyn (1975) had subjects carry out a task like the fly/elephant one, but with new stimuli replacing the fly and elephant. These new stimuli were squares shown to the subjects at the start of the experiment. A square could be either large or small (like the elephant and fly), and it could also be either simple or complex. In the simple case, the square was subdivided into four cells; in the complex case, it was divided into sixteen cells.

On each trial of this task, the subject heard what type of square to imagine (large or small; simple or complex) and then an object to imagine next to it (such as goose). Then the test word was given, as before, and the subject indicated whether it was part of the imagined object. The results showed effects of square size like those found for the fly and elephant: RT was greater when the object was to be imagined next to a large square than a small one, as would occur if the large square left less room for the imagined object and thus forced a reduction in its detail. But there were also effects of complexity independent of the effects of image size: RT was greater when the object was to be imagined next to a complex square than

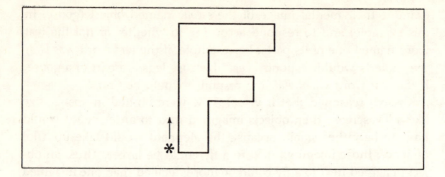

Figure 7.6   Stimulus used in task of Brooks (1968), indicating starting point and direction for categorization procedure. [After Brooks, 1968. Copyright © 1970 Canadian Psychological Association. Reprinted by permission.]

when next to a simple one. This suggests that the formation of the complex square's image might have used up some limited imaginal capacity, thus reducing the amount of detail it was possible to represent in the visual code of the object. In other words, we might say that forming images is mental work and that increasing the complexity of such images uses up more of the working capacity.

Other research also indicates that capacity is utilized by image generation and maintenance, and it suggests that there is a capacity specific to visual STM. The evidence comes from studies showing that processing of visual codes in STM competes with processing of visual information from external stimulation. One such study was devised by Brooks (1968). In his task, a subject was first shown a block letter with a star at one corner, like that in Figure 7.6. Then the letter was taken away, and the subject was required to remember it. The subject was to start at the starred corner and scan clockwise around the letter, saying "yes" whenever he or she viewed a corner that was on the very top or very bottom of the letter, and "no" if a corner was not on the top or bottom. For example, the correct responses for Figure 7.6 would be "yes, yes, yes, no, no, no, no, no, no, yes," (To vary the situation so the subject can't memorize the response sequence, different letters can be used from trial to trial, and the "yes" response can be required for corners on the extreme right or left rather than on the top or bottom.)

Brooks has shown that this task requires the use of visual processing capacity by contrasting it with a similar task that requires nonvisual, acoustic processing. The second task requires subjects to hold a sentence in memory, then go through it word by word, responding "yes" whenever a word is a noun and "no" when it is not. For example, if the sentence were, "A bird in the hand is not in the bush," the correct response sequence would be "no, yes, no, no, yes, no, no, no, no, yes." (Again, the task can be varied by using different sentences and by replacing the yes-if-a-noun criterion with the rule that the subject says "yes" whenever a word is from some other class.)

Brooks found that the letter and sentence tasks differed in certain critical respects. Consider two ways the subjects can respond in these tasks: They can either say the "yes" or "no" responses aloud, or they can point to the word "yes" or "no" on a response sheet. In the latter case, the sheet has several rows, each containing a yes and a no, with the words' positions varying from row to row. The subject points to one of the words for each response, starting at the top row and moving down the page for successive responses. Thus, the response requires visual monitoring.

We now have two tasks—a letter task, which presumably requires processing a mental image in STM, and a sentence task, which should lead to processing an acoustic representation of a series of words. We also have two kinds of responses—pointing, which demands visual monitoring of the locations of the responses, and vocalization, which involves acoustic representations. If there were limited capacities specific to the visual and acoustic domains, the visual demands of the letter task and pointing response should compete with one another, as should the sentence task and vocal response. Brooks's results were consistent with these predictions. Subjects were faster at making vocal responses with the letter task and faster with pointing responses in the case of the sentence task. Thus, they were faster in the conditions which would not be expected to compete for the same capacity, and slower when the task and response were within the same domain, both visual or both verbal.

Research of Baddeley and associates (Baddeley, Grant, Wight and Thomson, 1975) has also been used to study the limited capacity of visual STM. Their experiments are similar to the studies of working memory by Baddeley and Hitch (1974) discussed in Chapter 5, where subjects simultaneously performed a memory-span task and another task assumed to require "work" on verbal items. Baddeley et al. asked subjects to perform two types of visual processing at once. One was processing an external source of information called a pursuit rotor. The rotor consists of a light moving around in a circle, which subjects attempt to track by keeping a pointer on it as it rotates. The amount of time the pointer is on target can be manipulated by adjustment of the rate at which the target light moves. The rate is set fast enough so that the subject must continually monitor the visual information provided by the light and pointer; it is a demanding task.

At the same time as they tracked on the pursuit rotor, the subjects performed a second task that involved imagery. One task studied by Baddeley et al. was the letter task of Brooks (1968) just described (with the vocal response). From the work of Brooks, we know that this task demands visual processing capacity. And as we would expect, Baddeley et al. found that subjects' tracking suffered when they simultaneously performed the letter task. The letter-task-plus-rotor subjects were on target 78 percent of the time, whereas subjects who performed only the rotor task were on target 91 percent of the time. In contrast, Brooks's sentence task did not produce such impairment of tracking; subjects who did the sentence and rotor tasks simultaneously were on target 88 percent of the time. Thus, they were able to perform about as well as the subjects who did tracking alone. These results clearly demonstrate that it is not merely the presence of a second task that impairs rotor performance; it is the visual processing demands of the second task. Specifically, when the second task involves image maintenance and scanning, then processing of perceptual information, as measured by tracking with the pursuit rotor, is inhibited.

The experiments of Brooks and Baddeley et al. indicate that active processing of visual images uses a specifically visual capacity. Similar studies were described for the acoustic domain in Chapter 5. For example, you may recall that the acoustic similarity of simultaneously processed verbal information—such as items in a list, or a set of to-be-remembered items and a distractor task—affects performance, and storing a list of verbal items interferes with other operations on acoustic codes. Comparing these results to the competition for visual capacity we have just discussed suggests that very similar phenomena are found in both the visual and acoustic modes.

Rehearsal and Transfer of Visual Information to LTM

We have suggested that STM is limited in the capacity to process visual codes, much as it is limited in capacity for processing acoustic codes. Can we draw another analogy between the two types of coding, namely, with respect to rehearsal? (Perhaps we should call it "reseesal" for visual codes!) Recall that, in the case of acoustic codes, two kinds of rehearsal were distinguished—maintenance (Type I) and elaborative (Type II). The first refers to the act of maintaining an item in STM without enhancing (or minimally so) its long-term retention, the second to meaningful encoding operations that do facilitate memory. We shall consider the case for these sorts of rehearsal with visual codes.

Maintenance Rehearsal.   To a certain extent, we have discussed the maintenance of visual codes in STM. The experiments of Kosslyn, for example, revealed that subjects could maintain an image of a map for as long as they wished. In this case, the subjects were taught about the map in advance, and they generated the to-be-maintained image from knowledge in LTM. Rehearsal of a verbal code, however, generally follows the external presentation of the item. Can short-term visual codes be maintained under these circumstances, as well as when the code is generated from LTM? The data of Posner's task, previously discussed, are particularly relevant to this question. In that task, the reaction-time advantage for identity matches over name matches was found to decrease over an interval of a couple of seconds. Consequently, we assumed that the visual code on which the identity match was based could not be fully maintained over that interval, but that instead some information was lost from it.

It is possible to reconcile the maintenance in tasks like Kosslyn's with the evident decay of the visual code in Posner's task if we assume that the "decay" represents some partial loss of information, to the point where identity matches are no longer faster than name matches, but not a complete elimination of the visual code (Klatzky and Ryan, 1978; Klatzky and Stoy, 1978). In fact, we suggested that a partially decayed visual code might be comparable to one generated from LTM. It would not convey as much information as was available just after the stimulus was presented, but it would still constitute a visual code.

In support of this assumption, there is substantial evidence that a stimulus can be retained as a visual code for intervals longer than a couple of seconds in tasks similar to Posner's. For example, Parks and Kroll (1975; Kroll and Parks, 1978) found that an advantage (that is, shorter RT) for identity matches over name matches in the Posner task can last over a 12-second interstimulus interval rather than the 2-second interval observed by Posner (see Figure 7.3). They used pairs of letters as stimuli, and they found such an identity-match advantage even when subjects rehearsed the names of the first stimulus letters during the interval. This suggests that a visual code was used even though the names were available.

A somewhat different demonstration of relatively long-lasting visual STM codes was provided by Bencomo and Daniel (1975). Like Posner, they asked subjects to indicate whether two stimuli—in this case, pictures of common objects or their verbal labels—had the same or different names. An interval of 30 seconds separated the two stimuli. The most important evidence that pictures were maintained over this period in visual form was the pattern of RTs on trials where the two stimuli did not have the same name (and a "different" response was given). In this case, when the stimuli were pictures, RT was longer when they were visually similar (for example, a nail and a pencil) than when they were not (a nail and a dress). This same effect did not occur when the stimuli were words that merely named visually similar objects. Thus the similarity of the pictures actually presented, not simply the similarity of the underlying concepts (which are represented by the words as well as the pictures), seems to be instrumental here. Presumably, the detrimental effect of pictorial similarity occurred because the subjects compared the second picture to a visual code representing the first picture, and similarity between the two hindered their "different" response. These results therefore suggest that the visual code of a picture can be maintained over at least a half-minute period after its occurrence.

Given that visual codes can be maintained in STM, whether they remain after presentation of a visual stimulus or are generated from LTM in response to a label, we can ask if the maintenance facilitates long-term retention. If we find that it does not, then we can say that this maintenance process is like Type I rehearsal of verbal codes; it retains stimulus information for the short term without affecting LTM. One way to address this question would be to use a procedure like that used to study rehearsal of words, but with items that would presumably be coded visually. The techniques used to study maintenance rehearsal are rather new, however, and they have generally not been adapted to visual coding. Instead, data are available from a visual analogue to a manipulation presumed to affect *elaborative* rehearsal of words. The manipulation varies the presentation rate of words in a list-learning task.

As we saw in Figure 2.3C, presenting a list of words at a slow rate leads to better retention than presenting them at a fast rate. Presumably this is because, with a slower rate, the subjects are better able to rehearse each word after its presentation, before the next word occurs. Similar manipulations have been performed with lists of pictures, with the assumption that subjects will attempt to rehearse the pictures during the postpresentation interval, just as they attempt to rehearse words. However, the results of the picture studies indicate that the rehearsal, if it occurs, is ineffective. The ability to recognize pictures from a list has been found *not* to vary when the time between successive pictures is manipulated, holding constant the duration of exposure for each picture (Shaffer and Shiffrin, 1972).

This finding is relevant to our discussion of maintenance rehearsal, even though the experiments were derived from studies with words that reveal elaborative rehearsal. Although it might be argued that presentation-rate effects were not found because subjects did not try to rehearse each picture in the interval after presentation, this seems doubtful given the evidence that they rehearse in similar tasks with words. Let us presume, instead, that they did try to rehearse. In addition, it seems likely that subjects could maintain at least some of the visual information from the picture during the interval after its presentation. The absence of presentation-rate effects in this case therefore suggests that the maintenance was really Type I rehearsal—it did not enhance long-term retention.

The evidence for a process analogous to verbal maintenance rehearsal for visual codes is indirect to be sure, but in any case the contrast between effects of presentation rate on pictures and words is striking. In the case of word lists, as we saw in Chapter 5, it was relatively difficult to devise a task where subjects would maintain stimuli without elaborating on them. Generally, they take advantage of slow presentation rates to rehearse. By contrast, subjects seem not to elaboratively rehearse pictures after their presentation even if it should be advantageous to do so, and even if the postpicture interval is long.

The suggestion that pictures are not elaboratively rehearsed is also supported by the failure to find serial-position effects with picture lists (Loftus, 1974; Weaver and Stanny, 1978). You may recall that the usual advantage for recall of the initial items in a list (the primacy effect) is attributed to greater rehearsal of those items. When such an advantage is not found for pictures, the suggestion is again that elaborative rehearsal is not occurring.

The situation is complicated, however, by some studies that do show evidence for elaborative rehearsal of pictures. For example, Tabachnick and Brotsky (1976) found weak serial-position effects with picture stimuli, especially when the pictures were not complex. And some experimenters have found effects of the poststimulus interval on picture retention as well (Tversky and Sherman, 1975; Weaver, 1974). Just what variations among experiments lead to the differences in results is not clear. However, we can summarize the data on maintenance rehearsal as follows: There is evidence that subjects can maintain stimuli as visual codes in STM. There are also studies where under circumstances that should motivate maintenance of pictures, maintenance appears not to affect the ability to remember the pictures in a test of long-term retention. Taken together, these data suggest a maintenance rehearsal process may be occurring with visual codes in STM, although the conditions when pure maintenance will occur are unclear.

Elaborative Rehearsal of Visual Codes.   As we have discussed, there is some evidence for elaborative rehearsal of visual codes. It consists of serial-position and presentation-rate effects on memory for lists of pictures, found in at least some studies. This raises the question of what elaborative operations subjects might perform on visual codes. Do they mediate and chunk as they do with words? Although the elaboration and chunking of visual information as an aid to long-term retention has not been studied nearly as extensively as that of verbal items, there is evidence that such processes occur in the visual domain.

One body of studies that offers evidence for such processes has been conducted by Jean Mandler and her associates (Mandler and Johnson, 1976; Mandler and Parker, 1976; Mandler and Ritchey, 1977). These experiments compare subjects' retention of objects depicted in meaningful pictures to that of objects in nonmeaningful, disorganized pictures (such as those in Figure 7.7). The idea behind the Mandler et al. studies is that a meaningful picture can be interpreted through use of certain knowledge in LTM, called a *scene schema*. Just as elaborating verbal items by relating them to LTM knowledge is found to enhance memory, the interpretation of a picture through such a schema is assumed to provide an effective encoding in LTM.

Like the schemata discussed in relation to the prototype theory of pattern recognition, a schema for a scene would be a prototypical representation, a framework depicting the objects and the relationships that would generally occur. For example, a schema for a classroom scene might indicate the presence of a teacher, a pupil at a desk, a blackboard, and so on. If a meaningful picture of a classroom is presented, it would be likely to fit in with the scene

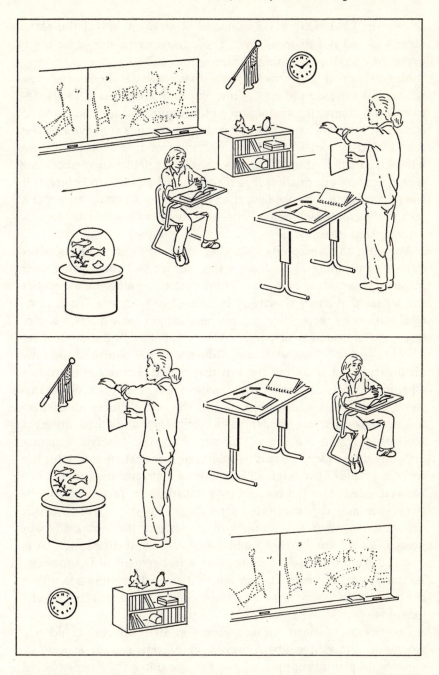

Figure 7.7 Organized and disorganized versions of a classroom scene. [After Mandler and Parker, 1976. Copyright 1976 by the American Psychological Association. Reprinted by permission.]

schema in LTM, whereas a nonsensical arrangement of the same objects would not fit in as well. Thus, the schema would be more useful in encoding meaningful scenes into LTM.

Mandler et al.'s work suggests that subjects do in fact use schemata to encode pictures of meaningful scenes. The data are derived from comparing memory for meaningful and for disorganized scenes. If a certain aspect of a meaningful scene is conveyed by the relevant schema in LTM, then integration of that aspect with the LTM information should improve memory relative to memory for corresponding information in a disorganized picture. In contrast, if the schema cannot be applied, then memory for a certain aspect of a meaningful scene will be no better than memory for that aspect of a disorganized picture.

Applying this reasoning, Mandler et al. showed subjects a sequence of meaningful or disorganized scenes and then tested their memory in a variety of ways, designed to determine the aspects of the scenes that could effectively be related to schemata. Their principal tools were recognition tests, where subjects saw a series of pictures and indicated which were old—seen before in the original set of scenes—and which were new. Moreover, the nature of the new pictures presented during the test was varied. For example, to test whether subjects remember the specific appearance of an object in a scene, such as a schoolteacher, one of the new pictures, or distractors, can be a scene similar to the original but with a different schoolteacher. To the extent that subjects avoid falsely "recognizing" this distractor, they can be said to demonstrate memory for the specific details of the original. Similarly, a distractor picture that has been changed from the original by a substitution for one of the objects (such as a cat substituted for a dog) tests the extent to which subjects remember the identity of the object that originally appeared. In yet another test, subjects are shown a distractor that is changed from the original by spatial rearrangement of two objects. To the extent that subjects can tell that such distractors are unlike the original, they can be said to retain information about the objects' locations.

The results of these studies indicated that subjects could use schematic knowledge about scenes to encode certain aspects of meaningful pictures but not others. For one thing, they remembered information about the relative locations of objects and their identities better when those objects were depicted in meaningful, rather than disorganized, scenes. On the other hand, descriptive information about the particular features of objects was remembered no better when the scenes were meaningful. Thus, it seems that a classroom schema may indicate where a pupil usually is relative to a teacher (leading to superior retention of location information in a meaningful scene), but it apparently does not specify the particular features of the pupil. This agrees with our intuition about what prototypical features of scenes might be.

We shall return to the concept of a schema in Chapter 8; for the present, it is the evidence that such LTM information is applied at all when pictures are encoded that is important. This is a form of elaborative encoding, and it supports the idea that elaborative rehearsal of visual stimuli does occur. The data of Mandler et al. indicate that meaningful elaboration enhances the retention of certain types of visual information much as it enhances retention of verbal information. Elaborating a collection of objects by integrating it into the unit "classroom scene" is not so different from encoding a collection of words like *bread, bake, heat, yeast* through knowledge of their meaningful relationships to the concept *making bread*. We shall see another example of elaborative encoding of visual stimuli in Chapter 12, where we will find that experienced chess players seem to remember meaningful configurations of chess pieces by interpreting them with respect to the game.

MENTAL IMAGES: LIKE INTERNAL PICTURES?

We have considered evidence that STM can retain information about visual stimuli in a manner that conveys physical properties. Studies of mental rotation and image scanning suggest further that visual STM codes are processed analogously to physically present objects. The nature of these codes is much contested in cognitive psychology. They have been called *mental images*, a label suggesting that they are like internal copies of pictures. The contention focuses on just how picturelike visual codes really are.

There are arguments against the idea that short-term visual codes are exact copies of pictures we see in the real world (see Pylyshyn, 1973). One says that since visual codes can be generated from information in LTM, they can only have as much detail as is stored there. For example, if I show you a picture of a zebra and then, at a later time, ask you to form a mental image of it, you might think you could generate a very clear one. However, it is doubtful that you would have generated it in such detail that you could count the stripes. Mental images are assumed to be fuzzy, relatively incomplete representations of real objects; they may have gaps and holes. They must be more like the products of pattern recognition—what we perceive about an object—than the object itself.

Psychologists also debate whether mental images are internally represented as some sort of spacelike entity or whether they are represented in an abstract form that does not resemble space at all. What does it mean to be "spacelike," as the first alternative proposes? One commonly cited characteristic of space is that it is continuous. For example, a map represents not only the locations of cities but also the space between them. Such a representation, which conveys the intermediate locations as well as the cities themselves, is called an *analogue* representation. An analogue representation of a spatial entity is, in this sense, analogous to space itself. For another example, the usual clock face with hands might be said to represent time in an analogue fashion because the hands move continuously, forming a new position for each reasonably measurable instant of time. In contrast, consider the digital clock with numbers that pop into position instead of hands. The numbers are a discrete representation of time, changing relatively slowly and leaving gaps betwen successive digits. Moreover, the digital clock provides an abstract representation of time that can only be understood through knowledge of digit symbols; there is no change in the configuration of the display as time passes. In contrast, the clock with hands provides a more concrete analogy, portraying the passage of time by the passage of hands over space.

In theories of memory, the principal alternative to a spacelike representation is called a *propositional* code. Such a code is like a digital clock in that it adequately represents the corresponding stimulus, but it does not do so by being analogous to it. It is more abstract than a picture, and it is not continuous, but discrete. For example, the propositional representation of two points in space might convey, "There is a point 1 at location x_1, y_1; there is a point 2 at location x_2, y_2." It would indicate the locations of the points, but it would not represent the space in between. If asked to compute the distance between the points, the user of this propositional representation would apply a formula for computing distance from the coordinates of two points, whereas the user of an analogue representation would measure the space between the points.

As we shall see in subsequent chapters, propositional representations have often been theorized to represent nonvisual information in memory. If they can describe visual objects and events as well, only one form of mental representation need be postulated. This would be an advantage, allowing memory theorists to integrate their ideas about visual and nonvisual codes. Theorists who advocate propositional representations have therefore pointed out that visual codes need not look like pictures in order to represent visual properties, and they have attempted to adequately account for data like those suggesting spacelike codes with propositionally based models.

For example, Anderson (1978) and Palmer (1975) have suggested that a propositional model can account for the data of Shepard and associates suggesting mental rotation. They argue that it is not necessary to assume that images are rotating in memory like physical objects; the propositional model simply computes the changes in the object that would occur if it were rotating, rather than directly rotating it. If it computes the changes in small steps, it would take longer to compute a rotation the more degrees it involved, which would produce the usual rotation data. This representation would be similar to a digital clock, which, moving minute by minute, takes longer to compute ten minutes of time than five.

If both picturelike images and more abstract representations like propositions can account for the data on rotation and scanning we have discussed, the implications of these data for the structure of visual codes become less important than their implications for the content those codes provide. What studies of visual coding in STM do tell us is that a great deal of information about the visual appearance of items can be maintained and processed in STM. Moreover, at least some of the mental processes that act on visual codes appear to be analogue, in the sense that they convey intermediate states that objects would go through when similar processing occurred in the physical world.

The questions we have raised about visual codes in STM will recur when we discuss the nature of coding in LTM. As we shall see, when the controversy about imagery is carried over to LTM, the question also arises as to whether visual information is separated from verbal information in permanent storage.

In this chapter we have stressed similarities rather than differences between immediate processing of visual and verbal items. We have seen that such concepts as limited capacity for storage, working memory, and elaborative rehearsal apply to both types of codes. At the same time, however, we have made a distinction between these two aspects of STM on a coding basis. That is, we have assumed that information can be represented in STM in terms of its visual properties as well as its acoustic ones. On this basis, then, we maintain a separation between the two aspects of STM, regardless of their commonalities.

8

Long-Term Memory: Structure and Processing of Knowledge

Long-term memory, we have said, stores our knowledge of the world. It is material in LTM that enables us to recall events, solve problems, recognize patterns; in short, to think. All the knowledge that underlies human cognitive abilities is stored in LTM.

Some aspects of LTM have been mentioned in previous chapters. We know that abstract representations of patterns are stored in LTM, and that these representations can be matched with incoming stimuli. We have seen that information can be chunked with the help of various rules— rules of spelling, rules for recoding digit series, rules of English syntax—all stored in LTM. We have seen that word meanings and facts are stored in LTM. The Peterson and Peterson (1959) experiment on STM forgetting made use of the rules for arithmetic that are stored in LTM. Who wrote *Macbeth?* The answer is probably in your LTM. If John runs faster than Mary, and Sally runs faster than John, who runs fastest? As you answer the question, you are working with information in LTM. The sheer amount of information in LTM is astounding.

Given the quantity of information in LTM, it seems surprising that we can use it with such facility. When you attempt to recall who wrote *Macbeth*, for example, you do not have trouble finding the answer among all the other data in memory. Somehow, the nature of LTM makes rapid retrieval possible. As we shall see, information seems to be arranged in LTM in a very orderly fashion. Facts are connected to other facts in a nonrandom way; one word is connected to other words related in meaning. Thus, when you recall that Shakespeare wrote *Macbeth*, you may also recall others of his plays without laborious searching.

SEMANTIC AND EPISODIC MEMORY

Long-term memory may seem complex already, but in fact it has been suggested that we should talk about two LTMs instead of just one. Tulving (1972) proposed a distinction between *semantic* and *episodic* LTM. Both memories store information for relatively long periods, but they differ in the kinds of information stored.

The reason for this distinction may become clearer if we consider a typical experiment used to study LTM. Suppose we give a subject a list of 20 words, followed by a retention interval of an hour or so, and then a recall test. Suppose that one of the words in the list is *table*. When the subject encodes the list into LTM, is it true that the word *table* is being stored? The subject certainly had knowledge about *table* in LTM before the word list was presented. Instead, what is encoded and stored is some new knowledge like, "On my list in an experiment was the word *table*." The prior knowledge about the word *table* is what Tulving means by semantic knowledge; the concept of a table will remain the same in LTM whether it is studied in a list or not. Semantic information does not depend on such conditions of occurrence. On the other hand, the knowledge that table was studied in a list is entered into episodic memory, because it is an "episode" in the life of the subject. It is specific to a context, that of the experiment. Episodic information is "autobiographical"; it does convey conditions of occurrence.

It is semantic memory that holds all the information we need in order to use language. It includes not only words and the symbols for them, their meaning and their referents (what they represent), but also the rules for manipulating them. Semantic memory holds such things as the rules of English grammar, chemical formulas, rules for adding and multiplying, knowledge that autumn follows summer—facts that do not depend on a particular time or place, but are just facts. Episodic memory, in contrast, holds temporally coded information and events, information about how things appeared and when they occurred. It is our memory for personal history, such as "I broke my leg in the winter of 1970." It stores things that depend on context—"It is not every night that I have fish for dinner, but I had it last night."

In addition to differences in what they store, semantic and episodic memories are assumed to differ in their susceptibility to forgetting. Information in episodic memory can become inaccessible rather easily, for new information is constantly coming in. When you retrieve something from either memory—for example, you multiply 3×4 (which uses information from semantic memory) or recall what you did last summer (information in episodic memory)—the actual act of retrieving is itself an event. As such, it must be entered into episodic memory, and you will store the knowledge that you multiplied 3×4 or that you recalled what you did last summer. Thus, episodic memory is in a constant state of change, and information there is often transformed or made unretrievable. Semantic memory probably changes much less often. It is not affected by the act of retrieval, and information in it is more likely to stay there.

Tulving's distinction has important implications for the use of word lists to study memory. As we have seen, experiments of this sort are studying episodic, rather than semantic, LTM. But experiments with lists form the bulk of memory research from the time of Ebbinghaus to the time of Tulving's distinction! The study of semantic memory has been relatively neglected.

Only in the last decade or so has semantic memory become the focus of a great deal of research. Much of that research has concerned the structure of LTM, that is, the manner or format in which information is stored over a lifetime. Researchers have also studied the way in which that information is processed: how knowledge about the meaning of concepts is retrieved and utilized in a variety of experimental tasks. In the remainder of this chapter, we shall consider some of these investigations. In particular, we will discuss some of the models, or theories, of LTM knowledge and its structure that have been proposed. We will also discuss the experimental tests of these models and the basic facts they have revealed. Our emphasis in this chapter will be on semantic memory, although we will touch on episodic knowledge from time to time.

Psychologists have made extensive use of computer simulations to develop theories about the way people represent and process meaning. In part, this interest has been fueled by computer scientists in the area of "artificial intelligence" or AI. The field of AI attempts to develop computer programs that are "intelligent," capable of complex information-processing activities, such as assigning meaning to and utilizing language. In order to develop such capacities in a computer, it becomes necessary to provide it with extensive knowledge about the world, so that it knows what linguistic utterances refer to and can evaluate them. The problem of the best way to store this knowledge for effective use has led workers in AI to become interested in the representation of knowledge. This interest is shared by psychologists, and the two fields have worked on problems in semantics with great mutual interest and cooperation. The fusion of psychologists and computer scientists has even been called a field in its own right and has been given the name *cognitive science*, and the use of the computer to develop and test models of memory has become quite common. We will examine representative examples of two general types of models of LTM, called *network* and *feature* models.

A NETWORK MODEL OF LTM

Constructing a model of LTM is a difficult job. We might start by considering the nature of the information stored there. As we have said that one type of knowledge stored in LTM is the meanings of words, let us begin by considering LTM as a "mental dictionary." Like a real dictionary, it would have a listing of words. On the other hand, we have suggested that LTM is arranged so that items with similar meanings are easily retrieved together. It therefore seems unlikely that LTM would have the alphabetical organization of a dictionary, for this would not be conceptually useful. Consider, for example, aardvark and zebra, both rather unusual animals. They are closely related conceptually, and they might be reported close together if you were asked to list unusual animals, but they would be maximally separated in an alphabetically organized dictionary. In LTM, they would presumably be more closely associated.

One way to represent the meaningful connections between words would be to use associations, or ties, between them. A short tie (or strong association) could be used between closely related words like *apple* and *orange*; there would be a weaker association between *apple* and *walnut*, and perhaps no association at all between *apple* and *hearse*. This sort of model, consisting of interconnected concepts, is called a *network* model of LTM. Network models are not unlike the S-R conception of memory as a bundle of associations. However, these models differ from traditional associationism in some fundamental ways. For one thing, most such models assume that different kinds of associations can be formed; not all associations are the same. This means that when two concepts are associated, the relationship between the two is known; the association is more than a simple bond. This approach has been called *neo-associationism* (Anderson and Bower, 1973).

We have compared LTM to a dictionary organized by meaning rather than alphabetically. However, dictionaries have not only a listing of words, but definitions for them as well. How can we accomplish this in our model? If we look at the dictionary for suggestions, one thing we discover is that the definitions are circular. Suppose we were to look up the meaning of the word *client* in the dictionary. We might find "client, n., (klī'ĕnt) 1. A dependent; one under the protection of another. 2. One who employs the services of any professional, as a lawyer." What we have found is a rather detailed description of the word: *Client* falls in the class noun, meaning it is a "thing." It has more than one meaning, or sense, and we are given the meanings. Suppose, however, we were unfamiliar with English. Unfortunately, the word *client* is defined in terms of other words we would not know, such as *professional*. We might look up *professional*, and find, "adj., of or pertaining to a profession." Not much help. We might look up *lawyer*, and find, in part, ". . . lawyer, the general term, applies to anyone in the profession; attorney and solicitor are strictly applied to the lawyer transacting business for his client." In short, we find a mess: *Client* is defined with the terms *lawyer* and *professional*; *lawyer* is defined with the terms *professional* and *client*; *professional* is defined with the term *lawyer*, and so on. That's what we mean by circular. Words are defined with other words.

The situation is much the same in our model. Since concepts are associated with related concepts, we might find that the client concept is associated with the concepts employ and lawyer; lawyer is tied to client, solicitor, and professional; and so on. In fact, the pattern of connections can be considered to be the definition of client. That is, it is defined by its ties to other concepts, as a dictionary entry is defined by its connections to other entries. Thus, the network provides definitions for concepts by listing and connecting them.

Note that we have been saying that, in the dictionary, words are connected to one another, whereas, in the network, it is concepts rather than words that are interconnected. This distinction between words and the concepts they represent is often made in models of LTM. The general knowledge about concepts is assumed to reside in semantic memory. The words are just arbitrary labels for the concepts, so they are held in a separate part of memory, called the *lexi-*

con (another term for dictionary). Each word is connected to its concept; however, it is the concepts themselves that are represented in meaningful ways in LTM.

Quillian's TLC

We have come up with a network model of LTM that is based on one developed by Quillian (1969; Collins and Quillian, 1969) called TLC (for *Teachable Language Comprehender*). It was the first attempt to use a network structure for a detailed model of LTM. Quillian's model attempted to simulate the ability of a person to comprehend and use language in a natural way. It was embodied in a computer program, and we might think of it as an attempt to enable the computer to "speak." We shall initially consider a simplified version of Quillian's model; later we will discuss an expanded version proposed by Collins and Loftus (1975).

According to Quillian's model, factual information in LTM is made up of three types of structures—units, properties, and pointers. The first two are places, or "nodes," in the LTM network that correspond to information about concepts. The difference between units and properties lies in the kinds of concepts they represent. A unit is a structure that corresponds to an object, event, or idea; things that in English would be represented by nouns or noun phrases, or— if sufficiently complex—even sentences. Essentially, a unit represents "thingness." (Examples of units include the concepts *dog*, *America*, *father*, *beautiful weather*, *good vibes*, and so on.) In contrast, a property is a structure that tells about a unit; in English grammar it would correspond to the predicate of a sentence, or an adjective, adverb, and so on. (Examples would include *solid*, *graceful*, *quickly*, and *loves cats*. Keep in mind that although we use English words here as examples, units and properties are more abstract structures than words. They are the LTM entries that correspond to these words, not the words themselves. However, using the English term is a convenient way to refer to the unit or property in LTM.)

In order to see how pointers, together with units and properties, form the structure of LTM, it will be useful to refer to Figure 8.1, where we find the structure in memory corresponding to just one concept, that of the word *client*. Thus, the figure depicts just one tiny portion of LTM. We can see from the figure that the word *client* is external to the LTM network structure; it resides outside the network in the lexicon. However, it points to the place in the network that corresponds to the word *client*. That place is the unit for *client*.

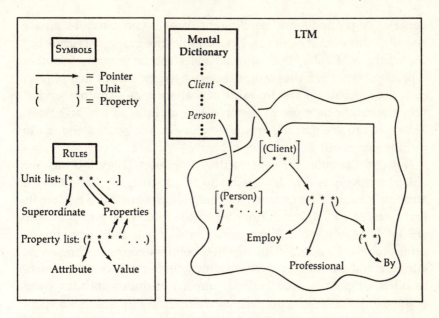

Figure 8.1 Information in TLC's memory corresponding to the concept *Client*. [After Quillian, *Communications of the ACM*, Vol. 12, August 1969. Copyright 1969, Association for Computing Machinery, Inc. Reprinted by permission.]

The association between the word *client* and the unit *client* is called a *pointer*. Essentially, pointers are TLC's associations. They serve to associate lexical labels with concepts in LTM, and they also associate units and properties inside the LTM network with one another. In doing so, they serve to define those units and properties; in fact, definitions correspond to the patterns of associations.

According to the TLC model, the nature of units and properties is described by a small number of rules. Let us look at the rules for making up a unit (see Figure 8.1). They say that a unit consists of an ordered list of pointers. The first pointer of the unit must point to a second unit—specifically, the immediate superordinate of the first unit. (For example, in the unit for *client*, the first pointer points at the unit corresponding to *person*, because person is a concept that includes *client*. In fact, it is the immediate superset of *client*—the smallest higher-order category that includes the category *client*.) The remaining pointers of the unit point to properties. There can be any number of such pointers. In the present example, however, we cite only one; it goes to a property called *employs professional*.

Like units, properties consist of ordered lists of pointers. To see what they point to, we must first consider the nature of properties in general. A property can be thought of as some attribute plus a specific value of that attribute. For example, the property *is white* has the attribute of color; the value of that attribute is white. Another type of property is a prepositional phrase like *on hill*. In that phrase, *on* is the attribute; *hill* is the value of that attribute. Another kind of property might be more like a predicate, such as *throws basketballs*. Thus, we can see that the attribute-value form is general enough to include just about any kind of property.

Now, to the rules for constructing properties. They include two obligatory pointers. The first points to an attribute; the second to the attribute's value. The property of client shown in Figure 8.1 has its first pointer to *employs* (attribute); its second to *professional* (the value). Thus, we see that a property of clients is that they employ professionals. In addition to the two pointers corresponding to its attribute and value, a property can include any number of pointers to other properties. Our current property includes such an extra pointer. It points to the property *by client*. Thus, we see that a client is a person who employs a professional; a professional is employed by a client. We could easily expand Figure 8.1 so that it filled this book. We would show the properties of the unit *person* and the properties of the units and properties involved in its definition. *Person* might include *living thing* in its definition; think of all the pointers it would take to define that, and to define the things they point to.

The structure that evolves is a huge interconnected set of concepts. They are of two types, units and properties, and the pattern of interconnections serves to give them meaning. Units are defined by other units and properties; properties are defined by other properties and units. It should also be noted, although the TLC model does not make it specific, that concepts must also be defined by their connections to the world through the sensory system. LTM cannot be totally self-contained. For example, what good would it do to define a concept like *white* by its relationships with such concepts as hospitals, daisies, most bedsheets, hats worn by "good guys," and so on, unless we had a memory of seeing it? Thus, ultimately, the models of LTM must explain how it interacts with the world, as well as how its internal parts are interrelated.

In summary, Quillian's model of LTM depicts a vast associated network. What is associated are concepts—ideas like *client* or *having color*, or acting in various ways. What ties them together are pointers, which are essentially associations. These associations differ from the traditional S–R bonds in that there are distinct types of associations: The superordinate association, the property association, the attribute association, and the value association. The depiction of LTM as a set of locations connected by labeled associations is the fundamental characteristic of network models of LTM.

The associationistic structure proposed for LTM is only part of the picture. A model of LTM would not go far with structure alone. In order to simulate human behavior, or make predictions about experimental data pertaining to semantic memory (which we shall discuss shortly), a model must also stipulate *processes*. Processes act on the structure and work with it to encode, store, and retrieve information.

It is necessary to explain, for example, how TLC acquires new information, comprehends linguistic inputs (which is essential for its acquisition of new information), and answers questions. The most important process used in these tasks is called the *intersection search*. Suppose TLC is trying to comprehend a sentence that we give it as input, such as *A wolf can bite*. In the sentence, certain concepts are named (such as *wolf* and *bite*). The search process is simultaneously activated in LTM at the location of each concept named, then proceeds outward from those concepts along the pointers or paths leading from them. Each time a pointer leads the search to a new concept, that concept is given a mark to indicate it has been passed in the search and from what concept it was reached. At some point, it is probable that a pathway being followed will lead to a concept that has already been marked (that is, has been reached previously in the search). At that point, we have an intersection. Finding an intersection means that the same point (the intersection) has been reached from two concepts. Thus, it indicates the two concepts are related. The intersection is then evaluated. That is, by checking the marker at the point and tracing back the steps leading to the intersection, the process determines just which concepts intersected and how those concepts are related. If the relation between the concepts in LTM is compatible with the relation in the input sentence, the sentence can be said to be comprehended.

The TLC intersection search can be illustrated with the aid of Figure 8.2, which shows a portion of the LTM network (in a somewhat neater form than Figure 8.1, with units and properties labeled), including the concepts of certain animals and their properties. Suppose we give TLC a sentence like *A canary is a fish*. The search process will originate in the network at *canary* and *fish*. From *canary*, the concepts *bird*, *sing*, and *yellow* will be marked. From *fish*, the concepts will include *fins*, *swim*, and *animal*. Finally, when the search emanating from *canary* hits the concept *animal*, it will find a marker

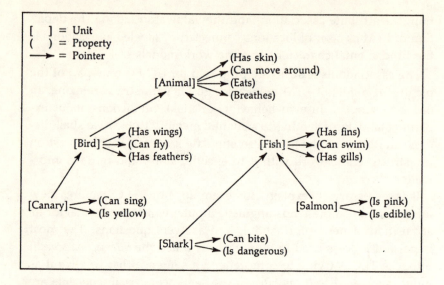

Figure 8.2 Portion of a hierarchy in TLC's memory, showing relationships among the units and properties within the category *Animal*. [After Collins and Quillian, 1969.]

trom *fish* there. By tracing back along the paths that led to *animal*, the relationship between *fish* and *canary* will be found. It is not compatible with the relationship in the sentence, which says *a canary is a fish*. However, if the sentence said that *canary is related to fish*, it would be verified. Similarly, the search could verify that *a canary has skin* (by finding the path from *canary* to *bird*, *bird* to *animal*, and *animal* to *skin*), or find that *a canary can fly* (from the path saying *a canary is a bird*, a bird *can fly*).

SEMANTIC MEMORY DATA

Having introduced a model for LTM that depicts it as a network of interconnected concepts, we must ask how well the model performs. In order to answer this question, we must first consider some basic data from experiments on semantic memory, for TLC, or any model, is evaluated according to its ability to account for the way people actually use their semantic memory in experimental tasks.

In general, research on semantic memory tries to tap nonepisodic knowledge, knowledge that exists independently of the time or place it was acquired. We know that one example of this kind of knowledge is word definitions. Almost everyone knows that *A canary is a bird* and that *All diamonds are stones*. It is not surprising, then, that word definitions have served as a source of many experiments investigating semantic memory. One of the most commonly used research procedures is the sentence-verification task. A subject is given a sentence and asked whether it is true or false. For example, the sentence might be *A canary is a bird* or *A canary is a fish*. Not surprisingly, subjects can perform such sentence-verification tasks with very few errors. The dependent variable in the task is reaction time (RT), usually the time between presentation of the sentence and the subject's response.

The type of sentence commonly used in verification tasks has the form, *A subject (S) is a predicate (P)*. Such sentences were used by Collins and Quillian (1969) to test the TLC model. The variable of particular interest to them concerned the relationship between the S and P words, in terms of the LTM structure described by TLC. Suppose, for example, that the S word in a sentence is *canary*, and the P word is *bird*, *animal*, or *living thing*. We know that, in LTM as depicted by Quillian's model, a concept is connected by a single pointer to its immediate superordinate. The superordinate is connected to its superordinate, and so on. This means that *canary* is separated from *bird* (its immediate superordinate) by one pointer; from *animal* (the superordinate of *bird*) by two pointers (connecting *canary* to *bird*, and *bird* to *animal*); and from *living things* by three pointers (*canary* to *bird*, *bird* to *animal*, *animal* to *living thing*). We know, too, that TLC uses a process called intersection search to verify sentences, and the search process acts by following pathways from words in the sentence, looking for connections between them. Assuming that following each pointer in the pathway takes about the same amount of time, it should take more time to follow the three pointers connecting *canary* to *living thing* than to follow the two pointers connecting *canary* to *animal*, which would take more time than to follow the one pointer connecting *canary* to *bird*. In short, the depiction of LTM proposed by Quillian makes a prediction about RT in the sentence-verification task: The RT measure should be greater, the greater the number of concepts separating the S and P words in the network.

Collins and Quillian (1969) found that this prediction was confirmed in sentence-verification tasks. That is, RT was greater for sentences of the type *A canary is an animal* than for those of the type *A canary is a bird*. And the RT for sentences like *A canary is a living thing* was the greatest of all. This phenomenon has been called the *semantic distance effect*, for it shows that verification RT increases with the distance between the S and P terms, as measured in semantic hierarchies like that depicted in Figure 8.2.

The TLC model is supported by the semantic-distance data just described. However, the version of the model we have discussed runs into problems with other data from semantic-memory experiments. One finding comes from sentence-verification tasks where a variable called *typicality* is manipulated. Typicality refers to how good an example of its superordinate category a concept seems to be; for example, how typical *canary* is of *birds*. To construct measures of typicality, subjects can be given a set of word pairs, each consisting of a category name (like *bird*) and an instance of the category (like *canary*). The subjects are asked to rate how typical the instance is of the category or how closely related the two words are (Rips, Shoben, and Smith, 1973; Rosch, 1973). The various instances of a category are found to be quite different in typicality. For example, a robin is a far more typical bird than a chicken.

Consider the prediction TLC might make about the effects of the typicality of the S word, relative to the P, in a sentence-verification task. For example, suppose we measured RT to say "true" to two sentences: (1) *A robin is a bird*. (2) *A chicken is a bird*. According to TLC as we have described it, RT depends only on the number of pointers separating the S and P words in LTM. Since both *robin* and *chicken* are separated from *bird* by a single pointer, RT should be the same for both. However, RT is actually found to be less for the *robin-bird* sentence than for the *chicken-bird* sentence. And, in general, RT is less the greater the typicality (or relatedness) of the S word relative to the P category.

Another problem with the TLC model comes from reversals of the predicted semantic-distance effects. Consider the following example (Rips et al., 1973). Given the three words *bear*, *mammal*, and *animal*, we would say that *mammal* is the superordinate of *bear*, and *animal* is the superordinate of *mammal*. Thus, more pointers should separate *bear* and *animal* in LTM than separate *bear* and *mammal*. We would predict from TLC, then, that RT should be greater for the sentence, *A bear is an animal* than for *A bear is a mammal*. However, the first sentence is actually verified faster. This result is inconsistent with our prediction; yet it is consistent with the effects of typicality, where sentence-verification RT was found to decrease as the judged relatedness of the S and P words increased. The relatedness of *animal* and *bear* is judged to be greater than the relatedness of *mammal* and *bear*, and RT is less for the sentence with the more related S and P words.

Given results like these, it seems that the relatedness of the S and P words in a sentence is a better predictor of the verification time for that sentence than distance in the TLC hierarchy. Relatedness is found to facilitate RT for true responses: The more related the S and P words, the faster subjects respond "true." This is called the *positive relatedness effect*, because it applies to positive (true) sentences. But relatedness is also found to affect RT to negative (false) sentences, such as *A canary is a fish*. The more related the S and P words are in such untrue sentences, the longer subjects take to say "false." That is, the negative relatedness effect is the reverse of the positive; relatedness inhibits, rather than facilitates, sentence falsification. For example, subjects find it more difficult to determine that *A tree is an animal* (both are living) is false than to determine that *A diamond is an animal* is false.

A SEMANTIC FEATURE MODEL OF LTM

If semantic distance as defined by TLC does not provide an adequate account of the data we have described, we must turn to alternatives. One model that can account for such relatedness effects, called the *semantic feature* model, is proposed by Smith, Rips, and Shoben (Rips et al., 1973; Smith, Shoben, and Rips, 1974). The feature model suggests that a concept is defined not by a network, or pattern of connections to other concepts, but by a set, or collection, of features. These features are like the properties of the TLC model in that they describe attributes of an object. For example, the concept *bird* can be considered to have such features as *has wings*, *can fly*, *lays eggs*, and so on. The semantic features of a concept combine to provide its meaning.

The featural approach to the meanings of concepts is not new, either to linguists or psychologists (for example, Katz and Fodor, 1973; Miller, 1972; Osgood, 1952). However, the model of Smith, Shoben, and Rips is novel in the assumptions it makes about the nature of these features and in the way it relates the assumptions to the data of semantic-memory research. In addition, Smith, Shoben, and Rips have attempted to provide evidence for the feature idea.

This attempt began with the collecting of relatedness ratings for sets of concepts. Rips et al. (1973) asked subjects to indicate how closely related each of several instances (*chicken*, *sparrow*, etc.) was to its category name (*bird*) and to other instances of the category. They then translated those ratings into distances, *not* measured by steps in a hierarchy like TLC's, but rather distances in a "semantic space." This was accomplished by the use of computerized "multidimensional scaling" methods. In general, these methods take estimates of the similarity between members of some set and then describe an arrangement for the members in a hypothetical multidimensional space, so that the distance between items in the space is greater, the less similar they were originally estimated to be.

In the Rips et al. study, subjects' ratings of the relatedness between concepts were converted to a representation of the concepts as points in a space, where the closer the concepts, the more similar their meanings had been rated. And what is most important for evaluating the featural model, the dimensions of the space were indicative of the underlying mental basis on which the ratings were made. To make this point clearer, consider Figure 8.3, where the two-dimensional spaces derived from the ratings of *bird* and *mammal* concepts are shown. Rips et al. assume that in making the initial relatedness judgments, subjects were relying on semantic features in LTM. To the extent that two concepts had features in common, they would be judged as related. That means in turn that the dimensions of the derived two-dimensional spaces could serve to indicate the semantic features the subjects used in making the ratings of relatedness. It seems reasonable, looking at the figure, to give the horizontal axis the name *size*. In the bird space, hawk and eagle, the large birds, are at one end of that dimension, and small birds like robins are at the other. In the mammal space, the large mammals like deer and bear are at one end of the horizontal dimension, and mouse is at the other. The vertical dimension in both spaces can be called something like *predacity*—the extent to which the animals prey on others. Wild mammals and farm animals are at opposite ends of this dimension in the mammal space; predatory birds are separated from tame birds in the bird space. Since the two spaces were derived independently, the consistency of the dimensions is remarkable, and it supports the idea that the dimensions represent some consistent basis for relatedness. In this case, judgments of relatedness seem based on semantic features related to size and predacity.

The feature model has been shown to provide a good account of the relatedness effects on sentence verification that we have described. In order to understand how it does so, we must consider the assumptions the model makes about the way sentences are verified. Essentially, the model assumes that when presented with a sentence of the form *An S is a P*, a subject compares the features of the S and P concepts and determines how similar they are. If they are found to match, a decision can be made that the sentence is true; the S concept is a member of the P category. If they are found not to match, a decision is made that the sentence is false. It is further

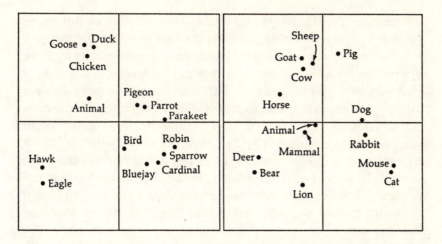

Figure 8.3 Two-dimensional spaces derived from subjects' ratings of the relatedness of members of the categories *Birds* (*left*) and *Mammals* (*right*). [From Rips, Shoben, and Smith, 1973.]

assumed that the speed with which these decisions are made depends on the degree of similarity. When the S and P terms have many features in common and the to-be-verified sentence is true, the featural overlap will produce a relatively fast positive decision. On the other hand, if the S and P terms have features in common but the sentence is false (for example, *A tree is an animal*), the overlap of features will hinder the decision, for it misleadingly suggests that the S concept is in the P category.

In short, the model states that shared features will facilitate "true" responses and inhibit "false" responses in sentence-verification tasks. It can then account for the observed positive and negative relatedness effects through its assumption that relatedness ratings are based on the degree to which concepts share features. That is, the model predicts that the shared features of related concepts will speed up responses to true sentences and slow down those to false sentences.

HOW DIFFERENT ARE THE MODELS?

A principal difference between the feature model and the network model lies in their depiction of categories. A superordinate category in the network model is depicted as being pointed to by all of its members. This means that all instances in the category are removed from the superordinate concept by the same amount—one pointer.

Furthermore, there is never any doubt about whether or not an instance is in a superordinate category; it either points to the category or it does not. Yet, an important implication of such effects as those of typicality on verification RT is that not all instances are equally good members of a category. In fact, many semantic categories are "fuzzy" sets; they do not have clearly defined members (McCloskey and Glucksberg, 1978; Oden, 1977). Kintsch (1974) gives as an example the set of students at the University of Colorado. Is John a student if he is officially enrolled but has not attended classes for months? Is Mary a student if she does attend classes but has not registered? It seems that there are varying degrees of studentdom; it is difficult to find the strict cutoff that says, "These are students; those are not."

The feature approach to meaning makes it possible to deal with the fuzziness of categories, for it allows instances to vary in the extent to which their features match those of their superordinate category. Chickens are not very good birds; they don't fly and come in a rather large size, but they can still be birds by virtue of the bird features they possess. Robins are very good birds because they have more of the desired features.

But features are not the only way to handle the problem of varying degrees of category membership. Collins and Loftus (1975) have described a version of Quillian's TLC that can also do so. In this version, it is assumed that not all connections between nodes in the network are equal. Rather, associated with each pointer is a strength value that indicates how quickly it can be followed in the search process. And the strength reflects relatedness: More typical instances of a category have stronger connections to the category concept, leading to faster verification of typical instances.

Furthermore, Quillian's model assumes that when a sentence is to be verified, an intersection search attempts to find a connection between its named concepts. If it is successful, the connection is evaluated. Collins and Loftus modify the model by assuming that an evaluation that follows a successful intersection search can take several forms. For one thing, if it is determined that one of the intersecting concepts is a superordinate of the other, that determination can produce a decision. But another possible means of evaluating an intersection is very much like the comparison process suggested by Smith et al. (1974): The properties of two intersecting concepts can be compared, and a decision can be reached on that basis. Essentially, Collins and Loftus incorporate the Smith et al. model directly into their network model by assuming that it describes a possible means of evaluation.

Collins and Loftus argue that their network model is superior to that of Smith et al. because it is flexible. Because it allows a feature comparison to underlie at least some semantic decisions, it can account for the same data as the model of Smith et al. But because it allows other bases for decisions as well, it can account for other data. For example, Holyoak and Glass (1975) have shown that, in some cases, relatedness does not have the usual effect of impairing RT for negative responses. One case is the sentence *All fruits are vegetables*, which is falsified faster than *All fruits are flowers*, even though fruits are more related to vegetables than to flowers. The reason is that we have learned that fruits and vegetables are distinct categories, and this knowledge enables us to make a quick negative decision. Collins and Loftus assume that when the knowledge that particular sets are distinct is available, it can be used to make decisions; this is part of the flexibility of decision making. But the Smith et al. model, which postulates a single decision process, cannot readily account for the cases in which the usual negative relatedness effect is reversed.

The Collins-Loftus model also differs somewhat from our description of TLC in its interpretation of intersection search. It depicts the search as an activation that spreads out from processed concepts. When a concept is accessed (for example, when it is named in a sentence-verification task), its location in memory (node) is activated, causing the flow of energy along pathways from that location. (This concept is similar to the activation we discussed in Chapter 4, when we examined automatic and attentional processes.) When a new concept is reached by the spreading activation, *its* node is activated. (This serves the function of what we referred to as marking the node in our initial discussion of TLC.) If a node is a point of intersection, it will receive activation from two different sources. This activation then will combine to excite the intersection still further, and if the combined activation is large enough to pass a criterion, the intersection is then evaluated.

The emphasis on spreading activation from processed concepts in memory is an important aspect of the Collins/Loftus model, for there is evidence that such activation occurs during semantic processing. One source of evidence comes from a procedure called the *lexical decision task*, which requires a subject to decide whether or not a string of letters is a word (for example, *pacon* is not; *pecan* is). The measured variable in this task is RT—the time between the onset of the letter string and the response. Meyer and Schvaneveldt (1971) first used the task and discovered that processing of one word appeared to spread activation to facilitate processing of another word related to the first. They had subjects make decisions about two strings of letters printed one above the other. The subjects were to respond "yes" if both strings were words. Of special interest was the case of a "yes" response where the two words were meaningfully related (for example, one was *bread* and the other *butter*). The RT was faster in this case than on trials where the letter strings were two unrelated words (like *nurse* and *butter*).

The idea of spreading activation can readily be invoked to provide an account of the Meyer and Schvaneveldt finding (Meyer and Schvaneveldt, 1976). First, assume that the subject decides that a letter string is a word through a process like that described in the logogen model of pattern recognition (Chapter 4). That is, the string will be recognized as a given word if the word's logogen— presumably a component of the word's entry in the lexicon—receives enough excitation to pass a certain criterion. If no logogen receives enough excitation, a nonword decision is made. If the first letter string in a Meyer/Schvaneveldt task is a word, its visual features excite its logogen so that the word is recognized. Identification of the word then causes activation to spread from the word's location in the lexicon to the location of the corresponding concept in semantic memory, and thence through the semantic-memory network to the locations of related words (see Figure 8.4). From these locations the activation spreads back to the lexicon to excite the logogens for those words. If the second string of the trial is a word related to the first, its logogen will receive some of this excitation. When processing of the second string begins, it will therefore have a "head start;" that is, the excitation from the first word will reduce the amount of additional activation needed to reach the decision criterion. As a result, less processing of the second string will be required before the response can be made, and it will be made more quickly.

Further evidence for activational effects has been found with a variety of tasks. One is the study of Neely (1977) described in Chapter 4, where subjects made a lexical decision about a string of letters that was presented following a prime word. When the prime word was the name of some category and the letter string was a word that named one of its members, responses appeared to be automatically facilitated. This suggests that processing of the category name (the prime) spread activation to its members. In general, when subjects make two consecutive semantic decisions, RT is facilitated if those decisions are made about related items (e.g., Loftus, 1973; Loftus and Loftus, 1974; Meyer, 1973). This suggests that the initial semantic processing spreads activation, which speeds later processing.

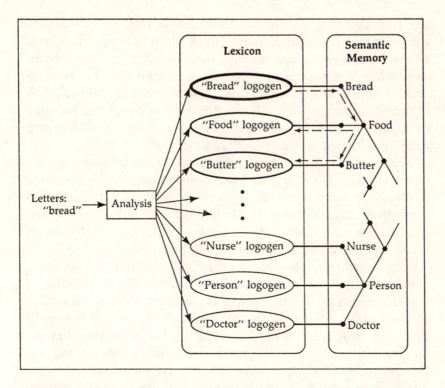

Figure 8.4 Spreading activation in the lexical decision task. When a letter string is presented, it is analyzed and information about its features is sent to logogens. If the string is a word, its logogen's excitation (indicated by darkness of border) passes criterion and activates semantic memory. Activation (broken arrows) spreads through semantic memory to related words, then returns to activate their logogens. [After Meyer and Schvaneveldt, 1976. Copyright 1976 by the American Association for the Advancement of Science.]

The time-course of spreading activation has also been investigated. Fischler and Goodman (1978) used a lexical-decision task in which a prime word preceded the to-be-decided-on letter string by as little as 40 msec. They found that, even at this brief interval, and even though subjects did not have to make any overt decision about the prime word, "yes" responses were faster when the prime and the letter string were related words than when they were unrelated words. This suggests that activation can occur very rapidly, and the speed of its inception supports the idea that it can occur automatically (since, presumably, attention would take longer to apply). Meyer, Schvaneveldt, and Ruddy (1972) also studied changes in activation over time by manipulating the interval between two successive letter strings about which lexical decisions were to be made. The usual advantage (shorter RT) for trials in which the two strings were related words was obtained, but, more importantly, the related-word advantage was found to decrease as the interword interval increased from 0 to 4 seconds. This suggests that the activational effects from processing the first word dissipated over time, reducing its impact on processing of the second word. Such a decline in activation is assumed in the Collins/Loftus model.

Which model provides the best account of semantic memory remains an issue. The idea of semantic features is compatible with the fuzziness of many semantic categories, but the feature model of Smith, Rips, and Shoben seems to be restricted in the range of data to which it applies. The model of Collins and Loftus can account for many different findings because it assumes a variety of decision-making processes; however, it pays for its breadth by becoming rather complicated. Collins and Loftus argue that a complicated model is necessary in order to account for the complexity of semantic processing, but not all theorists agree. The situation is complicated further by a demonstration of Hollan (1975), showing that feature models can be rewritten and represented as network models. This suggests that arguments about which type of model is best are somewhat misplaced, for the differences between them may be minimal. It is possible that the argument about which model is "best" will ultimately hinge on which model has been most adequately simulated by a computer program. Procedures have been better developed for simulating networks, which gives such models an advantage.

PROPOSITIONS AND KNOWLEDGE IN LTM

We have indicated that one way concepts are represented in LTM is as locations, or nodes, in a network, connected to other concepts by a variety of associations. But this depiction tells only part of the story, for we have been restricting our discussion of knowledge in memory to concepts named by single words; yet knowledge concerns more than that. Intuitively, you may feel that the "basic unit" of knowledge is more like a fact than a single concept— *George Washington was the first President of the United States*, rather than *George Washington*. In fact, it has been suggested that the basic unit of knowledge (episodic as well as semantic) is a combination of concepts called a *proposition*.

A proposition may be the basic unit of knowledge, but its exact nature is rather difficult to pin down. Some characteristics of a proposition have been proposed by Anderson (1978). First, a proposition is something like a sentence but more abstract; that is, it is more like the meaning of the sentence than the sentence itself. Two quite distinct sentences might be represented by the same proposition; for example, *John saw Mary*, and *Mary was seen by John*. Therefore, although we might represent propositions with words, we should keep in mind that they are not actually words. Another characteristic of a proposition is that it makes sense to ask whether it is true or false. For example, *The boy ran* is either true or false, but *The boy* is not. A third characteristic is that a proposition is formed according to certain rules. The rules may vary from theorist to theorist, but the important thing is that the proposition adhere to some formal structure.

Propositions may seem like a completely new aspect of LTM, but we have actually seen them before. For example, in the TLC model, the combination of a unit and a property it points to forms a proposition, such as, *A dog has fur*. In general, network models can incorporate propositions as higher order structures, collections of nodes and associations formed according to rules. The network can be considered to contain many mini-networks of propositions. And the propositions, not the single nodes or associations, are the units of factual knowledge.

One network model that places great emphasis on propositional structure is called ACT. It was developed by Anderson (1976), based on an earlier model of Anderson and Bower (1973) called HAM. The rules in ACT for constructing propositions from nodes and associations are quite simple (see Figure 8.5). A proposition combines two nodes, or concepts, with a subject-predicate association. One node is the subject of the proposition; the other is the predicate. The subject can be thought of as what the proposition is about, the predicate as what is known about the subject. Another type of association that can enter into the proposition is the relation-argument association. A relation is generally a verblike entity, and the argument is a concept that is affected by or enters into the relation. When two nodes are connected by a relation-argument association, as Figure 8.5 shows, they form a new node that can serve as either the subject or the predicate of a proposition. The nodes representing propositions can themselves enter into associations, so that higher-order propositions can be formed from combinations of propositions. The result can become quite complex.

Propositions provide a means of representing factual knowledge in a model, but the question arises as to whether people actually represent knowledge in propositional units. This question has been

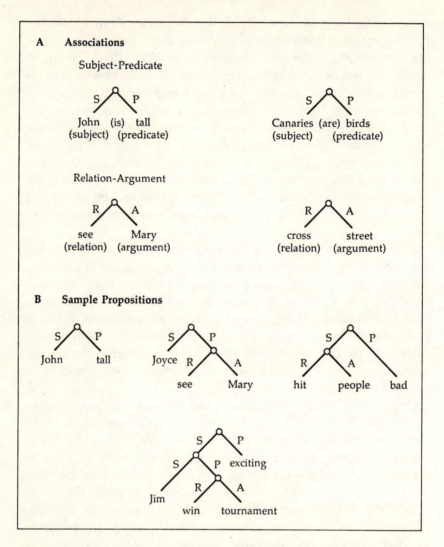

Figure 8.5 Propositions in the ACT model. (A) The two types of associations. (B) Some sample propositions (corresponding to the sentences: John is tall. Joyce sees Mary. Hitting people is bad. Jim's winning the tournament is exciting).

investigated in experiments in which the propositional nature of the stimulus material is varied. Kintsch (1974) has provided a variety of evidence for what he calls the "psychological reality" of propositions. In one study (Kintsch and Keenan, 1973), subjects were given sentences to read that varied in their propositional makeup while remaining about the same in length. For example, one sentence was "Romulus, the legendary founder of Rome, took the women of the Sabine by force." This sentence is made up of four simple propositions (roughly corresponding to: Romulus took women by force; Romulus founded Rome; Romulus was legendary; and, The women were of the Sabine). Another sentence was, "Cleopatra's downfall lay in her foolish trust in the fickle political figures of the Roman world." Although this sentence is about the same length as the first, it contains eight propositions. Kintsch and Keenan found that the more propositions a sentence contained, the longer subjects took to read the sentence. This is consistent with the idea that the propositions, and not single words, correspond to units of comprehension, with each additional proposition adding to comprehension time.

Moreover, patterns of sentence recall reflected the number of propositions in a sentence (Kintsch, 1974). Sentences with two or three propositions were only partially recalled more often than sentences with the same number of words but based on just one proposition. This suggests that a single proposition formed a more integrated sentence than two or three propositions in combination. Results such as these therefore support the idea that a proposition is a basic unit of knowledge.

REPRESENTATION OF VISUAL INFORMATION IN LTM

The concept of propositions occurred previously when we discussed mental images in visual STM. The possibility of images, or picture-like representations, arose when we considered data like those from the mental rotation paradigm and mental map-scanning studies. As an alternative to the idea that the actively processed visual information in these tasks is analogous to a picture, the proposition was introduced.

A similar question arises when long-term storage of visual information is considered. Again, theorists have debated whether visual data have a unique, modality-specific format, or, alternatively, whether visual and nonvisual modes of information in LTM have a common format. The common format that has been suggested most often is propositional.

Long-Term Storage of Visual Information

The possibility of a specialized code for visual information in LTM is suggested in part by experiments indicating that people have a vast capacity for storing visual details. For example, Shepard (1967) showed subjects a set of over 600 colored pictures. He then gave them a recognition test in which they were shown pairs of pictures, one previously seen and one new, and were required to indicate which member of each pair was in the original set. The recognition score was a phenomenal 97 percent, more accurate than retention of words under similar circumstances. Standing, Conezio, and Haber (1970) carried this sort of demonstration even further. They showed subjects 2,560 slides for 10 seconds each. Later, on a recognition test of a subset of those slides, subjects scored 90 percent. With such high recognition levels for pictures relative to words, it has been argued that subjects must have remembered something about pictures other than simple verbal descriptions of them. There must have been some sort of information about pictorial detail that facilitated memory.

A different sort of evidence that pictorial detail is retained in LTM has been provided by Shepard and Chipman (1970). In this case the experiment can be assumed to tap what Tulving (1972) would call semantic information, in contrast to the episodic information tapped by the picture-memory tasks. Shepard and Chipman asked subjects to go through a deck of 105 cards. On each card were the names of two states of the United States, selected from a group of fifteen states. (The 105 cards exhausted all paired combinations of the fifteen states.) The subjects were asked to rank order the 105 cards according to the similarity of the shape of the two states represented on them. Thus, the two states most similar in shape would be ranked first; the two next-most similar ranked second, and so on. The rank ordering is essentially an estimate of the similarity of shape, with lower ranks corresponding to higher similarity. The rank ordering can also be thought of as a distance measure, with low rank order (and therefore high similarity) corresponding to minimal distance between the two states with respect to shape.

Given such similarity measures for the 105 pairs of states, Shepard and Chipman fed that data into a multidimensional scaling program like that used by Rips et al. (1973) to study semantic memory. You may recall that multidimensional scaling takes similarity measures among pairs of items and describes an arrangement of the items in a multidimensional space. Moreover, the dimensions of the resulting space can be used to make inferences about the basis of subjects' similarity ratings. For the fifteen states of the Shepard and Chipman experiment, the two-dimensional solution to the scaling routine based on estimates of shape similarity is shown in Figure 8.6. There seem to be four groupings of states: small, irregular, and wiggly-bordered (*spread across the bottom*); rectangular and straightbordered

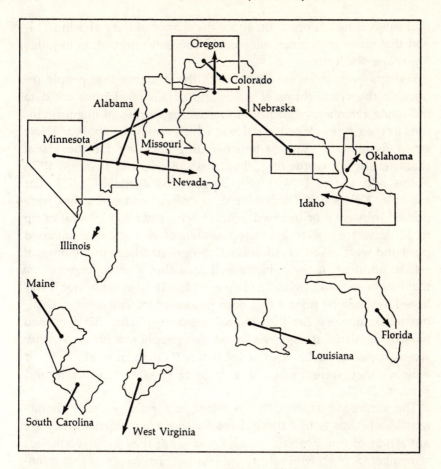

Figure 8.6 Two-dimensional spaces derived from subjects' ratings of how similar states were in shape. Two such spaces are shown, superimposed. One was derived from subjects' ratings when they were given the states' names (points in this space correspond to heads of arrows); the second is derived from subjects' ratings when given outline drawings of the states (points in this space correspond to tails of arrows). The drawing of each state has been centered on its location in the second space, and its name is printed by its location in the first space. [After Shepard and Chipman, 1970.]

(*grouped at the top*); vertically elongated states with irregular shapes (*far left*); and states with a handle, or elbow (*on the right*). Thus, the multidimensional solution reflects the visual properties of the states, even though the subjects were given only their names when they made the ratings of similarity. In fact, as the figure shows, essentially the same solution was obtained when the subjects were shown outlines of the states rather than state names. This finding suggests that subjects had information about the shapes of the states in LTM, and that given the names, they could use that information in judging shape similarity.

Perhaps even more surprising than the evidence that people remember the visual forms of states and details of pictures are data indicating retention of such unimportant properties of linguistic inputs as their typeface or the voice in which they were spoken. There are a number of studies demonstrating memory for the visual characteristics of words (e.g., Hintzman, Block, and Inskeep, 1972; Kolers and Ostry, 1974; Light, Berger, and Bardales, 1975). For example, Kolers and Ostry had subjects read sentences that were printed in normal or inverted print. After a retention interval of up to 32 days, they were given test sentences in normal or inverted print and were asked to indicate which ones had been in the original set. In addition, if the subjects indicated that a sentence was one that had been read originally, they were to say whether or not it was tested in the same print it had been presented in. The subjects demonstrated memory for the original print even after 32 days had passed. Similarly, it has been found that people remember whether words consisted of block or script letters (Hintzman et al., 1972) or whether they were spoken in a male or female voice (Craik and Kirsner, 1974).

The surprising aspect of such retention for the physical characteristics of items is that these characteristics are incidental; they are not a part of the meaning of the items. That they are nevertheless remembered, even without explicit instructions, suggests that retention of physical attributes is a fundamental property of LTM.

Theories of Visual Representations in LTM

Given the evidence that LTM can contain a great deal of information about the physical attributes of items, it is not surprising that the question of how that information is represented has arisen. We can divide theories about physical representations into two general camps. In discussing these theories, we shall primarily consider memory for visual properties, although it is clear that other kinds of physical attributes, such as sounds or smells, are remembered. Many of the points raised in our discussion of visual codes will apply to these other properties as well.

The Dual-Code Theory.   One theory proposes that knowledge about visual events is held in LTM in a different kind of store than that which retains knowledge about verbal information. This theory is called the dual-code, or dual-systems, view, and one of its principal advocates is Paivio (1969; 1971; 1978). Essentially, the theory assumes that LTM includes two systems for representing information (like two LTMs). One, called the *verbal* system, is specialized for knowledge that is usually expressed in words. The other system is nonverbal; it is called *imaginal*. Codes in the imaginal system— *mental images*—are what we termed *analogue* in Chapter 7; that is, they are capable of representing information continuously, as a picture represents space. The two systems are assumed to be strongly connected, so that a concept represented as an image in the imaginal system can be converted to a verbal label in the other system, or vice versa.

However, the systems are also assumed to differ in certain ways. One of the most important differences is that the imaginal system deals with only certain kinds of information; it is specialized for the representation of concrete concepts, those that can readily be pictured or imagined. It would represent concepts like dog or bicycle, for example, but it would not do well with abstract concepts like truth or justice. We might say that the mental dictionary corresponding to imaginal LTM would contain concrete words but not abstract ones.

The dual-code theory easily accounts for the data on visual memory we have cited. It simply assumes that information about pictures is held in the imaginal system and that codes in that system are retained particularly well. As you would expect, this theory is also very compatible with the data cited in Chapter 7, which indicate that actively processed visual information has analogue properties so that it can continuously represent space or transformations over space such as rotation. The dual-code model assumes that what is processed in this case is an analogue image.

The dual-code theory also can account for data from studies comparing memory for lists of concrete and abstract verbal items. Generally, the concrete lists are better remembered. The dual-code model assumes that concrete items can be represented in both the imaginal and the verbal system, whereas abstract items are represented only in the verbal. Two memories are presumably better than one, so the concrete items have an advantage.

There are a number of problems with the dual-code model that offset the advantages mentioned above, however. To begin with, we might ask what mental images "look like." As was mentioned in Chapter 7, it seems unlikely that LTM stores exact copies of visual stimuli. Pylyshyn (1973) has argued that there are many logical difficulties inherent in this idea. For instance, the storage of detailed copies of all the scenes we remember would seem to impose immense demands on LTM's capacity. Another point to consider is how we would use those stored scenes. They would somehow have to be retrieved, which would require reperceiving and analyzing them to "see" what was there. But if the stored pictures have to be reperceived before they are used, they might as well be stored as already perceived entities rather than as copies of visual events. Pylyshyn argues, using points like these, that the images, or whatever we may call them, must exist in memory as analyzed entities rather than as raw sensory material. They cannot look just like the world outside the sensory register but are more like a description of what has been perceived.

Dual-code advocates might readily concede that mental images are not like explicit copies of pictures but instead contain what has been encoded from visual displays after perceptual analysis and pattern recognition. Thus, images would be organized to segregate figures from background, representing objects as units with clearly defined contours (Kosslyn and Pomerantz, 1977). Of course, they would still be analogue representations. This view answers the objections to the idea that imaginal LTM stores templates of viewed scenes, without giving up the idea of imaginal LTM itself.

Even this version of the dual-code theory has been questioned, however. The attempt to equate images with the output of the perceptual process suffers from the fact that we are not really sure just what that output is like. If it is still very like a picture, then many of the problems raised by the concept of mental images as copies of pictures still stand. For example, the processes that retrieve information from such images must be specified (see Kosslyn and Pomerantz, 1977). On the other hand, we could assume that the products of perception are not picturelike at all; that they resemble the LTM codes representing sentences. This assumption would bring us to the unitary view, which proposes that there is a single representational format for pictorial and verbal stimuli.

Unitary Codes for Pictures and Words. One source of experimental evidence for the unitary view of visual and verbal coding consists of studies indicating that meaningful interpretations of pictures, not just the remnants of perception, are stored in LTM. The work of Mandler and associates (see Chapter 7), indicating that scenes are encoded with meaningful schemata, suggests this view. Further support comes from studies of memory for nonsensical pictures.

Such pictures are difficult to interpret without a label, but they become meaningful (and often amusing) when one is supplied. (For a simple example,○○ might be labeled "a pig approaching in a fog.") When subjects are given such pictures without labels, their ability to reproduce them later is relatively poor; supplying the meaningful label improves their memory (Bower, Karlin, and Dueck, 1975). Moreover, when subjects who saw such pictures with meaningful labels take part in a recognition test (that is, they must indicate which of a series of test items are previously seen pictures and which are new, distractor items), they are particularly adept at detecting distractor items that change the meaning of the original, rather than those that change the original item without altering its meaning (Rafnel and Klatzky, 1978). (In terms of the above example,○ ○ would change meaning;○ ○ would not.) This finding suggests that, during the test, subjects did not merely compare the test items with internal copies of the original pictures. Rather, they were comparing what they had previously decided was in the pictures to their current interpretation. Studies like these do not attempt to refute the idea that physical details of pictures are stored, but they emphasize that semantic analysis is highly important to retention of pictorial stimuli, as it is to verbal items.

Another argument for the unitary code comes from a study by Light and Berger (1976), which casts doubt on the idea that incidental properties of words such as their typefaces are retained through mental images. They tested a rather strong version of the imagery notion, which states that if a printed word were stored as an image, the image code should contain all of the word's visual properties. For example, if the word were printed in red capital letters, the resulting image would convey both that the letters were capital and that they were red. This means that if subjects remembered one attribute of a given word, such as its color, they should also remember the other. For if one attribute were remembered, that would indicate an image had been retained, and the image would also convey the second attribute. This prediction was not confirmed, however. When subjects were given a list of words that varied in both case (whether or not they were capitalized) and color, the data indicated that the two attributes were retained independently. (This means that if we know that a subject remembered the case of a given word, we are no better at predicting he or she remembered its color than if we don't know case was retained.) These results argue that storage of one attribute is not tied to storage of another. Thus the stored representation cannot be like a picture of a colored word, which would tie the color of the item to its form by representing the two together. The independent storage of the two attributes observed by Light and Berger is consistent with a more abstract representation such as a proposition, which could as readily describe either attribute alone as both, or neither.

An alternative explanation of these results might be that the words were retained as images but that the attributes of case and color could fade independently from an image. After all, a photograph can represent the form of an item without its color. However, Light and Berger argue against this proposal. If this were true, subjects who were instructed to remember a word's case and its meaning could afford to store the word as a colorless image. But subjects who were instructed to remember a word's color and meaning would have to store an image clear enough to read, so they would also retain information about the word's case. If both types of subjects were then tested on the attribute they were *not* told to remember, the remember-color subjects should do better at remembering case (which was necessarily conveyed by their image) than the remember-case subjects do at remembering color (which could be dropped from their image). Thus the remember-color subjects should do better on an attribute-memory task. This outcome was not observed, however; the two groups performed about equally when asked to recall both case and color. In short, this study offers little support for the idea that the visual attributes of words are retained as images. Presumably, they are held as more abstract representations of the sort that can convey nonvisual attributes as well—in other words, unitary codes.

Theorists who postulate a unitary representation for visual and verbal codes in LTM generally assume that the format is propositional. Within this approach, however, theories vary in the extent to which they distinguish between the propositional representations of visual and nonvisual information. One view, for example, has proposed that there are two types of propositions to represent visual and verbal items (Kieras, 1978). In contrast is the idea that there is but one type of proposition. According to the latter view, one can speak of visual and verbal codes, but the differences between them are minimal, pertaining only to the content of the information they convey. That is, the one-proposition theory states that all propositions convey information about the meaning of items. Sometimes that meaningful information is about an item's physical appearance; sometimes it is not. But even if a proposition conveys physical attributes, it still represents an interpretation of those attributes and is essentially the same as the representation of a sentence about those attributes.

Theorists who do not make a distinction between propositions representing visual and nonvisual inputs must still explain data, like those we considered above, suggesting that visual and nonvisual information are dealt with differently in LTM. One approach is to reinterpret the data so as to minimize the differences between the visual and nonvisual domains. For example, consider the phenomenon of very robust long-term retention of pictures. To counter this evidence for visual/verbal storage differences, it has been argued that studies overestimate the capacity for remembering pictures. For one thing, such studies have usually used recognition tests on which subjects could perform adequately even if they remembered little about the appearance of a picture. The distractor items (new items which the subject is to discriminate from previously seen pictures) are from a different class than the original pictures, which would allow accurate performance if subjects remembered only the concept represented by the picture and not the picture itself. In support of this argument is the finding that picture recognition is not nearly so accurate when items in the originally presented list and distractor items are all drawn from a highly similar pool. When subjects were presented with as few as 14 pictures of snowflakes, for example, their recognition performance was only 36 percent accurate on a test (with snowflake distractors) immediately following presentation (Goldstein and Chance, 1970). This is rather different from the 90 percent or greater accuracy with several hundred pictures observed in other studies.

Another argument that has been offered to explain the generally observed good memory for pictures is that pictures contain more information than their corresponding labels. If part of the information in a picture is forgotten, therefore, it will still be discriminable from distractors on a recognition test because enough other information remains. In contrast, forgetting of part of a word will make it highly similar to other words, leading to recognition errors. If we assume that the extra information in a picture that leads to better memory is stored propositionally, like any other information, this argument can account for high rates of picture recognition within the one-proposition model.

An experiment by Nelson, Metzler, and Reed (1974) offers some support for the one-proposition model by providing evidence that subjects' ability to remember pictures does not necessarily mean they store highly specific visual details about them. Nelson et al.

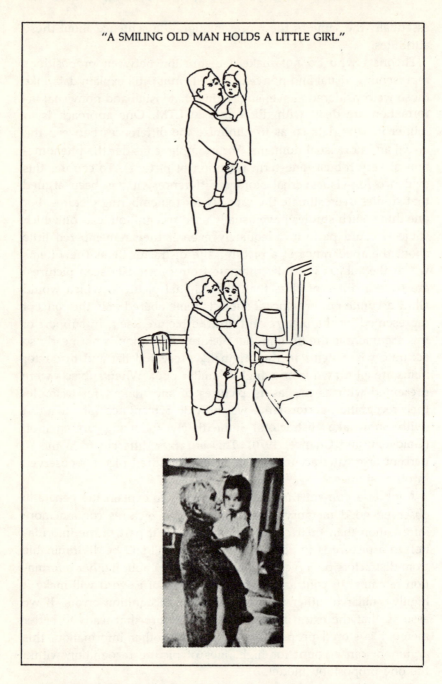

Figure 8.7 Example of an item that can be represented by *(from top to bottom)* a phrase, a drawing with little detail, a detailed drawing, and a photograph. [From Nelson, Metzler, and Reed, 1974. Copyright 1974 by the American Psychological Association. Reprinted by permission.]

constructed four types of stimuli for the same scenes (see Figure 8.7). A given scene was represented by a photograph, a one-phrase description of the photo, a detailed drawing of the photo, and a nondetailed drawing of it. Each subject viewed one of the four types of stimuli and was then given a recognition test, where the stimuli were to be discriminated from distractors not seen before. Nelson et al. found that recognition performance for any pictorial stimuli (photos, detailed drawings, or nondetailed drawings) was better than that for the verbal descriptions; this is the usual pictorial capacity effect. However, the recognition scores for the various types of pictorial stimuli did not differ from each other; that is, amount of detail did not affect recognition. This suggests that the superior memory for pictures is not due to their being stored in LTM as detailed copies, for in that case greater detail should have led to better performance. The fact that recognition was as good for nondetailed pictures as for detailed pictures *is* consistent with the idea that subjects store interpretations of the stimuli, since interpretations could be sufficiently abstract that they would describe nondetailed and detailed pictures equally.

The large capacity of picture memory is not the only phenomenon that one-proposition theorists must explain; another is the superiority of memory for lists of concrete items over memory for abstract item. It has been suggested that the two types of items differ on more than just concreteness. Concrete and abstract words may also differ in complexity or in the number of meanings they have (Anderson and Bower, 1973); sentences made up of concrete words may be more comprehensible than those made up of abstract words (Johnson, Bransford, Nyberg, and Cleary, 1972). These alternative explanations of concreteness effects seem intuitively plausible; however, when experimenters control for differences other than concreteness between such items—for example, by comparing concrete and abstract words rated as equal in meaningfulness—effects of concreteness are not eliminated (Moeser, 1974; Paivio, Yuille, and Rogers, 1969). Concreteness effects have proved rather difficult to explain in terms of other attributes (Kieras, 1978).

The difficulty of showing that the concreteness variable is really due to some other underlying difference between words is a problem for the one-proposition view. Another problem comes from findings related in Chapter 7. When subjects take part in tasks that request them to form mental images, it is found that performance competes for capacity with visual perception. Moreover, the mental images subjects form upon being given such a request show indications of being processed continuously over space—in analogue fashion. For example, the time required for rotating an image varies with the distance in space over which it is to be rotated. These effects are found even when subjects are given a verbal label and generate the images from information in LTM, so that they must reflect the content of visual information stored there.

The problem posed by these findings is how the visual codes they suggest exist in LTM could be conveyed by propositions, especially when those propositions are the same type that convey the meanings of sentences. Consider the picture below, for example.

A verbal interpretation of this picture might be, "It is a square with a dot in the lower left corner and a star in the upper right corner." This description would not convey the distances between the dot and the star. Yet, we could predict from the study of Kosslyn, Ball, and Reiser (1978) that if we taught subjects about the square and then had them form an image of it and mentally scan from one corner to the other, the time required would depend on the actual distance between corners. This would not occur if the only information about the square in their LTM was that conveyed by our interpretation. In short, the idea that visual information in LTM is at an abstract interpreted level seems somewhat at odds with the visual details that information seems to convey.

Evaluation of the Visual Coding Theories

We have considered two general approaches to the question of how visual information is represented in LTM. One emphasizes the differences between visual and nonvisual representation, assuming they are held in dual systems. This model accounts well for our common subjective impression of having images and for data indicating highly accurate and capacious visual memory. The second approach emphasizes the common elements in visual and nonvisual coding; a strong version assumes that a picture is represented much as a verbal description of its contents is stored. This approach accords with the evidence that pictures are stored in an abstract interpreted form.

Which approach is better is a question of some controversy. However, the differences between the two views of visual coding in LTM may not be quite as great as they first appear. Consider first the experimental data. Studies may seem to support first one approach, then the other, but in fact they have served the function of constraining the theories so that they do not make extreme claims. Thus they may move the approaches toward a common middle ground as much as supporting one in favor of the other. For example, the studies showing that semantic interpretations are important to retention of pictures rule out an extreme dual-code view, which proposes that pictures are held as mental templates. And studies demonstrating retention of pictorial detail rule out the possibility that pictures are retained only as simple sentencelike descriptions.

The two views of visual coding may ultimately be reconciled by models that combine attributes of both. For example, to accomodate the idea that LTM stores detailed visual information, it is not necessary to discard the idea that all of the information is propositional. As mentioned previously, the suggestion has been made that two types of propositions exist—one to convey visual detail, the other for semantic interpretation (Kieras, 1978; see also Kosslyn and Schwartz, 1977). Presumably, the two types of propositions would differ not only in content, but also in the rules by which they were formed. The possible relations among concepts in a visual proposition might be different from those in a nonvisual proposition, for example. This sort of model accomodates both similarities and differences in processing pictures and verbal material, for it assumes both types are represented propositionally, yet that the propositions differ.

The idea that dual-code and unitary theories may not be as different as they first appeared has been presented in even stronger form by Anderson (1978). He suggests that both an imaginal and a propositional model can be developed to account for the form of any set of data. Differences in the representational format of information postulated by the models are accomodated by differences in their assumptions about the processes that work with the representations. Thus, choosing one type of model as superior becomes extremely difficult. The choice must be made on the basis of which provides the superior account in other respects, such as which is simpler or more efficient. Anderson's argument suggests that a better goal for cognitive psychologists may be to investigate visual information processing without attempting to determine the nature of the underlying representation. Still, the case is far from closed, and the study of the format as well as the content of visual information in LTM remains a provocative endeavor.

HIGHER-ORDER KNOWLEDGE STRUCTURES

So far, we have considered two levels of meaningful information in LTM. At the more elemental level, there are individual concepts. At another level, concepts are assumed to be associated in configurations called propositions, which we have called basic units of knowledge. Theorists have also suggested that still higher-order units combine propositions pertaining to a common topic. In a network model, for example, propositions about canaries, robins, and seagulls are all connected to a node representing the superordinate concept of birds. Of particular interest are higher-order units that represent general knowledge about some topic; these units have been called *frames* (Minsky, 1975), *scripts* (Schank and Abelson, 1977), or, as we have called them previously, *schemata*.

Perhaps the best way to convey the nature of such a structure is to give examples. One illustration is provided by the work of Schank and Abelson, who have developed a computer program called SAM (for Script Applier Mechanism). SAM is given stories that it is to "understand"; it shows its comprehension by paraphrasing a story, summarizing it, or drawing inferences from it. All this is accomplished by SAM's use of scripts. For example, part of SAM's knowledge includes a "restaurant script," a general depiction of the events that occur in a restaurant. The roles in the script are those of the customer, waiter, cook, cashier, and owner. The "props," the basic items needed to conduct a restaurant scenario, are tables, a menu, food, the check, and money. In the first scene, entering the restaurant, the customer comes in and does such things as looks at the tables, moves to one, and sits down. The next scene, ordering the meal, consists of subscenes: the customer getting the menu (picking it up if it is already on the table or requesting it from the waiter) and then choosing the food, the waiter ordering from the cook, and the cooking. Further scenes describe the general characteristics of eating and exiting.

There are several points to note about the restaurant script that characterize scripts—or as we shall call them, schemata— in general. First, a schema is a fairly general description. In our present example, each particular restaurant event—called an *instantiation* of the restaurant script—would have particular characters, items, and events that would fit into the more general framework of the script. For example, the script provides for a character called the customer; the customer might be instantiated by my friend Jim. Thus, a schema has a fill-in-the-blanks kind of structure; the blanks are filled in when the schema is instantiated. Secondly, a schema provides for the typical events that occur; it is a stereotyped description. Obviously, the restaurant script cannot provide for every restaurant event in detail, for such an event might include incidents that did not fit the script. A third characteristic of a schema is that it can be depicted as a hierarchy of components. That is, it has very general components at one level, which can be broken down into more specific components, these in turn being subdivided into still others, until some final level of specificity is reached. The usual diagram of a schema puts the most general components at the top and the most specific at the bottom (leading, as we noted in Chapter 4, to the top-down/bottom-up distinction). In the restaurant script, for example, the component "Customer orders" can be subdivided into "Waiter brings menu; customer reads menu; customer signals waiter," and so on. Note that a component can itself be thought of as a schema. Signaling the waiter, for example, is a schema with its own components.

SAM uses scripts to infer the cause-and-effect relationship between events. For example, if it is told, "John went into a restaurant and the waiter brought him a menu," it can use the restaurant script to infer that the waiter brought the menu because John was hungry and wanted to order food. Schank and Abelson suggest that people use scripts for the same purposes. Like SAM, we would have more difficulty with, "John went into a forest and the waiter brought him a menu," because there is no obvious way the restaurant script can be made to apply.

The script concept of Schank and Abelson emphasizes higher-order knowledge structures for everyday events. We have seen that a similar concept is invoked as a representation for objects (Chapter 4) and scenes (Chapter 7). Rumelhart (1975) has suggested that people have knowledge structures for still other entities, in particular, stories. He has devised a *story grammar*, a set of rules specifying the general framework or schema for simple stories. A version of his grammar is depicted in simplified form in Figure 8.8A, in the form of *rewrite rules*. (To read such rules, interpret the arrow as "can be rewritten as," and transform the entity on the left so that it is written as the components on the right.) The rules indicate that, like the restaurant script, a story can be subdivided into (rewritten as) a series of components. The major components of a story, as indicated by the first rule, are a goal (that is, a desired state), followed by an episode or a sequence of episodes, followed by a resolution (a state corresponding to the final outcome of the story). Each of these com-

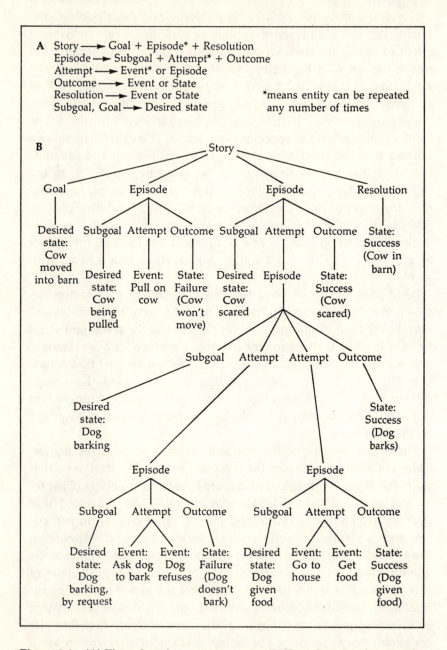

A   Story ⟶ Goal + Episode* + Resolution
Episode ⟶ Subgoal + Attempt* + Outcome
Attempt ⟶ Event* or Episode
Outcome ⟶ Event or State
Resolution ⟶ Event or State   *means entity can be repeated
Subgoal, Goal ⟶ Desired state   any number of times

Figure 8.8   (A) The rules of a story grammar. (B) Tree diagram showing the structure of the farmer story, according to the grammar. [After Thorndyke, 1977.]

ponents can in turn be subdivided according to other rules. For example, the second rule indicates that the components of an episode are a subgoal (to be accomplished on the way to the major goal of the story), an attempt or series of attempts at that subgoal, and an outcome of the attempt or attempts.

In Figure 8.8B, the rules have been applied to the following simple story:

> A farmer had a cow that he wanted to go into his barn. He tried to pull the cow, but it would not move. So the farmer asked his dog to bark and scare the cow into the barn. The dog refused to bark unless it had some food. So the farmer went to his house to get some food. He gave it to the dog. It barked and frightened the cow, which ran into the barn.

The result of the application of the grammar to this story is a "tree" diagram, which shows successive applications of the rewrite rules below one another. For example, the rule for subdividing a story is the first one to be applied, and its components—goal, episodes, and resolution—branch out below the story unit. The rules for subdividing each of these components have in turn been applied, and their components branch out below each of them, and so on until no further breakdown can be accomplished. As a result, the diagram puts general concepts at the top and more specific units below them, and ultimately the branches terminate with the specific events of the farmer story. Essentially, the diagram is a way of describing how this particular story fits into—or instantiates—the general schema described by the rules of grammar.

Thorndyke (1977) conducted a set of studies based on the story grammar of Rumelhart, and his results suggest that people do in fact use such a knowledge structure when they comprehend stories. In one of his experiments, subjects were presented with a story and later asked to recall it. Thorndyke manipulated the extent to which the story fit into the grammar, by constructing different versions of an original, normal story. One version put the main point of the story (the goal of putting the cow in the barn, in the first sentence of our farmer story) at the end; another version had the main point eliminated; another version simply told the story as a set of facts without tying together causes and their effects, and another version had randomly ordered sentences. He found that the more the presented story fit the normal form described by the grammar, the better subjects recalled it. Apparently, when subjects comprehended the story, part of their comprehension process involved fitting the story into the rules of the grammar. Their ability to do so affected their later ability to recall the story. This is similar to the findings of Mandler and her associates described in Chapter 7, where it was proposed that subjects used a scene schema, containing general knowledge about visual configurations (such as a classroom) when they encoded pictures of regular scenes, but could not use such a schema as effectively to encode disorganized scenes.

In another experiment, Thorndyke had subjects learn two stories in sequence. The second story either repeated the structure of the first but used new characters, or repeated the characters of the first but with a new structure. You might intuitively think that, because repetition of the characters means that many words would be the same in the two stories, character repetition would lead to superior recall of the second story. But this is not the case: Recall of the second story was worse if it used the same characters as the first but in a new structure, than if it did not repeat any aspect of the first story. However, recall of the second story *was* facilitated if it repeated the structure of the first. These results indicate that the structure of the story is one of the things subjects learn. In fact, structure appears to be retained independently of the specific characters or actions that fill in that structure, so it can be applied to new characters and actions. This is very consistent with the theory that the general structure of stories is part of our knowledge in LTM.

Whether we call them scripts, frames or schemata, evidence for knowledge structures representing complex events is compelling. These structures are assumed to combine information from many propositions; moreover, they combine the information in a highly organized way. Are these the highest in the hierarchy of knowledge structures in LTM? It seems doubtful. For example, scripts could be combined into still higher order scenarios to produce "macro-scripts" like "A night on the town" (combining theatre and restaurant scripts). The potential for the breadth and complexity of knowledge in LTM seems virtually limitless.

9

Encoding Information into Long-Term Memory

This chapter begins a series on what we might call the topic of re-membering. You may recall from Chapter 1 that in order for infor-mation to be remembered, three things occur. First, the information is encoded—prepared for memory. Second, the encoded informa-tion is held in storage. Finally, the information is retrieved from the memory store. Although we shall treat them somewhat separately, we shall see that these three components of remembering are in-terdependent. For example, the nature of encoding affects the fate of information in storage and its retrievability.

The encoding process is the focus of the current chapter. But we have discussed encoding in previous chapters as well. When we re-ferred to the entry of letters into a visual register, for example, we suggested they were encoded by processes that isolated visual fea-tures and separated figures from background. In reviewing storage in STM, we assumed that items were usually encoded in terms of their acoustic labels. We indicated, too, that encoding of verbal in-formation into STM can be quite complex, involving elaborative de-vices such as chunking.

Encoding in LTM is closely related to the elaborative processes we considered in discussing STM as working memory, processes that incorporate existing information in LTM into the to-be-remem-bered input. These very processes—sometimes called elaborative rehearsal—are assumed to enhance long-term retention and thus to constitute effective encoding devices. In this chapter, we will discuss such elaborative encoding into LTM in detail. We will find that integrating new information with data in LTM is highly important for producing later remembering.

The encoding devices we will discuss in this chapter pertain primarily to preparing information for storage in what Tulving (1972) calls episodic memory, in contrast to the emphasis of the preceding chapter, which was on the structure and processing of semantic knowledge. One reason for the shift of emphasis is that much more is known about the encoding of episodic information. It is episodic information that is tapped in studies using list-learning procedures like free recall. The concept of encoding is also more relevant to episodic memories, for the nature of semantic data—general knowledge about the world and symbolic representations—suggests that we have many exposures to it; that is, there is usually no single incident of encoding. Episodic information, on the other hand, tends to be encoded in a single episode, making it more amenable to experimental study. Of course, semantic information is used when episodes are encoded.

NATURAL-LANGUAGE MEDIATORS

Elaborative encoding in LTM takes many forms. One of the simplest was discussed earlier—the conversion of a nonsense syllable (consonant-vowel-consonant or CVC) to a word, for example, encoding FEL as *fuel*. This is an example of a general category of encoding devices called NLMs, or natural-language mediators. The label NLM simply refers to the fact that the mediating information in LTM that is related to the to-be-remembered item is part of natural language—spelling patterns, word meanings, and so on.

The use of NLMs is certainly not confined to single syllables. Montague, Adams, and Kiess (1966) investigated their use in a procedure called *paired-associate learning*. In this type of task, a subject is given a list of items to remember. Each item consists of two parts, termed the stimulus and the response. The subject is to learn to associate the two parts, so that he or she can recall the response term when presented with the stimulus term. For example, a pair might be DAX–7; when given DAX–?, the subject should respond, "seven."

In the Montague et al. study, subjects were to write down any NLMs they formed while learning a list of paired associates, although they were not required to form them. For example, seeing the pair PAB–LOM, the subject might write down *pablum*. At the time of test, the stimulus terms were shown to the subject, and he or she was to recall for each stimulus not only the response, but also the NLM that had originally been formed with that stimulus (if any). Then the authors analyzed the extent to which the response terms were correctly recalled, separating the paired associates according to whether the subject had originally formed an NLM for a pair or had not and whether he or she remembered the NLM or not. They found that on the average for cases where no NLM was reported during the study of the list, the subject recalled only 6 percent of the response terms correctly. For cases where an NLM was reported, recall jumped considerably—but only if the subject could remember the NLM. On the average, if he or she had used an NLM and forgotten it, recall of the response was at 2 percent; if the NLM was remembered, recall was 73 percent.

Montague et al. also found that more NLMs were used when the paired associates were presented for study at a slow rate (30 seconds per pair) than at a faster rate (15 seconds), and that more NLMs were formed when the CVCs were high in "meaningfulness" than when they were low. The meaningfulness of a CVC (Noble, 1961) refers to the number of associations that are typically given to the CVC in a limited time period by a group of subjects. High *m* (meaningfulness) indicates a large number of associations. A syllable like WIS, for example, might lead to the associations *whiskey, Wisconsin, whisper, whistle,* and so forth; it would be high in meaningfulness. A low-*m* syllable might be something like GOQ. Thus, it seems that the more readily a CVC elicits associated words, the more likely it is to be used in NLM formation in a paired-associate task. And the more time is available to mediate, the more likely an NLM is to be formed. What these results mean, essentially, is that NLM formation takes time and a certain amount of work. It is not automatic or effortless. The subject must think up an NLM for a CVC, and, although this task is made easier if the CVC gives rise to a large number of associations, because there will be several candidates for the NLM, it still takes time.

A more complex NLM that can be used is an entire sentence. Learning of paired associates can be markedly influenced by the use of mediators that convert the pairs into sentences (Bobrow and Bower, 1969; Rohwer, 1966). For example, given the pair *boy–door*, we might mediate by thinking, "The boy is closing the door." If we did so, we would later be able to recall *door*, given *boy*, more readily than if we had not used the sentence mediator.

VISUAL MEDIATORS

A type of mediator that presents somewhat of a contrast with the language-based encoding devices we have been discussing is a visual mediator. Such a mediator can be said to be used when a subject encodes an input stimulus by relating it to visual information in LTM. One context in which this type of mediation has been proposed to occur is in the encoding of "high-imagery" nouns. We have already mentioned one measure that can be associated with a verbal item—meaningfulness. The m-value of a word is directly based on the number of associations given to that word in a free-association task within a fixed amount of time. Thus, the meaningfulness of the word reflects the extent to which it is interconnected with other words. Now, let us define a measure corresponding to how readily an image can be conjured up when a word is given. Subjects were asked by Paivio (1965) to indicate when they had an image for a given word; the image could be a mental picture or even a sound. The speed with which they indicated that an image had been produced was used to formulate an imagery measure, I, for the word. The higher the I value, the more readily a word could be used to produce an image. We might note also that I is highly related to concreteness; that is, the more the word refers to some concrete entity, the higher its I value tends to be. This is certainly not surprising, since we might expect words, like *dog*, that refer to concrete objects to activate information about visual properties in LTM more readily than do abstract words like *thought*.

As was mentioned in Chapter 8, the concreteness of nouns has proved to predict performance in memory tasks (reviewed in Paivio, 1971). In fact, the I-value of a noun has proved to have greater effects on performance in many tasks than has the m-value for the same noun. When lists of items are presented and memory for them is subsequently tested, concrete nouns (high I) lead to better performance than do abstract nouns (low I); this holds for a variety of testing procedures and retention intervals. It seems that the activation of visual information during encoding of a verbal item (which is more likely with concrete items) serves to enhance retention; verbal mediators are not unique in this regard.

More direct evidence for the effectiveness of visual mediation comes from list-learning procedures where subjects are given explicit imagery instructions. Bower (1972b) instructed subjects whose task was to learn noun paired associates to imagine the two nouns in each pair interacting in a mental picture. For example, the pair *dog–bicycle* might be represented as a mental image of a dog riding a bicycle. Other subjects, who were given standard instructions with no mention of images, did only two-thirds as well as the imagery group. Imagery instructions were similarly found to enhance performance in a serial-learning task, where a list of words was to be learned in a fixed order (Delin, 1969). (In this case, the subjects were to use image mediators to unite the first word with the second, then the second with the third, and so on.)

Just why are image mediators so effective? Several explanations have been offered, divided along lines like those that divide theories of visual LTM in general (as described in Chapter 8). According to the dual-code approach, the advantage of imagery is that it provides a code for words in the imaginal system of LTM as well as the verbal system. The imaginal code is assumed to be particularly effective at tying pairs of words together, for it unites them as a picture would. On the other hand, Anderson and Bower (1973) have offered unitary-code arguments for imagery effects. They propose that imagery instructions act like instructions to mediate with sentences; both simply induce subjects to perform elaborative encoding of the items. For present purposes, however, the point of these studies is to demonstrate the effectiveness of encoding verbal items by relating them to visual properties of their referents.

ORGANIZATION IN FREE RECALL

Thus far we have focused on the encoding of individual verbal items or pairs. We discovered that relating an item to LTM facilitates memory. But encoding can occur at a higher level, when many individual items are combined. This type of processing, called *organization*, has been extensively studied in the context of the free-recall task.

First, we must note that under the term *organization* are subsumed all of the encoding processes mentioned above. Whenever subjects act on incoming information to modify it systematically, they can be said to be organizing that information. In this sense, organization can occur at the level of perception. When subjects isolate the figure F from the page around it, they are organizing the visual field; when they group YMCAFBI into YMCA FBI, a process we discussed under chunking, they are organizing; when they think of *Wisconsin* as an NLM for WIS, they are organizing; and so on. In the free-recall procedure, however, we have one of the most natural situations in which to study organizational processes. In free recall, we have: (1)

full access to information in LTM (that is, we are tapping information beyond sensory levels when we recall word lists); (2) freedom to rearrange list words in accordance with organizational tendencies (because it is *free* recall); and (3) usually enough words in the list so that there is ample material to organize. With these conditions, then, organization should be most accessible to our inspection. Usually, we define organization in free recall as occurring when there are *consistent* discrepancies between the order of the list items as presented and their order as recalled. The idea is that such discrepancies arise because the subject is internally modifying (organizing) the input, and this systematically affects how the items are recalled.

Experimenter-Imposed Organization

Quite often, when organization has been studied in free recall, the organization has been manipulated by the experimenter's choice of words to use in the list. Consider, for example, some experiments by Jenkins, Russell, and Mink (Jenkins, Mink, and Russell, 1958; Jenkins and Russell, 1952). These experimenters constructed lists by manipulating the association value of pairs of words in the list. (The association value between two words reflects the number of times subjects give one word in a free-association task when the other word is given as a stimulus. For example, *butterfly* and *moth* are highly associated; *butterfly* and *garden* are less highly associated, and *butterfly* and *book* are nonassociates.) Jenkins and Russell, in one experiment, selected twenty-four pairs of highly associated words, such as *man–woman, table–chair*, and so on. They then separated the pairs, scrambled these words, and presented them in random order as a 48-word free recall list. They found that although the words had been scrambled at presentation, they tended to be unscrambled at recall. That is, words were likely to be reported together if highly associated. Even though we might separate *table* and *chair* by seventeen other words when we construct the list, subjects often report them together at recall. Moreover, Jenkins, Mink, and Russell found that the stronger the association between pairs of words in a free-recall list, the higher the recall score (the percentage of items recalled correctly) and the more likely that associated pairs would be recalled together. Thus, we see that word relationships are reflected both in the recall *score* and in the *manner* of recall. It seems that the subject has organized the list—has modified it in such a way that he or she can take advantage of associated words. We have strong evidence that the list-as-presented is not the list-as-encoded, just as a CVC presented may not lead to a CVC stored, but to an NLM instead.

We have seen that associations among word pairs interspersed in a free-recall list can be reflected in organized recall of the list. We could carry this further than pairs, certainly. We could include *groups* of associated words in our list. One fruitful example of just such an approach is the use of category instances in list generation. By that is meant the use of several words from each of several classes in the list. For example, we could take several members of the category *animal: dog, cat, bird, fish,* etc., or several members of some of those subcategories, such as *fish: trout, tuna, carp, smelt, sardine,* etc., and scramble them with members of other categories to make a list. We would find that when it is used in a free-recall list, categorical structure does have an effect much like the effect of associated word pairs.

Bousfield (1951; 1953) used categorical structure in free recall as follows. In one experiment, he used four categories to make up his list. From each, he took 15 words, to make a list of 60 words in all. The words were presented in random order for free recall. Bousfield found what he called "categorical clustering"—the tendency of subjects to recall members of the same category together, even when they were not originally presented together. This is, of course, much like the finding of Jenkins and Russell that highly associated pairs of words are recalled together, or clustered.

Presumably, words that are all members of a given category will also tend to be associated with one another. We could therefore ask whether categorical clustering is in any way different from the associative clustering of the Jenkins, Russell, and Mink experiments. The answer seems to be yes: The effects of categorical relationships can be distinguished from the effects of associative relatedness. Evidence comes from the finding that when a list is composed of words that have categorical relationships but that are not associated, categorical clustering nevertheless occurs (Bousfield and Puff, 1964; Wood and Underwood, 1967). For example, *spool, barrel,* and *baseball* all come from the category *round objects.* They are not associated with one another in terms of association value, but, under appropriate conditions, they will be recalled together. Another piece of evidence for the independent contribution of categorical relationships is that clustering is greater when words in a list are both categorically *and* associatively related than when their relationship is only associative (Cofer, 1965). For example, *bed* and *chair* are both in the same category and are highly associated; *bed* and *dream* are associated but in distinct categories. And lists made up of pairs of the first type are more highly clustered than lists constructed of the second type of pair.

Bousfield's explanation of the category-clustering effect (Bousfield and Cohen, 1953) is that, in the learning of a categorized list, all the instances of a given category will become associated to a higher-order structure representing the category itself. Later on, the recall of just one of the instances will tend to activate that superordinate structure, which will in turn facilitate the recall of the other instances of the category. Those instances will be recalled together, yielding a cluster. For example, if a list contains several animal names, remembering *lion* may activate the category *animal*, leading to recall of *dog*, *zebra*, etc.

Work subsequent to Bousfield's original discovery of categorical clustering has helped to clarify this type of organization. It seems that recall of categorized lists reflects at least three basic processes (Bower, 1972a): (1) learning which categories are represented by list words, (2) learning to associate the category name with instances in the list, and (3) recalling category names. The first two processes occur at the time of encoding the list; the last when it is retrieved.

First, the subject must determine what categories are represented in the list. We could make this job easier by presenting all the members of one category, then all the members of another, and so on—in blocks, rather than randomly interspersed. Indeed, presenting category instances in blocks increases both clustering and recall (Cofer, Bruce, and Reicher, 1966).

Second, the subject must learn, for each category, which members are present in the list. He or she must somehow store the occurrence of category members in the list, and associate those members with the category name, so that later, in recalling the category name, it will be possible to recall the members that were in the list. We would expect factors that represent increased association between members of the category and the category name to improve this second stage and therefore facilitate recall. And we do find this. For example, the frequency with which subjects report various instances when asked for examples of a category has been studied (Battig and Montague, 1969). It has been found that *iron* is a high-frequency response to the category *metal*, whereas *lead* is relatively low-frequency; that *dog* is a frequent instance of four-*footed animal* whereas *mouse* is low; and so on. What is relevant to the free-recall task is that if a categorized list is constructed from high-frequency category instances, it is recalled better than a list constructed from low-frequency category instances (Bousfield, Cohen, and Whitmarsh, 1958; Cofer et al., 1966).

Finally, we assume that recall leads off with retrieval of category names, which, in turn, cue retrieval of the category members that

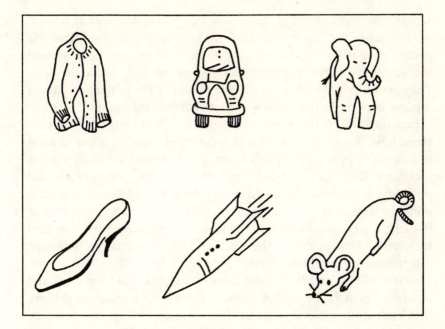

Figure 9.1 Stimuli that can be categorized by semantic category (*columns*) or orientation (*rows*), as used by Frost (1972). [After Hunt and Love, 1972.]

were in the list. The category members are then reported in recall. We therefore expect factors that improve retrieval of category names to lead to better recall of the list. For example, when Tulving and Pearlstone (1966) and Lewis (1972) told subjects, at the time of the recall test, which categories had been represented in the list, the recall scores of the subjects substantially improved.

Work of Frost (1972) indicates that the categories that underlie clustering can be based on the physical appearance of objects as well as on their meaning. She selected a set of 16 drawings of common objects (see Figure 9.1) that could be categorized on both a semantic basis—they were animals, articles of clothing, vehicles, or furniture—and a visual basis—the long axis was in one of four orientations. The drawings were shown to two groups of subjects, one who expected a recognition test, where they would be shown drawings and asked which ones had been in the initial set, and one who expected a free-recall test, where they would have to recall the object names. Then both groups of subjects were given a free-recall test.

Frost found that when subjects expected to recall, they showed the usual clustering on the basis of semantic category, recalling items from a given category together. But the group who expected a recognition test recalled in clusters based on visual as well as semantic characteristics. Frost's results suggest that when subjects expected to see the drawings during the test, they organized around the visual attributes of the objects as well as their semantic class. They could then use this visual information at the time of recall and retrieve clusters in the same way that semantic information is used.

Experiments on the recall of categorized lists help us to understand how organization works. It seems that learning items in a list is a complex process in which units are organized into larger units that can later be decoded into the original inputs. All the phenomena we have discussed under the general label of organizational processes fit into this pattern. Although specific properties of the larger units produced by organization may differ from one case to another (for example, the organization of words in semantic categories may produce different structures from those that simply associate related words or those based on visual characteristics), the building up of higher-order units, followed by a retrieval process that leads from retrieval of those units to recall of their components, seems to be the nature of organization in general. Organization thus encompasses chunking, the use of NLMs, the clustering of associatively related and categorized lists, and, as we shall see, subjective organization.

Subjective Organization

Subjective organization stands in contrast to the kind of organization we have just been discussing, in which the experimenter builds some structure into the list. In *subjective organization*, a term proposed by Tulving (1972), the subject builds structure into a list that the experimenter may have thought was truly disorganized. This is something like what happens when the subject thinks of *mother* given the ostensibly nonsensical stimulus MOT. Although subjective organization may differ from organization of a categorized list in this sense, similar processes are going on in the two situations.

Subjective organization is more difficult to assess than deliberately induced organization of the type imposed on categorized lists. How can we tell that a subject is organizing a free-recall list? One way is by observing the order in which words are recalled. We already know that if highly associated words are included in a list, they will tend to be recalled together, and that members of the same category will be recalled together from categorized lists. Thus, it would seem that the same sort of effect should be present in subjective organization—that words organized into the same structure should be recalled together, or clustered. This should occur no matter what order they were presented in, so that if we observed recall over a series of trials with the same list, the words that are organized together should be recalled together each time. In short, we would suspect that organization would reveal itself by the subject's recalling words in some consistent order, even though the input order of the words varied over trials. It is just this reasoning that leads to measures of subjective organization.

Two notable measures of subjective organization are Tulving's SO (subjective organization) measure and Bousfield and Bousfield's (1966) ITR (intertrial repetitions) measure. These measures are based on consistency of recall order—the more consistent the subject's recall order is from trial to trial, the more he or she tends to recall pairs of words in the same order from one trial to the next, the higher these measures will be. And the measures are assumed to indicate the amount of organizing the subject is doing. Thus, we think that the more he or she organizes, the more consistent the ordering of words in recall should be, and the higher the measure of subjective organization will be as a result.

Do the measures work? And if so, what do they do? For one thing, on the basis of what we know about the effect of organization on categorized lists, we would expect that subjective organization of a list would lead to better recall. Thus, we would expect that SO would correlate with recall; that is, the higher the SO score, the higher would be the recall score. By and large, experimental results have supported this view (e.g., Tulving, 1962; 1964). On the other hand, some theorists have claimed there is no great consistency in the correlation. In reply, supporters of the view have suggested that it is not the idea that organization leads to recall that is at fault—it is merely that we could use better measures of organization (Postman, 1972; Wood, 1972).

Other evidence for the existence of subjective organization, and for its effect on recall, comes from experiments in which a manipulation is found to affect both organization and recall similarly. For example, subjects learning a list in a free-recall task may be instructed to group certain items together. Such instructions tend to increase measures of both organization and recall (Mayhew, 1967). In contrast, instructions that emphasize encoding of each item as a separate unit tend to impair both organization and recall (Allen, 1968). This pattern of results supports the idea of subjective organization.

The subjective organization that occurs in free recall appears to share many characteristics with experimenter-imposed organization. The SO score is an index of the subjective counterpart of category clustering; thus, the data on SO scores indicate that subjects produce subjectively determined clusters in recall. Another similarity between subjective and experimenter-imposed organization is found in their positive effects on recall. Both categorical clustering and SO scores correlate positively with recall. This indicates that both types of organization, the subject's own and that controlled by the experimenter, operate in essentially the same way.

Further support for the essential similarity of categorical and subjective organization comes from a study by Mandler and Pearlstone (1966). In their experiment, subjects were given a set of 52 cards, each having a word printed on it. They were told to sort the cards into two to seven categories, however they wished. The cards were scrambled and then sorted by the subject repeatedly, until he or she had sorted the cards in the same way twice in succession. After the sorting task, each subject was asked to recall as many of the words as possible. The experimenters found that subjects recalled about five words for each category sorted, so the more categories they used, the more words they recalled. This is very similar to a finding for categorized lists (Cohen, 1966; Tulving and Pearlstone, 1966): If subjects manage to recall any members of a category, then they tend to recall the words from that category fairly well. Thus, in the categorized-list situation, the more categories from which any items are recalled, the higher the overall recall score. This general similarity between subjective and experimenter-determined organization supports the idea that the two work in a similar manner.

A point of clarification seems in order here concerning the relationship between chunking, which we discussed in connection with STM, and organization, discussed here in connection with LTM. In fact, these words refer to essentially the same processes, but they have been applied to different situations. The term *chunking* is generally applied in situations calling for immediate recall of a fairly short list of items, as in the memory-span task. The recaller is often required to reproduce an input list in its original order, and only one trial per list is given. *Organization* is a term used in the case where subjects freely recall longer lists, and they may receive and recall the same list over several trials (in fact, this is necessary to measure subjective organization). In the first case, the items are assumed to be recalled from STM; in the second case, from LTM. However, the two situations have in common the underlying process of combining more than one item into a unit; we call this chunking in the STM case and organization in the LTM situation. Where does the process occur? We have included chunking in the collection of processes called elaborative rehearsal and have assumed it takes place in the working memory of STM. Since we assume that elaborative rehearsal also serves to encode information into LTM, and since we view chunking and organization as essentially the same process, it would seem that organization too occurs in working memory. The differences between chunking and organization, then, seem to lie more in terminology than substance.

Encoding Specificity and the Role of Retrieval in Organization

At this point, we have a fairly well-developed idea of what organization is: the formation of superordinate units from collections of input items. This occurs across a variety of situations, where the information is held for a short time or for longer periods, and where the input has some formal structure (like a categorized list) or a structure perceived only by the person doing the organization. Just why is this ubiquitous process so effective? Although we have given this question some consideration, a bit more discussion is in order.

One reason for the facilitative effect of organization on memory is that a unit containing several items demands less storage space than the several items individually. This is particularly important for storage in STM, where space is limited and chunk formation reduces capacity demands. However, LTM is assumed to be far more capacious, and the space-saving function of organization is therefore less important, so we must look for another reason for its effect. If we assume that elaborative rehearsal is used to transfer information about items to LTM throughout the period the items are in STM, organization could facilitate long-term retention simply by enabling items to reside longer in STM. However, we have previously mentioned a different basis for organizational effects in LTM performance, and this basis is more important: When items are stored as organized units, retrieval from LTM is facilitated. In other words, we should consider organization as a process that encompasses both encoding and retrieval.

The interdependence between retrieval and encoding operations has been emphasized in work on the principle of *encoding specificity* (Thomson and Tulving, 1970). This principle says that "What is stored is determined by what is preceived and how it is encoded, and what is stored determines what retrieval cues are effective in providing access to what is stored" (Tulving and Thomson, 1973, p. 353). In other words, recall is the result of a rather complex interaction between encoding (or storage) processes and retrieval. In order to best get at information stored in memory, the retrieval operation should have available the same information that was present at the time of encoding. That means that the encoding of the input should match the cues for retrieval.

We have already mentioned an instance of encoding specificity in the context of the Tulving and Pearlstone (1966) study. They presented subjects with a categorized list in which all the instances of a given category were grouped together and preceded by the category name. Then, at the time of the test, one group of subjects was given the category names as cues for recall, whereas a control group was given no cues. The group given the recall cues remembered more words from the list than the control group. This indicates that making the information that had been available at the time of storage (in this case, the category names) also available at the time of testing had a facilitative effect on recall. Thus, this finding is consistent with the encoding specificity principle—recall was best when the encoding situation matched the testing, or retrieval, situation.

In related experiments, Tulving and Osler (1968) and Thomson and Tulving (1970) expanded on this finding. Their general method was in part as follows: The subjects were given a list of words for free recall. For some subjects, each to-be-remembered word was accompanied by an associate; for example, the word *eagle* might be accompanied by its associate, *soar* (the lists were set up so that the subject knew which of the two words was to be remembered and was instructed that the other was a word that might be helpful in remembering it). Other subjects got no associates with their list words. At the time of the test, some subjects in each group were given the associate of the list word as a recall cue; others got no cue. Thus, there were four groups: (1) associate at both input and at test, (2) associate at input only, (3) associate at test only, (4) no associates given. The results were clear. The first group, which got the associate at both the presentation of the list and the test, outperformed the other groups on recall. The second and third groups, which were given associates only at presentation or only at the time of the test, performed worse than the fourth group, which was given no associates at all. These results provide strong support for encoding specificity. When the conditions of encoding and recall are most similar, then recall will be best.

The principle of encoding specificity has been studied primarily in the context of using cues for recalling individual items. However, it can help us to round out our picture of free recall and organization, for the same principle seems readily applicable to recall of organized clusters of words. We can now summarize organization as follows: When subjects are given a list of words, they tend to organize the words as they encode. This means that they form higher-order units that combine several words. Later, at the time of recall, they use a retrieval process that decodes the higher-order units formed during encoding. This results in clustering of organized groups at output and facilitates recall as well. (A more detailed description of retrieval will be developed in Chapter 10.) All this will occur as long as the conditions of retrieval are compatible with the organizing that was done at the time of encoding. Moreover, supplying cues at the time of retrieval that help to bring back the conditions of encoding will facilitate retrieval.

ENCODING TEXT: ROLE OF KNOWLEDGE STRUCTURES

The material we have been discussing has become increasingly complex as we moved from nonsense syllables, to single words, to paired associates, to lists of items for free recall. Yet the general principle of encoding seems to be the same: The better incoming information is meaningfully related to existing information in LTM, the better it is remembered. At this point we turn to more complex material still—information presented in texts. This, too, appears to follow the general pattern. There is ample evidence that integrating texts with knowledge structures in LTM makes them more memorable.

A number of experiments make this point. One is the study of Thorndyke (1977) described in Chapter 8. He gave subjects stories that varied in the extent to which they followed the rules for normal text (the story grammar). Presumably, they varied as a result in the degree to which the grammar could be applied in encoding. Consistent with this idea, recall of a story was found to decrease as it departed more and more from the normal rules.

Another study that supports this idea was performed by Dooling and Lachman (1971). They used the following text:

> With hocked gems financing him, our hero bravely defied all scornful laughter that tried to prevent his scheme. "Your eyes deceive," he had said. "An egg, not a table, correctly typifies this unexplored planet." Now three sturdy sisters sought proof. Forging along, sometimes through calm vastness, yet more often over turbulent peaks and valleys, days became weeks as many doubters spread fearful rumors about the edge. At last from nowhere welcome winged creatures appeared, signifying momentous success.

Subjects were presented with the text and then asked to recall as much as they could about it. Some of the subjects were not given a title for the passage, but others were told that the passage was about Columbus discovering America. Those that were given the title were able to recall a great deal more of the passage than those who were not. Why should this be? When subjects were told the passage was about Columbus, they had a body of information in LTM they could apply to it. This enabled them to understand it better, leading to better encoding and better retention.

A similar demonstration was given by Bransford and Johnson (1972). They presented the passage in Figure 9.2 with either picture A or picture B. Picture A provides a more meaningful context for the passage, and, sure enough, subjects given that picture were able to recall more than those presented with picture B.

All these results show that encoding a text by interpreting it with respect to a larger body of knowledge aids retention. Because this encoding is not just passive reception of the text, but a process whereby the meaning is constructed from other knowledge together with the words presented, it has been called *constructive* processing. Such processing has been viewed as essentially synonymous with comprehending natural-language material (Bransford and McCarrell, 1974). In this view, the experiments just described show that comprehending a passage plays an important part in remembering it.

The effects of comprehension on recall can be related to the concept of a schema that was developed in Chapters 7 and 8 (Rumelhart and Ortony, 1977; Thorndyke and Hayes-Roth, 1979). The idea is that a higher-order knowledge structure in LTM, such as a schema for stories, is *instantiated* as a passage related to that knowledge is comprehended. In other words, comprehending the passage corresponds to filling in the blanks of the schema with the presented information. And integrating the ideas of a text into a schema provides a strong encoding for later recall, much as organizing a group of words from a list does.

You may question from the data given thus far, and rightly so, whether it is appropriate to infer that comprehensibility affects the *encoding* process. There is, in fact, experimental evidence that the effects of comprehension take place at the time of encoding. If they did not—for example, if they took place after the material had been stored or at the time of retrieval—it should be possible to facilitate retention by giving the comprehension-assisting material after the passage had been encoded. For example, if knowing that the above passage is about Columbus makes it easier to retrieve, then it should be sufficient to give the title just before retrieval, at the time when

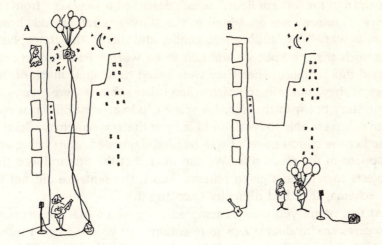

If the balloons popped, the sound wouldn't be able to carry, since everything would be too far away from the correct floor. A closed window would also prevent the sound from carrying, since most buildings tend to be well insulated. Since the whole operation depends on a steady flow of electricity, a break in the middle of the wire would also cause problems. Of course, the fellow could shout, but the human voice is not loud enough to carry that far. An additional problem is that a string could break on the instrument. Then there could be no accompaniment to the message. It is clear that the best situation would involve less distance. Then there would be fewer potential problems. With fact to face contact, the least number of things could go wrong.

Figure 9.2 A passage that is difficult to understand and remember. A meaningful context (A) aids memory; a nonmeaningful one (B) does not. [After Bransford and Johnson, 1972.]

subjects are asked to recall. But this generally does not work: Giving the title after the passage has been presented is not found to be effective (Dooling and Mullet, 1973). Similarly, giving picture A after presenting the passage of Figure 9.2 is no better than giving picture B or even than giving no picture at all (Bransford and Johnson, 1972).

Constructive effects have been observed with measures other than overall recall. It has been found that information presented at encoding affects the type as well as the quantity of material retained. One study illustrating this was performed by Bransford and Johnson (1973). They gave some subjects a story entitled "Watching a peace march from the fortieth floor," which described a view seen from far above. One sentence contained in the story was rather odd, however. It was, "The landing was gentle, and luckily the atmosphere was such that no special suits had to be worn." Few subjects reported this sentence when they were asked to recall as much of the story as they could. In contrast, when other subjects were given the same story but with the title, "A space trip to an inhabited planet," over half were able to recall an idea from the key sentence. Clearly, whether the critical material was recalled depended on its being appropriate to the given title. We can infer that the title induced the subjects to activate a given schema, and if the sentence did not fit the schema, they had difficulty encoding it.

At this point, you may be tempted to conclude that constructive processes are invaluable aids to retention; that you had better interpret inputs as much as possible in order to remember them. Though this may be true for most of what you are asked to remember, it can also backfire on occasion. We saw an example of this in the study just described, where subjects who were constructing a peace march had trouble remembering a space-landing sentence. Another illustration is provided by a study of Sulin and Dooling (1974). Subjects read the following passage after being told it was about a fictional woman named Carol Harris:

> Carol Harris was a problem child from birth. She was wild, stubborn, and violent. By the time Carol turned eight, she was still unmanageable. Her parents were very concerned about her mental health. There was no good institution for her problem in her state. Her parents finally decided to take some action. They hired a private teacher for Carol.

A second group of subjects was given the same passage, but with the name Helen Keller substituted for Carol Harris. Later, the subjects were presented with sentences like those from the passage and were asked to indicate whether or not each one was identical to a sentence in the original version. A key sentence in the test was similar to the second sentence from the original passage but read, "She was deaf, dumb, and blind." Subjects who had been told the passage was about Helen Keller showed a marked tendency to falsely recognize this test sentence. This was especially true when the test followed the initial presentation by a week; fewer errors were made if the test followed the passage by only a few minutes.

The results of the Sulin and Dooling study indicate that interpretation of a text through previous knowledge can in some cases lead to certain kinds of errors. This was apparently not too much of a problem for subjects if the test came fairly soon after the passage, for at that time they could remember the actual words fairly well. But as more time had elapsed, their memory for the passage apparently relied to a greater extent on their general knowledge in LTM about Helen Keller. This reliance increasingly led them to falsely recognize a test sentence that was highly congruent with that knowledge.

We will discuss further in Chapter 11 the kinds of errors that constructive processes in text encoding can provoke. At this point, one further warning is in order. Although it has been indicated that construction takes place at the time a passage is encoded, there is evidence for at least some constructive activity at other phases of remembering at well. That retrieval can rely on interpreting events with respect to world knowledge was demonstrated in a study by Anderson and Pichert (1978). They had subjects read a story about what two boys did at one of their homes when they stayed away from school. The subjects read the story after having been given information that set it in a certain perspective, such as the viewpoint of a burglar. The subjects recalled the story once, then some were given a second, new perspective, such as the viewpoint of a prospective home buyer. Then all subjects attempted to recall a second time. During this recall, the subjects who had been given a new perspective reported a substantial amount of previously unreported information that was particularly relevant to that new perspective. In contrast, there was little change in the reports of the subjects who were not given a new perspective. The perspective-change subjects reported that they had attempted to recall everything they could on their first attempt, but the new viewpoint seemed to lead them to think of new information relevant to it. The subjects' own reports suggested that the new perspective activated a second schema in memory, which then, by virtue of the general knowledge it conveyed, provided cues for the retrieval of previously inaccessible information.

The study just described provides an appropriate preface for our discussion of retrieval, for we shall depict the process of retrieving information as an active search through memory structures, directed by a cue. This depiction is quite consistent with the schema-directed recall suggested by Anderson and Pichert. Our discussion will make use of many topics covered in the present chapter, for, as we have mentioned, retrieval and encoding are highly interdependent. The present chapter also introduces a topic to which we will return in Chapter 11—inaccuracies in remembering. Chapter 11 will consider not only errors in recall of text, but also the progressive loss of memory accuracy that we call forgetting.

10

Retrieving Information from Long-Term Memory

In the preceding chapter, we began a discussion of remembering with an investigation of encoding processes—operations that work on input information to prepare it for storage in LTM. It became clear that encoding is inextricably tied to retrieval, the process of getting at information stored in LTM. In the present chapter, we will focus on retrieval.

It seems appropriate to begin by looking at the experimental procedures used to induce retrieval. Two such procedures are list-learning techniques we have discussed previously called recognition and free recall. In both situations, a subject is given a list of words, followed by a test. But the test differs for recognition and recall, and the way the subject seems to retrieve varies as a result. A great deal has been learned about the retrieval process by comparing these two procedures, and the resulting theories are the focus of this chapter. We shall begin our discussion by considering the nature of recognition and the theory of retrieval it suggests.

RECOGNITION

The Nature of Recognition Tests

In general, memory tests attempt to find out what knowledge subjects have about previously presented information. What makes a recognition test distinctive is that, during the test, the subject is presented with the material that is supposed to be remembered. The task would be very easy if this were the only material given on the test, but the subject is also given some other material, *not* part of the to-be-remembered information. The latter is called, appropriately enough, distractor material. The subject's task then becomes indicating which portions of the test material were part of the original set.

Within this basic definition of recognition testing, a number of variations are possible. Consider the case of subjects who are given a list of words to remember. Later, they may be given what is called a yes/no recognition test. The subjects are shown a series of items, one at a time. As each item appears, the subjects are to say "yes" if they think it was on the original list, and "no" if they think it was not. Usually, half the items on the test are from the original list, and the other half are distractors. The yes/no test is analogous to the true/false tests commonly encountered by students.

Another form of recognition testing is the forced-choice test. In a forced-choice procedure, the subject sees two or more items at a time during the test, not just one. One of those items was on the original list; the rest were not. The job is to pick out the item that was on the list. If the subject sees two items at a time, then the test is called a two-alternative forced choice; if three, a three-alternative forced choice; and so on. The forced-choice test thus is a kind of multiple-choice test.

Finally, a recognition test can use a batch-testing procedure, in which everything—all the list words and all the distractors—is presented at once. The subject then tries to indicate which words were on the original list. Often, all the test items are printed on a page and the subject circles those he or she thinks are from the originally presented list.

Recognition testing is sometimes used in combination with other list-learning procedures. For example, we could combine the recognition procedure with the use of paired associates by testing each stimulus term with a set of response alternatives. A subject who had first been presented with DAX–7 might be tested with:

DAX – ?   5 8 7 1   (*Pick one*)

Recognition can also be combined with tests of memory for the serial order of inputs. In that case, we might ask the subject to recognize which ordering of a set of items corresponded to the order in which they had previously been presented.

Recognition Performance

The basic difference between recognition and recall test procedures is that in recognition, subjects are given the original items during the test; in a recall test, they are given instructions to report the items without being shown them. What may seem a minor difference leads to rather major differences in the results of the tests. One of the important differences is that, in general, subjects can recognize list items much better than they can recall them. In fact, if we first give subjects a chance to recall a list, and then give them a recognition test, we will usually find that they can recognize many items they were unable to recall.

We have noted previously that people have a remarkable ability to recognize pictures (at least when the test uses dissimilar distractors). Shepard (1967) provided a demonstration of the ability of subjects to recognize large number of verbal items as well. In one of his experiments, subjects were presented with 540 words, each printed on a card. The subjects looked through the cards in order; then they were given a series of 60 two-alternative, forced-choice tests on the words. Shepard found that they could perform on the tests with a mean accuracy rate of 88 percent! This was not as high as performance of subjects who saw 612 colored pictures—their recognition accuracy was 97 percent—but it is impressive nevertheless. In another experiment, subjects shown 612 sentences scored 89 percent on a subsequent recognition test. Shepard was even able to persuade a couple of friends to look at 1,224 sentences, and they scored 88 percent in a recognition test that followed.

Shepard's results emphasize the fact that recognition performance is extremely high relative to recall. We might well ask if this is always true. It is not; it is possible to design recognition-testing situations in which performance is rather poor. For example, we can use as distractors items that are very similar to list items, as was done with snowflakes by Goldstein and Chance (1970). In the case of word recognition, we can use distractors that are strongly associated with list items. For example, we might present *cat* as a list word and use *dog* as a distractor. This sort of manipulation leads to decrements in recognition-test performance (e.g., Underwood, 1965; Underwood and Freund, 1968). Or we can use a large number of distractors; for example, we can present the list words on the test together with 90 alternatives. It is difficult to recognize list words in this situation (Davis, Sutherland, and Judd, 1961).

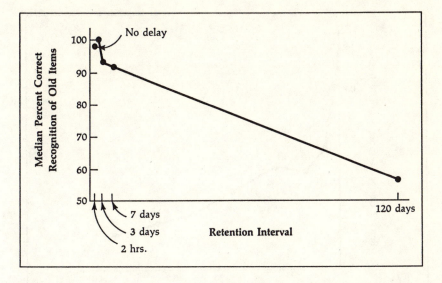

Figure 10.1 Correct recognition of old (previously presented) items, as a function of retention interval. [After Shepard, 1967.]

Another fact about recognition testing is that performance remains high even with long retention intervals. That is, forgetting of items appears to be very slow when it is evaluated with the recognition method. Postman and Rau (1957) found that performance on a test of recognition for short lists of CVCs or words stayed near 100 percent over a two-day retention interval. Shepard (1967), in one of the experiments mentioned above, tested retention of picture stimuli over a period of 120 days. He tested groups of subjects at retention intervals of no delay, 2 hours, 3 days, a week, and 120 days. As you can see in Figure 10.1, although forgetting took place, it did so very slowly.

The type of test administered also affects the measurement of forgetting over shorter intervals. Forgetting is notably slower when recognition tests are used than when testing uses recall as a measure. Short-term recognition was studied by Shepard and Teghtsoonian (1961). In their experiment, subjects were given a large deck of cards, with a three-digit number written on each. The subjects were instructed to go through the cards, indicating for each one whether or not they had seen it before. Of course, the first few cards all contained numbers that were new to the subjects. But the deck was so arranged that, after the first few cards, old cards (those containing a number the subjects had already seen) and new cards (those

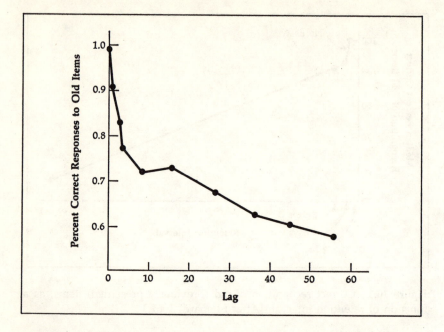

Figure 10.2 Percent correct responses to old items as a function of lag—the number of stimuli intervening between the first and second presentations of the item. [After Shepherd and Teghtsoonian, 1961. Copyright 1961 by the American Psychological Association. Reprinted by permission.]

containing a number not seen previously) occurred equally often in a random sequence. Except for a few cards at the bottom of the deck that occurred only once (to maintain the equal probability of old and new), each number in the deck occurred just twice.

Shepard and Teghtsoonian were particularly interested in how recognition would vary as a function of the distance between the first and second occurrence of a number. They defined this distance, which they called *lag*, as the number of cards that intervened between the first and second appearance of a given number. For example, if the series of cards seen during some period was: 147, 351, 362, 215, 111, 147, we can expect the subjects to say "new" to the first appearance of 147 and "old" to the second. We can define the lag here as four, because four items intervene between the two 147s. If we plot the percentage of correct responses to old items as a function of lag, the results are as shown in Figure 10.2. We see that performance is better than chance for lags of as many as sixty items, with chance meaning the level of correct responses a subject could get by merely guessing. Since each time the subjects respond there is a 50:50 chance of being correct (the item is either old or new), the guessing level is 50 percent. When subjects do better than 50 percent, we suspect that they are doing more than just guessing—they are working with information in memory, and this information helps them to do better than they would by chance. Thus, we see that the lag during which forgetting occurs in this situation is about sixty items.

We can contrast these results with some obtained in a similar experiment that measured recall rather than recognition: An approximate parallel in recall is found in the Waugh and Norman (1965) probe-digit task discussed in Chapter 6. There we had a lag, defined as the number of digits intervening between the first and second appearance of the probe. And there, too, we had a recall measure—recall of the digit adjacent to the probe. Waugh and Norman found that performance decayed to guessing levels when about 12 digits intervened. Thus, we see that although the forgetting curves look the same, with gradual decreases in memory as more and more items intervene, the number of intervening items necessary for what appears to be complete forgetting is quite different. In recognition there is still memory for an item after 60 subsequent items, whereas in recall, memory has vanished with 12. Thus, over the short term, to the extent that these experiments are comparable, forgetting measured with recognition methods seems to be less than forgetting measured by recall, just as it is over longer intervals.

Signal-Detection Theory and Recognition

With some of the basic facts about recognition at hand, it is time to look at a theoretical model of the recognition of an item in memory. This is the first retrieval model we shall discuss. It is the signal-detection model for recognition memory. The model enables us to derive an estimate of the amount of information in memory on which a subject bases recognition judgments. In addition, the model provides a means of dealing with a very important problem in recognition testing: the problem of response bias, or guessing effects.

To illustrate the problem, consider a hypothetical experiment in which we give two groups of subjects a list of items, followed by a yes/no recognition test. That is, the subjects are tested with a mixed sequence of list items and distractors and instructed to say "yes" if they think a given item was on the list, "no" if they think it is a distractor. Now suppose that, to one group of subjects (the "free" group), we indicate that performance on the recognition test will be scored on the basis of overall accuracy and that there will be no penalty for guessing. To a second group of subjects (the "conservative" group), we give somewhat different instructions: We indicate that performance on the recognition test will be scored on the basis of accurate use of the "yes" response, and that there will be a heavy penalty whenever they incorrectly identify a distractor as having been on the list. Clearly, the two groups of subjects would be well advised to use different strategies. Because the first group is not penalized for guessing, they should do so. Whenever they are unsure whether an item is old or new, they should attempt to guess. The second group, in contrast, must be very conservative in their use of the "yes" responses. This means that if they are not absolutely certain whether an item is from the list or a distractor, they should indicate that it is a distractor.

In view of their different strategies for responding, our two groups of subjects should perform differently. First, considering the correct recognition of list items—that is, the percentage of the time the subjects said "yes" to a list item on the test—we will probably find better performance by the free group. That is because subjects in that group were free to guess "yes," and some proportion of those guesses were probably correct. On the other hand, conservative subjects used their "yes" response more cautiously. Although a large proportion of their "yes" responses may be correct, they were forced to say "no" to many list items during the test. Thus, they have lower scores on recognition of list items. In addition, the overall accuracy of the free group may be better, for they were permitted their "best guess." To the extent that subjects in the conservative group were forced to say "no" to items that they felt were probably on the list but did not want to take a chance on, they were forced into error.

Now the point of this exercise can be seen. Although there is no reason to suppose that the two groups of subjects have different amounts of information about the list in memory, their recognition scores differ. If we were to use recognition performance to make inferences about their memory for list items, we would be in error. For it is our instructions that have biased the responses of the two groups and have caused them to perform differently. This means that in order to use recognition performance to assess what subjects actually remember, we must have some way to account for the effects of response bias and guessing.

Actually, there are several methods available for correcting for guessing, to obtain a good estimate of memory performance. One is to use yes/no or two-alternative, forced-choice tests and to give the subject a corrected score of number right minus number wrong. This assumes that the subject's guesses are random, with a 50:50 chance of being correct, and that every time he or she gets an item wrong, the response was a guess. In that case, we would expect the number wrong to represent only *half* of the guesses—because the other half of the guesses could be right purely by chance. Thus, we must subtract the number of correct guesses from the recognition score. For a two-choice test, the number of correct guesses would be equal to the number of incorrect guesses, so we would give the subject a corrected score of the total number correct minus the number wrong. For example, if he or she guessed ten times in answering one hundred questions, on the average there should be five right answers and five wrong answers. Thus, we must take five away from a score of ninety-five correct because the subject was guessing—not remembering—when five of the correct answers were given.

However, this particular method of correction is considered an inaccurate one by some psychologists. A problem is that in assuming that the subject has a 50:50 chance of being correct when a guess is made, it ignores the possibilities that the subject may be biased toward making a particular response, or that he or she may be better at recognizing old items than at recognizing distractors. As we shall see, the signal-detection approach provides a more reasonable correction for guessing. We will discuss this approach in some detail, because it is used as much more than a correction for guessing. It can also be considered a theory of retrieval.

The theory of signal detection actually originated with the study of auditory-detection tasks (Green and Swets, 1966). Typically, in such a task, a subject listens for some signal (for example, a tone) to occur against a background of white noise (a hissing, or static-like sound). He or she presses a button if the signal occurs within a certain period. In this situation, there are essentially four things that can happen within any given period: If the signal occurs and the subject presses the button, a *hit* is recorded. If the signal occurs and the subject misses it and fails to press the button, a *miss* is recorded. If the signal does not occur, and the subject does not press the button, a *correct rejection* is recorded. If the signal does not occur, but the subject nevertheless presses the button, a *false alarm* is recorded. Thus, in the event of a hit or a correct rejection, the subject's response is correct, whereas in the event of a miss or false alarm, the subject has made an error.

The auditory signal-detection task has a direct parallel in the yes/no recognition situation. Consider an experiment in which a subject has first seen a list of items and then is performing on a yes/no test. That means a sequence of items is shown, and to each item the response "yes" (or "old") is made if it is thought to be from the original list, and "no" (or "new") is made if it is thought to be a distractor item. In this case, the occurrence of an old item (one that was actually on the list) is like the occurrence of the signal in the auditory-detection task, and the occurrence of a new item (a distractor) is like the absence of the signal. Another similarity to the auditory task is that as each item comes up on the test, there are four situations that can occur. These are shown in Figure 10.3. First, the item can be an old item (that is, previously on the list), and the subject can say "old"; this is the correct response, and as in the auditory task, it is called a *hit*. Second, the item can be old but the subject may incorrectly say "new"; this is called a *miss*. Third, the item can actually be new, and the subject can say "new"; again, as in the auditory task, this is a *correct rejection*. And last, the subject can say "old" when the item is really new; this is a *false alarm*. Thus, signal detection and recognition testing are analogous, and it is for this reason that the theory originally developed for signal detection has been applied to recognition memory.

Note that the four cells (compartments) in Figure 10.3 are not independent. This means that by knowing the rate of occurrence of only some of the events, we can figure out the rate of occurrence of the others. Suppose, for example, that we give the subject a yes/no test on 20 list items. There are 40 items on the list, 20 old and 20 new. Now, suppose we know that the subject is correct on 15 old items; that is, 15 out of the 20 times an old item was presented on the test, the response was "old." The subject is said to have a *hit rate* of 75 percent (which represents the 15 hits made out of the 20 that were possible). Now, we can fill in the cell marked "miss," because we know the subject missed 5 of the 20 old items. That is, we know there were 20 old items, and we know the hit rate was 75 percent; that a correct response was made to 15 of those old items. The subject must have been wrong with the other 5; that is, he or she must have said they were "new," and this is what defines a miss. The *miss rate* is 25 percent, equal to the 5 out of 20 items that were missed. (In general, the hit rate and miss rate must add to 100 percent.) By similar reasoning, if we know the subject's *correct-rejection rate* is 40 percent, we know the response "new" was made to 40 percent or 8 of the new items. Then the subject must have said "old" to the other 12 new items, so we know the *false-alarm rate*—it is 12 out of 20 items, or 60 percent. Thus, we know all the cells of our table if we know one cell in each column. Most commonly, therefore, only two cells, one in each column, are ever referred to. These are usually the

		Subject has seen an old item.	Subject has seen a new item.
Subject says:	"Old"	Hit (——%)	False Alarm (——%)
	"New"	Miss (——%)	Correct Rejection (——%)

TOTALS: Old items (100%) New items (100%)

Figure 10.3 Types of trials that can occur in a yes/no recognition test.

hit cell and the false-alarm cell. (Because they are used so frequently, the terms *hit rate* and *false-alarm rate* are often abbreviated HR and FAR.)

With the classificatory scheme of Figure 10.3 for the outcomes of yes/no recognition tests, we shall now consider the basic assumptions of the model that is applied to them. Its first assumption is that any information in LTM has a certain strength. This is similar to the assumption, discussed in Chapter 6, that information in STM has a certain strength. At this point, we won't attempt to stipulate just what "information" means. Instead, we can focus on single items in LTM, items that may be presented in a list. We can think of the strength of an item as the amount of excitation of a location in LTM that corresponds to the item. Strength can also mean the degree of familiarity—the stronger is the item in memory, the more familiar it will seem.

Our second assumption is that measurements of the strengths of items presented in a list will be distributed normally. Let us briefly expand on that assumption: Each item in the list, after its presentation, has a particular strength in the subject's LTM. The distribution of those values among items at any time is normal—many items have medium strength, a few have very high strength, and a few have very low strength. (You may wish to refer to an introductory psychology text for a review of normal distributions.) On the other hand, consider the items that were not presented but that will be used as new, or distractor, items at the time of the test. We shall assume that each of those new items also has its own strength and that the distribution of their strengths is also normal (see Figure 10.4). Moreover, we assume that the variability in the strengths of old items is as great as that of the distractors. Thus, we have two normal distributions to consider—one represents the strengths of the list items; the other represents the strengths of the distractors.

Third, we assume that presenting some item on a list has the effect of increasing its strength in the subject's LTM. That means that

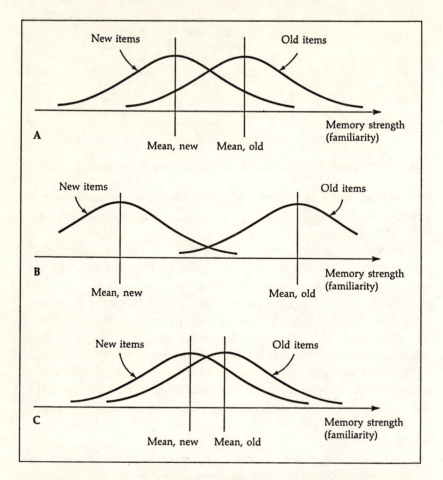

Figure 10.4 Possible relationships between the distributions of strengths for old (previously presented) and new (distractor) items in memory: (A) Moderate overlap: (B) old items stronger than new items; (C) old and new items similar in strength.

presenting the item moves its initial strength, or familiarity, from some starting value to some new, higher value. It also means that items that are not presented to the subject will stay at their initial level of strength, or familiarity. This third assumption is important, because it implies that the distributions for old items and distractors will have different mean strength values. Usually, the mean strength of the old items will be higher, because they have just been presented, and that has moved their strength values up. The new items will be lower in strength, at the level the old items were at before they were presented on the list. If we were to plot the strength distributions along some dimension of familiarity, the presentation of the list would serve to move the distribution of old items a jump along the dimension, tending to separate it from the distribution of distractor items.

The resulting arrangement of the two distributions, one for presented items and one for distractors, would vary according to their initial strength values. (Various possibilities are presented in Figure 10.4.) For example, if the items chosen for presentation in the list had initial high strength values (they were very familiar or had been presented several times before), then presenting them might push their strength far beyond that of the distractors. More usually, we could expect some overlap of the two distributions. Although the mean strength of the old items would be greater than that of the new items, some new items would still be stronger than some old items.

From Figure 10.4, it is clear that the difference between the means of the distributions is a measure of their distance on the familiarity or strength continuum. The further apart the means are, the stronger the old items are relative to the new. In the signal-detection model this distance becomes a measure known as *d*-prime (d'), which is an indicator of how far apart the old and new items are. More precisely, d' is the distance between the means of the two distributions in standard-deviation units (that is, the difference between the two means, divided by the common standard deviation of the distributions). In addition to the d' value, there is a second theoretical value to consider, called *beta* (β). In terms of the model, β is used by the subject in making a decision. Beta is the criterion strength upon which the subject bases the decision. In order to see how this works, let us review what happens in the experiment.

When a subject is presented with a list of items, we assume: (1) Each item increases in strength. It had a starting strength that has now increased. (2) All items, regardless of their starting strengths, increase by this same amount; this has the effect of shifting the distribution of items presented on the list—now called *old* items—up along the strength continuum by some constant amount. Meanwhile, the items to be used as distractors on the test—called *new* items—remain at their old strength. Presumably, the mean strength of these new items will be less than the mean of the old items.

Now, consider what happens when the subject is tested on the list. A series of items is presented; half are old and half are new. The subject examines each item and decides whether it is old or new. A particular strength value (β) is adopted and used as a criterion for this decision. As each test item is presented, the subject evaluates its LTM strength (or decides how familiar it is). Suppose, for example, he or she determines that a given item's strength is 100. Whether the item is called old or new depends not only on its strength but also on β. If the item's strength is greater than β, the subject says "old." If it is less than β, the response is "new." So, for example, if β were 90, our item with strength 100 would be called old. To summarize, we now have a decision rule that says: Calculate the strength of the current item, and say "old" if that strength is greater than β; otherwise, say "new."

Now is the time for us to put these ideas about strength distributions, d', and β, together with the outcome labels *hit*, *miss*, *false alarm*, and *correct rejection*. This is done in Figure 10.5. Here the two strength distributions are presented, with d' and β drawn in. In the total area under the two distributions, four subareas of interest can be identified. What each represents is determined by whether it is under the old or new distribution and whether it is to the left or right of β. For example, consider the area under the old distribution and to the right of β. This area represents the times when an old item is presented on the test and the subject says "old"—in short, the times when hits occur. The size of the area indicates the proportion of hits—the hit rate. Similarly, the area under the old-item distribution and to the left of β indicates the miss rate. Taken together, these two areas comprise the total area under the old-item distribution, just as they add to 100 percent in our previous four-celled table (Figure 10.3). Under the new-item distribution, we can find the false-alarm and correct-rejection areas. The false alarms are to the right of β (where the subject says "old" to a new item by mistake) and the correct rejections are to the left of β. The total area under the two distributions contains four regions, and these regions correspond to the four possible outcomes of the yes/no test.

So far, our partly complete model of the recognition process includes the ideas of memory strength, distributions, and decision rules. In order to understand how this enables us to measure recognition performance independently of guessing, we must next consider what happens as d' and β vary. There are various possibilities, shown in Figure 10.6. In Figure 10.6A, we see what happens to the subject's performance as d' changes. An increase in d' corresponds to an increase in the difference between the strengths of old and new items. For very large d', the strengths are very different, and the subject should find it very easy to tell old items from new. However, if d' is small, it should be difficult to tell the two sets of items

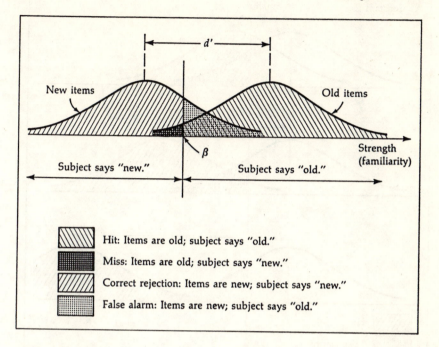

Figure 10.5 Concepts in the theory of signal detection as applied to recognition memory.

apart. Thus, we see that d' is essentially a measure of how sensitive we are to the difference between old and new items—in fact, d' is often referred to as "true" sensitivity. It represents the information that is in memory; it tells us the difference in LTM strength between presented items and distractors. It is d' that we want to get a pure estimate of by ruling out guessing. Note in Figure 10.6A that if β remains constant and d' increases (which corresponds to a true increase in what is available in memory, that is, a true increase in sensitivity), then the hit rate will increase but the false-alarm rate will not. That is because as the subject becomes more sensitive, he or she is better able to tell an old item when it occurs, relative to the new items.

Now consider Figure 10.6B. It shows what happens if β changes while d' remains the same. This means that the subject is changing the decision criterion, although there is no change in the amount of information in memory—no change in true sensitivity to old items. In effect, what is changing is the subject's guessing strategy. When β is very low, an item needs little strength for him or her to say "old." Consequently, the response will be "old" very often, with the subject being correct on most of the items that are actually old but

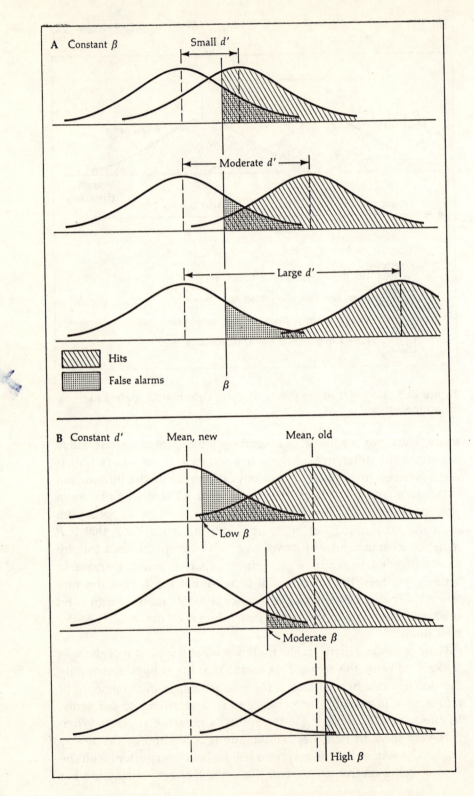

A Constant β

Small d′

Moderate d′

Large d′

Hits

False alarms

β

B Constant d′

Mean, new   Mean, old

Low β

Moderate β

High β

committing many errors on new items. In short, there will be a high hit rate, but also a high false-alarm rate. If β is high, the situation is reversed. The subject is very cautious, and seldom says "old" unless he or she is quite sure—which will be only for items with high familiarity. There will be a relatively low hit rate, for the subject will often say "new" to old items, simply because of caution. On the other hand, the subject will also have a low false-alarm rate, because the response "old" will not often be given to new items. Thus, we see that if d' remains constant, shifts in β will cause both the hit and false alarm rates to change, and in the same direction. As β goes up, both hit rate and false-alarm rate go down.

The pattern of changes in hits and false alarms with changes in d' and β enables us to use the signal-detection model to correct for guessing. For each pair of values of hit and false-alarm rates, there is a corresponding value of d'. It is that fact that allows the model to be used to eliminate guessing effects. For, given a change in β, the hit and false-alarm rates will both change, but their new values will be associated with exactly the same d' as before. That is, the subject may change his or her guessing strategy (as might occur if we institute a penalty for false alarms), and that may result in a new hit rate and a new false-alarm rate—but that new pair of values will correspond to the same d'. In contrast, if there is a change in the subject's true sensitivity to old items (as there might be, for example, if the list were presented a second time, causing the strengths of old items to be incremented), then there will be a change in hit rate without a concomitant change in false alarms. The resulting changed hit and false-alarm rates will correspond to a new value of d'. In short, it is the *pair* of values, hit rate and false-alarm rate, that determines the estimate of memory strength, not just the hit rate or false-alarm rate alone. And the manner in which those paired values change determines whether a change in true sensitivity (d') or response criterion (β) can be inferred.

Experimenters who use the signal-detection analysis have available special tables that list values of d' for each pair of values for the

---

Figure 10.6 Effects of variations in β and d' on recognition: (A) Effects of changes in d' when β remains constant. As d' increases, the hit rate increases without a corresponding change in false alarms. Estimates of d' will therefore increase. (B) Effects of variations in B when d' remains constant. As β increases, both the hit and the false-alarm rates will decrease, and estimates of d' will remain constant.

hit rate and the false-alarm rate. From the table, the experimenter can tell if an experimental manipulation that might have changed both the hit and false-alarm rates has actually changed d'. If what has changed is merely the subject's guessing strategy, then the hits and false alarms will have changed together, and d' will be the same for the new values as for the old. In this way, the use of d' rather than a simple percentage of correct responses enables the experimenter to correct for guessing in a theoretically meaningful way.

Moreover, the representation of the recognition task that this theory provides can actually be considered a theory of memory. Essentially, it says that presenting an item has the effect of increasing its strength, or exciting its location, or boosting the familiarity value for that item. (Which of these terms you use is not too important; all have been used at one time or another.) It also says that the subject is able to assess the familiarity of any item that is given and then use the assessment to decide if the item was on the list. If it is familiar enough to have been there, he or she will identify it as a list item. Various circumstances may alter the criterion for "familiar enough."

Let us use this theory to account for some of the data from recognition experiments. Consider, for example, what happens if we use as distractors words that are similar to the list words. That is, we might present *dog* as a distractor when *cat* was on the list. We know this tends to reduce recognition scores. An explanation in terms of our model is not hard to come by—we simply assume that when the list words are presented, similar and associated items also receive a boost in strength, somewhat indirectly. (This is like the spreading activation concept introduced in Chapter 8.) At the time of the test, their strength will therefore be higher than most other items that could be used as "new" items on the test, and the overlap of the distributions will be that much greater. Higher overlap means lower d'; thus, using similar or associated distractors will yield poorer recognition performance.

Consider another finding, namely, that recognition is usually better for infrequent words than frequent words (Shepard, 1967; Underwood and Freund, 1970). Here, the frequency of a word refers to how often it is used in natural language, for example, in literature. Tables of word frequency are readily available (e.g., Thorndike and Lorge, 1944), and frequency is often deliberately varied in experiments using words. The word-frequency effect on recognition performance can be explained in terms of signal-detection theory much as the effect of associated distractors was explained (Underwood and Freund, 1970). We assume that when a word is presented, its high associates are somewhat increased in strength by virtue of their association with the presented word. For high-frequency list words, there will be quite a few associated words receiving the strength increase, and most of the associated words will also be of high frequency. Some of the words that receive the indirect increase in strength will be list words themselves, whereas others will be among those presented as distractors. If we assume that the indirect strength increase has a greater effect on the relatively low-strength distractor items than it has on the already high-strength list items, then it follows that the magnitude of the increase of the distractors' strengths (which shifts the distribution of new items up on the strength continuum) will outweigh any effects on other list items. The net result will be considerable overlap between the old and new distributions when high-frequency words are presented, owing to the indirect increases in strength of those list words' associates.

Now consider a list of low-frequency words. These words will elicit relatively few associates and thus induce increases in strength of relatively few words. There will be very little shift in the strength of the distractor items, in general, and thus no great overlap in the distributions of old and new items. As a result, the d' measured will be greater for low-frequency words than for high-frequency words, and this accounts for frequency effects on recognition.

The signal-detection model can also be applied to forgetting, if we assume that the strength increment due to presentation declines in the course of time, and the distribution of old items slowly sinks back down the continuum into the distribution of new items. Thus d' decreases, and, if we wait long enough, it may eventually reach zero.

We see that this theory accounts for certain recognition phenomena and at the same time provides a means of separating the subject's memory (d') from the decision process (β). Admittedly, some of the explanations seem a bit after-the-fact, but they do fit with the theory. On the whole, then, let us be satisfied—at least temporarily—with the signal-detection model as a retrieval theory. It describes how information is reported from memory; the decision process is assumed to include a strength analysis of a presented item and internal comparison to a standard. Thus, it is a model of retrieval to the extent that it describes the processes that occur when information is obtained from memory.

At this point, it may seem that a more complex theory of retrieval is not really required for a model of recognition. That is, it may seem that there is little to retrieve when the thing to be retrieved is given to the subject at the time of the remembering. We shall see that retrieval, in the sense of looking for something in memory, does occur when an item is recognized. However, it is in recall that retrieval in this sense is most clearly important. For that reason, it is time to examine recall a bit more and to try to construct a retrieval theory that includes recall.

RETRIEVAL AND RECALL

We already know quite a bit about recall. We know, for example, about interpretations of the serial-position curve, about the effects of categorized lists, and about subjective organization. Before we proceed further with the discussion of free-recall phenomena, let us first try to characterize the basic nature of the task. It seems, intuitively, that recall is the experimental procedure that comes closest to tapping what we think of as "remembering," in the term's commonly used sense.

Bower (1972a) has noted the similarity between free recall of a list of words and recall in situations outside of the laboratory. He points out that, most generally, free recall corresponds to reproducing all the items that are members of a designated set. For example, you may be asked to recall all the words on a list you just saw, you may be asked to name the Presidents of the United States or the people you met at a party, or you may be asked to recall the retention intervals in the experiment of Peterson and Peterson (see Chapter 6). In the laboratory, of course, free recall is usually like the first example—remembering all the items in some previously presented list.

In general, we could describe recall as a procedure in which a subject is first given a set of information and then given some cue to retrieve and report that information. In a recall experiment, the experimenter may use a temporal cue—such as "Recall the list you learned last Monday"—or an ordinal cue—such as "Recall the list you learned before this one." In everyday remembering as well, a cue usually directs recall. It might be a direct request, as when you are asked a question on a test. Or it might be a smell that triggers a memory. Retrieval cues can also be internal, as when you begin to feel hungry and remember that you forgot to eat breakfast. In these cases, the cues are analogous to that given by an experimenter who says, "Recall the previous list."

The fact that recall generally occurs in the presence of a retrieval cue also points to a similarity between the free-recall and paired-associate procedures. In a sense, free recall is like remembering a paired associate: The stimulus term is the retrieval cue, and the response is actually a set of responses—all the items in the to-be-remembered set. For example, if there are two recall lists to be learned, each consisting of several items, then what is learned may be something like a pairing of the stimulus "first list" with one set of items and "second list" with the other set.

A Model of Recall

How might the recall process work? One fairly detailed theory of recall has been presented by Anderson and Bower (1972; 1973; Anderson, 1972) in the context of an associative-network view of memory (as presented in Chapter 8). This model does not divide LTM into semantic and episodic memory, but instead makes a distinction between semantic and episodic information. Both are assumed to reside in a common LTM network of nodes (locations) interconnected by associations (pathways). The difference between the two is that the propositions (built up from nodes and associations) describing episodic information indicate the situation (time or place, for example) where an item or event occurred—its episode. Semantic information does not include such contextual data. In this model, a subject who studies a list for later recall will combine semantic information about list items with indications that the items were part of a certain list. More specifically, several events occur when a list is encoded (see Figure 10.7). First of all, given a list word (such as *cat*), the subject marks its location in LTM by associating it with a "list marker." (For example, he or she may associate with that location a proposition indicating *on the list I studied* cat.) The subject also follows network pathways from that word, searching for other words that are marked to indicate they were on the list. For example, following a pathway in LTM connecting *cat* to *dog* (such as the proposition *Cats chase dogs*), he or she might find that *dog* is also associated with the list marker. If a pathway is found that connects the current list word (*cat*) to another word (*dog*) also on the list, the pathway itself is marked by an association with the list marker. (For example, the proposition connecting the two words *cat* and *dog* can be embedded in a proposition indicating its connection with the list.) In summary: When a given word is studied, it is marked as belonging on the list, and any pathways that are followed in a brief search through the network from the word are similarly marked if they lead to other list words. Essentially, this means that the subject *organizes*

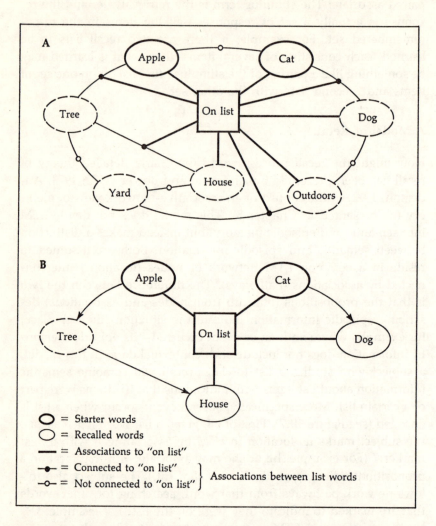

Figure 10.7   The recall model of Anderson and Bower. (A) When the list is studied, locations of list words in memory are connected to a list marker ("On list"). Pathways connecting list words are also marked, and a small set of starter words is formed. (B) When the list is recalled, a search process follows associative pathways from each starter word, and marked words that are found in that search are reported. Note that a word can be marked but not recalled, because it is not found in the search (an example is "Outdoors"); also, a word can be found in the search and not recalled, because it is not appropriately marked (an example is "Tree"). [After Bower, 1972a.]

the list while studying it. He or she is also assumed to select some small set of words that are particularly rich in connections with other list words. This *starter set* is given a special status in associating it with the list, for words in the set will be used as starting points in the retrieval process.

Retrieval in the Anderson-Bower model commences (after an initial recall of any words that may be in STM) with the words in the starter set. One word from the set is picked, and the associative pathways from that word's location in LTM are followed in a search for other words connected to the list marker. Only those pathways that were previously marked as leading to list words will be followed, for it would not be possible to follow every single path from a given word. When words are found to be marked to indicate they were on the list, they are reported. If the process ends at a word that has no marked pathways leading from it, then the process returns to the starter set, again picks up a word there, and begins following pathways. The recall process ends when there are no more words in the starter set—all have been used.

Errors occur in the recall process, according to this model, because the process of marking word locations and associative pathways is probabilistic. That is, it is not certain that a word that is studied will be marked as belonging to the list, and it is not certain that a pathway connecting two list words will be marked. Nor is it certain that the starter set will contain connections rich enough so that every word in the list can be reached from one starter word or another. All these factors lead to errors in recall.

In general, the Anderson-Bower model of recall might be described as follows: First, study of the to-be-remembered items serves to organize them; to associate them with some common label and with one another. Then, recall is initiated by a retrieval cue (such as an instruction to recall the list). This cue signals the LTM location from which recall is to begin. The recall process then consists of following associative pathways from various words connected with the cue. This might be called the search process, for it is a search for marked items from the to-be-remembered set. When such items are found, they are reported. We might note that finding and reporting requires another step. As the search proceeds along pathways in LTM, sooner or later it is bound to run into items that are not in the proper set. For example, if asked to recall the Presidents, you might retrieve Eisenhower and then Stevenson. But just because Stevenson is associated with Eisenhower, he is not necessarily one of the Presidents. Thus, there must be some decisions about the items found during the course of the search. Are they in the to-be-remembered set or are they not? (In the Anderson-Bower model, the question is phrased, "Are they appropriately marked or are they not?") Thus, we can think of recall as comprising a search for items and decisions about those that are found.

This characterization of recall will lead us to some problems; our description of the process is not as comprehensive as it might seem. However, we can learn a great deal about recall from Anderson and Bower's associative-network model: it helps, for example, to explain the effects of organization discussed in the previous chapter. It seems that a good general rule about recall is: Anything that facilitates associations among the items in the TBR set will facilitate later recall. That is because it will make the study and search processes— the marking of items and following of pathways—a bit easier. There should be more and better pathways connecting items on a list when the list has an associative structure than when it does not.

COMPARING RECOGNITION AND RECALL

At this point, we have two hypotheses or theories of "remembering." We can think of them as retrieval theories, for they address the question of how information that is in memory is regained. However, the two theories are quite different. Our theory of recognition is based on the notion of strength and a rather complex decision process. Our theory of recall relies on such concepts as associative pathways and searches. Retrieval seems to employ different processes, depending on whether we study recognition or recall. But do the retrieval processes of recognition and recall differ? If so, how do they differ?

The Threshold Hypothesis

The question of how recognition differs from recall is not a new one. The problem has interested psychologists ever since recognition and recall were first defined, and the superiority of performance with recognition testing was noted (McDougall, 1904). One of the first attempts to account for the difference was the "threshold" hypothesis. It states, quite simply, that both recognition and recall performance depend on the strength of items in memory. It suggests that an item must have a certain amount of strength before it will be recognized; this criterion value is called the *recognition threshold*. There is also a certain amount of strength necessary in order for an item to be recalled; this amount is the *recall threshold*. The threshold for recall is assumed to be higher than the threshold for recognition. That, essentially, is the threshold hypothesis.

Consider what this means. It means that some items, with very high strength, will be both recalled and recognized. Others, with very low strength, will not be remembered in either fashion. A third set of items, with intermediate strength (above the recognition threshold but below the threshold for recall) will be recognized but not recalled. This accounts for the fact that recognition testing produces results superior to recall testing.

Kintsch (1970) has reviewed the evidence for and against the threshold hypothesis in a detailed comparison of recognition and recall. He points out that it is evidence for the hypothesis when a variable is found to affect both recognition and recall in the same way. An example of evidence supporting the hypothesis is the finding, noted in this chapter, that although the time-course of forgetting differs, forgetting is a function of the number of items that intervene between presentation and test, for recognition as for recall, and the form of the forgetting function is similar in the two situations. Variables such as the presentation rate of the list and the number of presentations also have similar effects in both tasks, and both recognition and recall give rise to a serial-position function having primacy and recency effects (Shiffrin, 1970; also see Chapter 2). All these results can easily be explained by a threshold hypothesis (and thus support it), if one assumes that such manipulations push the strengths of items up or down the strength continuum, and that recognition and recall go up or down together.

But if even a single variable were found that affected recognition and recall differently, the validity of the threshold hypothesis would be in doubt. For example, suppose we found a manipulation that improves recognition performance and impairs recall. The better recognition performance implies that the manipulation has improved the strength of items in memory, but the impaired recall implies just the reverse. Thus, because the threshold hypothesis attempts to explain both measures by the same idea, it may be possible to show that it is wrong. For if there is only one mechanism underlying both recognition and recall, then a given manipulation can only produce changes in performance in one direction: Performance for both recognition and recall can go up, or down, but the directions of change cannot differ.

Are there such variables that affect recognition and recall differently? In fact, there are several (Kintsch, 1970). The most important is word frequency. You may recall that the frequency rating of a word is determined by how often it appears in English text. It is a very common finding that frequent words are recalled better than infrequent words. Other things being equal, if we give subjects a list of words and ask them to recall the words, they will do much better if those words are frequent words than if they are not. But in recognition, the outcome is just the reverse. Frequent words, when used in a list and tested with recognition tests, lead to worse performance than do infrequent words; it is easier to recognize infrequent words. With this variable (and others that affect recognition and recall differently), the threshold hypothesis is shown to be inadequate as an explanation of the difference between recognition and recall.

The Dual-Process Hypothesis

A second hypothesis about the difference between recognition and recall is the dual-process hypothesis (Anderson and Bower, 1972; Kintsch, 1970). This hypothesis has received much attention in recent years. It has the advantage of unifying theories of recognition and recall, as well as accounting for differences in the data resulting from the two procedures. The dual-process hypothesis reconciles our discrepant notions of strength (as applied to recognition) and search processes (as applied to recall) by assuming that recall includes recognition as a subprocess. You should remember that our previously described theory of recall includes the processes of search (following pathways in LTM and finding items), and decision (deciding whether or not those items are appropriate to report). The dual-process model accepts this sequence of events as a model for recall and further suggests that recognition corresponds to the decision process. That is, it suggests that recall includes search and recognition. The decision stage of recall is assumed to involve the same processes as are involved in recognition, the processes described by the signal-detection theory. Thus, we see that recognition is essentially recall with the search processes removed. (Because the dual-process model assumes that the subject generates candidates for recall during the search process and then recognizes them, it has also been called the *generation-recognition* model.)

The dual-process interpretation appears to have much to recommend it. By assuming that there are separable processes involved in recall and recognition, it allows for variables that affect the two situations differently. In addition, by retaining the concept of strength for recognition memory, it can explain all the findings that the signal-detection model explains. And it still allows for the search processes of recall, which account for the effects on recall performance of the organizational manipulations we have previously discussed. Thus, it would seem that the dual-process hypothesis, by integrating our separate theories for recognition and recall, combines the advantages of both.

What kind of evidence is there for the dual-process model, aside from the after-the-fact explanatory power it appears to have? We could claim evidence for it if we found manipulations that separately affected the search and decision components of the process. Such a finding would indicate at least that the search and decision stages could be separated, which is certainly an essential aspect of the theory. One such experiment has been conducted by Kintsch (1968). He measured memory for categorized lists using both recognition and recall tests. Two kinds of lists were used: high-association lists, in which each of the list words was highly associated with the name of its category, and low-association lists, which used category members only weakly associated to the category name. By manipulating category membership in this way, Kintsch was essentially manipulating the extent to which the list was structured. He found that low structure led to worse free recall than did high structure, as expected, but there was no difference in recognition performance with the same lists. This finding is consistent with the idea that list structure affects the search portion of recall and does not affect the decision phase of recall or recognition. Others, too, have found that manipulating the organization of a list affects recall without affecting recognition performance (for example, Bruce and Fagan, 1970).

Although the dual-process model, as described so far, appears to account for many of the important phenomena of recall and recognition, Anderson and Bower (1972) have pointed out one modification that is needed. They suggest that the notion of "strength," as used in the signal-detection model for recognition (and therefore in the decision stage of the dual-process model for recall) is inadequate. The authors point out that a simple strength theory cannot explain what is called *list differentiation*. This refers to subjects' ability to distinguish among items on the basis of which of a series of lists contained them. This ability is very good; in fact, subjects can tell whether a given item appeared in the first and fourth of a series of lists, or whether it was in the second and third (Anderson and Bower, 1972). Or, for another example, if List 1 is presented ten times and List 2 is presented once, we would predict that items in the first list should have greater strength than that of items in List 2 on a test following List 2. List 1 items should therefore be falsely recognized when used as distractors in a test of List 2. On the contrary, discrimination of List 1 items from List 2 items is even better in this case than in the usual recognition procedure (Winograd, 1968). In short, a simple strength theory cannot explain how a subject can tell an item was from some list not being tested at present, even though its strength should be as great or greater than the items from the currently tested list. Thus, list differentiation poses a problem for strength theories.

Anderson and Bower (1972) suggest that list differentiation and recognition involve essentially the same processes; that is, recognizing that an item occurred in a certain list is essentially the same as recognizing that it occurred in the only list that was presented. Since simple strength is not adequate for list differentiation, according to this reasoning, it is not adequate for models of recognition and recall. As an alternative, they propose what we might call *contextual strength*. To see what this is, first consider the fact that when a list of words is presented, its presentation occurs in a context. The context includes such things as the temperature, the time of day, the state of the subject's stomach, the color of the experimenter's hair, and so on. All these contextual "elements"—stimuli associated with the context—add up to a totality of context. It is assumed that as the subject learns the list, these contextual cues become associated with the marker for "the list" in LTM. That in turn will become associated with the words in the list (just as in the model for free recall previously discussed).

Now, consider what happens at the time of the test, according to Anderson and Bower. The subject searches for and finds words in memory (or just goes right to them if it is a recognition test) and must decide whether each word found is on the list being called for. This is done by evaluating the item, not with respect to some simple strength or excitation, but instead with respect to the degree of association between that word and the context elements of the called-for list. For example, asked to recall items from List 2, the subject will retrieve some items. For each item, he or she checks to see whether it is sufficiently associated to the context elements of List 2. If so, the item is reported; if not, the item is rejected. It is easy to see how the ability to differentiate lists is predicted by this theory—each list will have occurred in a different context, even if the differences are slight. We could even expect subjects to be able to describe the context in which an item was presented, and they often can. And the theory can also be applied to straightforward recognition—that is, list "differentiation" with just one list.

To support their revised dual-process model, Anderson and Bower manipulated list context, and this resulted in separable effects on recognition and recall. They had subjects learn a series of lists. Each list contained 16 words, and those words were pulled from a master list of 32 words. Thus, the lists overlapped considerably, as each was taken from the same 32-word pool. In one of their experiments, after each list was presented, the subject first tried to recall as many of the words from the master list as possible. That is, he or she recalled all of the previously presented words, from any list. Next, the subject was instructed to indicate (recognize) which of the recalled words came from the most recently presented list. Of course, for the very first list, those words were the same as the ones recalled. However, as the subject received more and more lists, the situation changed. Recall of the master list improved steadily as more lists were presented. This is not surprising, for the retrievability of the total set of words (the master list) is expected to improve as the words are studied more and more often. However, the ability of the subject to recognize which of the recalled words had been most recently presented deteriorated with the number of lists. The authors explained this by assuming that presenting more and more of the overlapping lists results in attaching the same words to more and more contexts. This makes it increasingly difficult to use contextual elements to differentiate words on the most recent list from the others, causing "recognition" of those words to decline. Moreover, their experiment dissociates this decline in recognition from the improvement in recall, supporting the dual-process model.

A brief review is in order. We now have a dual-process hypothesis for retrieval. It says that recall works as follows: Given a retrieval cue, LTM is entered at an appropriate point. From this point, a search process moves out, following previously studied pathways of associations from one item to another. Whenever an item is found, a recognition process occurs—is this item in the set to be recalled? If so, it is reported; if not, the search goes on. From this retrieval theory follows the general rule that any factor that tends to facilitate the associations between the retrieval cue and to-be-remembered items or among the items themselves, such as categorical structure, a schema, or an NLM, will facilitate initial organization and search—and therefore recall.

Recognition Failure of Recallable Words

From our discussion thus far, it might seem that the dual-process model is unassailable. However, it runs into trouble from a

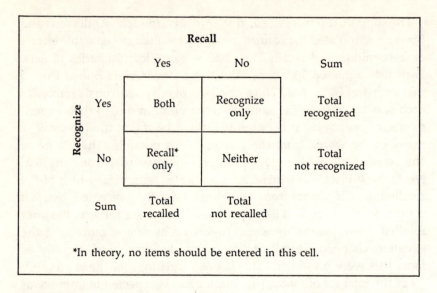

Figure 10.8 Possible outcomes when an item is tested with both recognition and recall tests.

phenomenon introduced in work of Tulving and Thomson (1973). The trouble arises from the dual-process model's assumption that recognition is a subprocess of recall. Tulving and Thomson pointed out that this means if an item can be recalled, it should also be recognizable. That is because subjects' ability to recall the item means that they can both find its location in LTM and make a decision that it was on an initial list, and making the decision is precisely what they must be able to do in order to be able to recognize the item.

The dual-process model actually has two implications, which can be described with the aid of Figure 10.8. The figure shows what can happen to an item from some initially presented list that is tested with both a recognition and a recall test. There are four cells into which an item can be placed, corresponding to four possible outcomes: The item can be recognized only and not recalled; it can be recalled only; it can be both recognized and recalled, or it can be neither recognized nor recalled. What the dual-process model says about this table is, first, *no* items should be in the recall-only cell; that is, whenever an item is recalled, it should also be recognized, so it will never be the case that it is recalled only. As a result, we have the second implication of the model: The total number of recognized items should always be at least as great as the total number recalled. For the total recognition score will include all the recalled items— because these items must also be recognized—plus whatever items are recognized and not recalled.

Step	Event	Example
1a	Present list items and cues, #1.	ground COLD
1b	Test, given cues, #1.	ground *cold*
2a	Present list items and cues, #2.	badge BUTTON
2b	Test, given cues, #2.	badge *button*
3	Present list items and cues, #3.	glue CHAIR
4	Free-association task	table *chair* *cloth* *bench* *dining*
5	Recognition test	table (*chair*) *cloth* *bench* *dining*
6	Recall test, given cues, on list #3.	glue *chair*

Figure 10.9 Procedure of recognition-failure experiment. [After Watkins and Tulving, 1975. Copyright 1975 by the American Psychological Association. Reprinted by permission.]

Tulving and Thomson (1973) provided data that violate both these implications of the dual-process model. The experiments that contradicted the model used a procedure like that shown in Figure 10.9. Subjects in this experiment went through a rather complex sequence of events. First, the subjects were given a list of to-be-remembered items. Each of the to-be-remembered items was written in capital letters, and above it was another item, written in lower-case, which was weakly associated with the to-be-remembered item. The subjects did not have to remember the lower-case items, but they were to be tested later on the capitalized items. Then the subjects took part in a recall test, in which they were given all the lower-case items from the list. They were told to write down as many of the previously seen capitalized items as they could remember, using the lower-case items to help them. (Because the lower-case items were presented with the to-be-remembered list and reappeared on the test to cue recall, they are called *list cues*.) We know, from the encoding-specificity procedure described in Chapter 9, that if the subjects encoded the capitalized words with reference to the list cues, they would benefit from the cues' reappearance at the test.

Next the subjects were given a second list and a second test, like the first except for the use of new words. Finally, a third list, similar to Lists 1 and 2, was presented. At this point the subjects may have expected the same type of test as they had had on the first two lists; if so, they were surprised. Instead, the subjects were given a free-association task. That is, they were shown new words, not seen before during the experiment. Each new word was a stimulus, and the subjects were to write down next to it four responses the stimulus brought to mind. What the subjects were not told is that each stimulus word was highly associated with one of the to-be-remembered words in the third list. It was therefore highly likely that one of the four responses they wrote down would be that very to-be-remembered item. In fact, the subjects were creating their own four-alternative forced-choice recognition test by writing down a list item as one response and three nonlist items as the other responses. They were next given that recognition test; that is, they were asked to look back over their free-association responses and circle any that they recognized as having been on the third list. Finally, the subjects were given a recall test on the third list. Like the previous recall tests for Lists 1 and 2, this test provided the list cues.

The Tulving-Thomson procedure is quite complex (in fact, this description has omitted a couple of steps), but the authors had a purpose for every step in it, all leading to their ultimate goal of contradicting the dual-process model. The first two lists were used in order to show the subjects that encoding each capitalized word in the context of its list cue would be effective. They would then use this strategy for the third list. The free-association and recognition tasks were used in order to mimic the processes assumed by the dual-process model to occur in recall: Subjects generated words as responses to stimulus words and then decided which of their responses were words from the previously presented list, just as the model assumes they internally generate and recognize items during recall. Finally, the recall test was used so that recall and recognition of the same words could be compared. The comparison had a rather surprising outcome—subjects were very poor at recognizing which of their free associates had been on the list. In contrast, they did very well on the recall test on the same list. In one experiment, for example, subjects produced 18 out of the 24 words that had been on the third list as responses when they were performing the free-association task. But they circled only about 4 of the words to indicate their having been on the list. This contrasts with their recall (given the list cues) of 15 of the list words. Thus, recognition performance was worse than recall, and subjects recalled some words without recognizing them. These results are incompatible with the dual-process model.

Tulving and Thomson's demonstration of "recognition failure," that is, recalling some words from a list without being able to recognize them, has been criticized for a variety of reasons. One area of criticism concerns the experimental procedures used to elicit the phenomenon. For one thing, it has been argued (Martin, 1975; Reder, Anderson, and Bjork, 1974) that the words used in the list actually have two meanings, and that a different meaning is tested with recognition than is tested with recall. For example, suppose that a list word is LIGHT, and the list cue for that word is *head*. This means that the subject initially encodes the word as *light-meaning-lamp*. It is this same meaning that will be tested in the recall test, when the word *head* will reappear as a list cue. Now, on the recognition test, suppose the subject is faced with the word LIGHT in the presence of the word *dark*. The subject is now being asked to recognize the word *light* in a context where it has the meaning *level-of-illumination*, rather than *lamp*. It would not be surprising, given this shift of meaning, if recognition suffered. However, in rebuttal to this argument, recognition failure has been obtained even when the list words are carefully selected to have a single meaning tapped by both the recognition and recall tests. (Tulving and Watkins, 1977).

It turns out, in fact, that recognition failure is robust enough to occur over a number of procedural variations. Tulving and Thomson would not have needed to do such a complicated experiment to produce it. This was shown by Watkins and Tulving (1975). Essentially, all you need in order to produce recognition failure is to use a context at recall that is compatible with initial encoding, and *not* to use that context in recognition. Recognition failure occurs, for example, even when the experimenter constructs the recognition test rather than having the subject generate it with a free-association task. Nor is it necessary that the distractor items on the recognition test be associated with the list item; unassociated distractors will do. A minimally complicated experiment that could produce recognition failure would simply present a single list, with each item paired with the usual list cue; then test list items with a conventional forced-choice recognition test (where the list cue is not given) and contrast this with a recall test where the list cues are present. Recognition failure of some words can even occur when total recall performance is inferior to recognition. In terms of Figure 10.8, this means that some items can be in the recall-only cell even when total recall is not greater than total recognition (Wiseman and Tulving, 1976).

Yet despite its robustness, serious problems with the recognition-failure paradigm remain. Santa and Lamwers (1974; 1976) have raised a number of other critical points, some related to the methodology of the experiments demonstrating the phenomenon, others related to its theoretical implications. One criticism of the procedure itself concerns exactly when we should say that recognition failure has occurred. Suppose just a couple of list items are in the recall-only cell, that is, they are recalled and not recognized. Should we call this recognition failure of recallable words? Is the phenomenon "real" in this case? In general, if we give subjects two tests in a row on the same material, even two recognition tests, we will find that performance is not identical. Some items will be remembered on one test and not on the other, simply through the vagaries of human performance, for example, moment-to-moment fluctuations in strength or response criterion. We could expect, say, a couple of items to be remembered on the second test and not on the first. But by this reasoning, if we see that two items are recalled (correct on a second test) and not recognized (incorrect on a first test), this may not be recognition failure; instead it may simply result from the same sort of variations that will generally produce some differences in any two successive tests. Psychologists usually rely on statistical procedures to solve this sort of problem and tell them how many items must show an effect in order for it to be "real," but Santa and Lamwers argue that the appropriate tests for this situation are not evident.

The theoretical arguments of Santa and Lamwers are even more provocative. To understand them, consider what recognition failure tells us about the dual-process model. The model assumes that recognition occurs implicitly when an item is recalled. Successful recall then means that the internal recognition was successful. This leads to the idea that if an item is recalled, it should be recognizable on an overt, external test. If it were not, as occurs with recognition failure, the model would appear to be wrong. But wait—this would be true if we used an external recognition test that precisely simulated the internal recognition that goes on during recall. In that case, successful recall would imply successful internal recognition, which should be duplicated in the external test. But since the internal recognition cannot be observed, we do not know if the recognition procedures used in the work of Tulving and associates are appropriate simulations. In fact, recognition performance is known to be quite sensitive to such test variations as the number and type of distractors used. It seems that it would be very difficult to externally simulate the internal recognition that is a component of recall. We would have to be very careful in attempting to make an overt test match an internal one, for even slight mistakes in selecting the test material could ruin our simulation. By this reasoning, recognition failure does not disprove the dual-process model, for it merely shows that correct recall will not always predict correct performance on an *experimenter's* recognition test. This is not the same as showing that recall will not predict performance on an *internal* recognition test, which is what must be shown in order for the model to be disproved.

As the foregoing argument suggests, the dual-process model can account for the recognition failure phenomenon of Tulving and Thomson by assuming that the recognition that occurs during recall and that which occurs during a recognition test are not identical. To see this, consider the following modification of the model, as depicted in Figure 10.10 (compare Anderson, 1976; Anderson and Bower, 1974). It says that what the subject encodes during the presentation of a list are propositions about the list words; these propositions are themselves formed into a proposition of the form, "_____ is on the list." Recall occurs when a subject searches for and retrieves a concept, and decides (recognizes) that the retrieved item was on the list (that is, finds the connection to the on-the-list proposition). Recognition testing may superficially seem the same as this decision process, but in fact it has its own search component. In recognition, the subject is given a potential list word, which sends him or her to a location in memory. At that point, propositions connected to that location are searched. The subject may or may not find the critical proposition, the one that was tied to the on-the-list proposition during the initial encoding. If not, recognition failure will occur.

In other words, the foregoing model says that encoding is more than accessing the given concept; it is a process of relating it meaningfully to other concepts, creating a sort of propositional package rather than marking a single word as Figure 10.7 suggests. Retrieving will be successful in this case if the package node, connected to "on the list," is recovered. Recognition testing, however, only gives the subject part of the package, the single word that was on the list. There is no guarantee that this will lead to retrieval of the critical proposition required for a correct response. Recall testing may in fact provide a better key to the package, especially when a cue that was present at encoding is given at recall. For example, if a subject encoded the list word COLD in the context of *ground*, then giving the subject the list cue GROUND at the test may prove to be a better means of leading to retrieval of a proposition pertaining to *ground*

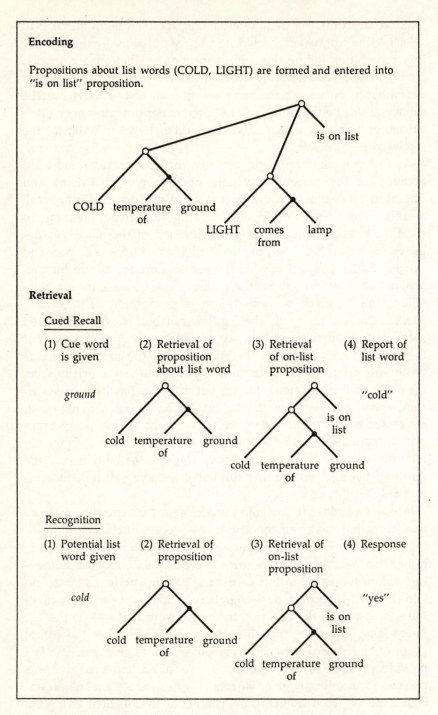

Figure 10.10   Modified dual-process model.

and *cold* than presenting the word COLD, even though the word *cold* is ultimately to be reported. In this case, recall may succeed when recognition fails.

The modified dual-process model suggests that recognition testing, where a to-be-remembered item is actually presented, does not guarantee that the subject will find the appropriate location in memory for the item. Instead, there may still have to be a search for a key proposition about the item. This idea is supported by evidence that recognition is not purely a decision process but involves a search component as well. This view has been espoused by Mandler and his associates (Mandler, 1972; Mandler, Pearlstone, and Koopmans, 1969), and in a model of Atkinson and Juola (1973). One line of evidence for search processes in recognition is that, in some experiments, the degree to which a list is organized affects recognition of list items. It is important to note that this result is not invariably found, as indicated by previously described experiments in which organization of a list was found to affect recall but not recognition (for example, Kintsch, 1968). However that list organization can affect recognition has been found with some consistency, particularly for highly structured lists (Bower, Clark, Lesgold, and Winzenz, 1969; D'Agostino, 1969; Lachman and Tuttle, 1965). Since organization is usually assumed to affect search and not decision processes, the implication is that recognition must include some search processes.

ENCODING SPECIFICITY AND MODELS OF RETRIEVAL

The revision in the dual-process model just described places a greater emphasis on the interdependence between encoding and retrieval. It assumes that a proposition about an item is encoded and must be retrieved, rather than that the item is represented and retrieved by itself. This is consistent with the encoding specificity principle presented in Chapter 9, which says that retrieval will be successful to the extent that its circumstances overlap with those of encoding. In making its new assumptions, the dual-process model becomes more similar to other models of retrieval that have emphasized the importance of encoding conditions (Kintsch, 1974; Flexser and Tulving, 1978). In all these theories, it is assumed that encoding is more complex than the mere marking of a location in memory to indicate that the corresponding item has occurred on a list. Instead, an item is encoded in the context of other items, even in the larger context of the subject's mental and physical state, and the extraexperimental surroundings. As a result, what must be retrieved is not an individual item but the encoding complex—the episode.

In line with this general view of retrieval, Kintsch (1974) depicts the retrieval process as a matching of episodes. (Similar ideas have been espoused by other theorists, e.g., Bower, 1967; Flexser and Tulving, 1978.) At both encoding and retrieval, a large set of information, including attributes of the sound, appearance, and meaning of the experimental material, and features of the subject's internal states and experimental setting as well, is assumed to combine to form episodes. During encoding, such episodes are stored in LTM; during retrieval, an episode is formed and matched against those in memory. If the retrieval task is a recognition test, the degree of match between the episode formed for a given test item and episodes in LTM will determine whether the item is recognized or not. If the task is a recall test, the match between a retrieval episode representing the list context and episodes in memory leads to the recall of some items. Moreover, as an item is recalled, all the information in the corresponding LTM episode becomes available, which cues the retrieval of other episodes and thus the recall of additional items.

A principal difference between recognition and recall in this view is like that given in the modified dual-process model; it resides in the information the two types of tests provide. The episode constructed during a recognition test for comparison with memory will incorporate features of the actual test item, whereas the episode constructed during recall must utilize the more general experimental context (or, if available, a more specific cue).

An advantage of the episodic view of retrieval, which says that what is encoded and retrieved is an episode or propositional package of information, is that it can be applied to retrieval of items other than single words. For example, consider what happens when a picture (for example, a teacup) is initially presented and retrieved. Included in the encoded package might be visual features of the picture. This package would later be compared with the episode formed during a recognition test. If the episodes matched, a positive decision would be made.

Consider in contrast what the initial version of the dual-process model might say about picture recognition. According to this model, locations in LTM corresponding to single concepts are marked during encoding. If what is encoded is a picture, then a location in LTM for that picture would be marked. We know, however, that if a different picture of the same object (a new teacup) is presented as a distractor on the recognition test, subjects will show the ability to tell it is a new item (Bahrick, Clark, and Bahrick, 1967). In order to explain how they do so, the initial model might suggest that the distractor will make contact with a different, unmarked, location in LTM. But this suggests that there would be in LTM a distinct location for each possible picture of the object. Just how these multiple locations for objects would be differentiated is unclear. If all we have is a marked node representing "cup," it should represent one cup as well as another. In contrast, by assuming that specific features of the presented picture are encoded into an episode, the revised model can more readily account for the ability to tell that another picture of the same sort of object is a distractor, for some features of the new object will differ from those of the episode.

The revised dual-process model and the episode-matching notion seem to converge on a conception of retrieval that is nicely tied to the conception of encoding derived in Chapter 9. Both concepts emphasize the active nature of remembering. Encoding is far different from the passive reception of incoming information; it is not like the way a camera's film receives a brief exposure to the outside world. Rather, people act on information to elaborate it and relate it to previous knowledge and the circumstances of its occurrence. Similarly, retrieval is an active process in which previously encoded information is accessed in a search of memory and evaluated with respect to the retrieval context. This process is aided when the initial input was meaningfully encoded, for in that case long-term knowledge can be applied. For example, knowledge about the structure of semantic categories can be used to guide the search process when it is known that category members have been presented. Similarly, when an attempt is made to recall a text that has previously been encoded in relation to a schema, schematic knowledge about complex sequences of events can be used to guide the retrieval process. (Some consequences of this sort of retrieval will be considered in the next chapter.) The elaboration of inputs and searches of LTM that we have described as components of encoding and retrieval may seem complex, but it is just this sort of seeking out and acting on information that characterizes the cognitive being.

11

Forgetting, Distortion, and Construction of Information in Long-Term Memory

This chapter might have been entitled "Inaccuracies in Remembering," because in it we discuss what happens when inputs to LTM cannot be correctly retrieved. As was mentioned in Chapter 1, inaccurate memories can result from failures of several types. The encoding process itself can be incomplete or inaccurate; material can be lost from storage; or the retrieval process can fail to access the proper stored information. In this chapter we will encounter all of these causes of inaccurate remembering.

Errors in memory performance have been variously attributed to forgetting, construction, and distortion of initially presented information. Although these terms are all related (and indeed can vary from one user to another), we can make some general distinctions among them. The term *forgetting* refers to a loss in the ability to retrieve material that was once encoded. The requirement that the material was coded at some earlier point in time is important, for it excludes from "forgetting" the inability to remember events that have not even been perceived. Indeed, we seem to make a similar distinction in everyday life. If someone says, "Did you forget about the meeting?" you might say, "I never heard about it in the first place."

Inaccurate remembering can result not only from the loss of information, as in forgetting, but from the addition to memory of information that was not part of an initial input. Adding to memory in this way is part of what we call *constructive processing* (see Chapter 9), and it is particularly prevalent in experiments that use natural-language texts as the stimulus material. Constructive processing and the errors it induces appear to be normal aspects of comprehending language. When sentences are presented, listeners commonly encode not only the meanings of the words presented, but implications and presuppositions (information that the utterer of a sentence supposes to be known by the listener) as well. Listeners integrate the information in sentences with their general knowledge about the world. All this means that the comprehension of a sentence is an act of construction, and errors can result from constructive processing.

The term *distortion* is usually applied to inaccurate remembering of the sort where what is reported is related, but not identical, to the original input. Distortions can result when incoming information creates cognitive or emotional discomfort, and they can be considered a form of constructive processing. For example, an illogical story may be remembered as more orderly than it actually was. And personality theorists have often noted that memory for anxiety-provoking events may deviate from the original incidents, as a result of psychological defense mechanisms.

THE NATURE OF FORGETTING IN LTM

We have defined forgetting as the loss of ability to retrieve once-encoded information. This definition is a broad one, but its breadth is necessary to enable it to include the various kinds of forgetting that occur. Consider, for example, the fact that you cannot remember what your first birthday was like, although you may even have had a birthday party. In general, you cannot remember the details of your infancy, or early childhood, at all. Since you were at that time a preverbal organism, and you had no verbal codes to store in LTM, the phenomenon of forgetting your infancy may be quite different from the forgetting you do as an adult. Even in adult life, forgetting has many meanings. For example, there is what we may think of as "ordinary" forgetting; you fail to bring something home from the market, or miss an appointment, or cannot fill in a blank during a test. There is also forgetting as a result of physical trauma—amnesia. Then there is repression—the deliberate forgetting of information that might be emotionally painful to recall. All of these occurrences fit our general definition of forgetting, for in each case information that was once stored cannot be retrieved.

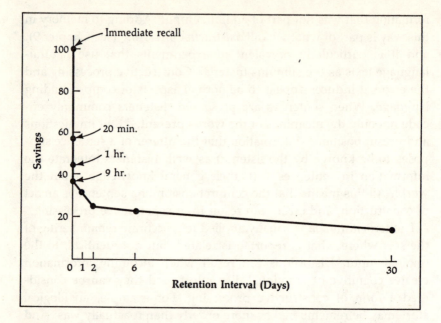

Figure 11.1 Ebbinghaus's forgetting function. Retention of previously learned lists of nonsense syllables, as measured by savings, is plotted as a function of the retention interval—the time between initial learning and the retention test. [After Ebbinghaus, 1885.]

Despite variations in the content that is forgotten, if we look at a forgetting function, that is, one that plots the amount of material remembered over a sequence of points in time (the retention interval), we discover that its form remains remarkably constant. That form is what we saw when we considered short-term forgetting in Chapter 6: The amount of information retained steadily declines, rapidly at first, and then at a slower rate. In STM experiments, the forgetting is essentially complete over a matter of seconds. However, we find similar forgetting functions when we look at information lost from LTM. Ebbinghaus did just this as early as 1885. His measure of how much was retained in memory is called *savings;* it measures how much study is needed to relearn a previously learned list after a given amount of time has elapsed. The more information that has been "saved" or retained in memory, the less study should be required to relearn. Figure 11.1 shows the function obtained by Ebbinghaus, which has the same general form as the forgetting obtained in STM studies such as that of Peterson and Peterson. However, it shows a decline in memory over an interval of days rather than seconds.

Squire and Slater (1975) show that forgetting in LTM occurs gradually even over a period of years. They tested adult subjects on recognition for the names of television shows and race horses that had been prominent during the years 1957 to 1972. Although younger subjects were somewhat better on recent events and adults on earlier ones, both groups of subjects showed gradual forgetting over the period of years since an event occurred.

The PI and RI Paradigms

Traditional procedures used to study forgetting in LTM are the techniques that produce PI and RI, introduced in Chapter 6. At this point, let us consider those procedures in more detail. You may recall that proactive inhibition, or PI, refers to the forgetting of some given material caused by interference from material learned previously. Retroactive inhibition, or RI, refers to forgetting caused by material learned after the to-be-remembered information. These two types of interference have been primarily studied in experiments using paired associates as stimuli.

A bit of notational information is in order here, before we continue. Recall that in the typical paired associate task, subjects are given a list of two-part items and required to recall the second part of each (the response term) when given the first part (the stimulus term). We will use the notation A–B list to refer to a paired-associate list in which stimulus items are taken from a set A and responses from a set B. For example, if the A terms were nonsense syllables and the B terms were digits, DAX–7 and CEB–3 would be typical members of an A–B list. An A–C list, similarly, refers to a list of paired associates using as stimuli the same A terms as the A–B list, but different responses—taken from a set C. For example, if the C terms were letters of the alphabet, DAX–B and CEB–X might be in an A–C list. Using this notation, the PI and RI procedures are as follows (see Figure 11.2):

For both PI and RI, an experimental group of subjects learns an A–B list of paired associates to a certain criterion, usually several perfect runs through the list. Then, they learn an A–C list; it has the same stimulus terms as the first list but different response terms. After a retention interval, the group is again tested. In the PI procedure, the test is on the A–C list. A control group learns only the A–C list (or sometimes learns an unrelated X–Y list before the A–C list), waits for the same retention interval, and then gets the A–C test. We then define PI as the interference generated in the experimental group by the learning of the A–B list. We can actually quantify PI (numerically measure it) in this situation. We do so by finding out how much worse the experimental group does than the control group. The actual mea-

PROACTIVE INHIBITION

Experimental Group	Learn A–B	Learn A–C	Retention Interval	Test A–C
Control Group	———	Learn A–C	Retention Interval	Test A–C

Time →

RETROACTIVE INHIBITION

Experimental Group	Learn A–B	Learn A–C	Retention Interval	Test A–B
Control Group	Learn A–B	———	Retention Interval	Test A–B

Time →

Figure 11.2 The PI and RI procedures. The course of an experiment with paired-associate lists is shown.

sure is: PI = percent correct on A–C test for the control group, minus percent correct for the experimental group, all divided by percent correct for the control group. That is, we take the difference in the mean percentage of correct responses for the two groups, and divide by the performance of the control group (the division makes it possible for us to take into account the difficulty of the A–C list in general; it is a device for making the PI measure here roughly comparable to others). For example, if we find the average for the control group is 75 percent correct, whereas the average for the experimental group is only 50 percent, we have

$$PI = (75 - 50)/75 = 1/3 = 33\%$$

The procedure for measuring RI is just the same as the measure of PI, except that the experimental group is tested on the first list learned and not the second. That is because we are interested in the decrement in first-list performance caused by learning the second list. So the experimental group learns an A–B list, then an A–C, and is then tested on the A–B list. The control group learns the A–B, then does nothing (or sometimes learns an unrelated X–Y list, depending on the experiment) and is later tested on the A–B list. Again, the experimental group will do worse than the control on the A–B test, and just how much worse is measured by: RI = percent correct for control group, minus percent correct for experimental group, all divided by percent correct for control group. This is much the same as the PI measure; all that differs, essentially, is that in RI the tested list is the first one learned, whereas in PI the tested list is the second.

The PI and RI procedures both lead to decrements in performance on the part of the experimental group. That is, we can think of these procedures as manipulations that induce forgetting; in fact, many theorists believe that this laboratory-induced forgetting is fundamentally the same as the forgetting of information outside the laboratory. The extent to which the PI and RI procedures produce forgetting depends on the number of trials with the interfering list (Briggs, 1957; Underwood and Ekstrand, 1966); an *interfering list* is one that the experimental group receives and the control does not. To restate, the amount of PI or RI varies with the number of trials that the experimental group has on the interfering list. For the PI procedure, that is the A–B list; for RI, the A–C list.

INTERFERENCE AND FORGETTING

Hypotheses about why the PI and RI procedures produce forgetting have usually been assumed to apply to all forgetting. They form a general class called the *interference theory of forgetting*. There are several such hypotheses, and we will discuss some of them in this chapter. Before we do, however, there are two points to keep in mind. The first is that these hypotheses are, for the most part, grounded in the S–R tradition. For this reason, the terminology used by interference theorists will at times seem inappropriate; we shall attempt to reconcile that language with the information-processing approach when confusion seems likely. Second, it is also important to keep in mind that most of the experiments to be discussed concern forgetting in episodic memory. Tulving (1972) suggests that semantic knowledge will not be so easily forgotten. So we must keep in mind that forgetting that the response *frog* goes with the stimulus DAX may not be the same as forgetting what a frog is.

Response Competition

One of the first hypotheses about LTM forgetting was McGeoch's (1942) response-competition hypothesis. It formulated forgetting in rather straightforward S–R terms in the context of the PI and RI paradigms. Essentially, McGeoch said that when we learn an A–B and an A–C list, we set up associations of varying strength: We get

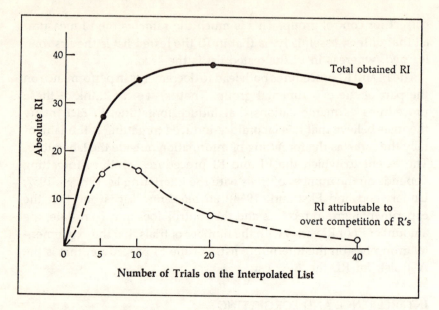

Figure 11.3 Total RI and RI attributable to response intrusions, as a function of the number of trials with the interfering list. [After Melton and Irwin, 1940.]

two associations for each stimulus term, and one will be stronger. When the subject is given the stimulus term on a test, the two responses compete and the stronger one wins; it intrudes and prevents the weaker response from occurring. For example, if a paired associate on the A–B list is DAX–7, and DAX–8 occurs on the A–C list, there might be an internal structure like this:

At the time of testing, when the subject is given DAX–?, he or she will report the 8. In the PI or RI procedure, it is possible that the stronger response will come from the interfering list rather than from the tested list.

The basic problem with McGeoch's hypothesis is that it predicts that errors that subjects make should take the form of intrusions from the interfering list. That is, if subjects err, they should respond "eight" given DAX, when the correct response is "seven," because DAX–8 came from the interfering list. They should *not* say "two" or "sixteen" or any other random response. However, errors do not follow the pattern predicted on this basis (Melton and Irwin, 1940). Figure 11.3 shows that RI and, correspondingly, errors on the tested list, increases and then decreases slightly with the number of trials on the interfering list. However, intrusion errors do not follow this pattern: Where RI attributable to intrusions is decreasing with trials on the interfering list, total RI still increases.

Extinction and Unlearning

Another hypothesis proposed to account for PI and RI is extinction, or "unlearning" (Melton and Irwin, 1940; Underwood, 1948a; 1948b): It proposes that a major determinant of forgetting is the unlearning of associations because of interference. The form of this unlearning is sometimes said to be analogous to the extinction that occurs in conditioning procedures. So, in order to get an idea of just what unlearning might be, let's briefly review classical conditioning.

A typical conditioning procedure might be used to train a dog to salivate when it hears a specific tone. We start out by taking an unconditioned stimulus (UCS) that produces the desired response without training (this might be some food, to produce salivation). We pair the UCS with a conditioned stimulus (CS)—in this case, the tone. We present the CS, then the UCS, and then the response occurs. (The occurrence of the UCS and the response after the CS is called the reinforcement.) This procedure, when repeated several times, constitutes the conditioning phase of the paradigm. It will ultimately result in the occurrence of the response following the CS alone. That is, without presentation of any food, the sound of the tone will produce salivation. The response is now said to be conditioned to the CS. But is this conditioning permanent? Suppose we repeatedly present the CS without the UCS, so there is no reinforcement. At first, the CS alone will produce the salivation, but eventually the response will diminish and then vanish. It is said to be extinguished, for lack of reinforcement. A third phase of conditioning can now take place: spontaneous recovery. Suppose we allow the dog to rest for a while, presenting neither CS nor UCS. We then present the tone again and find that the dog again responds by salivating. It seems as if the extinction phase was not really complete. The conditioned response is said to have spontaneously recovered from extinction, resulting in its reappearance in response to the tone. The response will reextinguish if we continue to present the tone without any reinforcement or will be reacquired if we present reinforcement.

These three phases of conditioning—the acquisition of the response, extinction, and spontaneous recovery—are applied to

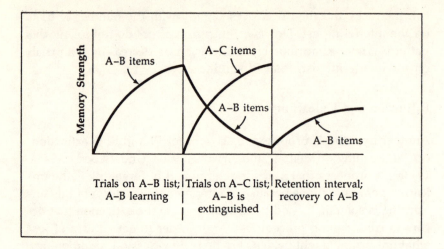

Figure 11.4 Theoretical functions corresponding to performance during an experiment with the PI and RI paradigms. During A–B learning (*first panel, left*) A–B responses increase in strength. During A–C learning (*second panel*), A–C strength increases, and A–B strength is assumed to decrease because of extinction of the A–B associations. During the retention interval (*third panel*), spontaneous recovery of the A–B associations occurs.

paired-associate learning in the unlearning hypothesis. To see how they are applied, examine Figure 11.4, which depicts the *theoretical* strength of responses in an experiment with the PI or the RI procedure. First, the subjects learn an A–B list. They are supposedly acquiring the responses to the stimuli in that list, much as the dog is acquiring the salivary response to the tone. Then, they learn the A–C list; the C responses are now conditioned, and the B responses previously learned are extinguished because they are not reinforced by presentation. During the retention interval, however, the A–B responses will undergo spontaneous recovery. The result will be that, if tested on A–C, the subjects will show PI, the relative improvement of A–B over the retention interval having led to a relative decrement in A–C performance. This decrement is presumably due to competition between B and C responses to A stimuli. On the other hand, if we test A–B, there will certainly be a decrement due to A–C learning, which has resulted in A–B extinction. Thus, RI will be observed.

To summarize, the extinction hypothesis proposes that in the A–B, A–C situation, A–B associations are extinguished, or unlearned, during A–C learning. Presumably this occurs because the presentation of A terms during the A–C phase leads to the awakening of the B responses, which are then not reinforced. During the retention interval, however, the B responses will show some spontaneous recovery. At the time of test, the B and C responses will compete when A terms are presented (much as in the McGeoch hypothesis), with the competition and its outcome depending on the relative strengths of the terms. (Because response competition is assumed to be a second factor contributing to forgetting, in addition to the unlearning, the hypothesis is sometimes called the two-factor hypothesis.)

The two-factor hypothesis has generated an immense amount of experimental work, far too much for us to attempt a comprehensive overview. However, there are certain experiments as well as theoretical views that have become "classics" in this area; we will try to cover the classics instead of reviewing the field as a whole. (For a review, see Postman and Underwood, 1973; their bibliography will also be helpful to interested readers.)

One obvious prediction of the hypothesis is that the amount of PI and RI observed at the time of test will depend on the retention interval. Since A–B strength increases as the retention interval goes on, it will lead to progressively greater decrements in A–C performance. In addition, the more time that A–B associations are given to recover, the better the performance on a subsequent A–B test should be. This means that with longer retention intervals there should be greater amounts of PI, and less RI. Underwood (1948a; 1948b) found this pattern of results.

Other strong empirical support for unlearning came from two experiments: the MFR experiment (Briggs, 1954) and the MMFR experiment (Barnes and Underwood, 1959). Both of these experiments tried to make the unlearning of A–B associations during A–C learning observable—to get inside the extinction process. Both used the A–B, A–C procedure; what varied were the instructions given the subject. In the MFR (modified free recall) experiment, subjects went through A–B, then A–C, learning and then were presented with each A item and asked to give the first response that came to mind. That is, they were not asked to give responses from a particular list, but whatever response they thought of first. Underlying this experiment is the assumption that the responses that were most strongly associated with the stimuli would be recalled first. Thus, the percentage of responses coming from a given list would be a measure of the strength of that list's stimulus–response associations. The results of the Briggs experiment, shown in Figure 11.5, provide strong evidence for unlearning. As learning of the A–B (or A–C) list pro-

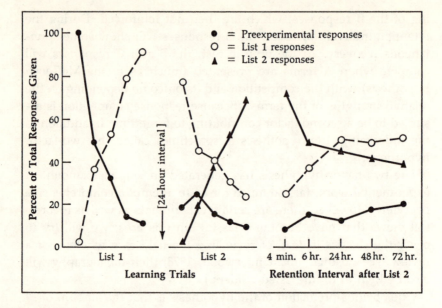

Figure 11.5 Results of the MFR experiment. The first and second panels (*starting at the left*) show the percentage of responses coming from each list during learning trials with the first and second lists, respectively. The third panel shows performance with responses from each list on the MFR test, as a function of the retention interval after the second list. Also shown in each panel is the percentage of responses that were preexperimental—those attached to the stimulus terms at the beginning of the experiment. These responses exhibit extinction and some spontaneous recovery. [After Briggs, 1954. Copyright 1954 by the American Psychological Association. Reprinted by permission.]

gressed, the percentage of responses from the A–B (or A–C) list increased. And when a final test was given after a short retention interval, more responses came from the C list than from the B list. But with longer intervals, the advantage of the C list declined, and there was actually a B-list advantage for retention intervals greater than 24 hours.

One problem with Briggs's study is that although it supports the unlearning idea, it does not show that the A–C learning actually resulted in the *un*learning of B responses. It could have been that the B responses were still in memory, but the subject merely did not report them because he or she thought of the C responses first. To correct this problem—that is, to find out if the unreported responses were still available—Barnes and Underwood (1959) used the MMFR (modified modified free recall) procedure—subjects were presented each A item and asked to recall both B and C responses, if possible.

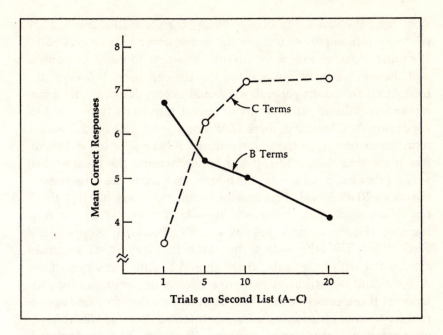

Figure 11.6 The mean number of correct responses on the MMFR test for both lists as a function of the number of trials with the second list. [After Barnes and Underwood, 1959. Copyright 1959 by the American Psychological Association. Reprinted by permission.]

The results, shown in Figure 11.6, suggest that the responses were actually *un*learned. As the A–C learning progressed, fewer and fewer B responses were given, even though subjects were asked to report them if they could: The B responses seemed to be gone from memory.

Although the experiments just described support the two-factor hypothesis of long-term forgetting, other research is not as supportive. Let us consider two aspects of the hypothesis that have not been verified experimentally. First, there has been equivocal evidence for what is called the elicitation hypothesis—namely, that A–B associations become extinguished because, during learning of the A–C list, the B responses are first elicited (awakened) and then not reinforced. Second, there has been some question about the occurrence of spontaneous recovery of B responses during the retention interval.

First, for the elicitation hypothesis. One form of this hypothesis might propose that, during A–C learning, if a subject actually says aloud the B responses, and the B responses are not then reinforced, the B responses will be extinguished. However, overt (aloud) intrusions from the first-list responses during the second-list learning are relatively infrequent, so unlearning cannot occur only on this basis. We must consider covert, or internal, attempts to use B responses, and their subsequent nonreinforcement. Even here, however, the evidence is mixed. In general, we would expect that any time a manipulation induced either overt or covert intrusions from the A–B list during A–C learning, there would be a great deal of RI, because more intrusions mean more unreinforced B-list responses and therefore more extinction. Thus, it is a result favoring the theory when we find that the more similar the B responses are to the C responses, the more RI is found. Presumably, similarity tends to elicit the B responses, resulting in more extinction—and more RI from the A–C learning (Friedman and Reynolds, 1967; Postman, Keppel, and Stark, 1965). The other side of the coin is that if the A–C responses are learned with little effort, there should be little extinction of the A–B list (and less RI) because there are fewer opportunities for elicitation of B responses during A–C learning and therefore few opportunities for those responses to be unreinforced. Yet this idea receives unimpressive experimental support (Postman and Underwood, 1973), weakening the case for the elicitation hypothesis.

The spontaneous-recovery portion of the unlearning hypothesis has even less evidence to support it. An obvious way to study spontaneous recovery would be to use the MMFR paradigm. We could give subjects an A–B list, then an A–C list, and then administer MMFR tests after several different retention intervals. We would expect to find an increase in B responses as the retention intervals grew longer, because the A–B associations should be recovering in the course of time. Yet, experiments that attempted to catch spontaneous recovery in action (Ceraso and Henderson, 1965; Houston, 1966; Koppenaal, 1963) found no increase in A–B recall over time. Perhaps the best attempts were those of Postman et al. (Postman, Stark, and Fraser, 1968; Postman, Stark, and Henschel, 1969)—"best" at least in terms of finding some evidence for recovery. They found that there was some recovery of B responses in about 25 minutes, a rather short retention interval in this paradigm. This is especially strange when we consider the fact that rather little PI is found at 20-minute retention intervals (e.g., Underwood, 1949) and that PI is supposedly caused by spontaneous recovery. The theory places the PI mechanism in the spontaneous recovery of B responses—how can we get strong PI when testing at intervals in which there is no recovery, and recovery at short intervals where PI is at a minimum?

A rather telling blow to the most basic assumption of the two-factor hypothesis—namely, that interfered-with associations are actually unlearned—comes from an experiment of Postman and Stark (1969). One condition of their experiment used a recognition test in the A–B, A–C paradigm. When tested on the A–B list after A–C learning, the subject was given a set of B terms and instructed to pick the one corresponding to a given A term. The subject did not have to recall the B terms, merely to recognize which ones matched the A terms. The results of this manipulation were startling—there was an insignificant amount of RI. It seemed that, far from being unlearned, responses from the A–B list were available for testing with the recognition method. It was the search for the B-list response terms, rather than the decision that those terms were associated with the A stimuli, that was difficult in the A–B, A–C paradigm. That is, the subjects did not have trouble remembering that DAX–7 was a paired associate on the first list so much as they had trouble recalling 7 when given DAX.

The idea that paired-associate learning involves, in part, learning to recall the response terms was not new. However, the idea that resulted from the Postman and Stark experiment—that PI and RI depend on the failure to generate response terms, rather than on the forgetting of associative links—is relatively new. Nor are the response terms actually lost, it seems. Instead, they are *unavailable* at the time of recall. If they were actually lost from memory, we would not expect the recognition test to lead to such good performance.

Response-Set Interference

The last hypothesis we shall discuss, called response-set interference (Postman, Stark, and Fraser, 1968), is compatible with the Postman and Stark results. It suggests that interference is a form of response competition but that the competition is not between individual responses. Instead, whole sets of responses compete with one another. For example, one set of responses might be the B terms of an A–B list—all of them. These would compete with the entire set of C responses on the A–C list.

Basically, the response-set hypothesis works like this (in the context of A–B, A–C learning): First, learning the A–B list activates the set of B responses. This activation includes the setting of a selector mechanism that makes B terms available at the expense of other responses. Then, during A–C learning, the selector shifts over to activate the C responses, inhibiting the B terms. Moreover, the selector mechanism has some inertia; it thus takes a little time to shift from one set to another. We will therefore observe RI if we test the A–B list shortly after A–C learning, for the selector is still activating the set of C responses.

The basic statement of the response-set interference hypothesis says that interference occurs at the level of whole response systems, not single associations. In addition to this basic claim, it includes other assumptions. First, it says that under appropriate conditions—those that manage to bypass the selector mechanism, for example—RI will not be observed. Presumably, the application of a recognition test (as in Postman and Stark, 1969) will do just that—bypass the selector by making responses available immediately through presenting the responses during the test. Second, the theory says that the amount of RI should decrease during the retention interval, because the inertia of the selector mechanism will be maximal immediately after A–C learning. With time, however, it will be easier for the selector mechanism to shift back to the A–B system. (This is related to spontaneous recovery.) Third, the hypothesis can handle the finding that RI increases as similarity among response sets increases. (That is, the more the C terms resemble the B terms, the more interference is generated.) This fact is explained by noting that the selector mechanism is sensitive to intralist similarities. Specifically, it is assumed that setting the response-selection mechanism will be effective only so far as there is a distinct response set to apply it to; that is, distinct criteria for its selection. When the mechanism is shifted, it must be directed by new criteria for response-set membership. Thus, if two response sets are not much different, the response selector may include responses from both in its current set.

The response-set hypothesis should not be construed as completely antagonistic to the two-factor hypothesis, because it includes many of the same ideas; for example, response competition (although it is presumed to be at a different level). Its principal departure from the assumptions of the two-factor hypothesis concerns the first factor assumed by that hypothesis to underlie forgetting—unlearning. For the response-set hypothesis does not propose that responses from one list are unlearned, in the sense of lost from LTM, due to learning responses of another list.

Interference and Forgetting in the "Real World"

The PI and RI paradigms have provided the basic data used to assess the various versions of the interference theory of forgetting. It has usually been assumed that the theory derived from experiments with these procedures will also apply to forgetting that occurs in other contexts. It is time now to ask how well interference theory as a whole fares when it ventures beyond the bounds of paired associates into everyday situations.

Some of the attempts to address this question have tried to induce forgetting, outside the laboratory, of information learned within the laboratory. For example, Underwood and Postman (1960) had subjects learn lists of frequent words (that is, words commonly used) and infrequent words. They reasoned that the forgetting of the frequent words should be greater, because the subjects would be more likely to use the words in common parlance. The extralaboratory associations corresponding to habitual use of the frequent words would interfere and lead to forgetting of the laboratory lists. Although somewhat supportive of this idea, the results were certainly not conclusive.

In a situation that was the reverse of the Underwood and Postman (1960) idea, Slamecka (1966) tried to have subjects unlearn associations they brought to the laboratory. First, he elicited responses to stimuli in free-association tasks. When the stimuli that had been used to elicit the associations were used in paired-associate lists with new responses (such as *cat*–rely instead of *cat*–dog), little interference was demonstrated. Tested for their free-association responses, the subjects had not forgotten a thing. In short, if you bring *cat*–dog into the laboratory, a few trials with *cat*–rely will not make you forget that dogs and cats go together.

Perhaps some of the problems that arise when attempts are made to have subjects forget laboratory material in the real world, or vice versa, can be explained by recourse to the response-set interference hypothesis. Presumably, real-world responses can be held in a different response set than laboratory responses, and once the subject is out of the lab, they can easily be regained. It seems therefore, that even though we want to get some idea of the role of interference in forgetting outside of the PI and RI procedures, we should avoid shifting between the laboratory and real-world setting, or we will get the complications of differing response sets. Of the two potential settings, the laboratory is preferred, for it provides us with the ability to conduct controlled experiments and reach unambiguous conclusions. But, at the same time, we want to mimic forgetting that occurs outside of an experimental setting.

One way to achieve this goal would be to conduct experiments using a more natural stimulus material than the usual paired-associate stimuli. We can do this by studying forgetting of natural language. By natural language, we mean just that—words connected to produce discourse in one's own language. As we shall see, the move to this type of material provides both gains and losses: It enables us to study forgetting in a broader context than the experiments discussed so far, but, at the same time, it seems to bring us into situations where the interference theory of forgetting has less explanatory power.

FORGETTING CONSTRUCTION, AND DISTORTION OF NATURAL-LANGUAGE INFORMATION

One difference between forgetting as it occurs in everyday life and forgetting in the interference procedures using paired associates is that the latter test retention of specific items, whereas in everyday situations we rarely have to remember the specific wording of information. Instead, what we usually retain in memory is the general meaning of information, or the "gist." So rare, in fact, is memory for specific wording that we may resent a teacher who tests for verbatim (word-for-word) retention. We feel, and rightly so, that the content of a message is usually more important than the specific words that conveyed that content.

Memory for Wording Versus Meaning

Experiments on memory for natural-language inputs have pointed out that it is important to make such a distinction between memory for meaning and memory for wording. A classic demonstration that our memory for content is much better than our memory for the specific form of a message (often called its surface structure) was performed by Sachs (1967). She had subjects listen to recorded passages. At some time after subjects had heard a sentence in the passage, they were presented with a new sentence, which could be either identical to the one in the passage or slightly changed. If changed, it could be different in wording (surface structure) but not meaning, or it could be different in meaning. For example, if the original sentence has been "The boy hit the girl," a surface change might be "The girl was hit by the boy"; a meaning change might be "The girl hit the boy." Sachs found that if the changed sentence was presented immediately after the original version, almost any change could readily be recognized. (Presumably, that is because recall at a short interval would utilize information in STM, which would contain the sentence verbatim.) However, as other verbal material intervened between the original presentation of a sentence and its second version, changes in meaning were much more recognizable than changes in wording only. In other words, the sentence could be distorted in form without the subjects' realizing it, but not in semantic content.

A similar phenomenon has been reported in work of Kintsch, McKoon, and Keenan (McKoon and Keenan, reported in Kintsch, 1974; McKoon, 1977). In the McKoon and Keenan study, subjects read a brief paragraph and then were given a test sentence, to which they were to respond true or false, according to the information given in the initial paragraph. The researchers varied whether the information tested in the subsequent sentence had been explicitly presented in the original paragraph or was implied by the paragraph but not explicit. For example, the subject might read a paragraph about the Arapahoe Indians, which indicated that when they first became acquainted with white culture, they were greatly amused by stairsteps. A true test sentence, testing material explicitly stated in the paragraph, would simply repeat one of its original sentences or clauses. A true test sentence on material that was only implicit in the paragraph might state that the Arapahoe had never used stairsteps before the whites arrived. (This is implied by their amusement at the stairsteps.) False test sentences were obtained by altering the true versions, making them negative or substituting a word. In addition, the time between the original reading of the paragraph and the test sentence was varied, from 0 seconds (test immediately after paragraph) to 48 hours.

The results of this experiment are shown in Figure 11.7. At the short retention intervals, subjects could be expected to still retain verbatim wording of the paragraph in STM, and thus they should find it easier to respond to sentences that tested the specific wording. That is, responses to sentences testing explicit information should be faster than to those testing implications of the paragraph. This in fact was the outcome, as the figure shows: At the 0 and 30-second retention interval, explicit-type sentences led to faster performance. At longer intervals, however, the two types of test became equivalent. This is consistent with the idea that memory for specific wording had vanished by the time 20 minutes had passed. At this point, the subject seemed to retain a representation of the passage that made answering questions about its implications as easy as those about explicitly presented information. Such a representation must convey the general meaning of the passage—not only what it said, but what it implied as well.

A similar result was also found by McKoon (1977). Subjects were tested on a passage either immediately after its presentation or after a 25-minute delay. With an immediate test, which should draw on

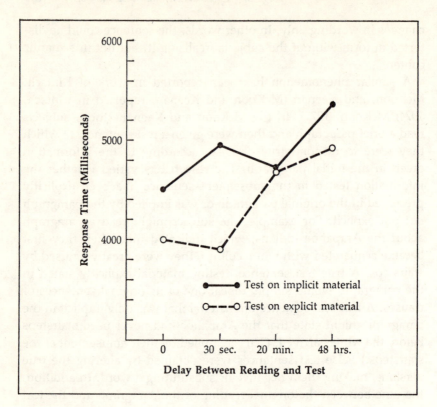

Figure 11.7   Response time for a test of material that was explicit or implicit in a previously read paragraph, as a function of delay of test. Explicit material is responded to faster at short delays but not at longer ones. [After Kintsch, 1974.]

specific wording of the passage retained in STM, subjects did not answer questions about important sentences (those pertaining to the overall topic, which would represent a high level in a schematic representation) any faster than those about relatively unimportant details. This is what we would expect if the subjects' responses were based on memory for the actual words of the passage, for the words of unimportant sentences would be just as well retained as those of important ones. But at the 25-minute test, subjects responded more quickly to the tests of important material from the passage. This suggests that the text was then represented in memory only in a more meaningful form, so that the important sentences had priority and were easier to access.

A study by Anderson and Paulson (1977) indicates that although memory for verbatim information rapidly declines after presentation, some verbatim data can be retained for longer intervals. In their experiment, subjects were given a sentence, then later tested on it. The test consisted of a newly presented sentence, which subjects indicated was either true or false with respect to the first. Two variables were of interest. The first concerned whether the test sentence, if true, was identical to the first sentence or changed in its wording. (For example, the initial sentence "The cat bit the dog" could be tested either with the same sentence or with "The dog was bitten by the cat.") Anderson and Paulson used what seems to be a relatively sensitive measure of the extent to which subjects retained the verbatim wording of a sentence. This measure was the amount of time required to respond "true" to a test sentence that was changed in surface form from the original, minus the time to respond to a true sentence that was identical to the original. An identical test sentence should have an advantage (that is, be responded to faster) over one changed in surface form only if subjects have retained information about the specific wording of the initial sentence, so that the identical sentence matches the retained information better than the changed sentence does. The magnitude of the advantage for the identical test sentence can then serve as a measure of the amount of information about the initial wording that has been retained.

The second variable of interest in this study, as in others we have discussed, was the delay between the initial sentence's occurrence and the test. The delay period was filled by a sequence of other sentences, alternating between new sentences receiving their initial presentation and sentences testing previously presented items. This delay varied from 0 (no intervening sentences) to about 7½ minutes (15 intervening new sentences and 15 tests). The data from this study, shown in Figure 11.8, show that the measure of verbatim retention declines over the first 30 seconds after presentation (one intervening new sentence and test), but thereafter remains steady. More importantly, the measure does not decline to zero. Instead, a small advantage for identical test sentences remains, suggesting that subjects retain some information about the wording of the initial sentence for intervals longer than those of STM storage.

Anderson and Paulson suggest that the difference between memory for wording and memory for meaning is that wording information is less likely to be transferred to LTM. Wording is well retained during its period of STM storage, but this is rather brief—memory for wording declines rapidly over a 30-second interval. Thereafter, memory for the surface form of a sentence depends on information

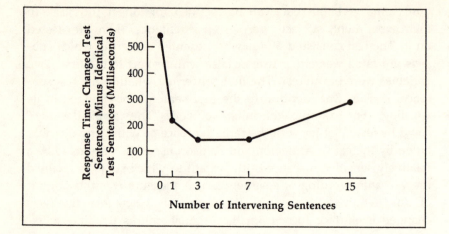

Figure 11.8 Difference in response times to true test sentences that were identical or changed from original sentences; this provides a measure of retention of original wording. The measure is shown as a function of delay (in number of intervening sentences) between original and test sentences; it declines with delay but does not reach zero. [After Anderson and Paulson, 1977.]

in LTM, and, though not completely absent, this appears to be secondary to the nonverbatim information about content stored there.

The experiments described above indicate that a distinction should be made between memory for wording and memory for meaning. Although it is possible to remember specific wording if we are motivated to do so (Cofer, Chmielewski, and Brockway, 1976), in everyday situations we seem to treat the content of a message as more important than its superficial form. This has implications for the application of the interference theory to natural-language materials, for the paired-associate procedure on which it is based clearly places emphasis on memory for specific wording. The paired-associate task requires subjects to remember specific terms associated in sequence with specific other terms, that is, to remember the surface aspects of an input. Moreover, paired associates are hardly natural material; they are virtually devoid of meaning. This raises the question of whether experiments with the PI and RI procedures reveal principles of forgetting general enough to apply to natural-language materials as well, especially to retention of the meaning of such materials.

The Interference Theory and Memory for Meaning

As applied to forgetting of natural-language inputs, the interference theory might be assumed to predict that any sort of text would interfere with any other. For example, if we presented people with a passage about baseball and then a passage about anatomy, we might predict that the baseball information would interfere with knowledge about anatomy. However, interference on this general level does not seem to occur. For example, if we give subjects successive prose passages and test their memory with a recognition test for general meaning (Slamecka, 1960a; 1960b), there is little forgetting.

According to Anderson and Bower (1973), it is inappropriate to predict interference from one passage with memory for the general meaning of another, dissimilar, passage. They suggest that interference will occur between two passages when they have more specific information in common, namely, similar underlying propositions. In particular, if subjects are presented with two successive propositions that share some elements and not others, interference will occur. For example, one proposition might be conveyed by the sentence "Harry hit the janitor"; the second proposition by "Harry followed the preacher" (or "The preacher was followed by Harry," which can be assumed to represent the same proposition). If we then give subjects the cue "Harry _____ the _____, " and ask for recall of the initial sentence, we should find that performance suffers because the second sentence also presents information about Harry's actions. That is, recall should be worse than if the second sentence had a propositional content unrelated to the first.

A somewhat larger perspective has been taken by Thorndyke and Hayes-Roth (1979). They suggest that successive passages that share the same schema may both interfere with and facilitate one another's retention. The facilitation arises because the repetition of the schema from one passage to another strengthens its representation in LTM. But the fact that details of the schema are changed from one passage (or instantiation) to the next produces interference between the passages, because the details are associated with the same schema and thus compete (much as competition occurs in the A–B, A–C procedure).

However, the situations where interference is predicted to occur with natural language still seem rather constrained. Interference is assumed to require the presence of highly similar (at least schematically) sets of material. In other words, the interference theory seems to apply to natural language in situations that resemble the PI and RI experiments. Yet knowledge expressed by language is remembered imperfectly in everyday life, despite the fact that we do not seem to be continually presented with sequences resembling A–B, A–C chains. To further understand failures of memory for natural-language materials, we must consider findings other than those associated with the interference theory. In particular, we will consider inaccuracies in remembering that occur when natural language is distorted and elaborated upon.

Inaccurate Memory for Meaning: Construction and Distortions

When subjects attempt to remember a meaningful passage, their attempts may take the form not only of paraphrasing the original material or forgetting it entirely, but of reporting more information than was originally given. A study by Bransford and Franks (1971) did much to bring this point to the attention of cognitive psychologists. This study demonstrated an effect in sentence remembering that is similar to one we previously described in discussing memory for visual forms. The visual effect was found by Franks and Bransford (1971), who demonstrated that when subjects were shown a set of complex visual forms, they appeared to abstract a prototypical form, or central tendency, for the set. The study of Bransford and Franks (1971) similarly began with a set of stimuli, in this case, sentences. The set was composed from four simple sentences, such as: *(1)* the ants were in the kitchen. *(2)* The jelly was on the table. *(3)* The jelly was sweet. *(4)* The ants ate the jelly. These sentence forms can be combined in twos, threes, or all four together to form new sentences. For example, combining 1 and 4 gives: The ants in the kitchen ate the jelly. Combining 3 and 4 gives: The ants ate the sweet jelly. Combining 2, 3, and 4 gives: The ants ate the sweet jelly that was on the table. All four combined give: The ants in the kitchen ate the sweet jelly that was on the table. That last sentence is the equivalent of the prototypical form in the Franks and Bransford visual-memory experiment, for it is a sentence that contains all the information in the basic ones *(1 through 4)*.

Bransford and Franks then presented subjects with a subset of the total set of sentences that could be derived from the four basic ones. The subset included two sentences out of the four simple ones *(1 through 4)*; two from the set made by combining them in twos, and two from the set made by combining them in threes. The sentences selected managed to represent all four of the basic forms in one combination or another, and, when presented, they were interspersed with sentences from other sets unrelated to ants, kitchens, and jelly, but derived in the same fashion. Then the subjects were given a recognition test and were asked to indicate how confident they were of their recognition judgment. The results were analogous to those of the experiment on visual forms: The subjects rated themselves most confident of having seen the sentence that was prototypical—the one that combined the four basic sentences. But that was a sentence that they had never been shown! In addition, subjects tended to rate their recognition of sentences combining three of the basic forms as more confident than that of sentences combining two; and their recognition of sentences combining two as more confident than that of the simple sentences. In short, whether a sentence had actually been seen or not was unimportant for its "recognition." What was important was how many of the simple forms a given sentence combined—the more it combined, the more likely it was to be "recognized."

Bransford and Franks suggested that their results occurred because the subjects abstracted and stored the combined content of the sentences they had been shown. They constructed a prototypical memory representation from the given raw material, and that representation built on—but was not restricted to—the information initially presented. Since their experiment was performed, others have challenged it on a variety of grounds; for example, pointing out that abstraction of a prototype does not occur under certain experimental conditions (Anderson and Bower, 1973; James and Hillinger, 1977), or offering an alternative to the view that the abstracted memory representation is a prototype (Reitman and Bower, 1973). As we have seen, however, the constructive effects demonstrated by these experimenters remain a focus of much research.

We have seen another example of construction-based errors in the study of Sulin and Dooling (1974). Their subjects appeared to store not only information explicitly presented in a paragraph, but elaborations based on the fact that information was about a famous person such as Helen Keller. A similar point was made in experiments by Barclay (1973) and Bransford, Barclay, and Franks (1972). Bransford et al. found that if subjects were presented with a sentence like "Three turtles rested on a floating log and a fish swam beneath them," they would falsely recognize "Three turtles rested on a floating log and a fish swam beneath it." The replacement of "them" by "it" represents an inference from the initial sentence—we know that if the turtles were on the log, then a fish swimming beneath the turtles (them) would also be swimming beneath the log (it). In contrast, if the original sentence is "Three turtles rested *beside* a floating log, and a fish swam beneath them," and the test sentence replaces "them" with "it," a similar recognition error does not occur. That is because the use of "beside" does not permit the same inference.

In these studies, subjects appear to have gone beyond the material given to them, storing an elaborated version. This seems rather far removed from forgetting as a source of memory inaccuracies, for the storing of implications from text is more like information addition than information loss. It could even be argued that the encoding of text in elaborated form should not be considered an inaccuracy at all, since it is part of the normal process of comprehending a linguistic input. On the other hand, in memory experiments concerned with verbatim retention, recalling an inference made from text as part of the text itself is indeed an inaccuracy.

A phenomenon that is related to errors in remembering due to acts of construction is distortion. As was mentioned previously, the term *distortion* is often applied to errors in remembering that are induced when to-be-remembered information is incompatible with knowledge in LTM, on either a logical or an emotional basis. One of the best known examples of distortions in memory is also one of the earliest. It was performed by Bartlett and published in 1932. He had subjects attempt to reproduce a story they had read. The story is a legend of a tribe of North American Indians called "The War of the Ghosts" (see Figure 11.9). When Bartlett's subjects, who were not Indians, tried to reproduce the tale, they were found to make rather systematic errors. Since the original passage did not necessarily fit into their cultural conceptions of what was logical and conventional, their errors of reproduction were distortions that tended to rearrange the story into what they considered a normal pattern. Bartlett proposed that subjects erred in this way because, in first reading the story, they formed an abstract representation of the story's general theme. Bartlett called the representation a *schema*, a term that we have seen is still used today with a similar meaning. Such a schema would of necessity be assimilated into the subject's personal system of beliefs, emotions, and so on. That assimilation would result in the systematic changes that were observed. In short, we might conclude that the subjects tried to fit the story into their existing LTM structure. They would "forget" certain aspects of the legend that did not fit in or were incompatible with their LTM structure.

Bartlett's ideas were ahead of their time, but psychologists have begun to catch up, spurred by studies of the role of constructive processes in memory for text. A more recent experiment demonstrating distortions like those Bartlett observed was performed by Spiro (1977). Subjects in his experiment read a story about two "friends" of the experimenter, Bob and Margie. To make the context as natural

The War of the Ghosts

One night two young men from Egulac went down to the river to hunt seals, and while they were there it became foggy and calm. Then they heard war-cries, and they thought: "Maybe this is a war party." They escaped to the shore, and hid behind a log. Now canoes came up, and they heard the noise of paddles, and saw one canoe coming up to them. There were five men in the canoe, and they said:

"What do you think? We wish to take you along. We are going up the river to make war on the people."

One of the young men said: "I have no arrows."

"Arrows are in the canoe," they said.

"I will not go along. I might be killed. My relatives do not know where I have gone. But you," he said, turning to the other, "may go with them."

So one of the young men went, but the other returned home.

And the warriors went on up the river to a town on the other side of Kalama. The people came down to the water, and they began to fight, and many were killed. But presently the young man heard one of the warriors say: "Quick, let us go home: that Indian has been hit." Now he thought: "Oh, they are ghosts." He did not feel sick, but they said he had been shot.

So the canoes went back to Egulac, and the young man went ashore to his house, and made a fire. And he told everybody and said: "Behold I accompanied the ghosts, and we went to fight. Many of our fellows were killed, and many of those who attacked us were killed. They said I was hit, and I did not feel sick."

He told it all, and then he became quiet. When the sun rose he fell down. Something black came out of his mouth. His face became contorted. The people jumped up and cried.

He was dead.

Subject's Reproduction

Two youths were standing by a river about to start seal-catching, when a boat appeared with five men in it. They were all armed for war.

The youths were at first frightened, but they were asked by the men to come and help them fight some enemies on the other bank. One youth said he could not come as his relations would be anxious about him; the other said he would go, and entered the boat.

In the evening he returned to his hut, and told his friends that he had been in a battle. A great many had been slain, and he had been wounded by an arrow; he had not felt any pain, he said. They told him that he must have been fighting in a battle of ghosts. Then he remembered that it had been queer and he became very excited.

In the morning, however, he became ill, and his friends gathered round; he fell down and his face became very pale. Then he writhed and shrieked and his friends were filled with terror. At last he became calm. Something hard and black came out of his mouth, and he lay contorted and dead.

Figure 11.9 Text of Bartlett's "War of the Ghosts" (1932) and a subject's reproduction. [Cambridge University Press.]

as possible, Spiro led the subjects to assume that they were in an experiment assessing reactions to interpersonal relations (rather than in a study of memory). The story concerned Bob's desire not to have children. He had delayed in telling this to Margie, his fiancee, and he was concerned that she should share his feelings. However, when he told Margie, she did want children very badly; thus her wishes were incompatible with Bob's. (Spiro also used a version in which Margie agreed with Bob, but, to avoid complicating matters, our discussion will be restricted to the version where they disagreed.) After a few minutes, the subjects were then casually told either that Bob and Margie married and are happy, or that the engagement was broken. The information that they had married was, of course, inconsistent with their disagreement on the subject of children. Spiro's principal concern was whether this inconsistency would lead to errors in memory for the story. To assess memory, he had subjects return from two days to six weeks later and recall the story as accurately as possible.

Spiro predicted that subjects who were told that Bob and Margie were happily married, information inconsistent with the original story, would tend to distort the story to accomodate the inconsistency and that subjects who were told the engagement had been broken would not distort in this fashion. Therefore, patterns of errors in recall should differ for the two groups. The group who received inconsistent information after the story should tend to make such errors as recalling the initial disagreement as less severe than it really was or minimizing its importance. In contrast, if subjects were told Margie and Bob did not marry, information consistent with the initial story about their disagreement, they should, if anything, enhance the magnitude of the disagreement or its importance in recall.

Spiro's predictions were confirmed. Subjects who were given inconsistent information following a story tended to distort the story in recall so as to reduce the inconsistencies. Spiro attributed this outcome to the subjects' assimilating their representation of the story into a more general, preexisting schema about interpersonal relations. This resulted in the loss of information specific to the story and a greater use of the general schema at recall. At recall, the subjects were assumed to reconstruct the story from the information available. They adhered to a rule of the general schema about interpersonal relations, which says that events and outcomes should be consistent. This directed the recall toward consistency, leading to the errors observed.

Constructive Processing: Encoding? Storage? Retrieval?

The inaccuracies of memory induced by constructive processing differ from the errors due to forgetting. As we have said, when construction occurs, it need not be the case that information is lost; in some cases, more is reported than was presented. And unlike forgetting, where we are usually aware of the inability to recall, subjects who distort don't necessarily realize they have lost information. In fact, in Spiro's experiment, subjects' confidence in distorted reports was as high as or higher than confidence in correct reports. Inaccuracies in remembering based on constructive processes differ from the traditional view of forgetting in another way as well. Forgetting is usually conceived of as happening during the interval when information is stored, after encoding and before retrieval. For example, RI is said to occur when new information, coming in after the initial input, causes a decrease in access to stored information about that input. Constructive processes, on the other hand, do not occur only during storage. In fact, emphasis usually has been placed on their occurrence at encoding, as is consistent with the idea that construction is an integral part of language comprehension. In Chapter 9 we reviewed a number of studies that made this point. We found, for example (Dooling and Mullet, 1973; Bransford and Johnson, 1972) that presenting a title with a difficult-to-interpret passage aided memory for the passage as long as the title was presented before encoding, but not if it was presented afterwards. This suggested that construction could occur only at encoding.

However, other data suggest that activity on the part of the subject can influence memory at retrieval. One relevant study is that of Anderson and Pichert (1978), cited in Chapter 9, where people given a new perspective at the time of a test on memory for a story recalled new information from it.

A study performed by Dooling and Christiaansen (1977) suggests that errors can be induced by constructive processes at the time of retrieval. It used the same story as Sulin and Dooling (1974), which was a biography of Helen Keller. Subjects read the story after being told it was about Carol Harris. At the time of a recognition test a week later, some subjects were told that the story had actually been about Helen Keller. The interest was in the extent to which they would then falsely recognize the sentence "She was deaf, dumb, and blind." To the extent that they did so, the subjects would appear to have reconstructed the passage using their Helen Keller knowledge, even though the relevant knowledge was activated after the story's initial encoding.

The results indicated, in fact, that false recognitions could be induced by knowledge activated after the initial text presentation. The subjects who were told the passage was about Helen Keller just before the test made more errors on the sentence related to Helen Keller than subjects who were never told it was about Helen Keller rather than Carol Harris. Apparently, constructive processing can take effect after initial encoding, even at the time of retrieval. Dooling and Christiaansen suggest that other studies (like those of Dooling and Mullet, and Bransford and Johnson) did not find any effects of giving a title after a text because they used relatively brief retention intervals. As more time passes after a passage is read, subjects seem to have less and less information about the actual words in the passage and come to rely more and more on general knowledge in LTM. At this point, they may use the general knowledge even if they are not told it is relevant until after the passage has initially been encoded. In line with this idea, Spiro (1977) found that the distortions in recall of subjects who heard information inconsistent with a previous story increased with the time between the inconsistent information and recall.

If construction can occur at encoding and retrieval, what about during storage? In Bartlett's experiments on memory, he often had a subject repeatedly attempt to reproduce a text after being presented with it just once. Generally, the reproductions changed over time, finally reaching some stereotyped form. Bartlett found that sometimes a subject partially introduced some change into one of the reproductions—for example, mentioning the change verbally but not writing it down—then fully introduced it in a later reproduction. This observation led him to speculate that during the time the stimulus was stored in memory, forces were working to bring the stimulus information into a certain form. For a time, a force might be held back by the subject, but gradually it would gain strength until the change could not be withheld and would at last appear in a reproduction. This idea suggests that distortions of material could be introduced in storage by some sort of mental force not under the subject's control.

The hypothesis that stored information changes spontaneously, without subjective control, was advocated even earlier by Wulf (1922), on the basis of experiments on memory for visual forms. Wulf found that subjects who attempted to repeatedly reproduce irregular forms did so in such a way as to make them simpler, more regular, or more similar to familiar objects. He hypothesized that the mental trace of a form changed "autonomously," due to neural forces. Riley (1962) reviewed the many subsequent studies that tested Wulf's idea, however, and concluded that the hypothesis of autonomous changes in storage is untestable. The problem is that an experimenter cannot control the internal forces that produce such change, precluding a direct test of the hypothesis. Then, too, many other factors could operate to produce results like Wulf's. For example, Wulf did not rule out the possibility that his subjects thought of a verbal label for a given form. Later, forgetting of the form's details could have led the subjects to draw in details suggested by the label, resulting in the changes Wulf observed. The changes would actually reflect a strategy for responding, rather than some sort of autonomous alteration in the internal representation of the form itself. In fact, Hanawalt and Demarest (1939) subsequently showed that giving subjects a label for a form at the time of reproduction influenced their drawing. Since the label was given so late, the changes in the drawing could not be the result of forces acting during the storage interval. Rather, these results suggest a response-strategy effect.

In summary, more evidence seems to indicate that elaborations and distortions produced by constructive processing occur at encoding or retrieval than indicates they occur during storage. (Part of the problem is that the storage hypothesis is difficult to test.) The assumption that construction occurs when information is actively processed at encoding and retrieval differentiates it from forgetting, which is generally characterized as a more passive loss of information over the time it is stored.

EXPERIMENTS ON "EVERYDAY" INACCURACIES OF MEMORY

The existence of constructive processing can have profound effects on our everyday life. Research of Loftus (1975; 1977; Loftus, Miller, and Burns, 1978) demonstrates one important situation in which construction can occur—when witnesses to some event testify about it in court. The general procedure used in this research first exposes a subject to some event, such as a film of a car crash. Then the subjects are questioned about the event. One of the questions is a critical item, for it introduces information that did not actually occur. For example, the critical question might be, "How fast was the car going when it passed the barn while traveling along the country road?" Note that the barn is not the focus of the question; subjects are not asked whether or not there was a barn. Rather, its existence is assumed by the question; it is presented implicitly as a fact. (In reality, no barn appeared.) Later, the subjects are given a test on their memory for the original film. The false presumption in the critical question is found to have an effect: Subjects who received the question about a barn "remember" actually having seen one more often than subjects who received a similar question without the barn. It seems that the presumption of the barn in the critical question is incorporated into subjects' memorial representation of the original event. It leads them to state later, even with confidence, that the original event included such an object. They do not realize that their memory for the event was reconstructed after the question occurred, inducing them to incorporate invalid information. This is a situation where the constructive nature of memory can be dangerous.

The studies of Loftus illustrate a construction-based error that might occur in a natural setting. Consider the following study, then, which provides a rather remarkable contrast, still in a natural context. Rubin (1977) asked college students to recall passages they were likely to have learned when growing up in the American school system. The passages were the Preamble to the Constitution, the Twenty-third Psalm, and Hamlet's soliloquy. The results showed virtually *no* sign of constructive processes at work; less than one word in six recalled by the subjects was not as in the original text. And recall was remarkably consistent across subjects, the only variation being in the total number of words recalled. This means that if we know the number of words a subject recalled, we can predict with virtually complete accuracy what those words were, just by looking at the stereotypical recall. For example, if we know that a subject recalled ten words from Hamlet's soliloquy, they are almost certainly "To be or not to be, that is the question," for those are the words most often recalled.

Unlike Bartlett's subjects, who seemed to first remember a general theme and then construct the details, Rubin's subjects seemed to recall in chains of associations between words. That is, they used the surface structure of the text as the framework for recall, rather than the underlying meaning. This was indicated in part by a tendency to recall in groups of words that were bounded by natural places in the text to stop for breath. The rhythm of the words seemed to be an important component of their recall strategy as well. A rather dramatic demonstration of this was obtained when Rubin asked subjects to recall the words of "The Star Spangled Banner" while listening either to repeated presentations of the appropriate tune or to the tune of "Stars and Stripes Forever." Subjects given the wrong music not only recalled less than those given the right music, they actually covered their ears on occasion! And subjects in the right-music condition clearly used the music to help them recall. They would hurriedly try to write the words corresponding to the current passage of music; then when the music outraced them, they would stop, wait until the tune came around to where they had stopped, and then rapidly write some more.

The use of surface-structure units defined by breath patterns and rhythm indicates that subjects were recalling a rather superficial representation of the texts. This is supported by the humorous article that occasionally appears in newspapers, reporting children's interpretations of memorized passages such as the Pledge of Allegiance, including such remarkable segments as, "and to the Republic for Richard Stans. . . ." This suggests that people may not ever have encoded the meaning of such passages; they must rely on memory for the surface. Nor is it surprising that their encoded representation is superficial, when we consider that rote memorization, rather than meaningful comprehension, was undoubtedly stressed when these texts were learned. Under these circumstances, it appears that forgetting can indeed be characterized by a deletion of information rather than an addition; subjects forget certain surface units of the passage and remember others.

Though they provide a contrast to the construction observed by Loftus, Rubin's subjects are also exemplifying forgetting as it occurs in an everyday setting (even if it is infrequently that we are asked to memorize passages verbatim). There appears to be room for theories that emphasize both constructive processes and verbatim loss. The human information processor is sufficiently variable so that both types of effects occur.

12

Memory
and Individuals

In the last eleven chapters, we have talked about memory in the abstract. We have compiled a picture of an "average" person's memory system and its use. In this chapter, we consider memory in individuals. As we shall see, not all memory systems are the same. Some people seem to perform rather spectacularly on memory tests; and, even within "normal" populations, memorial abilities vary. This sort of variation is the concern of this chapter.

EXPERTISE IN MEMORY

Some people seem to have an uncanny ability to remember. There are claims of memorizing the entire Bible, for example, and books like the best-selling *The Memory Book* (Lorayne and Lucas, 1974) attempt to provide the rest of us with similar abilities. Even if most of us remain unable to perform such feats ourselves, the study of memory experts expands our understanding of memory in more ordinary individuals as well. What we discover is that many of the devices the experts use are abilities we have studied in the preceding chapters, carried to unusual heights.

Mnemonics and Mnemonists

As was mentioned in Chapter 5, the term *mnemonics* refers to the use of learned devices and strategies to aid in remembering. Some mnemonic tricks are familiar to almost everyone, such as rhymes that define rules of spelling ("i before e except after c . . ."). Several devices can be used to remember lists of items. One is the method of loci described in Chapter 5, an ancient means of remembering a list by imagining each item in turn in one of a previously learned sequence of locations. Another device for remembering a list is to weave a story around the items.

Yet another way to remember a list is called the *peg-word* system. This system enables the mnemonist to remember lists of up to ten items, and it can easily be expanded to include more. First, the mnemonist must learn the following rhyme: "One is a bun; two is a shoe; three is a tree; four is a door; five is a hive; six are sticks; seven is heaven; eight is a gate; nine is a line; ten is a hen." Once you have the rhyme, the mnemonic device is much like that used in the method of loci. Suppose you are to learn the following list of items: *bread, eggs, mustard, cheese, flour, milk, tomatoes, bananas, butter, onions.* To remember the list, think of each item in its sequence as interacting with the corresponding item in the peg-word sequence. Think of a bun as growing out of the side of a loaf of bread; some broken eggs in a shoe, dripping out of the sole; a Christmas tree with cans of mustard hanging on it; and so on. Later, to recall the list of items, you just recall the peg-word rhyme. "One is a bun" leads to retrieval of the bun growing out of the loaf of bread; thus, you recall bread. "Two is a shoe" brings to mind the eggs, and so on. With the peg-word mnemonic, the entire list of items can easily be remembered.

Many mnemonic devices are easy to learn. Other mnemonics are not so easy; in fact, some are used only by especially skilled mnemonists—people who, for one reason or another, specialize in rote memorization. Bower (1973) reported his experiences with a group of such experts. He attended a convention of mnemonists, where each tried to impress the others with mnemonic twists and tricks. And their skills *were* impressive, Bower reported. One man could take four words called out by his audience and with great speed, write down the letters from one of the words upside down; those from another, backward; those from another both upside down and backward; and those from the fourth in normal fashion. But that's not all. While writing them down, he randomly interspersed the letters from one word with those from the others, at the same time retaining their proper sequence within each word. And if that were not enough, at the same time he recited "The Shooting of Dan McGrew"!

It is not difficult to document the skills of these amazing

mnemonists. Nor is it difficult to be impressed by them. What is difficult is to discover just how they do what they do. Bower asked the mnemonist who could scramble the words how he performed his feat. His answer was that he had practiced it so much that his hands just knew what to do while he thought about the words. His answer might seem surprisingly lacking in insight, but we might have just as much difficulty verbally describing how we play a piece on the piano, or how we arrive at the answer to "What is three times two?" or how we balance while riding a bicycle. Skills like these are not very amenable to introspective investigation.

Yet it is possible to study mnemonists in more rigorous ways. There are two highly skilled mnemonists who have been investigated in detail— one was studied by Luria (1968); the other by Hunt and Love (1972). These two men were similar in several respects, including the fact that the places where they spent their early lives were only 35 miles apart. On the other hand, their memory skills were somewhat different; for example, Luria's mnemonist reported much greater use of imagery than did Hunt and Love's.

Let us consider Hunt and Love's mnemonist in detail, for there is a great deal of experimental data available in his case. He is referred to as VP. The life of VP would not make an exciting book. He was born in Latvia in 1935, the only child in his family. He showed early promise of intelligence, reading by the age of 3½. He also showed some early indication of his memory skills—by age 5 he had memorized a street map of a city of half a million, and at the age of 10 he memorized 150 poems as part of a contest. He also began to play chess at 8 years of age. We might think that all these things indicate a person of high intelligence, and VP's scores on recently taken intelligence tests bear this out. His high scores on the IQ tests were primarily obtained on those tests relating to memory. He scored in the 95th percentile on a test in which short-term retention plays an important part. He also scored extremely well on a test of perceptual speed, the ability to perceive details quickly. On the whole, Hunt and Love point out, his test scores indicate an intelligent person, but they certainly do not predict an exceptional memorizer.

There is no doubt, however, that VP has exceptional memory skills. Hunt and Love were able to document this in a variety of experiments, many of which should by now be familiar. (Where appropriate, the number of the chapter in which an experimental procedure has been discussed will be noted.) Let us consider first VP's performance on tasks related to STM. One of the most basic tasks is the memory-span task, usually used to assess the chunk capacity of STM (Chapter 5). We know that the span is usually in the range of five to nine items. At first, VP's span for a series of rapidly presented digits did not appear to be exceptional. However, he soon developed a way to increase his span. When digits were presented at a rate of one each second, he reported grouping them in sets of three to five, then associating with each set some verbal code (1492, for example, is an obviously codable group). In this fashion, he increased his span to seventeen digits with little effort. Control subjects who were told about VP's coding device were able to improve their memory spans too, but not nearly as much.

The short-term forgetting data of the Peterson and Peterson task (Chapter 6) are also of interest. In that task, the subject tries to remember three consonants while counting backward by threes. In contrast to the usual rapid decay found over an 18-second retention interval in this task, VP showed little or no forgetting over 18 seconds. This held not only for the first trial (when PI is at a minimum, and maximum recall is found) but for the remaining trials as well. One possible explanation of these results was offered by VP. He said that when he was given a set of three consonants to remember, his knowledge of several languages enabled him to associate some word with it in almost every case. Thus, he converted it to a single chunk. His lack of forgetting is in that case predictable on the basis of what is known about the effect of the number of chunks in the Peterson task—forgetting is much greater for three chunks than for one. Moreover, the use of several languages might act, in effect, to produce a release from PI (as in the work of Wickens, Chapter 6) which would tend to decrease forgetting in this task. That is because each different language would act as a new class of to-be-remembered items, and switching to a new class generally produces a release from PI.

In view of the related effects of mediation and organization on long-term storage, we might expect VP's long-term retention to be as exceptional as his short-term retention. In fact, this is the case. Hunt and Love tested VP on several LTM tasks. One was with Bartlett's story, "War of the Ghosts," which most listeners tend to distort in recall (Chapter 11). The story was read to VP; then he counted backward by sevens from the number 253 until he reached zero. He then reconstructed designated parts of the story at intervals ranging from 1 minute later to 6 weeks later. On each occasion, his retention of the story was remarkable. He could not recall it verbatim, but he did recall it with great fidelity. And his retention was as good after 6 weeks as after a 1-hour retention interval.

How does VP perform so well on such tests of memory? To some extent at least, his performance appears to result from an ability to quickly derive schemes to chunk and elaborate on unrelated stimuli. In this he is aided by an ability to perceive details rapidly, which helps him to find a basis for using the mnemonic technique. VP's STM span does not appear to be markedly different from that of other individuals, but the chunking increases the amount of information his STM can hold, and the elaboration leads to better encoded data in LTM.

It is interesting to note that VP is primarily a verbal mnemonist; he does not use imaginal techniques to a great extent. One indication that he does not use imagery very often comes from his performance on Frost's visual-clustering task (Chapter 9). Both VP and control subjects first viewed Frosts's picture stimuli (which can be categorized semantically or by visual orientation), and then, after a delay, they were given a surprise free-recall test. The control subjects showed strong clustering by visual orientation, but VP showed only semantic clustering. Thus, it appeared that he did not store the visual characteristics in visual form. Not all mnemonists eschew images, however; Luria's mnemonist used them extensively, and the Lorayne/Lucas book stresses the use of image mediators for aiding memory (Chapter 9).

One factor that may have contributed to VP's ability is early training. Both VP and the mnemonist studied by Luria grew up on similar school systems (even in the same geographical area), which emphasized rote learning. In such a situation, it behooves the student to improve rote-memorization ability. It is extremely speculative, to be sure, but it is tempting to conclude that this early training may have provided VP with the impetus to hone his mnemonic skills.

Chess Experts and Memory

It is interesting to note that VP is a superior chess player. He has played in exhibitions where he simultaneously undertook seven blindfold games of chess! He also carries on large numbers of games in correspondence with others, in which he does not need a written record to keep track of what is happening. Such feats are impressive exhibitions of memory, and, as such, they are consistent with what we know of VP as an outstanding memorizer. But it is somewhat surprising to consider that such feats are not uncommon in the realm of chess. Most chess players at the level of master or grand master are able to reproduce almost perfrectly a configuration of chess pieces after viewing it for only 5 seconds (de Groot, 1965;

1966). This holds true when the configuration is meaningful in the context of the game. However, for randomly placed pieces, the ability of masters to reproduce a chess board is no better then that of weak players. The latter result indicates that it is not some exceptional STM capacity of masters that underlies their ability to reproduce the board; instead, it must have something to do with their knowledge of the game.

The capacity of chess masters to reproduce playing configurations has been studied in a series of papers by Simon and others (Simon and Barenfeld, 1969; Chase and Simon, 1973; Simon and Gilmartin, 1973). One outcome of this research is a computer simulation of chessboard memory. This computer program is of special interest because it illustrates how the capacities and processes of perception, short-term storage, and long-term memory combine to form the basis for a memorial skill.

Simon and Barenfeld (1969) first concentrated on the perceptual aspects of chessboard reproduction. In particular, they were concerned with the ways in which chess players looked at the chessboard in the first few seconds after being presented with a novel configuration of pieces. The data on memory for such configurations indicates that good players can pick up a remarkable amount of information in just those first few seconds. Moreover, when eye movements of chess players are recorded, it is found that vision is concentrated on the pieces on the board that are strategically most important.

Simon and Barenfeld proposed a model of chessboard perception that they implemented as a computer program. Essentially, their program assumes that the chess player first fixates on an important piece on the board. When fixated on a particular piece, the player at the same time gathers information about its neighbors, through peripheral vision. In particular, he or she takes note of neighboring pieces bearing a meaningful relation to the piece—attacking it, defending it, attacked by it, or defended by it. Then the player shifts to one of the related pieces, fixates on that, and so the process continues. What this means is that the player's visual attention is pushed around the board from one important piece to another, directed by the meaningful relations among the pieces. With these assumptions, the simulation program produced much the same eye movements as those produced by human chess players.

Efficient visual encoding of the chess board is but one aspect of reproducing a chess configuration. How does the player retain the configuration, having perceived it? Somehow, the player is able to reproduce the board immediately after a 5-second viewing. With such a short retention interval, we would suspect that it is STM capacity that is tapped in the performance. But if STM has a limited capacity, the chess information must be stored as no more than several chunks. Thus, it seems that the reproduction task requires chunking the information from the board and storing it in STM, once it has been perceived.

The role of STM in chessboard reproduction was studied by Simon, Chase, and Gilmartin. Their starting point was the hypothesis that chess masters were adept at reproducing chessboards because they could use their knowledge to chunk configurations on the board. According to this hypothesis, skilled chess players looking at the board will recognize certain combinations of pieces as familiar (in the sense that they match a schema in LTM). To such a cluster they are able to assign some label or code that enables it to be chunked (much as YMCA, consisting of four letters, can be a single chunk). By combining various clusters of pieces into chunks, the players can reduce the demands on STM. They are then able to store the information on the board and use it to reproduce the pattern. Less experienced players would undoubtedly be far less able to recognize and encode clusters of pieces as chunks, and this would mean that their reproductive capacity would suffer. Masters and weak players would be equally unprepared to encode random configurations, for in these cases the clusters of pieces would not be recognizable as meaningful. This would explain why masters do no better than lesser players at reproducing random boards.

Chase and Simon tested this hypothesis by having players at levels from master to novice take part in two tasks (see Figure 12.1). One was a test of memory; the board reproduction task we have been discussing, in which the player tries to reconstruct a chessboard after seeing it for only 5 seconds. The other was a perception task, in which the player tried to reproduce a board that was in plain sight. A videotape machine recorded the player's glances back and forth between the stimulus board and the reproduction.

For the perception task, Chase and Simon defined as a chunk any set of pieces that were placed on the reproduction board between successive glances at the to-be-reproduced board. For the memory task, a chunk was defined as all the pieces placed on the board with very short intervals (2 seconds or less) between them. If a longer interval occurred between placement of two pieces, they were assumed to be in different chunks. This definition is plausible if we assume that the subject should place all the chess pieces contained

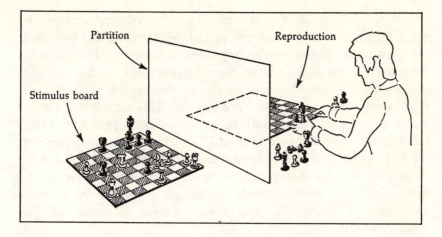

Figure 12.1 Diagram of the chessboard reproduction tasks used by Chase and Simon (1973). For the memory task, the partition is removed and replaced five seconds later; the subject then tries to reproduce the stimulus board. For the perception task, the partition is removed but not replaced. The subject then reproduces the stimulus board as quickly as possible.

in a single chunk quickly, then pause while attempting to decode the next chunk, quickly place the pieces in that chunk, pause, and so on.

Chase and Simon recorded the average number of chunks and the number of pieces per chunk for a master, a class-A player, and a beginner (listed in decreasing order of expertise). They found that, for the memory task, chunk size was related to the skill of the player. The number of pieces per chunk decreased from the master to the class-A player, and from the class-A player to the novice. This is consistent with the hypothesis that experienced players can reproduce chessboards better than weak players because they can pack more pieces into a chunk. Another difference between the players was found in the perception task. Although chunk size in that task was about the same as in the memory task, unlike the memory task, chunk size did not vary with level of player—the number of pieces per glance at the to-be-reproduced board was about the same for the novice as for the master. However, the better the player, the less time was taken to glance at the board. This indicates that, in the perceptual task, the master took much less time than the novice but picked up as much information. Thus, we find that masters can perceive and encode the board faster, and they can chunk more of what they have perceived.

A final point noted by Chase and Simon concerns the nature of

the chunks that master players form. The configurations corresponding to single chunks in the memory task fell into a rather restricted
set of patterns. These patterns represented meaningful relations in
the context of the game. In fact, over 75 percent of all of the master's
chunks fell into only three categories of chessboard patterns, and
those were all highly familiar and regular. This means the master
could accomplish chunk formation by using a relatively small
number of configurations stored in LTM. Thus, the results support
the hypothesis that chess masters use stored schemata in LTM to
recode chessboard configurations rapidly, facilitating their short-
term memory for chessboards. Although it occurs in a more
specialized domain, this skill seems similar to those of the
mnemonist VP.

Eidetic Imagery

A 10-year-old boy has been seated in front of an easel on which a
picture, depicting Alice in Wonderland looking at the Cheshire Cat
in a tree, was exposed for 30 seconds. The boy was instructed to
scan all over the picture while it was in view; now it is gone, and he
is asked by an experimenter whether he still sees something there.

> The boy replies: I see the tree, grey tree with three limbs. I see the cat
>   with stripes around its tail.
> The experimenter: Can you count those stripes?
> The boy: Yes (pause); there's about sixteen.
> Experimenter: You're counting what? Black, white, or both?
> Boy: Both.

The boy is right (after Leask, Haber, and Haber, 1969, p. 30).

This child is a subject in an experiment studying eidetic imagery, a
memory skill rather different from the abilities we have been discussing. *Eidetic imagery* is commonly called photographic memory,
but, as we shall see, an eidetic image is generally not like a photograph.

One method of studying this phenomenon is like the description
above. Subjects are shown a picture and told to scan around it; then
the picture is removed and the subjects report what they see. The
presence of an eidetic image is suggested by certain general criteria
(Haber and Haber, 1964; Leask et al., 1969). Perhaps the most important indications are the subjects' own confident reports that they actually see an image localized in front of them; they are not simply
remembering a picture but are currently experiencing it. In addition, subjects scan the image by moving their eyes around it, with-

out its appearing to move (as a perceptual afterimage would), and their eye movements correspond to the positions of the items they are reporting in the original picture. The image is also in the same color as the original picture (again unlike most afterimages). An image is typically reported to last from a half minute to several minutes, although subjects can terminate it by blinking their eyes; and most eidetikers cannot bring an image back once it has vanished (Leask et al., 1969).

One thing that clearly distinguishes an eidetic image from a photograph is that it seems to be formed in segments and vanish in segments, rather than appearing and disappearing all at once (Jaensch, 1930; Leask et al., 1969). Moreover, although some researchers report a general correlation between an eidetiker's accuracy at reporting details from an image and other characteristics such as image duration or the frequency with which an image is reported (Haber and Haber, 1964), these findings are not universal (see Gray and Gummerman, 1975). Thus, accuracy is not generally considered among the best indicators of image ability, which again distinguishes this ability from a so-called photographic memory—which should be very accurate.

We now know what an eidetic image is, but who forms them? Eidetic imagers are most likely to be children. In a review of studies performed over the last two decades or so, Gray and Gummerman point out that surveys of normal children have found an average of 5 percent to qualify as eidetikers. In the same period, only a single study (Gummerman, Gray, and Wilson, 1972) tested normal adults, and it found none to be eidetic. This may seem to suggest that eidetic imagery is an ability that we all have initially but that is lost as our verbal skills develop. However, Gray and Gummerman find relatively little consistent support for this idea. And, as they point out, the greater incidence in children may simply reflect a greater willingness on their part to respond according to what they sense the experimenters wish, even if the experimenters don't explicitly demand a certain sort of response.

The possibility that children may simply be complying with implicit demands to report detailed images points out a problem with the self-report method of studying eidetic imagery. What this method lacks is control over what the subject is seeing; too much reliance is placed on the subject's own reports. Another technique has been used, therefore, to which this criticism cannot be applied. In this case, the subject is first shown a picture that is meaningless by itself. The subject forms an eidetic image of this picture, then attempts to superimpose that image over a second picture, and reports what is seen. The second picture is so constructed that it, too, is nonsensical by itself; however, when it is superimposed on the first picture, the two together make sense. Thus, if the subject really has an eidetic image of the first picture, which can be superimposed on the second, he or she should be able to report the sense of the composite picture formed by the two together. On the other hand, if the subject has no eidetic image, then he or she will see only the second picture and will be unable to report the composite's meaning.

The superimposition method has had mixed results. Leask et al. (1969) reported subjects who were successful at fusing an image and a second picture and reporting the composite, but Gray and Gummerman (1975) point out that their pictures were sufficiently simple so that subjects may have been able to guess what the composite would be from just viewing its parts. In contrast, Gummerman et al. (1972) did not find any subjects who could fuse a complex pair of pictures (patterns of seemingly random black squares that, when superimposed, produced a geometric form), even though two of their subjects were children who had been classified as eidetic by the more usual self-report method.

There is one reported case, however, of an eidetiker who could pass the superimposition test (Stromeyer, 1970; Stromeyer and Psotka, 1970). Known as Elizabeth, she appears to be capable of an amazing eidetic ability, quite different from that of the imagers we have been discussing. One of her most impressive performances was superimposing an image on a picture where the stimuli were extremely complex. They were made of patterns developed by Julesz (1964), which, when viewed alone, look like random patterns of dots. When the patterns are viewed simultaneously, each by one eye (this can be acomplished by the wearing of special glasses, as with a 3-D picture), a three-dimensional figure appears. It is impossible to guess what the figure will be from the individual pictures, so that Elizabeth would have to have formed the composite in order to report the figure. She could in fact do so. In one case, she formed an image of a one-million dot pattern with one eye and superimposed it on another pattern viewed with the other eye. She could do this successfully even with a delay of several hours between the time the image of the first pattern was formed and the time the second pattern was seen, indicating she had the ability to retain her eidetic image in LTM.

Elizabeth's ability is truly amazing, so much so that it has not thus far been duplicated with another subject. This very difficulty raises questions about how to interpret the phenomenon. It is hard to draw conclusions from a single subject about what is purported to be a characteristic of at least a small percentage of the population at large. It seems more appropriate to treat this case as a rare exception and to draw conclusions on the basis of the eidetic phenomenon as it is more generally demonstrated. Gray and Gummerman thus conclude that eidetic imagery is really just a very vivid sort of visual memory, no different from the visual memory we have discussed in preceding chapters. The general failure of the superimposition method to demonstrate images that are picturelike, and the general similarity between reports about eidetic images and other memory images, support their conclusions. In their view, eidetic imagers may be more talented imagers than most of us, but the difference is one of quantity rather than the presence of a unique ability.

The various kinds of memory expertise we have reviewed suggest that the experts may not be so different from the nonexperts as we once imagined. They seem to have finely honed talents, but they are talents that also exist in the "average" information processor we have been studying, even if they appear in lesser form. This does not mean that all of us can develop equal skills if we try, although we could undoubtedly improve our memory abilities with practice. Just as superstar athletes seem to have natural gifts that they can develop to higher levels than other people, memory experts may have enhanced talents to begin with, which they then bring to the level of ability observed.

INDIVIDUAL DIFFERENCES IN PROCESSING INFORMATION

We've looked at the experts and found that they are not as unique as we might initially have thought. On the other hand, there are differences in individuals' memory-related abilities, even among the nonexperts. It is this variation among ordinary individuals that has led to the many tests of intelligence that follow us through the educational system. Such tests, although they may be called tests of general intelligence, rely to a great extent on memorial abilities like those we have been discussing. We have previously noted, for example, that the measure of memory span is a common component of IQ tests. Other common components test the amount of world knowledge a person has and the ability to manipulate symbols, both reflecting information stored in what we have called semantic memory. Individual differences in intelligence and memory seem to be rather intertwined.

When we consider the extent to which traditional tests of intellectual ability tap memory, one question that arises is how these tests relate to the information-processing skills that we have discussed. A traditional IQ test may produce a single number that reflects an individual's "measure of intelligence." This seems less informative than knowing how that individual performs at pattern recognition or chunking, how large his or her attentional capacity is, or how efficient that person is at retrieving information in long-term memory. For this reason, a number of theorists have attempted to determine how the more general concept of intelligence is related to the fundamental structures and processes of the human memory system that cognitive psychologists study.

A rather extensive body of studies in this area have been conducted by Hunt and his associates (Hunt, 1978; Hunt, Frost, and Lunneborg, 1973; Hunt, Lunneborg, and Lewis, 1975). In one series of experiments, Hunt, Lunneborg, and Lewis divided students at the University of Washington into two groups, one having scored below the median level of college-bound high school juniors on a verbal aptitude test, and the other having scored near the top of the students taking the test. These "low-verbal" and "high-verbal" students took part in a series of information-processing tasks. A number of differences in the performances of the two groups were found.

The students took part in the task of Posner (Chapter 7), where subjects indicate whether two letters have the same name. The difference between the time it takes to respond when the two letters are physically different but the same in name (Aa) and the time it takes when the letters are physically identical (AA) can be assumed to reflect the additional time required to name the letters and compare them by name in the nonidentical case. Naming time, as measured by this difference, was faster for the high-verbal subjects.

The high-verbal subjects also performed better on a variety of tests of short-term retention, especially if they tapped memory for the order in which items were presented. For example, in the task of Peterson and Peterson (Chapter 6), high-verbal subjects made fewer errors of the sort where a letter was reported out of its position in the original order. They also made fewer errors in reporting the identities of the to-be-remembered letters. As a whole, these results suggest that there might be a difference between low- and high-verbal groups in STM in general. Just what the difference is, how-

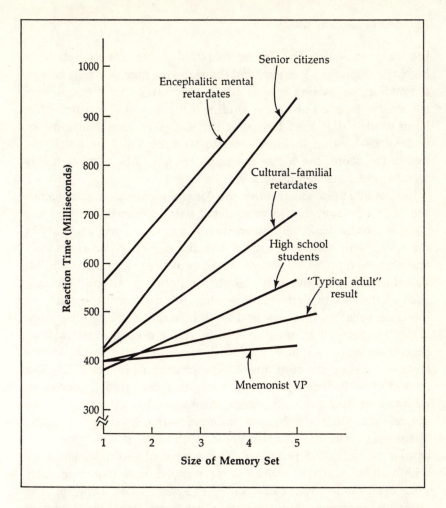

Figure 12.2 Reaction time in memory-scanning task as a function of size of memory set, for several groups of subjects. [After Hunt, 1978. Copyright 1978 by the American Psychological Association. Reprinted by permission.]

ever, is not clear, as we saw from a previous discussion (Chapter 5). There is evidence against the idea that the difference derives from greater ability of the high-verbal subjects to form chunks, for example.

A number of other tasks also show individual differences. One is the task developed by Sternberg (1966; see Chapter 5), which can be used to measure the rate at which information is retrieved from STM. Theoretically, the slope of the function relating reaction time to memory-set size represents the time to retrieve an item in STM and compare it to a test stimulus (the lower the slope, the faster the assumed rate of retrieval and comparison). Figure 12.2 shows such functions for a number of different groups of subjects, as well as for the mnemonist VP. The slopes for retarded subjects are relatively high; the slope for VP is low; and the slope for normal adults falls in the middle, suggesting at least a rough correlation with overall verbal ability. In addition, some studies (Chiang and Atkinson, 1976; Hunt et al., 1973) have looked at the slopes of such functions for individuals varying in intelligence-test scores and found that the higher the score, the lower the slope tended to be, although this result is not consistently obtained.

Results like these suggest that the general measures of intelligence can in fact be analyzed in more detail with information-processing methods. Individuals varying on such general measures also vary in the speed with which they can derive the names of verbal symbols and retrieve from STM, and in the amount they can retain in STM. The studies cited above demonstrate a number of other differences, such as the rate of performing mental arithmetic and the ability to integrate syllables into words. In summarizing such results, Hunt (1978) suggests that we can divide differences in information-processing abilities into two general classes. One is simply knowledge—the sheer amount and variety of information in LTM. The second class includes processes, such as those used in encoding information and retrieving from memory. This class Hunt subdivides into processes that are automatic—that is, do not demand attentional capacity (Chapter 4)—and those that are controlled, attention-demanding processes. The controlled processes can vary within an individual as well as between individuals; that is precisely what it means to say they are under the person's own control. The automatic processes, Hunt suggests, are more stable, representing individual abilities that are not so changeable.

On the other hand, we must be careful in the extent to which we treat individual differences as fixed, immutable characteristics of a person. Just as you can emulate mnemonists and increase your performance on remembering lists of items, so too can performance on tests of general intelligence change under such influences as training and motivation, or simply with changes in age (Anastasi, 1976). This suggests that information-processing skills would change under the same influences. In fact, such aspects of performance as the rate of retrieval from STM in the Sternberg task are known to change with practice (for example, Monsell, 1978). The virtue of the information-processing approach to measuring intelligence, then, is not its ability to uncover fixed capacities of individuals, but its promise to cast further light on the fundamental structures and processes that contribute to an individual's intellectual functioning at any one time.

ALTERED STATES OF MEMORY

As we have seen, the memory system we have developed varies across individuals. But memory can vary within the individual as well, as a result of changes in a person's emotional and physical state. Such fluctuations could occur, for example, as a result of illness, emotional trauma, or aging. It could also be produced by the ingestion of drugs. It is the effects of drugs, especially alcohol, on memory that we will next consider.

One effect of alcohol on memory is the alcoholic "blackout," the loss of memory for events that occurred during a period of drinking. We are familiar with the stereotype of the individual who "ties one on," then can't remember a thing about it the next day. But one need not drink a lot to show memory impairment; relatively small doses of alcohol are known to produce poor performance in memory tasks (e.g., Parker, Alkana, Birnbaum, Hartley, and Noble, 1974).

Researchers have attempted to determine the component of memory that is primarily affected by alcohol ingestion. A principal concern is whether memory performance under alcohol shows impairment because the alcohol hinders the encoding and initial storage of items or, alternatively, because even adequately stored items cannot be retrieved. To investigate this, Parker, Birnbaum, and Noble (1976) chose tasks that were assumed to minimize the role of retrieval, especially the search component. For example, one task used recognition testing to assess memory for a list of colored photographs. Subjects saw and were tested on the photographs after drinking either an alcoholic beverage or a placebo drink. The alcohol was found to interfere with recognition, with the placebo drinkers performing best and a group who had a relatively high dose of alcohol performing worst. The existence of a memory decrement due to alcohol in a task where retrieval is made relatively easy suggests that the alcohol caused the encoding process to suffer.

Further work of Birnbaum, Parker, Hartley, and Noble (1978, Experiment 2; a similar study was performed by Miller, Adesso, Fleming, Gino, and Lauerman, 1978) supports the assumption that encoding is a principal locus of alcoholic deficits. They had all their subjects encode a list of categorized words in a sober state. Then a week later, the subjects took part in recall tests after having had either an alcoholic or a placebo drink. In this study, the two groups of subjects should have encoded and stored the list equivalently, because both were treated the same when it was presented and until the time of the tests. The one difference, then, is that one group tried to retrieve the list while intoxicated, the other while sober.

The results of this study showed a remarkable similarity between the two groups. In terms of performance on a free-recall test, the two groups were equivalent in both overall recall level and measures of clustering. The rates of free recall were also equivalent. Both groups also benefited equally from receiving the category names as cues, leading to equal levels of performance on a cued-recall test. In short, the alcohol seemed to have no effect at all when given after the items were encoded and stored, at the time of retrieval. These results, therefore, present evidence that the primary effects of alcohol occur prior to the time information is retrieved. As long as the words were encoded and stored in a sober state, their recall was unimpaired by intoxication.

The information-processing approach to remembering has been applied to another drug-related phenomenon called state-dependent learning. This phenomenon is a counterpart of the encoding specificity effect discussed in Chapter 9. In an experiment of Thomson and Tulving (1970), subjects received a list of items either accompanied or unaccompanied by associated items. At the time of the test, the associates were either reinstated or they were not. It was found that the best recall performance occurred when the associates were given at both presentation and test. Somewhat poorer performance was obtained when there were no associates given at either time. Performance was worst when associates were present only at encoding or only at retrieval. These results suggested that the encoding of the items occurred in a specific context, and if some new context was introduced at the time of retrieval, performance suffered.

Similar effects have been observed when administration of drugs essentially replaces the associates in the Thomson and Tulving procedure. The typical experiment on this topic uses four conditions similar to those just described. Subjects are presented with information when they are in either a normal or a drugged state (for example, alcohol had been ingested), and are tested in either the same or the alternate state. State dependence is said to occur if performance on the memory test is higher when the state of encoding matches the state of retrieval—both normal or both drugged—than when the two states do not match. When state dependence is found, it is often asymmetric (Eich, 1977); that is, the two conditions with nonmatching states at encoding and retrieval do not lead to identical results. Performance is better when initial encoding occurs in a normal state and retrieval occurs in a drugged state than when the reverse holds.

In a review of the phenomenon of state dependence, Eich (1977) pointed out that not all tasks lead to the pattern described above. In

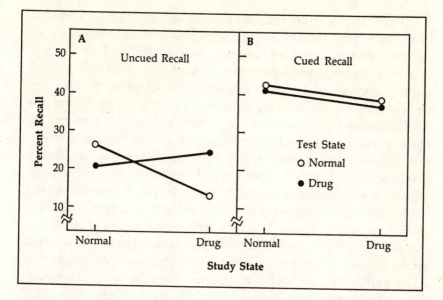

Figure 12.3   Recall in a normal or drug state, following study in a normal or drug state. (A) Uncued-recall test; the state-dependent pattern is shown. (B) Cued-recall test; no state dependence is evident. [After Eich, Weingartner, Stillman, and Gillin, 1975.]

a study by Eich, Weingartner, Stillman, and Gillin (1975), subjects were given a list of words to learn, either in a normal state or after smoking a marijuana cigarette. The list contained words that fell into categories (for example, flowers). The subjects were later tested on the words in either the same or alternate states. Two types of tests were administered—the standard free recall, or recall given the category names as cues. As was pointed out in Chapter 9, the presence of the cues should make the retrieval process much easier, for it would help the subjects to find the organized category units in memory. The contrast between these two tests is shown in Figure 12.3. Panel A shows the usual state-dependent pattern (performance is better when encoding and retrieval occur in the same state); it was obtained with the free recall. Panel B shows the results of the cued-recall test. In this case, the usual state dependence does not occur. People who studied after smoking marijuana did equally well if tested with the drug or without it; people who were not drugged at encoding did equally well whether they did or did not receive the drug at the time of the test.

These results suggest that state dependence occurs because it is easier to perform a successful search for items in memory if the state at the time of the search matches the state at the time of encoding. If the search component of retrieval is made less difficult, for example, by presenting category cues, the detrimental effect of being in a state different from the state of encoding will be alleviated. In support of this argument, Eich reviewed a number of studies and pointed out that uncued recall, which presumably requires memory search, showed the state-dependence pattern in 14 out of 17 cases; whereas cued-recall and recognition tests, which are assumed to require much less search, showed the typical result in only 9 out of 30 cases.

It is noteworthy, however, that state dependence is not always manifested even when the memory task has a difficult retrieval component. If state dependence had been evident in the previously described study of Birnbaum et al. (1978), subjects who retrieved in the alcohol condition, having stored in a sober condition, should have suffered from the change in state. This should at least have occurred on the free-recall test, where search processes were required, even if it did not on the cued-recall test, where retrieval would be easier. But no such effect was found. We know that subjects often show less of a deficit if they encode while sober and retrieve while intoxicated than if they encode while intoxicated and retrieve while sober, but these results seem to show no deficit in the former condition at all. A similar outcome was obtained in the Miller et al. (1978) study.

It is somewhat difficult to reconcile the results of studies that do not show state dependence with those that do. The differences possibly can be explained by procedural variations such as higher levels of learning in the studies that don't find state dependence (Miller et al., 1978). In any case, Birnbaum et al. point out that using a test that requires a relatively difficult retrieval process, as their free-recall task should have done, does not guarantee that state dependence will be observed, although retrieval difficulty may be a requirement for its occurrence.

The studies we have discussed suggest some general conclusions about drug (especially alcohol) effects on memory. First, there seems to be good evidence that encoding items while intoxicated can lead to memory impairment. However, some studies suggest that subjects who attempt to retrieve items that were encoded during intoxication may alleviate the memory impairment somewhat if they retrieve while intoxicated (Weingartner, Adefris, Eich, and Murphy, 1976). This state-dependent pattern is more likely to be found if the retrieval task is difficult. The case for effects of alcohol solely on retrieval is less clear, for if subjects initially encode information while sober, they may be able to retrieve it quite well when intoxicated.

Even these general conclusions are somewhat problematic, however. For the effects of alcohol have been found to vary with the dosage (Parker et al., 1976). The nature of the test can also have an effect, as we saw from the Eich et al. study comparing free and cued recall. Other test factors that have been found to change the effects of alcohol are the retention interval and the type of words used in the memory task. For example, Weingartner and Murphy (1977) found no effect of intoxication in a task where words were recalled immediately after presentation, but recall of those words 20 minutes later was impaired by the alcohol. It has also been found that the state-dependence pattern is more pronounced in tasks that use low-imagery words than in those using high-imagery words (Weingartner et al, 1976). The effects of alcohol on memory are clearly complex, and understanding the roles of encoding and retrieval and of various task factors appears to be a difficult endeavor. However, the application of information-processing theories of memory promises to be of aid in that endeavor.

A FINAL COMMENT

In addition to introducing some of the ways in which the memory system can vary, this chapter has provided a retrospective glance at some of the topics we have covered in this book. Considering the abilities that underlie the performances of spectacular mnemonists, eidetikers, and chess masters; the ways in which individuals differ; and the effects of drugs on memory, has brought us to consider all of memory, from the initial inputs to their final analysis and storage. Knowledge of encoding, storage, and retrieval processes has proven fruitful for the analysis of these special topics. Cognitive psychologists believe that it will also prove fruitful for a more general understanding of human memory and its role in intellectual functioning.

References

Aaronson, D., and Scarborough, H. S. Performance theories for sentence coding: Some quantitative evidence. *Journal of Experimental Psychology: Human Perception and Performance,* 1976, 2, 56–70.

Aaronson, D., and Scarborough, H. S. Performance theories for sentence coding: Some quantitative models. *Journal of Verbal Learning and Verbal Behavior,* 1977, 16, 277–304.

Adelson, E. H. Iconic storage: The role of rods. *Science,* 1978, 201, 544–546.

Allen, M. Rehearsal strategies and response cueing as determinants of organization in free recall. *Journal of Verbal Learning and Verbal Behavior,* 1968, 7, 58–63.

Anastasi, A. *Psychological Testing.* New York: Macmillan, 1976.

Anderson, J. R. FRAN: A simulation model of free recall. In G. H. Bower (ed.), *The Psychology of Learning and Motivation,* Vol. 5. New York: Academic Press, 1972.

Anderson, J. R. *Language, Memory, and Thought.* Hillsdale, N.J.: Erlbaum, 1976.

Anderson, J. R. Arguments concerning representations for mental imagery. *Psychological Review,* 1978, 85, 249–277.

Anderson, J. R., and Bower, G. H. Recognition and retrieval processes in free recall. *Psychological Review,* 1972, 79, 97–123.

Anderson, J. R., and Bower, G. H. *Human Associative Memory.* Washington, D.C.: V. H. Winston & Sons, 1973.

Anderson, J. R., and Bower, G. H. A propositional theory of recognition memory. *Memory & Cognition,* 1974, 2, 406–412.

Anderson, J. R., and Paulson, R. Representation and retention of verbatim information. *Journal of Verbal Learning and Verbal Behavior*, 1977, 16, 439–452.

Anderson, R. C., and Pichert, J. W. Recall of previously unrecallable information following a shift in perspective. *Journal of Verbal Learning and Verbal Behavior*, 1978, 17, 1–12.

Atkinson, R. C., and Juola, J. F. Factors influencing speed and accuracy of word recognition. In S. Kornblum (ed.), *Attention and Performance*, Vol. 4. New York: Academic Press, 1973.

Atkinson, R. C., and Shiffrin, R. M. Human memory: A proposed system and its control processes. In K. W. Spence and J. T. Spence (eds.), *The Psychology of Learning and Motivation: Advances in Research and Theory*, Vol. 2. New York: Academic Press, 1968.

Averbach, E., and Coriell, A. S. Short-term memory in vision. *Bell System Technical Journal*, 1961, 40, 309–328.

Averbach, E., and Sperling, G. Short-term storage of information in vision. In C. Cherry (ed.), *Fourth London Symposium on Information Theory*. London and Washington, D.C.: Butterworth, 1961.

Baddeley, A. D. Retrieval rules and semantic coding in short-term memory. *Psychological Bulletin*, 1972, 78, 379–385.

Baddeley, A. D. The trouble with levels: A reexamination of Craik and Lockhart's framework for memory research. *Psychological Review*, 1978, 85, 139–152.

Baddeley, A. D., and Dale, H. C. A. The effect of semantic similarity on retroactive interference in long- and short-term memory. *Journal of Verbal Learning and Verbal Behavior*, 1966, 5, 417–420.

Baddeley, A. D., Grant, S., Wight, E., and Thomson, N. Imagery and visual working memory. In P. M. Rabbitt and S. Dornic (eds.), *Attention and Performance*, Vol. 5. New York: Academic Press, 1975.

Baddeley, A. D., and Hitch, G. Working memory. In G. H. Bower (ed.), *The Psychology of Learning and Motivation*, Vol. 8. New York: Academic Press, 1974.

Bahrick, H. P., Clark, S., and Bahrick, P. Generalization gradients as indicants of learning and retention of a recognition task. *Journal of Experimental Psychology*, 1967, 75, 464–471.

Banks, W. P., and Barber, G. Color information in iconic memory. *Psychological Review*, 1977, 84, 536–546.

Barclay, J. R. The role of comprehension in remembering sentences. *Cognitive Psychology*, 1973, 4, 229–254.

Barnes, J. M., and Underwood, B. J. "Fate" of first-list associations in transfer theory. *Journal of Experimental Psychology*, 1959, 58, 97–105.

Baron, J., and Thurston, I. An analysis of the word-superiority effect. *Cognitive Psychology*, 1973, 4, 207–228.

Bartlett, F. C. *Remembering: A Study in Experimental and Social Psychology*. Cambridge: Cambridge University Press, 1932.

Battig, W. F., and Montague, W. E. Category norms for verbal items in 56 categories: A replication and extension of the Connecticut category norms. *Journal of Experimental Psychology Monograph*, 1969, *80* (3, Pt. 2).

Bellugi, U., Klima, E. S., and Siple, P. A. Remembering in signs. *Cognition*, 1975, *3*, 93–125.

Belmont, J. M., and Butterfield, E. C. What the development of short-term memory is. *Human Development*, 1971, *14*, 236–248.

Bencomo, A. A., and Daniel, T. C. Recognition latency for pictures and words as a function of encoded-feature similarity. *Journal of Experimental Psychology: Human Learning and Memory*, 1975, *1*, 119–125.

Bennett, R. W. Proactive interference in short-term memory: Fundamental forgetting processes. *Journal of Verbal Learning and Verbal Behavior*, 1975, *14*, 123–144.

Biederman, I. On processing information from a glance at a scene: Some implications for a syntax and semantics of visual processing. In S. Treu (ed.), *User-Oriented Design of Interactive Graphics Systems*. New York: ACM, 1977.

Biederman, I., Glass, A. L., and Stacy, E. W., Jr. Searching for objects in real-world scenes. *Journal of Experimental Psychology*, 1973, *97*, 22–27.

Birnbaum, I. M., Parker, E. S. Hartley, J. T., and Noble, E. P. Alcohol and memory: Retrieval processes. *Journal of Verbal Learning and Verbal Behavior*, 1978, *17*, 325–335.

Bjork, R. A. Short-term storage: The ordered output of a central processor. In F. Restle, R. M. Shiffrin, N. J. Castellan, H. R. Lindeman, and D. B. Pisoni (eds.), *Cognitive Theory*, Vol. 1. Hillsdale, N.J.: Erlbaum, 1975.

Bjork, R. A., and Whitten, W. B. Recency-sensitive retrieval processes in long-term free recall. *Cognitive Psychology*, 1974, *6*, 173–189.

Bobrow, S. A., and Bower, G. H. Comprehension and recall of sentences. *Journal of Experimental Psychology*, 1969, *80*, 455–461.

Bousfield, A. K., and Bousfield, W. A. Measurement of clustering and of sequential constancies in repeated free recall. *Psychological Reports*, 1966, *19*, 935–942.

Bousfield, W. A. Frequency and availability measures in language behavior. Paper presented at annual meeting, American Psychological Association, Chicago, 1951.

Bousfield, W. A. The occurrence of clustering in the recall of randomly arranged associates. *Journal of General Psychology*, 1953, *49*, 229–240.

Bousfield, W. A., and Cohen, B. H. The effects of reinforcement on the occurrence of clustering in the recall of randomly arranged associates. *Journal of Psychology*, 1953, *36*, 67–81.

Bousfield, W. A., Cohen, B. H., and Whitmarsh, G. A. Associative clustering in the recall of words of different taxonomic frequencies of occurrence. *Psychological Reports*, 1958, *4*, 39–44.

Bousfield, W. A., and Puff, C. R. Clustering as a function of response dominance. *Journal of Experimental Psychology*, 1964, *67*, 76–79.

Bower, G. H. A multicomponent theory of the memory trace. In K. W. Spence and J. T. Spence (eds.), *The Psychology of Learning and Motivation*, Vol. 1. New York: Academic Press, 1967.

Bower, G. H. Organizational factors in memory. *Cognitive Psychology*, 1970, 1, 18–46.

Bower, G. H. A selective review of organizational factors in memory. In E. Tulving and W. Donaldson (eds.), *Organization of Memory*. New York: Academic Press, 1972. (a)

Bower, G. H. Mental imagery and associative learning. In L. Gregg (ed.), *Cognition in Learning and Memory*. New York: Wiley, 1972. (b)

Bower, G. H. Memory freaks I have known. *Psychology Today*, 1973, 7, 64–65.

Bower, G. H., Clark, M. C., Lesgold, A. M., and Winzenz, D. Hierarchical retrieval schemes in recall of categorized word lists. *Journal of Verbal Learning and Verbal Behavior*, 1969, 8, 323–343.

Bower, G. H., Karlin, M. B., and Dueck, A. Comprehension and memory for pictures. *Memory & Cognition*, 1975, 3, 216–220.

Bower, G. H., and Springston, F. Pauses as recoding points in letter series. *Journal of Experimental Psychology*, 1970, 83, 421–430.

Bower, G. H., and Winzenz, D. Group structure, coding, and memory for digit series. *Journal of Experimental Psychology Monograph Supplement*, 1969, 80, 1–17.

Bransford, J. D., Barclay, J. R., and Franks, J. J. Sentence memory: A constructive versus interpretive approach. *Cognitive Psychology*, 1972, 3, 193–209.

Bransford, J. D., and Franks, J. J. The abstraction of linguistic ideas. *Cognitive Psychology*, 1971, 2, 331–350.

Bransford, J. D., and Johnson, M. K. Contextual prerequisites for understanding: Some investigations of comprehension and recall. *Journal of Verbal Learning and Verbal Behavior*, 1972, 11, 717–726.

Bransford, J. D., and Johnson, M. K. Considerations of some problems of comprehension. In W. G. Chase (ed.), *Visual Information Processing*. New York: Academic Press, 1973.

Bransford, J. D., and McCarrell, N. S. A sketch of a cognitive approach to comprehension. In W. Weimer and D. Palermo (eds.), *Cognition and the Symbolic Processes*. Hillsdale, N.J.: Erlbaum, 1974.

Briggs, G. E. Acquisition, extinction, and recovery functions in retroactive inhibition. *Journal of Experimental Psychology*, 1954, 47, 285–293.

Briggs, G. E. Retroactive inhibition as a function of the degree of original and interpolated learning. *Journal of Experimental Psychology*, 1957, 53, 60–67.

Broadbent, D. E. *Perception and Communication*. London: Pergamon Press, 1958.

Brooks, L. R. Spatial and verbal components of the act of recall. *Canadian Journal of Psychology*, 1968, 22, 349–368.

Brown, J. A. Some tests of the decay theory of immediate memory. *Quarterly Journal of Experimental Psychology*, 1958, *10*, 12–21.

Bruce, D., and Fagan, R. L. More on the recognition and free recall of organized lists. *Journal of Experimental Psychology*, 1970, *85*, 153–154.

Ceraso, J., and Henderson, A. Unavailability and associative loss in RI and PI. *Journal of Experimental Psychology*, 1965, *70*, 300–303.

Chase, W. G., and Simon, H. A. Perception in chess. *Cognitive Psychology*, 1973, *4*, 55–81.

Cherry, E. C. Some experiments on the recognition of speech with one and two ears. *Journal of the Acoustical Society of America*. 1953, *25*, 975–979.

Chi, M. T. H. Short-term memory limitations in children: Capacity or processing deficits? *Memory & Cognition*, 1976, *4*, 559–572.

Chiang, A., and Atkinson, R. C. Individual differences and interrelationships among a select set of cognitive skills. *Memory & Cognition*, 1976, *4*, 661–672.

Cofer, C. N. On some factors in the organizational characteristics of free recall. *American Psychologist*, 1965, *20*, 261–272.

Cofer, C. N., Bruce, D. R., and Reicher, G. M. Clustering in free recall as a function of certain methodological variations. *Journal of Experimental Psychology*, 1966, *71*, 858–866.

Cofer, C. N., Chmielewski, D. L., and Brockway, J. F. Constructive processes and the structure of human memory. In C. N. Cofer (ed.), *The Structure of Human Memory*. San Francisco: W. H. Freeman and Company, 1976.

Cohen, B. H. Some-or-none characteristics of coding behavior. *Journal of Verbal Learning and Verbal Behavior*, 1966, *5*, 182–187.

Cohen, R. L., and Sandberg, T. Relation between intelligence and short-term memory. *Cognitive Psychology*, 1977, *9*, 534–554.

Collins, A. M., and Loftus, E. F. A spreading-activation theory of semantic memory. *Psychological Review*, 1975, *82*, 407–428.

Collins, A. M., and Quillian, M. R. Retrieval time from semantic memory. *Journal of Verbal Learning and Verbal Behavior*, 1969, *8*, 240–247.

Conrad, R. Acoustic confusions in immediate memory. *British Journal of Psychology*, 1964, *55*, 75–84.

Conrad, R. Short-term memory in the deaf: A test for speech coding. *British Journal of Psychology*, 1972, *63*, 173–180.

Conrad, R., and Hull, A. J. Information, acoustic confusion, and memory span. *British Journal of Psychology*, 1964, *55*, 429–432.

Conry, R., and Plant, W. T. WAIS and group predictions of an academic success criterion: High school and college. *Educational and Psychological Measurement*, 1965, *25*, 493–500.

Cooper, L. A., and Shepard, R. N. Chronometric studies of the rotation of mental images. In W. G. Chase (ed.), *Visual Information Processing*. New York: Academic Press, 1973.

Cooper, W. E., and Blumstein, S. E. A "labial" feature analyzer in speech perception. *Perception & Psychophysics*, 1974, *15*, 591–600.

Craik, F. I. M., and Kirsner, K. The effect of speaker's voice on word recognition. *Quarterly Journal of Experimental Psychology*, 1974, *26*, 274–284.

Craik, F. I. M., and Lockhart, R. S. Levels of processing: A framework for memory research. *Journal of Verbal Learning and Verbal Behavior*, 1972, *11*, 671–684.

Craik, F. I. M., and Tulving, E. Depth of processing and the retention of words in episodic memory. *Journal of Experimental Psychology: General*, 1975, *104*, 268–294.

Craik, F. I. M., and Watkins, M. J. The role of rehearsal in short-term memory. *Journal of Verbal Learning and Verbal Behavior*, 1973, *12*, 599–607.

Crossman, E. R. F. W. Discussion of Paper 7 in National Physical Laboratory Symposium. In *Mechanisation of Thought Processes*, Vol. 2. London: H. M. Stationery Office, 1958.

Crowder, R. G., and Morton, J. Precategorical acoustic storage (PAS). *Perception & Psychophysics*, 1969, *5*, 365–373.

D'Agostino, P. R. The blocked-random effect in recall and recognition. *Journal of Verbal Learning and Verbal Behavior*, 1969, *8*, 815–820.

Darwin, C. T., Turvey, M. T., and Crowder, R. G. An auditory analogue of the Sperling partial report procedure: Evidence for brief auditory storage. *Cognitive Psychology*, 1972, *3*, 255–267.

Davis, R., Sutherland, N. S., and Judd, B. R. Information content in recognition and recall. *Journal of Experimental Psychology*, 1961, *61*, 422–429.

de Groot, A. D. *Thought and Choice in Chess*. The Hague: Mouton, 1965.

de Groot, A. D. Perception and memory versus thinking. In B. Kleinmuntz (ed.), *Problem Solving*. New York: Wiley, 1966.

Delin, P. S. The learning to criterion of a serial list with and without mnemonic instructions. *Psychonomic Science*, 1969, *16*, 169–170.

Deutsch, D. Tones and numbers: Specificity of interference in immediate memory. *Science*, 1970, *168*, 1604–1605.

Deutsch, J. A., and Deutsch, D. Attention: Some theoretical considerations. *Psychological Review*, 1963, *70*, 80–90.

Dillon, R. F. Locus of proactive interference effects in short-term memory. *Journal of Experimental Psychology*, 1973, *99*, 75–81.

Dillon, R. F., and Bittner, L. A. Analysis of retrieval cues and release from PI. *Journal of Verbal Learning and Verbal Behavior*, 1975, *14*, 616–622.

Dillon, R. F., and Thomas, H. The role of response confusion in proactive interference. *Journal of Verbal Learning and Verbal Behavior*, 1975, *14*, 603–615.

Donders, F. C. Die Schnelligkeit psychischer Processe. *Arch. Anat. Physiol.*, 1862, 657–681.

Dooling, D. J., and Christiaansen, R. E. Episodic and semantic aspects of memory for prose. *Journal of Experimental Psychology: Human Learning and Memory*, 1977, *3*, 428–436.

Dooling, D. J., and Lachman, R. Effects of comprehension on retention of prose. *Journal of Experimental Psychology*, 1971, *88*, 216–222.

Dooling, D. J., and Mullet, R. L. Locus of thematic effects in retention of prose. *Journal of Experimental Psychology*, 1973, *97*, 404–406.

Ebbinghaus, H. *Über das Gedächtnis*. Leipzig; Duncker & Humblot, 1885.

Efron, R. The relationship between the duration of a stimulus and the duration of a perception. *Neuropsychologia*, 1970, *8*, 37–55.

Eich, J. E. State-dependent retrieval of information in human episodic memory. In I. M. Birnbaum and E. S. Parker (eds.), *Alcohol and Human Memory*. Hillsdale, N.J.: Erlbaum, 1977.

Eich, J. E., Weingartner, H., Stillman, R. C., and Gillin, J. C. State-dependent accessibility of retrieval cues in the retention of a categorized list. *Journal of Verbal Learning and Verbal Behavior*, 1975, *14*, 408–417.

Eimas, P. D., and Corbit, J. D. Selective adaptation of linguistic feature detectors. *Cognitive Psychology*, 1973, *4*, 99–109.

Eriksen, C. W., and Eriksen, B. A. Visual perceptual processing rates and backward and forward masking. *Journal of Experimental Psychology*, 1971, *89*, 306–313.

Fischler, I., and Goodman, G. O. Latency of associative activation in memory. *Journal of Experimental Psychology: Human Perception and Performance*, 1978, *4*, 455–470.

Flexser, A. J., and Tulving, E. Retrieval independence in recognition and recall. *Psychological Review*, 1978, *85*, 153–171.

Franks, J. J., and Bransford, J. D. Abstraction of visual patterns. *Journal of Experimental Psychology*, 1971, *90*, 65–74.

Freud, S. [A note upon the "Mystic writing–pad."], J. Strachey, trans. *International Journal of Psycho-Analysis*, 1940, *21*, 469.

Friedman, M. J., and Reynolds, J. H. Retroactive inhibition as a function of response-class similarity. *Journal of Experimental Psychology*, 1967, *74*, 351–355.

Frost, N. Encoding and retrieval in visual memory tasks. *Journal of Experimental Psychology*, 1972, *95*, 317–326.

Frumkin, B., and Anisfeld, M. Semantic and surface codes in the memory of deaf children. *Cognitive Psychology*, 1977, *9*, 475–493.

Gardiner, J. M., Craik, F. I. M., and Birtwistle, J. Retrieval cues and release from proactive inhibition. *Journal of Verbal Learning and Verbal Behavior*, 1972, *11*, 778–783.

Glenberg, A., Smith, S. M., and Green, C. Type I rehearsal: Maintenance and more. *Journal of Verbal Learning and Verbal Behavior*, 1977, *16*, 339–352.

Goldstein, A. G., and Chance, J. Visual recognition memory for complex configurations. *Perception & Psychophysics*, 1970, *9*, 237–241.

Gould, J. D. Looking at pictures. In R. A. Monty and J. W. Senders (eds.), *Eye movements and Psychological Processes*. Hillsdale, N.J.: Erlbaum, 1976.

Gray, C. R., and Gummerman, K. The enigmatic eidetic image: A critical examination of methods, data, and theories. *Psychological Bulletin*, 1975, *82*, 383–407.

Green, D. M., and Swets, J. A, *Signal Detection Theory and Psychophysics.* New York: Wiley, 1966.

Gummerman, K., Gray, C. R., and Wilson, J. M. An attempt to assess eidetic imagery objectively. *Psychonomic Science*, 1972, *28*, 115–118.

Guttman, N., and Julesz, B. Lower limits of auditory periodicity analysis. *Journal of the Acoustical Society of America*, 1963, *35*, 610.

Haber, R. N., and Haber, R. B. Eidetic imagery: I. Frequency. *Perceptual and Motor Skills*, 1964, *19*, 131–138.

Haber, R. N., and Standing, L. G. Direct estimates of apparent duration of a flash followed by visual noise. *Canadian Journal of Psychology*, 1970, *24*, 216–229.

Halle, M., and Stevens, K. N. Analysis by synthesis. In W. Wathen-Dunn and L. E. Woods (eds.), *Proceedings of the Seminar on Speech Comprehension and Processing.* Bedford, Mass.: Air Force Cambridge Research Laboratories, 1959.

Halle, M., and Stevens, K. N. Speech recognition: A model and a program for research. In J. A. Fodor, and J. J. Katz (eds.), *The Structure of Language: Readings in the Psychology of Language.* Englewood Cliffs, N.J.: Prentice-Hall, 1964.

Hanawalt, N. G., and Demarest, I. H. The effect of verbal suggestion in the recall period upon the reproduction of visually perceived forms. *Journal of Experimental Psychology*, 1939, *25*, 159–174.

Hayes-Roth, F. Critique of Turvey's "Contrasting orientations to the theory of visual information-processing." *Psychological Review*, 1977, *84*, 531–535.

Hebb, D. O. *The Organization of Behavior.* New York: Wiley, 1949.

Hebb, D. O. *A Textbook of Psychology.* Philadelphia: W. B. Saunders, 1958.

Hintzman, D. L., Block, R. A., and Inskeep, N. R. Memory for mode of input. *Journal of Verbal Learning and Verbal Behavior*, 1972, *11*, 741–749.

Hollan, J. D. Features and semantic memory: Set-theoretic or network model? *Psychological Review*, 1975, *82*, 154–155.

Holyoak, K. J., and Glass, A. L. The role of contradictions and counterexamples in the rejection of false sentences. *Journal of Verbal Learning and Verbal Behavior*, 1975, *14*, 215–239.

Houston, J. P. First-list retention and time and method of recall. *Journal of Experimental Psychology*, 1966, *71*, 839–843.

Hubel, D. H., and Wiesel, T. N. Receptive fields, binocular interaction, and functional architecture in the cat's visual cortex. *Journal of Physiology*, 1962, *160*, 106–154.

Hunt, E. Mechanics of verbal ability. *Psychological Review*, 1978, *85*, 109–130.

Hunt, E., Frost, N., and Lunneborg, C. Individual differences in cognition: A new approach to intelligence. In G. Bower (ed.), *The Psychology of Learning and Motivation*, Vol. 7. New York: Academic Press, 1973.

Hunt, E., and Love, T. How good can memory be? In A. W. Melton and E.

Martin (eds.), *Coding Processes in Human Memory*. Washington, D.C.: V. H. Winston & Sons, 1972.

Hunt, E., Lunneborg, C., and Lewis, J. What does it mean to be high verbal? *Cognitive Psychology*, 1975, 7, 194–227.

Huttenlocher, J., and Burke, D. Why does memory span increase with age? *Cognitive Psychology*, 1976, 8, 1–31.

Jacobs, J. Experiments in "prehension." *Mind*, 1887, 12, 75–79.

Jacoby, L. L., Bartz, W. H., and Evans, J. D. A functional approach to levels of processing. *Journal of Experimental Psychology: Human Learning and Memory*, 1978, 4, 331–346.

Jaensch, E. R. *Eidetic Imagery and Typological Methods of Investigation*, O. Oeser, trans. New York: Harcourt, Brace, 1930.

Jakobson, R., Fant, G. G. M., and Halle, M. *Preliminaries to Speech Analysis: The Distinctive Features and Their Correlates*. Cambridge: M.I.T. Press, 1961.

James, C. T., and Hillinger, M. L. The role of confusion in the semantic integration paradigm. *Journal of Verbal Learning and Verbal Behavior*, 1977, 16, 711–721.

James, W. *The Principles of Psychology*, Vol. 1. New York: Henry Holt and Co., 1890.

Jenkins, J. J., Mink, W. D., and Russell, W. A. Associative clustering as a function of verbal association strength. *Psychological Reports*, 1958, 4, 127–136.

Jenkins, J. J., and Russell, W. A. Associative clustering during recall. *Journal of Abnormal and Social Psychology*, 1952, 47, 818–821.

Johnson, M. K., Bransford, J. D., Nyberg, S. E., and Cleary, J. J. Comprehension factors in interpreting memory for abstract and concrete sentences. *Journal of Verbal Learning and Verbal Behavior*, 1972, 11, 451–454.

Johnson, N. F. Sequential verbal behavior. In T. R. Dixon and D. L. Horton (eds.), *Verbal Behavior and General Behavior Theory*. Englewood Cliffs, N.J.: Prentice-Hall, 1968.

Johnston, J. C. A test of the sophisticated guessing theory of word perception. *Cognitive Psychology*, 1978, 10, 123–153.

Julesz, B. Binocular depth perception without familiarity cues. *Science*, 1964, 145, 356–362.

Kahneman, D. *Attention and Effort*. Englewood Cliffs, N.J.: Prentice-Hall, 1973.

Katz, J. J., and Fodor, J. A. The structure of a semantic theory. *Language*, 1963, 39, 170–210.

Keele, S. W. *Attention and Human Performance*. Pacific Palisades, Ca.: Goodyear, 1973.

Keppel, G., and Underwood, B. J. Proactive inhibition in short-term retention of single items. *Journal of Verbal Learning and Verbal Behavior*, 1962, 1, 153–161.

Kieras, D. Beyond pictures and words: Alternative information-processing models for imagery effects in verbal memory. *Psychological Bulletin*, 1978, *85*, 532–554.

Kinney, G. C., Marsetta, M., and Showman, D. J. *Studies in Display Symbol Legibility, Part XII. The Legibility of Alphanumeric Symbols for Digitalized Television.* Bedford, Mass.: The Mitre Corp., November 1966, ESD-TR-66-117.

Kintsch, W. Recognition and free recall of organized lists. *Journal of Experimental Psychology*, 1968, *78*, 481–487.

Kintsch, W. Models for free recall and recognition. In D. A. Norman (ed.), *Models of Human Memory*. New York: Academic Press, 1970.

Kintsch, W. *The Representation of Meaning in Memory*. Hillsdale, N.J.: Erlbaum, 1974.

Kintsch, W., and Keenan, J. M. Reading rate and retention as a function of the number of the propositions in the base structure of sentences. *Cognitive Psychology*, 1973, *5*, 257–274.

Klatzky, R. L., and Ryan, A. S. Category-structure effects in picture comparisons. *Perception & Psychophysics*, 1978, *23*, 193–204.

Klatzky, R. L., and Stoy, A. M. Semantic information and visual information processing. In J. W. Cotton and R. L. Klatzky (eds.), *Semantic Factors in Cognition*. Hillsdale, N.J.: Erlbaum, 1978.

Kolers, P. A., and Ostry, D. J. Time course of loss of information regarding pattern analyzing operations. *Journal of Verbal Learning and Verbal Behavior*, 1974, *13*, 599–612.

Koppenaal, R. J. Time changes in the strengths of A–B, A–C lists; spontaneous recovery? *Journal of Verbal Learning and Verbal Behavior*, 1963, *2*, 310–319.

Kosslyn, S. M. Information representation in visual images. *Cognitive Psychology*, 1975, *7*, 341–370.

Kosslyn, S. M., Ball, T. M., and Reiser, B. J. Visual images preserve metric spatial information: Evidence from studies of image scanning. *Journal of Experimental Psychology: Human Perception and Performance*, 1978, *4*, 47–60.

Kosslyn, S. M., and Pomerantz, J. R. Imagery, propositions, and the form of internal representations. *Cognitive Psychology*, 1977, *9*, 52–76.

Kosslyn, S. M., and Schwartz, S. P. A simulation of visual imagery. *Cognitive Science*, 1977, *1*, 265–296.

Kroll, N. E. A., and Parks, T. E. Interference with short-term visual memory produced by concurrent central processing. *Journal of Experimental Psychology: Human Learning and Memory*, 1978, *4*, 111–120.

LaBerge, D., and Samuels, S. J. Toward a theory of automatic information processing in reading. *Cognitive Psychology*, 1974, *6*, 293–323.

Lachman, R., and Tuttle, A. V. Approximation to English and short-term memory: Construction or storage? *Journal of Experimental Psychology*, 1965, *70*, 386–393.

Landauer, T. K. Rate of implicit speech. *Perceptual and Motor Skills*, 1962, *15*, 646.

Leask, J., Haber, R. N., and Haber, R. B. Eidetic imagery in children: II. Longitudinal and experimental results. *Psychonomic Monograph Supplements*, 1969, *3* (3, Whole No. 35).

Lettvin, J. Y., Maturana, H. R., McCulloch, W. S., and Pitts, W. H. What the frog's eye tells the frog's brain. *Proceedings of the IRE*, 1959, *47*, 1940–1951.

Lewis, M. Q. Cue effectiveness in cued recall. Paper presented at the annual meeting of the Psychonomic Society, St. Louis, 1972.

Light, L. L., and Berger, D. E. Are there long-term "literal copies" of visually presented words? *Journal of Experimental Psychology: Human Learning and Memory*, 1976, *2*, 654–662.

Light, L. L., Berger, D. E., and Bardales, M. Tradeoff between memory for verbal items and their visual attributes. *Journal of Experimental Psychology: Human Learning and Memory*, 1975, *1*, 188–193.

Locke, J. L., and Locke, V. L. Deaf children's phonetic, visual, and dactylic coding in a grapheme recall task. *Journal of Experimental Psychology*, 1971, *89*, 142–146.

Lockhart, R. S., Craik, F. I. M., and Jacoby, L. Depth of processing, recognition, and recall. In J. Brown (ed.), *Recall and Recognition*. New York: Wiley, 1976.

Loftus, E. F. Activation of semantic memory. *American Journal of Psychology*, 1973, *86*, 331–337.

Loftus, E. F. Leading questions and the eyewitness report. *Cognitive Psychology*, 1975, *7*, 560–572.

Loftus, E. F., Shifting human color memory. *Memory & Cognition*, 1977, *5*, 696–699.

Loftus, E. F., Miller, D. G., and Burns, H. J. Semantic integration of verbal information into a visual memory. *Journal of Experimental Psychology: Human Learning and Memory*, 1978, *4*, 19–31.

Loftus, G. R. Acquisition of information from rapidly presented verbal and nonverbal stimuli. *Memory & Cognition*, 1974, *2*, 545–548.

Loftus, G. R., and Loftus, E. F. The influence of one memory retrieval on a subsequent memory retrieval. *Memory & Cognition*, 1974, *2*, 467–471.

Loftus, G. R., and Mackworth, N. H. Cognitive determinants of fixation location during picture viewing. *Journal of Experimental Psychology: Human Perception and Performance*, 1978, *4*, 565–572.

Loftus, G. R., and Patterson, K. K. Components of short-term proactive interference. *Journal of Verbal Learning and Verbal Behavior*, 1975, *14*, 105–121.

Lorayne, H., and Lucas, J. *The Memory Book.* New York: Ballantine, 1974.

Luria, A. R. *The Mind of a Mnemonist*. New York: Basic Books, 1968.

Lyon, D. R. Individual differences in immediate serial recall: A matter of mnemonics? *Cognitive Psychology*, 1977, *9*, 403–411.

MacKay, D. G. Aspects of the theory of comprehension, memory, and attention. *Quarterly Journal of Experimental Psychology*, 1973, *25*, 22–40.

Mandler, G. Organization and recognition. In E. Tulving and W. Donaldson (eds.), *Organization of Memory*. New York: Academic Press, 1972.

Mandler, G., and Pearlstone, Z. Free and constrained concept learning and subsequent recall. *Journal of Verbal Learning and Verbal Behavior*, 1966, 5, 126–131.

Mandler, G., Pearlstone, Z., and Koopmans, H. S. Effects of organization and semantic similarity on recall and recognition. *Journal of Verbal Learning and Verbal Behavior*, 1969, 8, 410–423.

Mandler, J. M., and Johnson, N. S. Some of the thousand words a picture is worth. *Journal of Experimental Psychology: Human Learning and Memory*, 1976, 2, 529–540.

Mandler, J. M., and Parker, R. E. Memory for descriptive and spatial information in complex pictures. *Journal of Experimental Psychology: Human Learning and Memory*, 1976, 2, 38–48.

Mandler, J. M., and Ritchey, G. H. Long-term memory for pictures. *Journal of Experimental Psychology: Human Learning and Memory*, 1977, 3, 386–396.

Marslen-Wilson, W. D., and Teuber, H. L. Memory for remote events in anterograde amnesia: Recognition of public figures from newsphotographs. *Neuropsychologia*, 1975, 13, 353–364.

Martin, E. Generation-recognition theory and the encoding specificity principle. *Psychological Review*, 1975, 82, 150–153.

Massaro, D. W. Preperceptual auditory images. *Journal of Experimental Psychology*, 1970, 85, 411–417.

Massaro, D. W. *Experimental Psychology and Information Processing*. Chicago: Rand McNally, 1975.

Massaro, D. W., Cohen, M. M., and Idson, W. L. Recognition masking of auditory lateralization and pitch judgments. *Journal of the Acoustical Society of America*, 1976, 59, 434–441.

Mayhew, A. J. Interlist changes in subjective organization during free-recall learning. *Journal of Experimental Psychology*, 1967, 74, 425–430.

McClelland, J. L., and Johnston, J. C. The role of familiar units in perception of words and nonwords. *Perception & Psychophysics*, 1977, 22, 249–261.

McCloskey, M., and Watkins, M. J. The seeing-more-than-is-there phenomenon: Implications for the locus of iconic storage. *Journal of Experimental Psychology: Human Perception and Performance*, 1978, 4, 553–565.

McCloskey, M. E., and Glucksberg, S. Natural categories: Well defined or fuzzy sets? *Memory & Cognition*, 1978, 6, 462–472.

McDougall, R. Recognition and recall. *Journal of Philosophical and Scientific Methods*, 1904, 1, 229–233.

McGeoch, J. A. *The Psychology of Human Learning*. New York: Longmans, Green, 1942.

McKoon, G. Organization of information in text memory. *Journal of Verbal Learning and Verbal Behavior*, 1977, 16, 247–260.

Melton, A. W., and Irwin, J. M. The influence of degree of interpolated learning on retroactive inhibition and the overt transfer of specific responses. *American Journal of Psychology*, 1940, *53*, 173–203.

Meyer, D. E. Correlated operations in searching stored semantic categories. *Journal of Experimental Psychology*, 1973, *99*, 124–133.

Meyer, D. E., and Schvaneveldt, R. W. Facilitation in recognizing pairs of words: Evidence of a dependence between retrieval operations. *Journal of Experimental Psychology*, 1971, *90*, 227–234.

Meyer, D. E., and Schvaneveldt, R. W. Meaning, memory structure, and mental processes. *Science*, 1976, *192*, 27–33.

Meyer, D. E., Schvaneveldt, R. W., and Ruddy, M. G. Activation of lexical memory. Paper presented at the meeting of the Psychonomic Society, St. Louis, 1972.

Miller, G. A. The magical number seven, plus or minus two: Some limits on our capacity for processing information. *Psychological Review*, 1956, *63*, 81–97.

Miller, G. A. English verbs of motion: A case study in semantics and lexical memory. In A. W. Melton and E. Martin (eds.), *Coding Processes in Human Memory*. Washington, D.C.: V. H. Winston & Sons, 1972.

Miller, G. A., and Isard, S. Some perceptual consequences of linguistic rules. *Journal of Verbal Learning and Verbal Behavior*, 1963, *2*, 217–228.

Miller, G. A., and Nicely, P. An analysis of perceptual confusions among some English consonants. *Journal of the Acoustical Society of America*, 1955, *27*, 338–352.

Miller, G. A., and Selfridge, J. A. Verbal context and the recall of meaningful material. *American Journal of Psychology*, 1950, *63*, 176–187.

Miller, M. E., Adesso, V. J., Fleming, J. P., Gino, A., and Lauerman, R. Effects of alcohol on the storage and retrieval processes of heavy social drinkers. *Journal of Experimental Psychology: Human Learning and Memory*, 1978, *4*, 246–255.

Milner, B. The memory defect in bilateral hippocampal lesions. *Psychiatric Research Reports*, 1959, *11*, 43–58.

Minsky, M. A framework for representing knowledge. In P. H. Winston (ed.), *The Psychology of Computer Vision*. New York: McGraw-Hill, 1975.

Moeser, S. D. Memory for meaning and wording in concrete and abstract sentences. *Journal of Verbal Learning and Verbal Behavior*, 1974, *13*, 682–697.

Monsell, S. Recency, immediate recognition memory, and reaction time. *Cognitive Psychology*, 1978, *10*, 465–501.

Montague, W. E., Adams, J. A., and Kiess, H. O. Forgetting and natural language mediation. *Journal of Experimental Psychology*, 1966, *72*, 829–833.

Moray, N. Attention in dichotic listening: Affective cues and the influence of instructions. *Quarterly Journal of Experimental Psychology*, 1959, *11*, 56–60.

Moray, N., Bates, A., and Barnett, T. Experiments on the four-eared man. *Journal of the Acoustical Society of America*, 1965, *38*, 196–201.

Morris, C. D., Bransford, J. D., and Franks, J. J. Levels of processing versus transfer appropriate processing. *Journal of Verbal Learning and Verbal Behavior*, 1977, *16*, 519–533.

Morton, J. A functional model for memory. In D. A. Norman (ed.), *Models of Human Memory*. New York: Academic Press, 1970.

Moscovitch, M., and Craik, F. I. M. Depth of processing, retrieval cues, and uniqueness of encoding as factors in recall. *Journal of Verbal Learning and Verbal Behavior*, 1976, *15*, 447–458.

Murdock, B. B., Jr. The retention of individual items. *Journal of Experimental Psychology*, 1961, *62*, 618–625.

Murdock, B. B., Jr. The serial position effect of free recall. *Journal of Experimental Psychology*, 1962, *64*, 482–488.

Navon, D. Forest before trees: The precedence of global features in visual perception. *Cognitive Psychology*, 1977, *9*, 353–383.

Neely, J. H. Semantic priming and retrieval from lexical memory: Roles of inhibitionless spreading activation and limited-capacity attention. *Journal of Experimental Psychology: General*, 1977, *106*, 226–254.

Neisser, U. Visual search. *Scientific American*, 1964, *210*, 94–102.

Neisser, U. *Cognitive Psychology*. New York: Appleton-Century-Crofts, 1967.

Neisser, U. *Cognition and Reality*. San Francisco: W. H. Freeman and Company, 1976.

Neisser, U., Novick, R., and Lazar, R. Searching for ten targets simultaneously. *Perceptual and Motor Skills*, 1963, *17*, 955–961.

Nelson, T. O. Repetition and depth of processing. *Journal of Verbal Learning and Verbal Behavior*, 1977, *16*, 151–172.

Nelson, T. O., Metzler, J., and Reed, D. A. Role of details in the long-term recognition of pictures and verbal descriptions. *Journal of Experimental Psychology*, 1974, *102*, 184–186.

Noble, C. E. Measurements of association value (*a*), rated associations (*a'*), and scaled meaningfulness (*m'*) for the 2100 CVC combinations of the English alphabet. *Psychological Reports*, 1961, *8*, 487–521.

Norman, D. A. *Memory and Attention*. New York: Wiley, 1969.

Noyd, D. Proactive and intrastimulus interference in short-term memory for two-, three-, or five-word stimuli. Paper presented at the Meeting of the Western Psychological Association, Honolulu, Hawaii, 1965.

Oden, G. C. Fuzziness in semantic memory: Choosing exemplars of subjective categories. *Memory & Cognition*, 1977, *5*, 198–204.

O'Neill, M. E., Sutcliffe, J. A., and Tulving, E. Retrieval cues and release from proactive inhibition. *American Journal of Psychology*, 1976, *89*, 535–543.

Osgood, C. E. The nature and measurement of meaning. *Psychological Bulletin*, 1952, *49*, 197–237.

Paivio, A. Abstractness, imagery, and meaningfulness in paired-associate learning. *Journal of Verbal Learning and Verbal Behavior*, 1965, *4*, 32–38.

Paivio, A. Mental imagery in associative learning and memory. *Psychological Review*, 1969, *76*, 241–263.

Paivio, A. *Imagery and Verbal Processes*. New York: Holt, Rinehart and Winston, 1971.

Paivio, A. Mental comparisons involving abstract attributes. *Memory & Cognition*, 1978, *6*, 199–208.

Paivio, A., Yuille, J. C., and Rogers, T. B. Noun imagery and meaningfulness in free and serial recall. *Journal of Experimental Psychology*, 1969, *79*, 509–514.

Palmer, S. E. Visual perception and world knowledge: Notes on a model of sensory-cognitive interaction. In D. A. Norman, D. E. Rumelhart, and the LNR Research Group, *Explorations in Cognition*. San Francisco: W. H. Freeman and Company, 1975.

Parker, E. S., Alkana, R. L., Birnbaum, I. M., Hartley, J. T., and Noble, E. P. Alcohol and the disruption of cognitive processes. *Archives of General Psychiatry*, 1974, *31*, 824–828.

Parker, E. S., Birnbaum, I. M., and Noble, E. P. Alcohol and memory: Storage and state dependency. *Journal of Verbal Learning and Verbal Behavior*, 1976, *15*, 691–702.

Parks, T. E., and Kroll, N. E. A. Enduring visual memory despite forced verbal rehearsal. *Journal of Experimental Psychology: Human Learning and Memory*, 1975, *1*, 648–654.

Peterson, L. R., and James, L. H. Successive tests of short-term retention. *Psychonomic Science*, 1967, *8*, 423–424.

Peterson, L. R., and Peterson, M. J. Short-term retention of individual verbal items. *Journal of Experimental Psychology*, 1959, *58*, 193–198.

Pollack, I. Message uncertainty and message reception. *Journal of the Acoustical Society of America*, 1959, *31*, 1500–1508.

Posner, M. I. Abstraction and the process of recognition. In J. T. Spence and G. H. Bower (eds.), *Advances in Learning and Motivation*, Vol. 3. New York: Academic Press, 1969.

Posner, M. I., Boies, S. J., Eichelman, W. H., and Taylor, R. L. Retention of visual and name codes of single letters. *Journal of Experimental Psychology*, 1969, *79* (1, Pt. 2).

Posner, M. I., Goldsmith, R., and Welton, K. E., Jr. Perceived distance and the classification of distorted patterns. *Journal of Experimental Psychology*, 1967, *73*, 28–38.

Posner, M. I., and Keele, S. W. On the genesis of abstract ideas. *Journal of Experimental Psychology*, 1968, *77*, 353–363.

Posner, M. I., and Konick, A. F. On the role of interference in short-term retention. *Journal of Experimental Psychology*, 1966, *72*, 221–231.

Posner, M. I., and Mitchell, R. F. Chronometric analysis of classification. *Psychological Review*, 1967, *74*, 392–409.

Posner, M. I., and Rossman, E. Effect of size and location of informational transforms upon short-term retention. *Journal of Experimental Psychology*, 1965, *70*, 496–505.

Posner, M. I., and Snyder, C. R. R. Attention and cognitive control. In

R. L. Solso (ed.), *Information Processing and Cognition: The Loyola Symposium*. Hillsdale, N.J.: Erlbaum, 1975 (a).

Posner, M. I., and Snyder, C. R. R. Facilitation and inhibition in the processing of signals. In P. M. A. Rabbitt and S. Dornic (eds.), *Attention and Performance*, Vol. 5. New York: Academic Press, 1975 (b).

Postman, L. A pragmatic view of organization theory. In E. Tulving and W. Donaldson (eds.), *Organization of Memory*. New York: Academic Press, 1972.

Postman, L., Keppel, G., and Stark, K. Unlearning as a function of the relationship between successive response classes. *Journal of Experimental Psychology*, 1965, *69*, 111–118.

Postman, L., and Phillips, L. Short-term temporal changes in free recall. *Quarterly Journal of Experimental Psychology*, 1965, *17*, 132–138.

Postman, L., and Rau, L. Retention as a function of the method of measurement. *University of California Publications in Psychology*, Berkeley, 1957, *8*, 217–270.

Postman, L., and Stark, K. Role of response availability in transfer and interference. *Journal of Experimental Psychology*, 1969, *79*, 168–177.

Postman, L., Stark, K., and Fraser, J. Temporal changes in interference. *Journal of Verbal Learning and Verbal Behavior*, 1968, *7*, 672–694.

Postman, L., Stark, K., and Henschel, D. Conditions of recovery after unlearning. *Journal of Experimental Psychology Monograph*, 1969, *82* (1, Pt. 2).

Postman, L., and Underwood, B. J. Critical issues in interference theory. *Memory & Cognition*, 1973, *1*, 19–40.

Prytulak, L. S. Natural language mediation. *Cognitive Psychology*, 1971, *2*, 1–56.

Pylyshyn, Z. W. What the mind's eye tells the mind's brain: A critique of mental imagery. *Psychological Bulletin*, 1973, *80*, 1–24.

Quillian, M. R. The teachable language comprehender: A simulation program and theory of language. *Communications of the Association for Computing Machinery*, 1969, *12*, 459–476.

Rafnel, K. J., and Klatzky, R. L. Meaningful-interpretation effects on codes of nonsense pictures. *Journal of Experimental Psychology: Human Learning and Memory*, 1978, *4*, 631–646.

Reddy, D. R., Erman, L. D., Fennell, R. D., and Neely, R. B. The HEARSAY speech understanding system: An example of the recognition process. Proceedings of the Third International Joint Conference on Artificial Intelligence, Stanford, Ca., 1973.

Reddy, R., and Newell, A. Knowledge and its representation in a speech understanding system. In L. W. Gregg (ed.), *Knowledge and Cognition*. Hillsdale, N.J.: Erlbaum, 1974.

Reder, L. M., Anderson, J. R., and Bjork, R. A. A semantic interpretation of encoding specificity. *Journal of Experimental Psychology*, 1974, *102*, 648–656.

Reicher, G. M. Perceptual recognition as a function of meaningfulness of stimulus material. *Journal of Experimental Psychology*, 1969, *81*, 275–280.

Reitman, J. S. Mechanisms of forgetting in short-term memory. *Cognitive Psychology*, 1971, 2, 185–195.

Reitman, J. S. Without surreptitious rehearsal, information in short-term memory decays. *Journal of Verbal Learning and Verbal Behavior*, 1974, 13, 365–377.

Reitman, J. S., and Bower, G. H. Storage and later recognition of exemplars of concepts. *Cognitive Psychology*, 1973, 4, 194–206.

Repp, B. H. Perception of implosive transitions in VCV utterances. Status Report on Speech Research, SR–48. New Haven, Conn.: Haskins Laboratories, 1976.

Repp, B. H., Liberman, A. M., Eccardt, T., and Pesetsky, D. Perceptual integration of acoustic cues for stop, fricative, and affricate manner. *Journal of Experimental Psychology: Human Perception and Performance*, 1978, 4, 621–637.

Riley, D. A. Memory for form. In L. Postman (ed.), *Psychology in the Making*. New York: Knopf, 1962.

Rips, L. J., Shoben, E. J., and Smith, E. E. Semantic distance and the verification of semantic relations. *Journal of Verbal Learning and Verbal Behavior*, 1973, 12, 1–20.

Rohwer, W. D., Jr. Verbal and visual elaboration in paired associate learning. *Project Literacy Reports*, Cornell University, 1966, No. 7, 18–28.

Rosch, E. On the internal structure of perceptual and semantic categories. In T. E. Moore (ed.), *Cognitive Development and Acquisition of Language*. New York: Academic Press, 1973.

Rosch, E., and Mervis, C. B. Family Resemblances: Studies in the internal structure of categories. *Cognitive Psychology*, 1975, 7, 573–605.

Rosch, E., Mervis, C. B., Gray, W., Johnson, D., and Boyes-Braem, P. Basic objects in natural categories. *Cognitive Psychology*, 1976, 8, 382–439.

Rubin, D. C. Very long-term memory for prose and verse. *Journal of Verbal Learning and Verbal Behavior*, 1977, 16, 611–621.

Rumelhart, D. E. Notes on a schema for stories. In D. G. Bobrow and A. M. Collins (eds.), *Representation and Understanding*. New York: Academic Press, 1975.

Rumelhart, D. E., and Ortony, A. The representation of knowledge in memory. In R. C. Anderson, R. J. Spiro, and W. E. Montague (eds.), *Schooling and the Acquisition of Knowledge*. Hillsdale, N.J.: Erlbaum, 1977.

Rundus, D. Analysis of rehearsal processes in free recall. *Journal of Experimental Psychology*, 1971, 89, 63–77.

Rundus, D. Maintenance rehearsal and single-level processing. *Journal of Verbal Learning and Verbal Behavior*, 1977, 16, 665–681.

Rundus, D., and Atkinson, R. C. Rehearsal processes in free recall: A procedure for direct observation. *Journal of Verbal Learning and Verbal Behavior*, 1970, 9, 99–105.

Sachs, J. D. S. Recognition memory for syntactic and semantic aspects of connected discourse. *Perception & Psychophysics*, 1967, 2, 437–442.

Sakitt, B. Iconic memory. *Psychological Review*, 1976, 83, 257–276.

Sakitt, B., and Long, G. M. Relative rod and cone contributions in iconic storage. *Perception & Psychophysics*, 1978, 23, 527–536.

Sakitt, B., and Long, G. M. Spare the rod and spoil the icon. *Journal of Experimental Psychology: Human Perception and Performance*, 1979, 5, 19–30.

Santa, J. L., and Lamwers, L. L. Encoding specificity: Fact or artifact? *Journal of Verbal Learning and Verbal Behavior*, 1974, 13, 412–423.

Santa, J. L., and Lamwers, L. L. Where does the confusion lie? Comments on the Wiseman and Tulving paper. *Journal of Verbal Learning and Verbal Behavior*, 1976, 15, 53–57.

Salzinger, K., Portnoy, S., and Feldman, R. S. The effect of order of approximation to the statistical structure of English on the emission of verbal responses. *Journal of Experimental Psychology*, 1962, 64, 52–57.

Schank, R., and Abelson, R. *Scripts, Plans, Goals and Understanding.* Hillsdale, N.J.: Erlbaum, 1977.

Schneider, W., and Shiffrin, R. M. Controlled and automatic human information processing. I. Detection, search and attention. *Psychological Review*, 1977, 84, 1–66.

Selfridge, O. G. Pandemonium: A paradigm for learning. In *The Mechanisation of Thought Processes.* London: H. M. Stationery Office, 1959.

Shaffer, W. O., and Shiffrin, R. M. Rehearsal and storage of visual information. *Journal of Experimental Psychology*, 1972, 92, 292–296.

Shepard, R. N. Recognition memory for words, sentences, and pictures. *Journal of Verbal Learning and Verbal Behavior*, 1967, 6, 156–163.

Shepard, R. N. The mental image. *American Psychologist*, 1978, 33, 125–137.

Shepard, R. N., and Chipman, S. Second-order isomorphism of internal representations: Shapes of states. *Cognitive Psychology*, 1970, 1, 1–17.

Shepard, R. N., and Metzler, J. Mental rotation of three-dimensional objects. *Science*, 1981, 171, 701–703.

Shepard, R. N., and Teghtsoonian, M. Retention of information under conditions approaching a steady state. *Journal of Experimental Psychology*, 1961, 62, 302–309.

Shiffrin, R. M. Memory search. In D. A. Norman (ed.), *Models of Human Memory.* New York: Academic Press, 1970.

Shiffrin, R. M. Information persistence in short-term memory. *Journal of Experimental Psychology*, 1973, 100, 39–49.

Shiffrin, R. M., and Cook, J. R. Short-term forgetting of item and order information. *Journal of Verbal Learning and Verbal Behavior*, 1978, 17, 189–218.

Shiffrin, R. M., and Schneider, W. Controlled and automatic human information processing. II. Perceptual learning, automatic attending, and a general theory. *Psychological Review*, 1977, 84, 127–190.

Shulman, H. G. Similarity effects in short-term memory. *Psychological Bulletin*, 1971, 75, 399–415.

Shulman, H. G. Semantic confusion errors in short-term memory. *Journal of Verbal Learning and Verbal Behavior*, 1972, 11, 221–227.

Simon, H. A. How big is a chunk? *Science*, 1974, *183*, 482–488.

Simon, H. A., and Barenfeld, M. Information-processing analysis of perceptual processes in problem solving. *Psychological Review*, 1969, *76*, 473–483.

Simon, H. A., and Gilmartin, K. A simulation of memory for chess positions. *Cognitive Psychology*, 1973, *5*, 29–46.

Slamecka, N. J. Retroactive inhibition of connected discourse as a function of practice level. *Journal of Experimental Psychology*, 1960, *59*, 104–108. (a)

Slamecka, N. J. Retroactive inhibition of connected discourse as a function of similarity of topic. *Journal of Experimental Psychology*, 1960, *60*, 245–249. (b)

Slamecka, N. J. Differentiation versus unlearning of verbal assocations. *Journal of Experimental Psychology*, 1966, *71*, 822–828.

Smith, E. E., Shoben, E. J., and Rips, L. J. Structure and process in semantic memory: A featural model for semantic decision. *Psychological Review*, 1974, *81*, 214–241.

Sperling, G. The information available in brief visual presentations. *Psychological Monographs*, 1960, *74* (Whole No. 498).

Sperling, G. Successive approximations to a model for short-term memory. *Acta Psychologica*, 1967, *27*, 285–292.

Sperling, G., and Speelman, R. G. Acoustic similarity and auditory short-term memory: Experiments and a model. In D. A. Norman (ed.), *Models of Human Memory*. New York: Academic Press, 1970.

Spiro, R. J. Remembering information from text: The "State of Schema" approach. In R. C. Anderson, R. J. Spiro, and W. E. Montague (eds.), *Schooling and the Acquisition of Knowledge*. Hillsdale, N.J.: Erlbaum, 1977.

Squire, L. R., and Slater, P. C. Forgetting in very long-term memory as assessed by an improved questionnaire technique. *Journal of Experimental Psychology: Human Learning and Memory*, 1975, *1*, 50–54.

Standing, L., Conezio, J., and Haber, R. N. Perception and memory for pictures: Single-trial learning of 2560 visual stimuli. *Psychonomic Science*, 1970, *19*, 73–74.

Sternberg, S. High-speed scanning in human memory. *Science*, 1966, *153*, 652–654.

Sternberg, S. Memory-scanning: Mental processes revealed by reaction-time experiments. *American Scientist*, 1969, *57*, 421–457.

Stromeyer, C. F., III. Eidetikers. *Psychology Today*, November 1970, 76–80.

Stromeyer, C. F., III, and Psotka, J. The detailed texture of eidetic images. *Nature*, 1970, *225*, 346–349.

Stroop, J. R. Studies of interference in serial verbal reaction. *Journal of Experimental Psychology*, 1935, *18*, 643–662.

Sulin, R. A., and Dooling, D. J. Intrusion of a thematic idea in rentention of prose. *Journal of Experimental Psychology*, 1974, *103*, 255–262.

Tabachnick, B., and Brotsky, S. J. Free recall and complexity of pictorial stimuli. *Memory & Cognition*, 1976, *4*, 466–470.

Tejirian, E. Syntactic and semantic structure in the recall of orders of approximation to English. *Journal of Verbal Learning and Verbal Behavior,* 1968, *7,* 1010–1015.

Thomson, D. M., and Tulving, E. Associative encoding and retrieval: Weak and strong cues. *Journal of Experimental Psychology,* 1970, *86,* 255–262.

Thorndike, E. L., and Lorge, I. *The Teacher's Word Book of 30,000 Words.* New York: Teachers College Press, Columbia University, 1944.

Thorndyke, P. W. Cognitive structures in comprehension and memory of narrative discourse. *Cognitive Psychology,* 1977, *9,* 77–110.

Thorndyke, P. W., and Hayes-Roth, B. The use of schemata in the acquisition and transfer of knowledge. *Cognitive Psychology,* 1979, *11,* 82–106.

Townsend, J. T. Some results concerning the identifiability of parallel and serial processes. *British Journal of Mathematical and Statistical Psychology,* 1972, *25,* 168–199.

Treisman, A. M. Contextual cues in selective listening. *Quarterly Journal of Experimental Psychology,* 1960, *12,* 242–248.

Treisman, A. M. Verbal cues, language and meaning in selective attention. *American Journal of Psychology,* 1964, *77,* 206–219.

Tulving, E. Subjective organization in free recall of "unrelated" words. *Psychological Review,* 1962, *69,* 344–354.

Tulving, E. Intratrial and intertrial retention: Notes towards a theory of free recall verbal learning. *Psychological Review,* 1964, *71,* 219–237.

Tulving, E. Episodic and semantic memory. In E. Tulving and W. Donaldson (eds.), *Organization and Memory.* New York: Academic Press, 1972.

Tulving, E., Mandler, G., and Baumal, R. Interaction of two sources of information in tachistoscopic word recognition. *Canadian Journal of Psychology,* 1964, *18,* 62–71.

Tulving, E., and Osler, S. Effectiveness of retrieval cues in memory for words. *Journal of Experimental Psychology,* 1968, *77,* 593–601.

Tulving, E., and Patkau, J. E. Concurrent effects of contextual constraint and word frequency on immediate recall and learning of verbal material. *Canadian Journal of Psychology,* 1962, *16,* 83–95.

Tulving, E., and Pearlstone, Z. Availability versus accessibility of information in memory for words. *Journal of Verbal Learning and Verbal Behavior,* 1966, *5,* 381–391.

Tulving, E., and Thomson, D. M. Encoding specificity and retrieval processes in episodic memory. *Psychological Review,* 1973, *80,* 352–373.

Tulving, E., and Watkins, O. C. Recognition failure of words with a single meaning. *Memory & Cognition,* 1977, *5,* 513–522.

Turvey, M. T. Contrasting orientations to the theory of visual information-processing. *Psychological Review,* 1977, *84,* 67–88.

Tversky, B., and Sherman, T. Picture memory improves with longer on time and off time. *Journal of Experimental Psychology: Human Learning and Memory,* 1975, *1,* 114–118.

Underwood, B. J. Retroactive and proactive inhibition after five and forty-eight hours. *Journal of Experimental Psychology,* 1948, *38,* 29–38. (a)

Underwood, B. J. "Spontaneous" recovery of verbal associations. *Journal of Experimental Psychology*, 1948, *38*, 429–439. (b)

Underwood, B. J. Proactive inhibition as a function of time and degree of prior learning. *Journal of Experimental Psychology*, 1949, *39*, 24–34.

Underwood, B. J. False recognition produced by implicit verbal responses. *Journal of Experimental Psychology*, 1965, *70*, 122–129.

Underwood, B. J., and Ekstrand, B. R. An analysis of some shortcomings in the interference theory of forgetting. *Psychological Review*, 1966, *73*, 540–549.

Underwood, B. J., and Freund, J. S. Errors in recognition learning and retention. *Journal of Experimental Psychology*, 1968, *78*, 55–63.

Underwood, B. J., and Freund, J. S. Word Frequency and short-term recognition memory. *American Journal of Psychology*, 1970, *83*, 343–351.

Underwood, B. J., and Postman, L. Extraexperimental sources of interference in forgetting. *Psychological Review*, 1960, *67*, 73–95.

Watkins, M. J. The intricacy of memory span. *Memory & Cognition*, 1977, *5*, 529–534.

Watkins, M. J., and Tulving, E. Episodic memory: When recognition fails. *Journal of Experimental Psychology: General*, 1975, *104*, 5–29.

Watkins, M. J., Watkins, O. C., Craik, F. I. M., and Mazuryk, G. Effect of nonverbal distraction on short-term storage. *Journal of Experimental Psychology*, 1973, *101*, 296–300.

Watkins, M. J., Watkins, O. C., and Crowder, R. G. The modality effect in free and serial recall as a function of phonological similarity. *Journal of Verbal Learning and Verbal Behavior*, 1974, *13*, 430–447.

Watkins, O. C., and Watkins, M. J. Build-up of proactive inhibition as a cue-overload effect. *Journal of Experimental Psychology: Human Learning and Memory*, 1975, *1*, 442–452.

Waugh, N. C., and Norman, D. A. Primary memory. *Psychological Review*, 1965, *72*, 89–104.

Waugh, N. C., and Norman, D. A. The measurement of interference in primary memory. *Journal of Verbal Learning and Verbal Behavior*, 1968, *7*, 617–626.

Weaver, G. E. Effects of poststimulus study time on recognition of pictures. *Journal of Experimental Psychology*, 1974, *103*, 799–801.

Weaver, G. E., and Stanny, C. J. Short-term retention of pictorial stimuli as assessed by a probe recognition technique. *Journal of Experimental Psychology: Human Learning and Memory*, 1978, *4*, 55–65.

Weingartner, H., Adefris, W., Eich, J. E., and Murphy, D. L. Encoding-imagery specificity in alcohol state-dependent learning. *Journal of Experimental Psychology: Human Learning and Memory*, 1976, *2*, 83–87.

Weingartner, H., and Murphy, D. L. State-dependent storage and retrieval of experience while intoxicated. In I. M. Birnbaum and E. S. Parker (eds.), *Alcohol and Human Memory*. Hillsdale, N.J.: Erlbaum, 1977.

Wheeler, D. D. Processes in word recognition. *Cognitive Psychology*, 1970, *1*, 59–85.

Wickelgren, W. A. Acoustic similarity and retroactive interference in short-term memory. *Journal of Verbal Learning and Verbal Behavior*, 1965, *4*, 53–61.

Wickelgren, W. A. Distinctive features and errors in short-term memory for English consonants. *Journal of the Acoustical Society of America*, 1966, *39*, 388–398.

Wickelgren, W. A. The long and the short of memory. *Psychological Bulletin*, 1973, *80*, 425–438.

Wickens, D. D. Characteristics of word encoding. In A. W. Melton and E. Martin (eds.), *Coding Processes in Human Memory*. New York: V. H. Winston & Sons, 1972.

Wickens, D. D., Born, D. G., and Allen, C. K. Proactive inhibition and item similarity in short-term memory. *Journal of Verbal Learning and Verbal Behavior*, 1963, *2*, 440–445.

Winograd, E. List differentiation as a function of frequency and retention interval. *Journal of Experimental Psychology*, 1968, *76* (2, Pt. 2).

Wiseman, S. and Tulving, E. Encoding Specificity: Relation between recall superiority and recognition failure. *Journal of Experimental Psychology: Human Learning and Memory*, 1976, *2*, 349–361.

Wood, G. Organizational processes and free recall. In E. Tulving and W. Donaldson (eds.), *Organization of Memory*. New York: Academic Press, 1972.

Wood, G., and Underwood, B. J. Implicit responses and conceptual similarity. *Journal of Verbal Learning and Verbal Behavior*, 1967, *6*, 1–10.

Woodward, A. E., Jr., Bjork, R. A., and Jongeward, R. H., Jr. Recall and recognition as a function of primary rehearsal. *Journal of Verbal Learning and Verbal Behavior*, 1973, *12*, 608–617.

Wulf, F. Über die Veränderung von Vorstellungen. *Psychologische Forschung*, 1922, *1*, 333–373.

Zusne, L. *Visual Perception of Form*. New York: Academic Press, 1970.

Index of Names

Index of Subjects